THE TRIUMPH OF CONTRARIAN INVESTING

Crowds, Manias, and Beating the Market by Going Against the Grain

Ned Davis

McGraw-Hill
New York   Chicago   San Francisco   Lisbon   London   Madrid   Mexico City
Milan   New Delhi   San Juan   Seoul   Singapore   Sydney   Toronto

The McGraw·Hill Companies

Copyright © 2004 by The McGraw-Hill Companies, Inc. All rights reserved. Printed in the United States of America. Except as permitted under the United States Copyright Act of 1976, no part of this publication may be reproduced or distributed in any form or by any means, or stored in a data base or retrieval system, without the prior written permission of the publisher.

1 2 3 4 5 6 7 8 9 0 DOC/DOC 0 9 8 7 6 5 4 3

ISBN 0-07-143240-X

McGraw-Hill books are available at special quantity discounts to use as premiums and sales promotions, or for use in corporate training programs. For more information, please write to the Director of Special Sales, Professional Publishing, McGraw-Hill, Two Penn Plaza, New York, NY 10121-2298. Or contact your local bookstore.

This publication is designed to provide accurate and authoritative information in regard to the subject matter covered. It is sold with the understanding that neither the author nor the publisher is engaged in rendering legal, accounting, or other professional service. If legal advice or other expert assistance is required, the services of a competent professional person should be sought.
—*From a Declaration of Principles jointly adopted by a Committee of the American Bar Association and a Committee of Publishers.*

❂ This book is printed on recycled, acid-free paper containing a minimum of 50% recycled, de-inked fiber.

Library of Congress Cataloging-in-Publication Data
The triumph of contrarian investing : crowds, manias, and beating the market by going against the grain / [edited] by Ned Davis.
    p. cm.
Includes bibliographical references.
ISBN 0-07-143240-X (hardcover : alk. paper) 1. Investments—Psychological aspects. 2. Speculation—Psychological aspects. 3. Stock price forecasting. 4. Investments—Decision making. I. Davis, Nathan E.
HG4515.15.T74 2003
332.6—dc21
    2003013495

*Thanks for putting up with me every day—
Mickey, Evan, Brody, Dylan, and Connor.
Finally, I dedicate the book to our clients who have supported our research
process and to free thinkers, innovators, nonconformists, and peaceful
contrarians everywhere.*

The analysis contained herein is provided "as is," without warranty of any kind, either expressed or implied. Neither Ned Davis Research, Inc., nor any of its affiliates or employees (NDR) shall have any liability for any loss sustained by anyone who has relied on the information contained in an NDR publication. All opinions expressed herein are subject to change without notice, and you should always obtain current information and perform due diligence before trading. NDR, accounts that NDR or its affiliated companies manage, or their respective shareholders, directors, officers and/or employees, may have long or short positions in the securities discussed herein and may purchase or sell such securities without notice. The securities mentioned in this document may not be eligible for sale in some states or countries, nor be suitable for all types of investors; their value and income they produce may fluctuate and/or be adversely affected by exchange rates, interest rates or other factors. Further distribution prohibited without prior permission. Copyright 2003 © Ned Davis Research, Inc. All rights reserved.

Copyright © 2003, Standard & Poor's, a division of The McGraw-Hill Companies, Inc. Standard & Poor's including its subsidiary corporations ("S&P") is a division of The McGraw-Hill Companies, Inc. Reproduction of S&P 500 in any form is prohibited except with the prior written permission of S&P. Because of the possibility of human or mechanical error by S&P's sources, S&P or others, S&P does not guarantee the accuracy, adequacy, completeness or availability of any information and is not responsible for any errors or omissions or for the results obtained from the use of such information. S&P GIVES NO EXPRESS OR IMPLIED WARRANTIES, INCLUDING, BUT NOT LIMITED TO, ANY WARRANTIES OF MERCHANTABILITY OR FITNESS FOR A PARTICULAR PURPOSE OR USE. In no event shall S&P be liable for any indirect, special or consequential damages in connection with subscriber's or others' use of S&P 500.

Contents

    Foreword   vii

    Acknowledgments   xiii

1   Introduction   1

2   Scientific Studies on Crowd Psychology   19

3   Brief History of Manias and Panics   25

4   Headlines and Cover Stories   35

5   Indicators of Crowd Psychology   47

6   Postscript   61

    Addendum   65

    References   171

    Index   173

FOREWORD

In 1971, about the time I first knew Ned Davis and began sharing market timing ideas with him, I launched a stock market letter, *The Zweig Forecast,* which I wrote for 27 years, before coming to my senses and taking some things off of my plate. My market forecasts used a variety of indicators, including monetary, tape, and valuation. But the group, which I emphasized the most, included the sentiment indicators. To that end, I wrote a booklet, *Investor Expectations* (a fancy moniker for "investor sentiment"), which I sent to every new subscriber to the market letter. The introduction to that booklet is reprinted below. The booklet also included numerous articles that I had written for *Barron's,* primarily on sentiment indicators. I was fortunate that with one glaring exception, each article made a correct forecast of the market, beginning with one on options volume as an indicator of sentiment back in November 1970. It read bullish, and the market obligingly shot straight up.

That was followed by my invention of the puts-calls ratio in a *Barron's* article in the spring of 1971. I warned then of excessive optimism and the risk of a decline. That was followed by a severe intermediate correction, which lasted about 7 months. In those days, puts and calls were traded only over the counter through rather secretive options dealers. But I had gotten options data back to 1945 from the SEC, while finishing my Ph.D. dissertation in finance at Michigan State. I might have been the only one with the data at that time . . . and I found it a wonderful source of "investor sentiment." So, obviously, while Ned and I were strong believers in using investor sentiment, I not only had a theory, but also had a couple of right-on publicly made forecasts on my resume.

These were followed by more than 15 other *Barron's* "forecasting" articles over the years, with only one turkey in the group (if you ever see the article on floor traders shorts, please burn it!). And most of these articles featured "sentiment" indicators, some of which I invented (the total odd-lot short ratio), or just improved upon (public shorts ratio). Anyhow, the *Barron's* articles helped to promote the *Zweig Forecast,* which over the years was ranked first in risk-adjusted return in the Hulbert ratings among all the services. And in turn, that helped to launch my successful money management business, which bolted ahead in spades after both Ned and I called the 1987 market crash—primarily with the aid of sentiment indicators.

So I'm not just touting some theory in order to help Ned sell his book. Rather, I'm attempting, in a very brief way, to demonstrate that sentiment indicators have a lot of value. And in both my case and Ned's, it helped us to build extremely successful stock market businesses based not on theory, but on results. As the old saw goes: "The proof is in the pudding."

A SPECIAL REPORT—INVESTOR EXPECTATIONS: WHY THEY ARE THE KEY TO STOCK MARKET TRENDS

Economic factors, particularly monetary variables and interest rates, certainly influence the long-term values of common stocks, but it is *Investor Expectations* that exert the most dynamic impact on stock prices. If one were both able to measure the magnitude of Investor Expectations and to properly interpret them, *major* stock market movements could be anticipated within a reasonable degree of error.

WHAT ARE INVESTOR EXPECTATIONS?

Investor Expectations are simply the collective opinions of various groups of stock market participants . . . either investors or speculators. For convenience, such opinions may be expressed in terms of their relative degree of optimism or pessimism. Normally, it is optimal to segregate the marketplace into reasonably homogeneous groups of investors in order to obtain measurements of various types of sentiment. Such groupings, for example, might include odd-lot investors, short sellers, exchange members, mutual fund investors, foreign investors, etc. . . .

By obtaining many such samples of investor attitudes, one can decrease the probability of deriving a misleading reading of market expectations in the aggregate. In addition, it has been found that the expectations of some investor groupings are more reliable than those of others, and that the expectations of some groups are meaningful only under specified market conditions. Thus, as Investor Expectations are broken down into greater numbers of subclassifications, their predictive capacity is enhanced, as is the opportunity to corroborate one reading with another.

THE PREDICTIVE THEORY OF INVESTOR EXPECTATIONS

A forerunner to the theory of Investor Expectations was eloquently presented in 1962 by Professor Paul Cootner, then of M.I.T. Cootner hypothesized that stock market prices conform to a *random walk within reflecting barriers*. The reflecting barriers theory works as follows:

There exist two broad categories of stock market participants: *"professionals"* and *"nonprofessionals."* Professionals constitute a distinct *minority* and do not necessarily include all or even many of those who make their living in Wall Street. Professionals can obtain fairly reliable fundamental research at a very low marginal cost, and because they are relatively knowledgeable about *intrinsic values* of stocks, they have a fair idea as to the course of future stock prices.

On the other hand, the vast majority of investors are nonprofessionals (e.g., odd-lotters, the "public," etc.) who have poor access to research and very naïve ideas about intrinsic values. So, when they make their investment decisions, the nonprofessionals *on the average are as likely to be wrong as not.* Hence, when nonprofessionals are dominating market activity, prices will wander randomly about some central value.

Professionals, however, are aware of intrinsic values, and they carefully watch the random movements in prices created by the nonprofessionals. When these random movements cause prices to wander sufficiently far from intrinsic values (or to one of the hypothesized "reflecting barriers"), the professionals will then step in to profit on the differences between prices and values.

For example, suppose Stock XYZ shown in the figure is valued intrinsically by professionals at $50 per share. As long as the random prices generated by nonprofessionals do not deviate greatly from $50 in the short run (say between the barriers of $45 to $55), the professionals will do nothing. (Note, in the long run the barriers will shift upward or downward as intrinsic value changes). But, suppose that nonprofessionals become overly bullish for some reason and push prices to the $55 barrier. Now, the difference between prices and values is "large," and thus it behooves the professionals to sell or even to sell short. Similarly, if nonprofessionals become excessively bearish and sink prices down to the $45 barrier, the stock would be rated "undervalued" by the professionals, prompting them to enter the market as buyers and to push prices back up again.

Observe, that whenever the nonprofessionals become excessively enthusiastic or unduly pessimistic about prices and drive them to a reflecting barrier, the professionals enter the market and push prices away from the barrier in exactly the *opposite direction from that which the nonprofessionals anticipate!*

The general theory of investor expectations thus develops: WHENEVER NONPROFESSIONAL INVESTORS BECOME "SIGNIFICANTLY" ONE-SIDED IN THEIR EXPECTATIONS ABOUT THE FUTURE COURSE OF STOCK PRICES, THE MARKET WILL MOVE IN THE DIRECTION OPPOSITE TO THAT WHICH IS ANTICIPATED BY THE MASSES!

RANDOM WALKS WITHIN REFLECTING BARRIERS

Cootner verified his "reflecting barriers" hypothesis by means of some sophisticated statistical techniques, but he left open the question as to how (or even if) investors might actually profit from the theory. Hypothetically, profits could be made in one of two ways: either by following the professional investors or by going the opposite way of the nonprofessionals.

Unfortunately, the first alternative offers limited hope. Professionals, because they are relatively bright, are smart enough to cover their tracks until it is usually too late for one to follow them profitably. In addition, academic research has demonstrated that the number of true professionals . . . that is those who can consistently anticipate prices with accuracy . . . are unbelievably few in number, certainly far fewer than the number of investors normally considered "professionals;" thus, their activities are rarely visible. One exception is the trading activity of Corporate Insiders (officers, directors, and very large stockholders).

But all is not lost. Given the nonprofessionals' propensity to err, given their relatively vast numbers, and given the fact that there is abundant statistical data available with which to measure their expectations, one theoretically *can* achieve above normal profits by engaging in the *reverse* activity vis-à-vis that of the nonprofessionals . . . at least at those moments when their consensus

Random walks within reflecting barriers.
Courtesy of Marty Zweig, Investor Expectations.

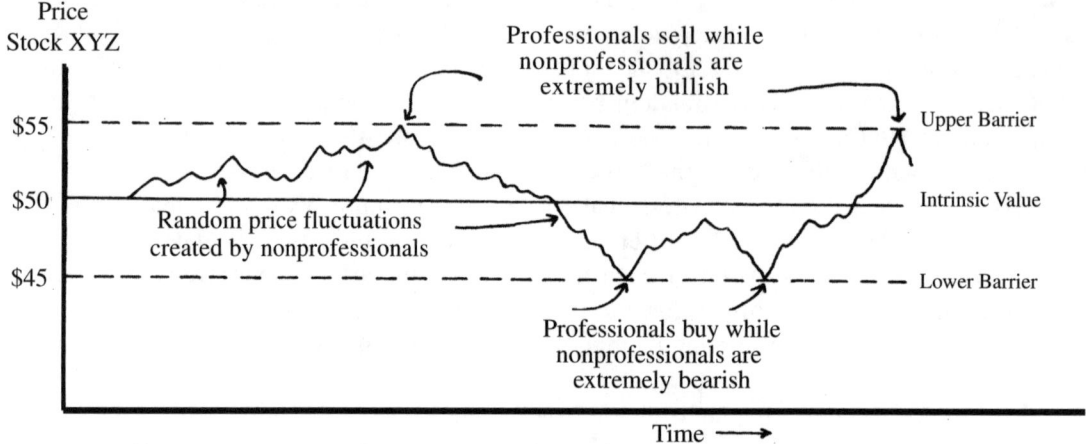

is historically "extreme." All the forecaster needs to do is: (1) develop a sound measurement system of nonprofessional opinion; (2) establish stable parameters which signify when that opinion is significantly "extreme"; (3) maintain the emotional stability to act in diametrically opposite fashion to that of the masses.

Step (1) is fairly easy to achieve. Step (2) is extraordinarily difficult, although years of careful research have uncovered useful parameters. But even where the first two steps have been successful, most investors fail at Step (3). *It is difficult to part company with the "crowd"* . . . to buy when nearly everyone is bearish and things "look" bleakest . . . or to sell when the masses are rampantly bullish and the economy appears strong. Yet, this is precisely what *must* be done in order to produce superior returns. After all, if one goes along with the majority of investors *all* of the time, he is doomed to duplicate the mediocre performance of the crowd.

WHY DOES THE INVESTOR EXPECTATIONS THEORY WORK?

Someone is bound to be skeptical. Why should the market drop when the masses are extremely bullish, or why should it rise when nearly everyone is bearish? The answer is simple. Suppose the overwhelming numbers of investors (call them nonprofessionals) become rampantly bullish on the market. The logical extension of highly bullish expectations results in the purchase of stocks right up to the respective financial limits of the masses. *At the very moment when the masses become most bullish, they will be very nearly fully invested!* They won't have the financial capacity to do more buying. Who then is left to create demand? Certainly not the minority of investors we call professionals. It is that group which recognizes over-valuations, and presumably has been the supplier of stock to the nonprofessionals during the time that both prices and the optimism of the masses were rising.

Thus, when the crowd has become extraordinarily bullish, a dearth of demand exists. The nonprofessionals are loaded with stocks and are cash-poor, while the professionals are liquid, but in no frame of mind to buy. Demand is saturated, and even minor increases in supply will cause stock prices to tumble. *At this point, prices are a strong bet to go but down!* Similarly, when the masses of nonprofessionals become heavily bearish, they panic and sell out. Supply soon evaporates and prices have strong odds to rise!

Martin Zweig
Managing Director
Zweig-DiMenna Associates L.L.C.

Acknowledgments

    I would like to thank my associates who helped me with this book including Ed Clissold and Sam Burns. I also want to thank my executive assistant Darlene Andronaco for typing, Andrea Justiniano-Blake for layout and design, Nancy Grab for compliance issues, and Lee Ann Tillis for helping to manage the process. We were aided by some initial work from interns Brody Davis (who also helped edit), Evan Davis, and Bradley Wilson. Tim Hayes, Julie Font, and Karen Tuttle also helped edit.

    In the first chapter I tried to list a number of people and sources that have influenced my thinking regarding contrary opinion and the madness of crowds.

CHAPTER 1

INTRODUCTION

> THE ROAD NOT TAKEN
> *Two roads diverged in a wood, and I—*
> *I took the one less traveled by,*
> *And that has made all the difference.*
>
> —Robert Frost

As a high school student, I first read Robert Frost's famous poem "The Road Not Taken" transcribed on a poster in a store, and I immediately bought it to hang on my wall. Since that day, something in my nature has driven me to be wary of the crowd and take "the road less traveled" both in the stock market and in my personal life. In life, forging one's own path is important, as it teaches the lessons of individuality and independence. (For those interested, this book includes a "postscript" on why I believe one should also consider "the road less traveled" in one's personal life.) Furthermore, in investing, taking the road less traveled can provide the key to understanding the stock market and profiting from it. In this book we will explore crowd psychology and how it manifests itself in the stock market and determine what we should do to remain open-minded. We will also examine studies on how crowds tend to control us and how crowd psychology has historically led to massive manias and busts. In addition we will focus on media cover stories that capture the popular social mood and on objective quantitative indicators that teach us when crowd psychology is at an extreme and warn us to use contrary opinion and take the road less traveled.

MORE BAD NEWS ON FORECASTING

(and are forecasts thus useless?)

My book *Being Right or Making Money* (published in 2000) begins by saying, "BAD NEWS ABOUT FORECASTING (Being Right)," and it states, "I've yet to find anyone who could consistently and reliably forecast an uncertain future." If it were really possible to forecast consistently and reliably, contrary opinion (the road less traveled) would not be so important. So I thought that it might be of interest to see how "the best and the brightest" have measured up in forecasting the stock market in the period since *Being Right or Making Money* was published. Figures 1-1 and 1-2 (from *InvesTech Research Market Analyst* on December 20, 2002) show the predictions of the panelists on the well-known Louis Rukeyser's Wall Street program for both 2001 and 2002, and Figures 1-3, 1-4, and 1-5 present the predictions of the top Wall Street strategists in *Barron's* magazine. As can be seen, the forecasting record was dismal. *Not a single* panelist had a prediction as low as the actual close for 2001 or 2002. Even *Barron's* says the strategists "missed by a mile."

FIGURE 1-1 *Wall Street Week* with Louis Rukeyser, 2001 panel predictions.

Wall Street Week With Louis Rukeyser 2001 Panel Predictions		
Panelist Close	DJIA Close	NASDAQ Close
▬▬▬▬▬▬▬▬	11,400	3,200
▬▬▬▬▬▬▬▬	13,050	3,450
▬▬▬▬▬▬▬▬	11,735	2,810
▬▬▬▬▬▬▬▬	12,100	3,800
▬▬▬▬▬▬▬▬	11,740	2,734
▬▬▬▬▬▬▬▬	11,400	3,450
▬▬▬▬▬▬▬▬	12,300	3,100
▬▬▬▬▬▬▬▬	12,500	4,600
▬▬▬▬▬▬▬▬	12,000	2,700
▬▬▬▬▬▬▬▬	12,250	3,400
▬▬▬▬▬▬▬▬	12,400	3,000
▬▬▬▬▬▬▬▬	12,504	2,842
▬▬▬▬▬▬▬▬	12,375	3,010
▬▬▬▬▬▬▬▬	12,100	3,000
▬▬▬▬▬▬▬▬	11,800	2,500
▬▬▬▬▬▬▬▬	12,000	3,000
▬▬▬▬▬▬▬▬	12,000	3,200
▬▬▬▬▬▬▬▬	11,900	2,250
▬▬▬▬▬▬▬▬	11,400	2,900
▬▬▬▬▬▬▬▬	13,000	3,500
▬▬▬▬▬▬▬▬	12,675	3,675
▬▬▬▬▬▬▬▬	13,170	2,570
Average Forecast	**12,173**	**3,122**
Actual Close	**10,021**	**1,950**

FIGURE 1-2 *Wall Street Week* with Louis Rukeyser, 2002 panel predictions.

Wall Street Week With Louis Rukeyser 2002 Panel Predictions		
Panelist	DJIA Close	NASDAQ Close
▬▬▬▬▬▬▬▬	11,200	2,400
▬▬▬▬▬▬▬▬	11,050	2,200
▬▬▬▬▬▬▬▬	11,100	2,220
▬▬▬▬▬▬▬▬	12,100	2,810
▬▬▬▬▬▬▬▬	10,235	2,404
▬▬▬▬▬▬▬▬	10,000	2,100
▬▬▬▬▬▬▬▬	11,500	2,450
▬▬▬▬▬▬▬▬	13,750	2,650
▬▬▬▬▬▬▬▬	11,050	2,130
▬▬▬▬▬▬▬▬	11,150	2,150
▬▬▬▬▬▬▬▬	10,800	2,260
▬▬▬▬▬▬▬▬	10,947	1,987
▬▬▬▬▬▬▬▬	12,345	2,579
▬▬▬▬▬▬▬▬	10,750	2,100
▬▬▬▬▬▬▬▬	10,950	2,280
▬▬▬▬▬▬▬▬	11,500	2,400
▬▬▬▬▬▬▬▬	11,900	2,240
▬▬▬▬▬▬▬▬	11,250	2,250
▬▬▬▬▬▬▬▬	10,750	2,000
▬▬▬▬▬▬▬▬	12,400	2,680
▬▬▬▬▬▬▬▬	11,600	2,146
▬▬▬▬▬▬▬▬	10,500	1,700
Average Forecast	**11,310**	**2,279**
Actual Close	**8,342**	**1,336**

FIGURE 1-3 *Barron's* **strategists' forecasts, 2000.**

2000

Strategist	Firm	DJIA	S&P 500 Profit Growth	30-Yr T-Bond
▓▓▓▓	▓▓▓▓	12,200	8-9%	6.5%
▓▓▓▓	▓▓▓▓	12,500	10.0%	7.0%
▓▓▓▓	▓▓▓▓	12,300	8.0%	6.7%
▓▓▓▓	▓▓▓▓	13,000	13.0%	6.0%
▓▓▓▓	▓▓▓▓	12,500	10.0%	6.0%
▓▓▓▓	▓▓▓▓	12,750	14.0%	6.5%
▓▓▓▓	▓▓▓▓	13,000	18.0%	6.5%
▓▓▓▓	▓▓▓▓	11,200	19.0%	6-6.25%
▓▓▓▓	▓▓▓▓	10,200	19.0%	6.8%
▓▓▓▓	▓▓▓▓	12,600	10.0%	6.0%
▓▓▓▓	▓▓▓▓	13,000	10.0%	6.0%
Average Forecast		12,295	12.7%	6.4%
Actual Close		10,787	3.8%*	5.5%

*Earnings estimates vary between reported actual and various measures of operating profits. We used reported profits for "actual close" earnings estimates for 2002. From Barron's published on 01/03/2000, 1/1/2001, and 12/31/2001.

FIGURE 1-4 *Barron's* **strategists' forecasts, 2001.**

2001

Strategist	Firm	DJIA	S&P 500	S&P 500 Profit Growth	10-Yr T-Bond
▓▓▓▓	▓▓▓▓	11,800	1,500	6.0%	5.5%
▓▓▓▓	▓▓▓▓	13,000	1,675	7.0%	4.8%
▓▓▓▓	▓▓▓▓	11,000	1,365	0-5%	4.75-4.90%
▓▓▓▓	▓▓▓▓	11,000	1,400	0.0%	5.5%
▓▓▓▓	▓▓▓▓	13,000	1,650	7-8%	5.5%
▓▓▓▓	▓▓▓▓	12,500	1,700	8.0%	5.3%
▓▓▓▓	▓▓▓▓	12,650	1,600	9.0%	5.0%
▓▓▓▓	▓▓▓▓	N/A	1,715	0-5%	4.75-5.0%
▓▓▓▓	▓▓▓▓	13,200	1,650	7.0%	5.6%
▓▓▓▓	▓▓▓▓	11,500	1,525	4.5%	5.4%
▓▓▓▓	▓▓▓▓	12,000	1,450	6.0%	5.5%
▓▓▓▓	▓▓▓▓	12,000	1,500	10.0%	5.5%
Average Forecast		12,150	1,561	5.8%	5.3%
Actual Close		10,021	1,148	-50.6%*	5.1%

*Earnings estimates vary between reported actual and various measures of operating profits. We used reported profits for "actual close" earnings estimates for 2002. From Barron's published on 01/03/2000, 1/1/2001, and 12/31/2001.

FIGURE 1-5 *Barron's* **strategists' forecasts, 2002.**

2002

Strategist	Firm	DJIA	S&P 500	S&P 500 Profit Growth	10-Yr T-Bond
▓▓▓▓	▓▓▓▓	N/A	1,570	4.0%	5.0%
▓▓▓▓	▓▓▓▓	12,000	1,350	15.0%	5.8%
▓▓▓▓	▓▓▓▓	11,850	1,363	14.0%	4.3%
▓▓▓▓	▓▓▓▓	11,500	1,300	15.0%	4.5%
▓▓▓▓	▓▓▓▓	11,500	1,350	13.0%	5.1%
▓▓▓▓	▓▓▓▓	11,400	1,375	9.0%	5.0%
▓▓▓▓	▓▓▓▓	10,000	1,200	8.0%	5.3%
▓▓▓▓	▓▓▓▓	10,800	1,350	1.6%	5.2%
▓▓▓▓	▓▓▓▓	10,400	1,200	0.0%	5.8%
▓▓▓▓	▓▓▓▓	11,050	1,225	7.0%	5.3%
▓▓▓▓	▓▓▓▓	8,500	950	-5.0%	4.8%
Average Forecast		10,900	1,294	7.4%	5.1%
Actual Close		8,342	880	14.7%*	3.8%

*Earnings estimates vary between reported actual and various measures of operating profits. We used reported profits for "actual close" earnings estimates for 2002. From Barron's published on 01/03/2000, 1/1/2001, and 12/31/2001.

Not to be outdone, the December 27, 1999, *BusinessWeek,* in its Fearless Forecast issue, published an article titled "Will the Bull Outrun Predictions Again?" that *chastises* the 55 stock market gurus to "stop underestimating the bull market's strength and resilience." The article ends by saying, "The odds are good that the consensus—and even some of the biggest bulls—will prove too bearish." The experts advised, on average, 69 percent in stocks, 24 percent in bonds, and 6 percent in cash. Their predictions for 2000 are shown in Figure 1-6. Note that the forecasts for 2000 and 2001 for the S&P 500 were within 1 point of each other. Fifty-two of the fifty-five experts (95 percent) who forecasted the S&P 500 for 2000 were too optimistic.

FIGURE 1-6 *BusinessWeek* market forecast survey.

BUSINESSWEEK MARKET FORECAST SURVEY				
	DJIA	**SP500**	**NASDAQ**	**RUSSELL 2000**
Actual 1999 Close	11,497	1,469	4,069	
2000 BW Survey	12,154	1,559	3,805	
Actual 2000 Close	10,787	1,320	2,471	
2001 BW Survey	12,015	1,558	3,583	
Actual 2001 Close	10,021	1,148	1,950	489
2002 BW Survey	11,090	1,292	2,236	520
Actual 2002 Close	8,342	880	1,336	383

In the December 25, 2000, *BusinessWeek,* an article titled "Why the Experts Are Upbeat" surveyed 38 "gurus" and found, for the consensus, an expected close of 12,015 on the Dow for 2001, 1558 on the S&P 500, and 3583 on the NASDAQ. They advised, on average, 66 percent in stocks, 26 percent in bonds, and just 8 percent in cash. *All but one* of those who were surveyed overestimated where the Dow, S&P, and NASDAQ would be at year-end.

On December 31, 2001, *BusinessWeek* again did its survey "of the smartest players on Wall Street," and this time it used 54 "experts," whose consensus predicted 11,090 for the Dow, 1292 for the S&P 500, and 2236 for the NASDAQ. They advised 70 percent in stocks, 20 percent in bonds, and 9 percent in cash. *Not a single* forecaster predicted an S&P 500 as low as 880 for the 2002 close. And it wasn't just the experts who got 2002 wrong. The collage shown in Figure 1-7, courtesy of the *Elliott Wave Financial Forecast* (January 3, 2003), echoes the high crowd optimism across the country at the start of 2002.

Furthermore it wasn't just investment experts and Wall Street media who were confident at the top of the bubble and hopeful during the bear market. The stock market is simply one of the best indicators of the *overall social mood.* Look at the chart in Figure 1-8 on consumer confidence and you can see that, at extremes, crowd psychology is so powerful that nearly everybody gets caught up in it. I first published this chart on March 8, 2000, two days before the all-time peak in the NASDAQ.

FIGURE 1-7 2002 forecasts collage.
© Elliott Wave Theorist International, Inc., January 2003.

2002 Forecasts

Business Bounces Back
—U.S. News & World Report 1/8/02

2002–Bring It On
Double-digit earnings growth and benign inflation environment will fuel a 20% gain in the S&P 500 to 1375 by year-end.
—Brokerage House Strategy, 12/17/01

The stock resurgence is here to stay, say the bulls
—BusinessWeek 12/31/01

BusinessWeek

Q&A: Still a True Believer in *Dow 36,000*
—December 31, 2001

The Outlook for Stocks
For investors, 2002 should be better than 2001.
—N.Y. Times, 1/2/02

DJIA 11,500

"There's no way prices can go down significantly. In other words, stay long, buy more and don't even think about going short."

The Case for a "Super-V"
Three stimulating economic factors may come together for 2002
—Barron's, 12/31/01

"It's hard to be bearish when the Fed is doing everything for the economy except dropping $100 bills out of airplanes."
—Money Manager, 1/1/02

Business Press: Forecasts of recovery spring forth
—Atlanta Journal Constitution 1/8/02

Stop Whining!
Gloomy Forecasters are forgetting history
—Barrons 1/14/02

Forecasters smell a recovery
Wall Street analysts pin hopes on consumer
—Atlanta Journal Constitution, 12/29/01

After Two Years of Suffering, Investors Hope for a Rebound
—Wall Street Journal, 1/2/02

The table shown in Figure 1-9, put together by Bianco Research on January 3, 2003, reports the results of a *Wall Street Journal* survey of leading economists regarding their forecast of the level and direction of interest rates 6 months forward. Currently, 55 economists are surveyed in this semiannual report. What the table shows is that fully 71 percent of the time (30 out of 42) *the consensus of economists could not even forecast the direction of rates, either up or down,* for 6 months forward. This record is so much worse than the probable outcome of a series of coin tosses that it argues that the tools that economists use are fatally in error.

Finally, *InvesTech Research Market Analyst* also featured the following forecast from *Fortune* in 1981 and 1983:

1981–1982 Recession

(July '81–Nov. '82)

A new batch of statistics from the Commerce Department, some dramatically revised from earlier estimates, demonstrate beyond reasonable doubt that a recession has begun. *It will, however, be one of the mildest of the postwar period.*

Fortune—**December 14, 1981**

It was the longest of the postwar period, spanning a year and a half, or nearly twice as long as the postwar average. Unemployment reached double digits for the first time in 40 years. Though

FIGURE 1-8 Consumer confidence versus DJIA.
The Conference Board.
© 2003 Ned Davis Research, Inc. All rights reserved.

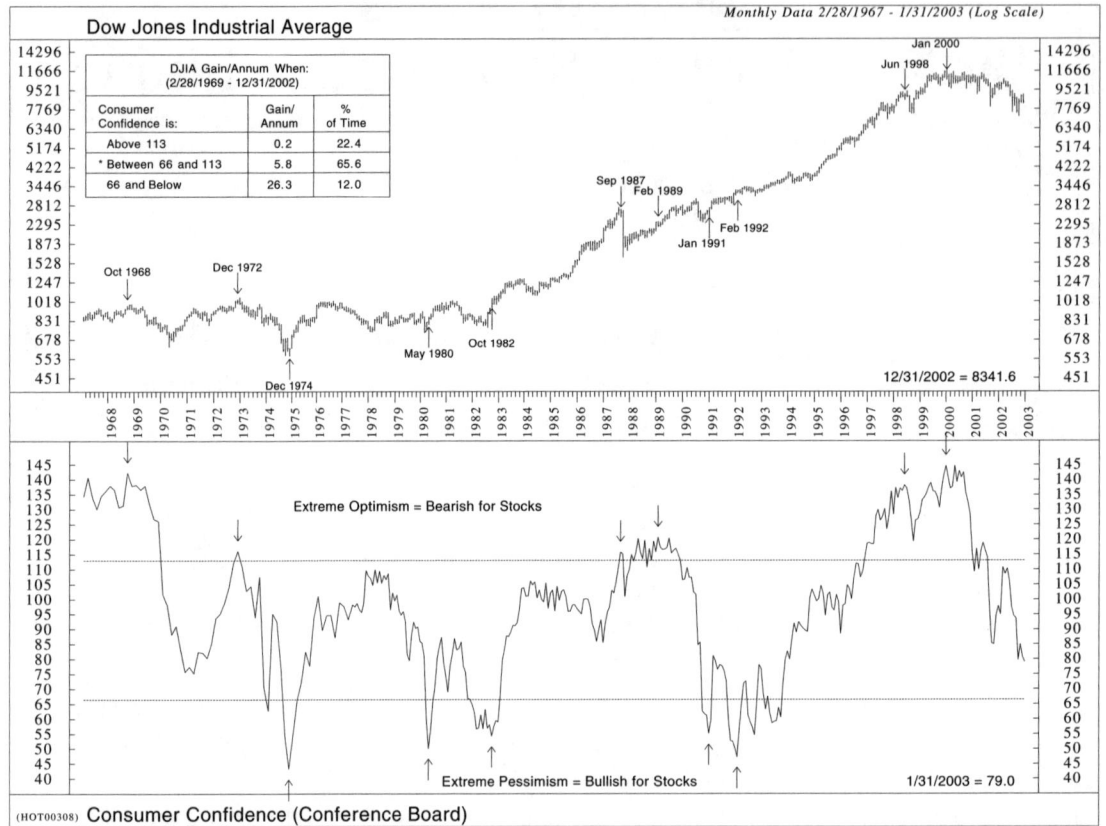

the decline in GNP was only 2.6%, it came after an aborted recovery from the 1980 recession—*prompting many to dub the slump the worst of the postwar period.*

Fortune—July 11, 1983

CLEARLY THERE HAS GOT TO BE A BETTER WAY TO INVEST THAN FOLLOWING THE FORECASTING CROWD!

And there is. Instead of arguing, as my book *Being Right or Making Money* did, that one should not forecast, this book will ironically argue that *forecasting can be useful because it allows one to go contrary to a strong bullish or bearish crowd psychology and make money doing so.* This

FIGURE 1-9 *The Wall Street Journal* forecasting survey.
Bianco Research, LLC.

		The Wall Street Journal **Forecasting Survey**				
		Long-Term Interest Rate Forecasts for the Next 6 Months				
Date of Survey	Yield When Survey Published	Yield Forecast for 6 mos. Forward	Forecasted Change in Yield	Actual Change in Yield	Absolute Diff. between Forecast & Actual	Was Forecast Direction Correct?
Jan-82	13.45%	13.05%	-0.40%	0.47%	0.87%	
Jul-82	13.92%	13.27%	-0.65%	-3.51%	2.86%	Yes
Jan-83	10.41%	10.07%	-0.34%	0.57%	0.91%	
Jul-83	10.98%	10.54%	-0.44%	0.89%	1.33%	
Jan-84	11.87%	11.39%	-0.48%	1.77%	2.25%	
Jul-84	13.64%	13.78%	0.14%	-2.11%	2.25%	
Jan-85	11.53%	11.56%	0.03%	-1.09%	1.12%	
Jul-85	10.44%	10.50%	0.06%	-1.17%	1.23%	
Jan-86	9.27%	9.42%	0.15%	-1.99%	2.14%	
Jul-86	7.28%	7.41%	0.13%	0.21%	0.08%	Yes
Jan-87	7.49%	7.05%	-0.44%	1.01%	1.45%	
Jul-87	8.50%	8.45%	-0.05%	0.48%	0.53%	
Jan-88	8.98%	8.65%	-0.33%	-0.13%	0.20%	Yes
Jul-88	8.85%	9.36%	0.51%	0.14%	0.37%	Yes
Jan-89	8.99%	9.25%	0.26%	-0.95%	1.21%	
Jul-89	8.04%	8.12%	0.08%	-0.07%	0.15%	
Jan-90	7.97%	7.62%	-0.35%	0.43%	0.78%	
Jul-90	8.40%	8.16%	-0.24%	-0.16%	0.08%	Yes
Jan-91	8.24%	7.65%	-0.59%	0.17%	0.76%	
Jul-91	8.41%	8.22%	-0.19%	-1.02%	0.83%	Yes
Jan-92	7.39%	7.30%	-0.09%	0.39%	0.48%	
Jul-92	7.78%	7.61%	-0.17%	-0.39%	0.22%	Yes
Jan-93	7.39%	7.44%	0.05%	-0.72%	0.77%	
Jul-93	6.67%	6.83%	0.16%	-0.33%	0.49%	
Jan-94	6.34%	6.26%	-0.08%	1.27%	1.35%	
Jul-94	7.61%	7.30%	-0.31%	0.26%	0.57%	
Jan-95	7.87%	7.94%	0.07%	-1.23%	1.30%	
Jul-95	6.64%	6.60%	-0.04%	-0.70%	0.66%	Yes
Jan-96	5.94%	6.00%	0.06%	0.95%	0.89%	Yes
Jul-96	6.89%	6.86%	-0.03%	-0.25%	0.22%	Yes
Jan-97	6.64%	6.52%	-0.12%	0.14%	0.26%	
Jul-97	6.78%	6.79%	0.01%	-0.86%	0.87%	
Jan-98	5.92%	6.02%	0.10%	-0.28%	0.38%	
Jul-98	5.64%	5.72%	0.08%	-0.55%	0.63%	
Jan-99	5.09%	5.04%	-0.05%	0.89%	0.94%	
Jul-99	5.98%	5.83%	-0.15%	0.50%	0.65%	
Jan-00	6.48%	6.38%	-0.10%	-0.58%	0.48%	Yes
Jul-00	5.90%	6.01%	0.11%	-0.40%	0.51%	
Jan-01	5.50%	5.35%	-0.15%	0.30%*	0.45%	
Jul-01	5.40%	5.30%	-0.10%	-0.38%	0.28%	Yes
Jan-02	5.02%	5.06%	0.04%	-0.22%	0.26%	
Jul-02	4.80%	5.20%	0.40%	-0.98%	1.38%	
Jan-03	**3.82%**	**4.42%**	**0.60%**	**????**	**????**	
Difference between forecast and actual (average of all periods)					0.84%	
Batting average						0.286

Starting with the July 2001 survey, the benchmark interest rate changed from the 30-year Treasury bond to the 10-year Treasury note.
*The actual change for January 2001 reflects the change of the 30-year bond.

supposition agrees with Bernard Baruch's idea, originally stated in 1932: "Without due recognition of crowd thinking our theories of economics leave much to be desired" (Mackay, 1989).

CROWD PSYCHOLOGY AND THE THEORY OF CONTRARY OPINION

A crusty Vermont libertarian, the late Humphrey B. Neill (1992), originally formulated the theory of "contrary opinion" more than 60 years ago. He wrote under the title of "The Ruminator," and originally all he tried to do was discover the prevalent market opinions and meditate ("ruminate") over their possible failings. Later the iconoclast Neill hosted gatherings in New Hampshire and then Vermont (very "far from the beaten path") called the Contrary Opinion Forum, at which I have been honored to speak several times. More and more over the years I saw Neill come to believe, as I do, that *mass psychology is of primary importance in market movements*. Here is what Neill wrote in the foreword of his book, *The Art of Contrary Thinking:*

> The art of contrary thinking may be stated simply: Thrust your thoughts out of the rut. In a word, be a nonconformist when using your mind.
>
> Sameness of thinking is a natural attribute. So you must expect to practice a little in order to get into the habit of throwing your mind into directions which are opposite to the obvious.
>
> Obvious thinking—or thinking the same way in which everyone else is thinking—commonly leads to wrong judgments and wrong conclusions.
>
> Let me give you an easily remembered epigram to sum up this thought:
> *When everyone thinks alike, everyone is likely to be wrong.*

Neill goes on to remind us, though, that people are not necessarily wrong in all of the choices they make in their everyday lives. Individuals, when they stop to think things through, may make perfectly reasonable decisions. It is when something occurs that has wide emotional appeal that the "crowd instinct" can take over due to people following their emotions, and their behavior then becomes different from how they would behave on their own.

Early in my career as an investment analyst, I was struck by how often the market seemed to be illogical and irrational in regard to the economic fundamentals. So "contrary opinion" analysis fascinated me. Yet I was not sold on it until I watched a series of incredible calls on the stock market by the late analyst Edson Gould, whom I met at Neill's Contrary Opinion Forum. In studying Gould's methods, I came across an essay he wrote. It would be fair to say that this essay expressed a force behind the market that changed and focused my attention in a different direction, toward psychology. In his essay "My Most Important Discovery," Gould relates how he realized psychology to be a driving force behind the stock market:

> I read a book, *The Crowd,* written in the late nineteenth century by a French social scientist, Gustave Le Bon. It was a study of the popular mind based largely upon the experience of crowds in the French Revolution. Here was the essential ingredient, the missing link, for which I had been searching. An apparently irrational stock market became comprehensible. Order emerged from chaos. Effect was finally linked to cause. I came to the initial realization, since reinforced, that *the action of the stock market is nothing more nor less than a manifestation of mass crowd psychology in action.*

Following Neill's and Gould's research, I have found in my own research that the market action is largely a result of mass psychology. Consequently, I have attempted to incorporate quantitative indicators of crowd psychology into our broader, multifactor market timing models. Examples of these indicators are discussed in Chapter 5.

EXPLANATION OF WHY CONTRARY OPINION WORKS

Thus, if you want to try to catch major market turning points, you can start with contrary opinion—wait for majority opinion to reach an extreme and then assume the opposite position. At turning points, contrary sentiment indicators are nearly always right. Almost by definition, *a top in the market is the point of maximum optimism, and a bottom in the market is the point of maximum pessimism.*

To better understand how contrary opinion operates, think of money as financial liquidity, and think of an extreme in liquidity as the direct opposite of an extreme in psychology. If people decided that the Dow Industrials would rise by 25 percent, for instance, they would rush out and buy stocks. Everyone would become fully invested, the market would be overbought, nobody would be left to buy, and the market wouldn't be able to go any higher. *When optimism is extreme, liquidity is low.*

On the other hand, if everyone were pessimistic and thought that the Dow would drop by 25 percent, the weak and nervous stockholders would sell, the market would be sold out, and nobody would be left to sell. In this case, the market couldn't go down any more. Whereas increasing optimism and confidence produces falling liquidity, rising pessimism and fear results in rising liquidity. Figure 1-10 illustrates the key relationship between psychology and liquidity.

My favorite way to describe this inverse relationship is to compare liquidity to a car's shock absorbers. As you drive down the road, you will inevitably encounter some potholes—some random, unpredictable, negative events. If your car has good shocks (abundant liquidity), you will be able to continue merrily along your journey after encountering a pothole. But if your car has poor shocks (no liquidity), you may crash.

Another way of looking at contrary opinion is to compare stockholders to nuts in a tree. An investor once wrote me and asked, "How do you get nuts out of a nut tree?" The answer, he said, is through a nut-shaking machine, which would be hooked to the nut tree. The machine would rattle the tree, and the nuts would drop until all the nuts had fallen out. In other words, when there is enough fear in the market, all the weak holders are shaken out, and there is no selling left to be done. "Have the nuts been shaken out," the contrarian asks, "or are all the speculative traders fully invested?"

In terms of shaking nervous holders out of the market, see Figure 1-11, which my company put out on September 11, 2001, the day of the terrible terrorist attacks. Note that in most cases, the short-term panic actually cleaned the market out for significant rallies. The figure shows that the DJIA dropped by a median of 5 percent during crisis events but rallied afterward. The implication of this is that after an initial negative reaction to a tragic event, a recovery can be expected. Of course, the list is subjective, and even the reaction dates are subject to interpretation in some cases.

FIGURE 1-10 Stock mutual funds cash-assets ratio versus S&P.
Source: Copyright © 2003, Standard & Poor's, a division of The McGraw-Hill Companies, Inc.
© 2003 Ned Davis Research, Inc. All rights reserved.

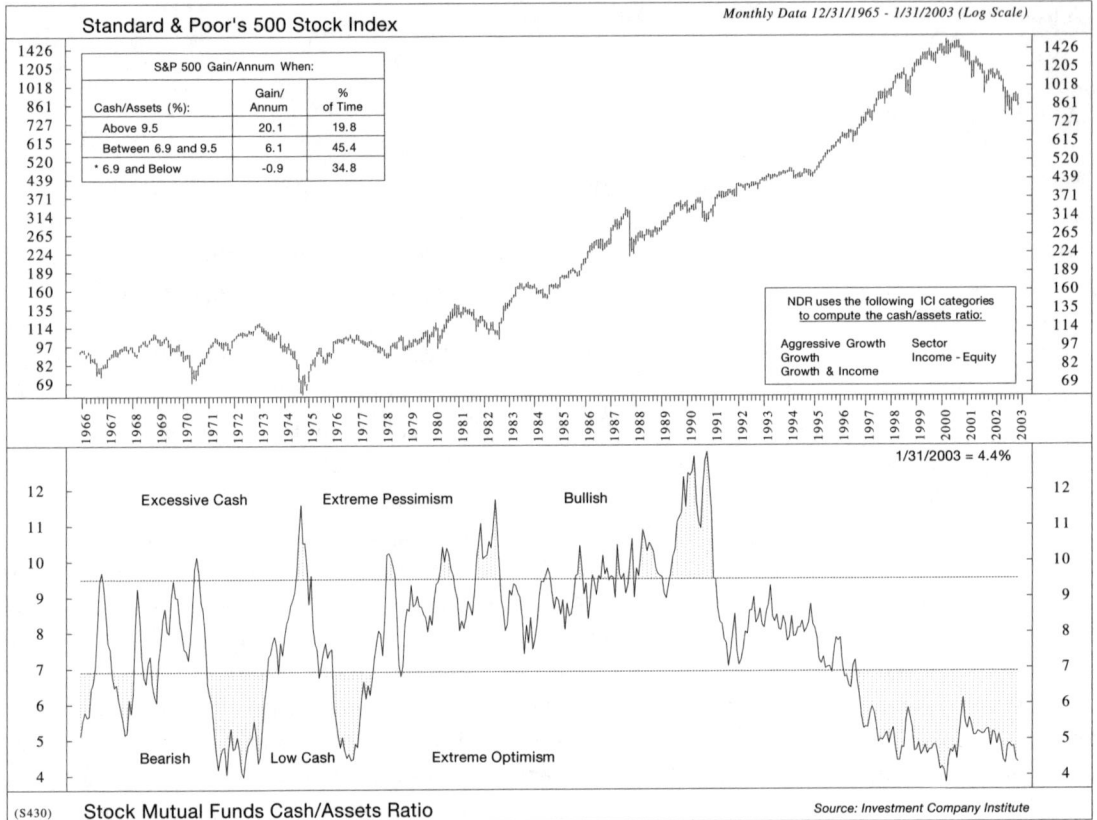

The impact of contrary opinion can also be illustrated by comparing the market to a theater. If someone yelled "fire" in a theater full to the rafters with people, panic would break out and people would get crushed. But if someone yelled "fire" in a theater with very few people, the people would get up and walk out in an orderly manner. In looking at any market, it is important to determine the degree to which the market is a crowded theater or an empty one.

What makes contrary opinion really valuable is that it opens your mind and keeps you from being swept up in the crowd—keeps you from being part of the herd shown in Figure 1-12. With an open mind you can say to yourself, "I know the majority is right, and I know the world is going to hell in a handbasket, but what if the minority is right? What if there is a silver lining in the cloud out there?" *Contrary opinion allows you to be flexible, enabling you to turn your emotions inside out and to act when you need to act.*

FIGURE 1-11 Crisis events—featured Chart of the Day.
© 2003 Ned Davis Research, Inc. All rights reserved.

Event	Reaction Dates	Date Range % Gain/Loss	DJIA Percentage Gain Days After Reaction Dates		
			22	63	126
Fall of France	05/09/1940 - 06/22/1940	-17.1	-0.5	8.4	7.0
Pearl Harbor	12/07/1941 - 12/10/1941	-6.5	3.8	-2.9	-9.6
Truman Upset Victory	11/02/1948 - 11/10/1948	-4.9	1.6	3.5	1.9
Korean War	06/23/1950 - 07/13/1950	-12.0	9.1	15.3	19.2
Eisenhower Heart Attack	09/23/1955 - 09/26/1955	-6.5	0.0	6.6	11.7
Sputnik	10/03/1957 - 10/22/1957	-9.9	5.5	6.7	7.2
Cuban Missile Crisis	10/19/1962 - 10/27/1962	1.1	12.1	17.1	24.2
JFK Assassination	11/21/1963 - 11/22/1963	-2.9	7.2	12.4	15.1
U.S. Bombs Cambodia	04/29/1970 - 05/26/1970	-14.4	9.9	20.3	20.7
Kent State Shootings	05/04/1970 - 05/14/1970	-4.2	0.4	3.8	13.5
Arab Oil Embargo	10/18/1973 - 12/05/1973	-17.9	9.3	10.2	7.2
Nixon Resigns	08/09/1974 - 08/29/1974	-15.5	-7.9	-5.7	12.5
U.S.S.R. in Afghanistan	12/24/1979 - 01/03/1980	-2.2	6.7	-4.0	6.8
Hunt Silver Crisis	02/13/1980 - 03/27/1980	-15.9	6.7	16.2	25.8
Falkland Islands War	04/01/1982 - 05/07/1982	4.3	-8.5	-9.8	20.8
U.S. Invades Grenada	10/24/1983 - 11/07/1983	-2.7	3.9	-2.8	-3.2
U.S. Bombs Libya	04/15/1986 - 04/21/1986	2.6	-4.3	-4.1	-1.0
Financial Panic '87	10/02/1987 - 10/19/1987	-34.2	11.5	11.4	15.0
Invasion of Panama	12/15/1989 - 12/20/1989	-1.9	-2.7	0.3	8.0
Gulf War Ultimatum	12/24/1990 - 01/16/1991	-4.3	17.0	19.8	18.7
Gorbachev Coup	08/16/1991 - 08/19/1991	-2.4	4.4	1.6	11.3
ERM U.K. Currency Crisis	09/14/1992 - 10/16/1992	-6.0	0.6	3.2	9.2
World Trade Center Bombing	02/26/1993 - 02/27/1993	-0.5	2.4	5.1	8.5
Russia Mexico Orange County	10/11/1994 - 12/20/1994	-2.8	2.7	8.4	20.7
Oklahoma City Bombing	04/19/1995 - 04/20/1995	0.6	3.9	9.7	12.9
Asian Stock Market Crisis	10/07/1997 - 10/27/1997	-12.4	8.8	10.5	25.0
U.S. Embassy Bombings Africa	08/07/1998 - 08/10/1998	-0.3	-11.2	4.7	6.5
Russian LTCM Crisis	08/18/1998 - 10/08/1998	-11.3	15.1	24.7	33.7
Mean		**-7.1**	**3.8**	**6.8**	**12.5**
Median		**-4.6**	**3.9**	**6.7**	**12.1**

Days = Market Days   T_900 9/11/2001

WINNERS WHO USE CONTRARY OPINION

In his book *How to Be Rich,* J. Paul Getty (1983), the "richest man in the world" at the time, wrote in his first chapter, entitled "How I Made My First Billion,"

> In business, as in politics, it is never easy to go against the beliefs and attitudes held by the majority. The businessman who moves counter to the tide of prevailing opinion must expect to be obstructed, derided and damned. So it was with me when, in the depths of the U.S. economic slump of the 1930s, I resolved to make large-scale purchases and build a self-contained oil business. My friends and acquaintances—to say nothing of my competitors—felt my buying spree would prove to be a fatal mistake.

FIGURE 1-12   Stampede.
Diane Schmidt.

In 1962, Getty again bought stocks against the following headlines: "Black Monday Panic on Wall Street—Investors Lose Billions As Market Breaks—Nation Fears New 1929 Debacle." Getty said to a puzzled correspondent, "I'd be foolish *not* to buy." "Most seasoned investors are doubtless doing much the same thing," he said; and feeling like a schoolmaster conducting a short course in the first principles of investment, he continued by saying, "They're snapping up the fine stock bargains available as a result of the emotionally inspired selling wave."

In Charles Mackay's 1989 book, *Extraordinary Popular Delusions and the Madness of Crowds,* the legendary Bernard Baruch says in the foreword that "all economic movements by their very nature, are motivated by crowd psychology. . . . Without due recognition of crowd thinking (which often seems crowd-madness) our theories of economics leave much to be desired." But listen to how he sees crowd thinking: "Schiller's dictum: Anyone taken as an individual, is tolerably sensible and reasonable—as a member of a crowd, he at once becomes a blockhead."

The following, written by Baruch, in October 1932, prescribes a "potent incantation" to use against crowd thinking:

> I have always thought that if, in the lamentable era of the "New Economics," culminating in 1929, even in the very presence of dizzily spiraling prices, we had all continuously repeated, "two and two still make four," much of the evil might have been averted. Similarly, even in the general moment of gloom in which this foreword is written, when many begin to wonder if declines will never halt, the appropriate abracadabra may be: They always did.

Peter Lynch in *Beating the Street* written in 1993 says, "Over the past three decades, the stock market has come to be dominated by a herd of professional investors. Contrary to popular belief, this makes it easier for the amateur investor. You can beat the market by ignoring the herd."

Marty Zweig, in his 1986 book, *Winning on Wall Street,* has this important qualification regarding the use of contrary opinion:

> The idea is that if you use contrary opinion, you should go against the majority. But that's an oversimplification and certainly not true in the middle of a bull market. Just because 51% of the crowd is bullish and 49% bearish is no reason the market cannot go higher. In fact, it probably will advance at that point. The time to be wary of crowd psychology is when the crowd gets extraordinarily one-sided.

In the book *Market Wizards* (1989) by Jack Schwager, Paul Tudor Jones stated "I learned that even though markets look their very best when they are setting new highs, that is often the best time to sell. He [Eli Tullis] instilled in me the idea that, to some extent, to be a good trader, you have to be a contrarian."

In the book *The Warren Buffett Way* (Hagstrom, 1994), fundamentalist value investor Warren Buffett is quoted as saying he has "long felt that the only value of stock forecasters is to make fortune tellers look good." Buffett is also quoted as saying:

> The most common cause of low prices is pessimism—sometimes pervasive, sometimes specific to a company or industry. We want to do business in such an environment, not because we like pessimism but because we like the prices it produces. It's optimism that is the enemy of the rational buyer . . . we simply attempt to be fearful when others are greedy and to be greedy only when others are fearful.

Legendary investor Leon Levy (2002) says in his book, *The Minds of Wall Street,* "the only course in which I ever got an A+ was abnormal psychology. What better preparation could there be to tackle the role of psychology in markets?" He quotes the great British economist and philosopher John Maynard Keynes as saying, "Markets can remain irrational longer than you can remain solvent." Levy asks, "Why should the markets be any more perfect than the very human emotions and calculations that drive it? Investors overreact and so do markets. Investors get swept up in moods and so do markets. And this interplay creates investment opportunities."

Finally, in the 2001 book *Stock Market Wizards* by Jack Schwager (published near the end of the bull market), when successful trader Steve Cohen was asked if he had any feelings about how the current long-running bull market will end, he responded, "It's going to end badly: it always ends badly. Everybody in the world is talking stocks now. Everybody wants to be a trader. To me that is the sign of something ending, not something beginning. You can't have everybody on one side of the fence. The world doesn't work that way."

MY PERSONAL EXPERIENCE WITH CONVENTIONAL WISDOM

When I came into the investment business, the conventional wisdom of nearly everyone was as follows: "I've never met a rich technician." "You can't make money short-term trading."

"Eighty-five percent of people who trade options and futures lose money." "Worrying all the time about risks will paralyze you from capturing the rewards from stocks." And so on. I do not claim to be the world's greatest investor, and I've been much too conservative to hit a lot of home runs. Nevertheless, I believed in what I was doing. While my techniques are not for everyone, they were right for my psyche. So I mostly use technical analysis (with heavy doses of contrary opinion); I am a very short-term trader; I make big use of options and futures; and I constantly worry about risks. And taking the road less traveled has worked for me. Since I started Ned Davis Research in 1980, I've never had a losing year on my investments. I am not trying to tout my own investment techniques. The real point of sharing my personal experience is that you have to find what works for you and follow your own dream.

MAKING OUR OWN REALITY

I've often wondered about the psychological forces behind why the crowd and popular forecasts are so often wrong. Earlier I offered one theory for the stock market, which is that crowd psychology and liquidity (potential demand) are inversely related. Looking further, I have become fascinated with the concept that we all *create our own realities*. This is a difficult concept to grasp, so I will try to explain it and give a few examples.

An important truth I've learned is that people will view reality according to the way they *want* to perceive it or believe it *should be*. This was illustrated to me during a human relations class I took. I read that a long-time warden from New York's infamous Sing Sing prison said, "Few of the criminals in Sing Sing regard themselves as bad men. They are just as human as you and I. So they rationalize, they explain. . . . Most of them attempt by a form of reasoning, fallacious or logical, to justify their anti-social acts even to themselves. . . . the desperate men and women behind prison walls *don't blame themselves for anything.*" Rationalization is a powerful coping mechanism.

Another good example is people who seemingly *must* gamble. Despite the fact that casinos make hundreds of millions of dollars every year, I've almost never met a gambler who claimed to have been a loser. The gamblers will look you straight in the eye when they tell you that. It is my belief that the pain of losing is so great they actually forget the losses. *Denial is a powerful defense mechanism.*

Yet another illustration: In listening to the sexual harassment testimony given during the Clarence Thomas confirmation hearing, I found that it was impossible for me to discern who was telling the truth and who was lying, but clearly I knew that one of them had to be lying. That is, until I heard a wise psychiatrist say that she thought both of them were telling the truth. At least it was the *truth as far as each of them saw it. Illusion or delusion is a powerful psychological force.*

Some time ago I read a fascinating magazine interview with actor Ralph Fiennes who played the evil Nazi Amon Goeth in *Schindler's List*:

Q—Was there an emotional residue from the experience of playing a character he views as obscene and sick?

A—After a long pause he answers softly, "I think there was a price to pay for this one. When you're investigating behavior that is so negative, so intensely for three months, then you feel sort of peculiar because you might have at moments enjoyed it and at the same time you feel slightly soiled by it.... *It's not a rational thing, but it's an instinctive thing.*... If you're playing a role, you are immersing yourself in thinking about that character—how he moves, how he thinks. In the end he *becomes an extension of your own self. You like him.* It just throws up all kinds of question marks about acting, about human behavior, about how evil is probably a lot closer to the surface than we like to think.

A person's mind can sometimes get badly twisted under intense emotional pressure.

Then there's the O. J. Simpson case. Was he guilty? *After* the innocent verdict, 36 percent of whites said he was innocent compared with 73 percent of African-Americans. William Raspberry (1994), the black Pulitzer Prize-winning journalist, said, "How can that be? Are white people, less invested in Simpson's fate, being objective while blacks are being emotional? Have we come to the point where color is of such importance as to override every other consideration, to render us, black and white, *incapable* of a *shared reality?*"

My favorite example of imagination distorting reality is watching basketball games. Almost always the vast majority of home fans at a game will swear that the referees favored the opposing team (many even proclaim the other team has paid off the refs) even though their home team won the game, and even though objective statistics show that if there is a bias, the calls in an average game favor the home team. Crowd psychology is contagious and can influence even what we see with our own eyes. *One's perception equals one's reality* (see Figure 1-13).

Finally, the latest example of "making one's own reality" came after 9/11. Very quickly after the 9/11 attack, the U.S. government identified the 19 hijackers personally and individually by the Arab countries from which they came, by what they did in the United States, and by the fact that they were all linked to Osama bin Laden's Al-Qaeda network. With the hard evidence presented, almost the entire U.S. population pulled together behind President Bush in his determination to wipe out the Al-Qaeda terrorist organization. Figure 1-14 shows that 90 percent of the U.S. people polled gave President Bush their approval, the *highest* approval rating *ever* (also note the stock market usually does best when Presidential approval is low—contrary opinion at work). Five months after the attack, after nearly all the "hard evidence" was already made public, Gallup also polled a statistically significant 9924 Muslims of nine Arab countries. According to CNN, 61 percent said "they did not believe Arab groups carried out the September 11th terrorist attack." Furthermore, only 11 percent of these Muslims had a favorable view of President Bush, while 58 percent had unfavorable opinions. Of those surveyed, 77 percent said any U.S. military action in Afghanistan was morally unjustified compared with 9 percent who said it was justified. In case anyone feels it was a lack of free press in some of those countries that led to these anti-U.S. views, the story of French author Thierry Meyssan (2002) refutes that thought. Meyssan wrote a book entitled *9/11, The Big Lie* seeking to prove that the September 11 acts of terrorism were committed not by Arab terrorists but by U.S. special services. Meyssan believes the attacks were organized by "ultra-rightist" high-ranking officials. In any case, Meyssan achieved great popularity, and his book was on the top of the bestseller list in France for many months.

FIGURE 1-13 Crazy markets.
Artist: Andrea Justiniano-Blake.
© *2003 Ned Davis Research, Inc. All rights reserved.*

I know most people feel they have a good grasp of reality and that it is all these other people who are "lost in space." However, even among my siblings, when we talk about our parents and how we were raised, I sometimes get the feeling that our realities are so different I can't believe we had the same parents. So what I hope this section will show is that *people see and hear mostly what they want to believe* or what the group (crowd) to which they belong believes. The bottom line is that *people often create their own realities* based upon things that may have happened to them as far back as their very early years of life. We are all subject to that condition. We are human. This means what feels right, easy, and obvious in your gut is quite often wrong.

THE NED DAVIS RESEARCH RESPONSE TO ALL THIS

Given (1) all the evidence in this book which shows the crowd is almost always wrong at extremes, (2) the pressures toward, and the ease of, being swept up by the crowd, and (3) the pos-

FIGURE 1-14 Gallup poll presidential approval rating versus DJIA.
© 2003 Ned Davis Research, Inc. All rights reserved.

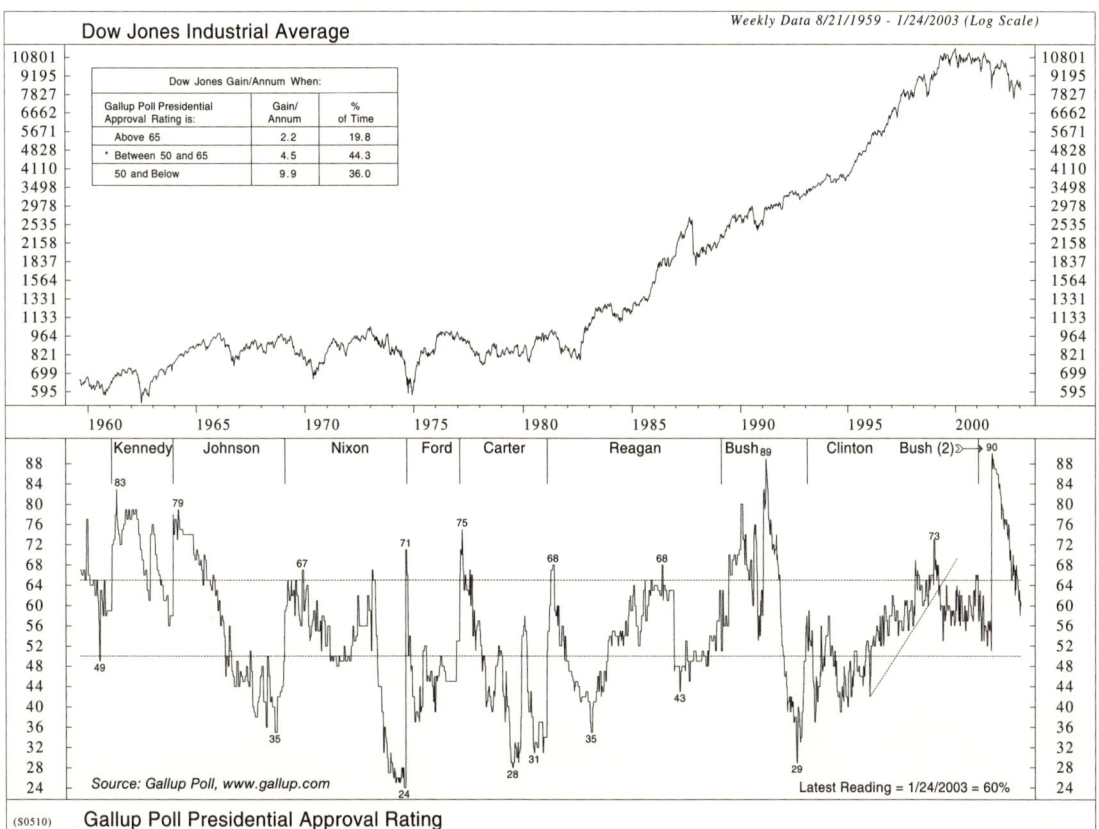

sibility that under stress, our own realities could become badly distorted, a clear study of crowd psychology and objective indicators to measure investor sentiment is critical. Such a study can open one's mind to thinking about other possibilities, keep us from getting swept up by mob fever, and, in many cases, encourage us to take the road less traveled. Since such a study can lead to increased profits, I have written this book to help both your investing and, possibly, your thought process in life. Also, it is because of the importance of crowd sentiment in the market that Ned Davis Research (NDR) builds so many indicators of crowd psychology; they can allow us to pass judgment devoid of emotionalism.

CHAPTER 2

SCIENTIFIC STUDIES ON CROWD PSYCHOLOGY

THE HISTORY OF FINANCIAL MARKETS IS RIFE with examples of irrational behavior by investors. But why do thousands of rational individuals, as a group, continue to make irrational decisions? At least part of the answer can be found in social psychology. Social scientists have conducted several experiments that indicate that it is human nature to be heavily influenced by crowds. Most of the experiments were not tested in the context of investor psychology. Instead, they show that people are influenced by crowds in many aspects of their lives, and investing is just one of them. The studies show that people make decisions based on their emotions, and their emotions are partially created by their surroundings. The stock market is nothing more than a reflection of investors' aggregate emotions, or as we like to say at Ned Davis Research, *the stock market is the manifestation of group psychology in motion.*

ANCHORING TO THE CROWD

One of the earliest studies on group conformity was conducted by Muzafer Sherif in 1935. As described by James McConnell (1980) in *Understanding Human Behavior,* Sherif's experiment consisted of students watching a pinpoint of light in a dark room. The light was stationary, but to the human eye it appeared to move (the phenomenon is known as the autokinetic effect). Sherif asked the students to estimate how far the light moved. For the first part of the experiment students made their decisions in private. Their answers varied widely, from a fraction of an inch to over a foot. For the second part of the experiment Sherif put the students into groups and had them answer in front of each other. Sherif found that answers anchored on the first response. In other words, each group created its own average, which was highly influenced by the answer given by the first respondent. Since the autokinetic effect is an illusion and is perceived differently by each person, there is no inherent reason someone would need to change his or her answer based on someone else's answer. Nevertheless, the subjects of the experiment felt compelled to conform to the crowd.

If one views the Sherif study in the context of the stock market being a reflection of investor sentiment, the connection to group psychology is obvious. Stock prices are determined by the aggregate opinion of investors, and the aggregate opinion is influenced by the voices heard by the most people. Twenty-four-hour news channels interview professional investors providing their opinions. Even those who do not watch financial news are exposed to commercials from financial services companies. Magazines, newspapers, and the Internet are full of opinions from analysts and money managers. Investors would have to try *not* to be exposed to the financial media in order to avoid them, and Sherif's findings indicate that investors are influenced by the exposure.

GROUP PRESSURE

Years after Sherif's experiment, psychologist Solomon Asch added a layer of complexity to group cohesion research. His study (McConnell, 1980) consisted of showing students an 8-inch line on a piece of paper. He told the students to study the line and then placed it out of sight. On another piece of paper he showed them three lines: one 8, one 8 3/4, and one 10 inches long. Asch then asked the students to tell him which of the three lines matched the line on the first piece of paper. When asked individually, students answered correctly 99 percent of the time.

Asch then altered the experiment. He had the students answer in groups. Each group included "stooges" who purposely answered incorrectly. (The students did not know the other participants were stooges.) When the stooges said that the 8 3/4-inch line was the correct line, about two-thirds of the subjects agreed. Even when the stooges said the 10-inch line matched the line on the first piece of paper, approximately one-third of the students agreed.

Just as interesting as the fact that people succumbed to group pressures were their reasons for yielding. About half of the students who answered incorrectly admitted that the pressure from the other members of the group overwhelmed them. They thought there was a trick they did not see, or they felt pressured not to go against the group. The other half *actually believed* they were giving the correct answer. They did not realize they were being led astray. Since virtually all the students answered correctly in private, this clearly illustrates human nature's ability to be influenced by group pressures.

Given the complex nature of the financial markets, the stock market can be compared to the 8 3/4-inch line in that the "correct" answer is not always obvious. Manias always appear obvious in hindsight. During the height of the stock market bubble, however, investors could be influenced, either knowingly or unknowingly, into believing a mania is not a mania. The recent NASDAQ Bubble is a case in point. Three years after the fact, it appears obvious the market was priced to perfection. At the time, however, the fact that everyone (at least it seemed like everyone) was getting rich on technology and Internet stocks made it easier to overlook overvaluations, oversupply, and overconfidence.

The previous examples illustrate that people are influenced by others when they are physically present. Most investors, however, are not on trading floors. They make their decisions in their office or at home. University of Texas professors Robert Blake and Henry Helson recognized and addressed this issue. Through their use of tape recorders, they proved that the stooges do not even have to be physically present to influence the subjects of the experiment.

CROWD PSYCHOLOGY AND INVESTING

Behavioral finance, the academic term for the study of investor sentiment, has long been considered to be on the outskirts of finance. However, the NASDAQ Bubble has given new credence to the field, so much credence that Daniel Kahneman was awarded the 2002 Nobel Prize in economics for his study of individual investor behavior with the late Amos Tversky. In his book *Beyond Greed and Fear,* Hersh Shefrin (2000) illustrates how Kahneman and Tversky pioneered the ideas of regret theory and loss aversion, which imply that people are sometimes motivated by minimizing their regrets rather than maximizing their wealth. While minimizing regret and maximizing wealth are typically compatible, occasionally they come into conflict. Kahneman and Tversky used this simple experiment to illustrate their point: You are faced with two choices. Option A is a certain loss of $7500. Option B is a 75 percent chance of a loss of $10,000 and a 25 percent chance of breaking even. The expected payoffs are the same for both scenarios:

Option A: -$7500*100% = -$7500
Option B: -$10,000*75% + $0*25% = -$7500

Yet Kahneman and Tversky found that most people choose option B. Why? Because most people want to avoid taking the loss. They found that a loss has to be about 2 1/2 times as large as a gain for the two to offset.

While the first experiment studied minimizing regret, Kahneman and Tversky's second survey studied maximizing wealth. The second scenario also presents two options: Option A is a sure gain of $2400. Option B is a 25 percent chance of a $10,000 gain and a 75 percent chance of breaking even. Despite the fact that option B has a higher expected payoff than A, most people chose the certain $2400 gain over the unlikely possibility of a $10,000 windfall.

Option A: $2400*100% = $2400
Option B: $10,000*25% + $0*75% = $2500

This experiment illustrates that people are loss-averse when looking at gains. Most people will take a slightly lower payoff if it is guaranteed over a larger, but uncertain, gain. The two surveys together indicate that people react differently when they are maximizing wealth versus minimizing regret. The study also illustrates that investors are influenced by *how* information is presented to them.

Hersh Shefrin and Meir Statman tested regret theory in the context of avoiding blame. Their study (Shefrin, 2000) consisted of a scenario with three investors who decided to buy certificates of deposit. Investor A had been invested in stocks, but he decided, through his own research, to switch to CDs. Investor B also switched to CDs from stocks, but he did so based on the advice of his financial adviser. Investor C had already owned CDs, so he just rolled over his CDs when they expired. Shefrin and Statman asked students which investor would be the most upset if stocks outperformed CDs over the subsequent few months. About 70 percent said A, 12 percent said B, 0 percent said C, and 18 percent said no one. Investors B and C have good "excuses" they can tell themselves. B can blame his financial adviser, and C can say he always invests in CDs anyway. Investor A, however, has no one to blame but himself.

One of the more common corollaries to Kahneman and Tversky's theories is the impact of crowd psychology on loss aversion. *If investors are trying to minimize their regret, then going along with the crowd can be the path of least resistance.* If an investor follows the crowd and is wrong, then at least he was not the only person to make the mistake. If an investor goes against the crowd and is wrong, then he must deal with not only the financial loss but also the psychological loss of watching other investors enjoy their windfall. Even if the investor believes the crowd is wrong, he may decide that the benefit of "safety in numbers" is greater than the potential pain of being wrong.

This type of crowd psychology could have played a role in the NASDAQ Bubble. The NASDAQ soared 85.6 percent in 1999, but as shown in Figure 2-1, 10 stocks accounted for 45.8 percent of the index's gains. The equal-weighted Value Line Composite and NYSE Advance/Decline line peaked in 1998, further demonstrating that most stocks were not participating in the final stages of the bull market. The narrow rally meant that almost everyone was invested in the same select names. As a result, the risks of going against the crowd were extraordinary. If an investor was underweight Technology and Internet stocks and they continued to soar, then he was guaranteed to underperform his peers. Conversely, if he followed the crowd and the market declined, then he was no worse off than anyone else.

Social psychologists have shown that it is human nature to be influenced by our surroundings. Why should investing be any different? History suggests that it isn't.

FIGURE 2-1 Top contributors as a percentage of the NASDAQ Composite Index (12/31/1998–12/31/1999).
© 2003 Ned Davis Research, Inc. All rights reserved.

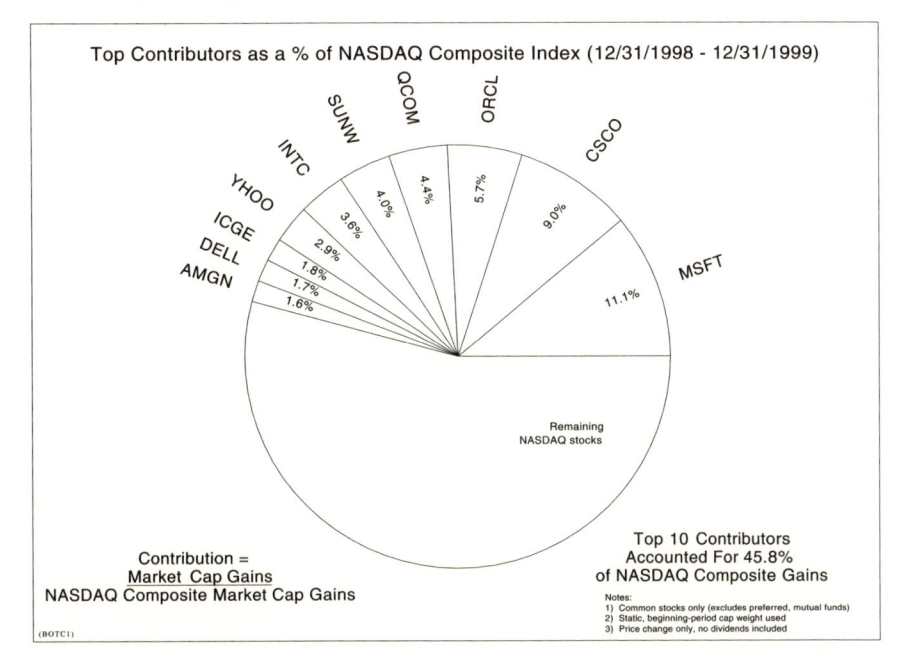

CHAPTER 3

BRIEF HISTORY OF MANIAS AND PANICS

THE PREVIOUS CHAPTER DESCRIBED PSYCHOLOGICAL studies illustrating how people are influenced by their surroundings when making decisions, including investment choices. The stock market is nothing more than an aggregate account of the opinions of millions of individual investors. Since the market is composed of the opinions of investors and since those opinions are influenced by their surroundings, the ebb and flow of the stock market reflects changes in crowd psychology. Therefore, almost by definition the peak in the market is the point of maximum optimism, and the trough is the point of maximum pessimism. The exact level of the peaks and troughs, however, varies in each cycle (see Chapter 5 for investor psychology indicators). Upon occasion, crowd psychology completely diverges from macroeconomic and company-specific fundamentals, resulting in manias and panics. In order to demonstrate this point, this chapter provides several examples of extremes in crowd psychology. Backgrounds, names, and geographies may differ, but the common link between all the stories is that the pressure of the crowd pushed investors to temporarily ignore the underlying economic environment.

MISSISSIPPI SCHEME

In 1841 Charles Mackay (reprinted in 1989) published a book entitled *Extraordinary Popular Delusions and the Madness of Crowds,* in which he explores different speculative episodes throughout history during which crowd psychology caused the rise and fall of economic systems. Mackay opens his book by retelling the story of the famous "Mississippi Scheme" engineered by the mad financial wizard John Law.

The death of King Louis XIV left France in financial disarray. The opulent king had accrued a phenomenal national debt, taxes were crippling, and sentiment was overwhelmingly pessimistic. Enter Law, a brilliant young man with a plan to right France. Law proposed that France grant him control of the Mississippi Company, an organization that had a monopoly over trade with the Mississippi-Louisiana area. Once he took control, he set up a national bank, which in turn inherited France's national debt. Speculators quickly bought bank bonds that were backed by stock in the Mississippi Company. Rampant buying pushed stock prices through the roof, and as people saw their friends change from pauper to millionaire virtually overnight, they ran to invest in the Mississippi Company. The French government, thrilled with the wealth with which Law was seemingly infecting France and blind to the terrible consequences of his system, poured money into the bank, sponsoring several similar banks around France. The French people were overcome with avarice and rushed to invest further. The future looked beautiful, and France's growing wealth seemed unstoppable.

One of many problems with Law's system, aside from the obvious problem that bank money was backed only with paper rather than some kind of gold or silver, was the Mississippi Company itself. The company actually served no function at all. France was not trading with nor developing the Mississippi region. The unbridled mass of buying the company stock was the only thing pushing the stock higher, rather than the success of the company itself. The Mississippi Scheme soon reached the height of its popularity, at which point virtually all France was invested. According to Robert Menschel (2002) in *Markets, Mobs, & Mayhem,* the price of Mississippi shares rose approximately 6200 percent over a 13-month period. With no one left to invest, the price began to drop. As people rushed to sell, the market collapsed. Perhaps if only the citizens had been invested, France could have survived the crash. However, with the French government so intimately entwined with Law's system, the whole economic system fell apart. Several days into the crash, 15 people were trampled to death trying to get money from the bank. According to Menschel, share prices tumbled 99 percent over the 13 months following the peak. The government and the country fell into an economic despair from which they did not recover for almost 100 years.

SOUTH SEA BUBBLE

One might be inclined to blame the conditions in France preceding the Mississippi Scheme for why Law's system could so thoroughly wreck the French economy. The people were destitute, left in financial ruin from the extravagant spending of Louis XIV, and starving for an easy way to right their problems. Certainly that was an environment rich for speculative opportunities. However, France's rise and fall was not a fluke. The pattern has been repeated throughout history. Even while England was watching France rise and fall, it was building a stock system of its own.

The English historical speculative disaster called the "South Sea Bubble" began in the 1700s. England was in a state of prosperity at this time; independent businesses flourished, and the economy was soaring. The solid state of the country would prove to be England's saving grace after the crash.

The South Sea Company was the section of England's trading companies that dealt with the South Sea region of the empire. Inspired by Law's Mississippi Scheme, the South Sea Company offered to take over England's national debt for the sole purpose of alerting the English public to the existence of the company. The ploy worked, and the company began selling off stock: £1 of stock for every £1 of debt it had taken. The stock's popularity was immediate; share prices rose more than 200 points in less than 2 months. However, the company did not stop there. The directors realized that they needed a new way to increase the cashflow into the company. They offered stockholders a loan—for every £100 the public had invested, investors could receive up to £250 in loans. The gimmick worked so well that the South Sea Company compounded the loan process three times, and the company's stock price eventually rose as much as 1000 percent over an 18-month period according to Menschel (2002) in *Markets, Mobs, & Mayhem*. England was swept up in financial success. Everyone was an investor, and new companies offering stock opportunities sprang up. These new companies, inspired by the South Sea Company, ultimately hurt the original organization by taking business away from the South Sea. Angered by a slowing in the number of investors, the directors of the South Sea Company appealed to Parliament, which passed a series of Bubble Acts forbidding the existence of all companies without a government charter. The Bubble Acts proved to be the pin that burst the South Sea Bubble. Unable to tell which companies were legitimate and which were fabrications, investors sold quickly as confidence plummeted, and South Sea shares tumbled approximately 84 percent in just 6 months. Perhaps if the South Sea Company had developed trade in the South Seas, it could have prevented its downfall. However, in reality, the South Sea Company was identical to the Mississippi Company—neither actually did anything except sell stock. The buying alone pushed prices higher rather than actual company success. The South Sea Company, facing bankruptcy, appealed to the Bank of England, begging the bank to buy large blocks of South Sea stock. The Bank of England refused the proposal, and the South Sea Company collapsed.

The situation in England differed from that in France because in France the speculative company actually controlled the bank system. Therefore, when the Mississippi Company fell apart, the entire economic system in France was overturned. In England, the Bank of England refused to get involved with the South Sea Company, so after its downfall, the Bank of England still remained somewhat intact. Also, England had a much sturdier economic base before the speculation, helping the British to salvage some of their original economy.

RUSSIA'S MMM MANIA

After reading those two stories, one might now concede that crowd psychology played a part in the financial ruin of England and France in the 1700s. Investors bought without considering the validity of either the company in which they were investing or the consequences of a bubble that would inevitably collapse. They simply followed the masses, blinded by riches. There were wise men who spoke out against the speculation; however, the very few who spoke publicly were regarded as fools, were ridiculed, and were ignored. Despite these facts, one might still argue that these examples happened almost 300 years ago, and this could never happen in modern society. In fact, an almost identical situation occurred less than a decade ago in Russia.

In his book *Contrarian Investment Strategies: The Next Generation,* author David Dreman (1998) explores the rise and fall of the MMM company in Russia. The year 1994 saw a Russia open for the first time to free enterprise and the world of capitalism. A brilliant and ambitious capitalist named Sergei Mavrodi opened MMM early in 1994. He advertised well, spending millions of dollars on TV and newspaper ads. Shares were first issued in February at $1 a share, a price that rose to $65 by mid-July. MMM estimated that, at the height of its popularity, it had between 5 million and 10 million shareholders. However, in mid-1994, the Russian government began investigating MMM only to discover there was actually no business at all behind MMM, making MMM an even more audacious scheme than that in England or France, where there was at least a semblance of a company. The government investigated MMM, and when it revealed its findings, the stock price collapsed, falling from $60 to $0.46. People trampled each other in the streets trying to redeem their worthless stock. Mavrodi, however, was far from finished. He claimed that MMM was getting ready to release new products that would be instant successes, and he offered to redeem the shares of the neediest citizens at $50 a share. The mobs turned around overnight, as enormous lines formed to buy more shares of MMM stock. Mavrodi was incarcerated for tax evasion, but, taking advantage of a Russian law allowing members of Parliament to avoid prosecution for almost all illegal activities, he ran for Parliament in a district with a large number of MMM investors. His platform promised to use the government to rescue MMM. Mavrodi won, and now free from prosecution, he admitted to the public that he had no intention of saving MMM.

Unlike England and France, the fall of MMM did not bring down the Russian economy. There were simply too many citizens not invested in MMM. However, millions of people lost everything they had as a result of obediently following the crowd, blind to the inherent risks.

CRASH OF 1929

It would be easy to dismiss these historic examples. After all, France and England suffered their economic collapses over 200 years ago, and Russia's lightning-quick rise and fall could simply be attributed to a response of a country experiencing capitalism for the first time. Those of us in developed economies can find reasons why the same forces could not overtake our markets and economies. Better information flow from corporations, detailed research from brokerage firms, government oversight to protect investors, and stabilizing tactics by monetary policy boards should ensure that investors in developed economies do not fall prey to the psychology of the masses.

Nevertheless, the U.S. financial markets are not immune to the effect of group psychology, and like other markets, the U.S. stock market has been engulfed in manias and panics. Perhaps the most notorious bubble led to the crash of 1929. While there are numerous reasons and explanations for the 1920s' bubble and subsequent Great Depression, the role of investor psychology cannot be ignored. As America entered the Roaring Twenties, the end of the Great War in Europe and excitement over the mass commoditization of new technologies such as the radio, the telephone, electrification, the automobile, and the airplane produced a wave of optimism. The impact these technologies made on society is arguably larger than the productivity gains via computers and the Internet in the late twentieth century. According to Robert Sobel (1965) in *The Big Board: A History of the New York Stock Market,* as the decade advanced, the optimism began to detach itself from reality. Installment buying made automobiles affordable to millions of Americans who otherwise could not pay for them. While clearly a positive for the auto industry, investors responded by pumping up General Motors' stock price to $222 from $146 over a 2-month period in early 1926 after GM CEO John J. Raskob said that his company's stock price was 100 points too low. Charles Lindbergh's flight across the Atlantic spurred imaginations about the possibilities of the airline industry. Investors, caught up in the speculation, pushed Wright Aeronautical, the company that built *The Spirit of St. Louis,* to $245 from $25 in the 19 months after the flight. While some worried that the speculation would result in a panic similar to the one in 1907, the general consensus, according to Sobel, was that a crash was not possible, "because of strong leadership on the Street, enlightened Federal Reserve policies, the strong economic structure of the nation, and the ability to profit from lessons learned from the past."

While the Federal Reserve worried about the speculation, it initially refused to raise interest rates because doing so would damage the fragile recovery in Europe and strain the English gold standard. Finally, in February 1929 the Fed tried to prick the bubble by warning banks against borrowing from the Fed to make margin loans. In direct defiance of the Fed, Charles A. Mitchell, the head of National City Bank and director of the New York Federal Reserve Bank, promised to loan $25 million to investors who were unable to obtain funds from the Fed. The move produced a new wave of optimism that Wall Street leaders would not let the market decline.

By early September, with the Dow Jones Industrial Average up 30 percent over the previous 3 months, public infatuation with the stock market reached saturation. The downward momentum built throughout October and climaxed on October 28 and 29 with the DJIA tumbling 12.8 percent and 11.7 percent, respectively. Wall Street leaders attempted to stymie the crash and buoy investor sentiment with staged public buying, but the decline was too severe for even the titans of Wall Street to prevent.

Too many individuals and too many corporations had tied their fortunes to the stock market for the crash not to impact the economy. Capital market conditions did not permit companies to issue stock or borrow, which set off a downward spiral of slower growth, rising unemployment, decreasing demand, lower investment, slower growth, etc. The DJIA finally hit its nadir in July 1932, 89 percent below its peak, and did not recover to precrash levels until 1954. Earnings for the S&P 500 did not surpass 1929 levels until the post-World War II boom in 1948.

The following quote by Alan Greenspan, published in the June 25, 1999, issue of *InvesTech Research,* summarizes the boom and bust of the 1920s and 1930s from the perspective of monetary policy as well as investor sentiment:

> . . . the excess credit which the Fed pumped into the economy (in the 1920s) spilled over into the stock market—triggering a fantastic speculative boom. Belatedly, Federal Reserve officials

attempted to sop up excess reserves and finally succeeded in breaking the boom. But it was too late! By 1929 the speculative imbalances had become so overwhelming that the attempt precipitated a sharp retrenching and a consequent demoralizing of business confidence.

Greenspan made this comment in 1966, more than 30 years before he found himself fighting the next great bubble in the stock market.

NASDAQ BUBBLE

The crash of 1929 left an indelible impression on the psyche of U.S. investors. Surely the lessons of the crash would prevent investors from being swept into another bubble. In the late 1990s, however, investors, business leaders, and the economy fell victim to another crowd mania. The surges in markets around the globe and billions of dollars in international inflows into the U.S. stock market suggest the phenomenon was global in nature; however, the NASDAQ Composite was the widely accepted epicenter. Several positive fundamental factors in the previous two decades laid the foundation for the boom. Demographic trends broadened the appeal of investing to baby boomers; the secular decline in interest rates increased the relative attractiveness of stocks; corporations restructured to become more competitive in the global economy; the fall of Communism in Eastern Europe spurred the popularity of American-style capitalism to record heights. Perhaps most importantly, the late 1980s and 1990s witnessed a technology and productivity boom not seen since the 1920s. Computers became an integral part of American life and, soon after that, an important part of life all over the world. Millions of families bought computers, as the Internet became the main way to research information and stay in touch with friends and family. As far as the economy was concerned, computers carried an even larger and more vital implication: They increased productivity. Computers did not need a salary and worked many times faster than any human; thus, increased computer usage cut expenses and raised profits. Brilliant and courageous entrepreneurs believed that dot-com companies would soon replace brick and mortar buildings filled with actual workers, and as a result, dot-com companies like Amazon.com, eBay, Monster.com, and E*Trade became investor favorites.

In her book *Ride the Wave,* Sherry Cooper (2001) points out that from a valuation standpoint, "New Economy" stocks created a problem. How does one value a company whose assets are human capital and concepts? Industrial companies use real assets. Accounting rules provide a relatively simple way to measure these assets. The assets are placed on the balance sheet and depreciated over time. However, the costs of acquiring New Economy assets, such as brand equity, are expensed during the period the money is spent, leaving no assets on the balance sheet. In addition, very few Internet companies produced profits according to generally accepted accounting principles, and so investors valued companies based on price-to-pro forma earnings, price-to-sales, or even price-to-concept ratios. The new valuation metrics provided companies with incentives to spend lavishly to build brand recognition. Cooper relates the tale of one dot-com CEO, Michael Budowski, who was in charge of a company called OurBeginnings. The company had only 12 employees and had revenues of about $1 million. However, it paid over $4 million for three commercials during the 2000 Super Bowl, and as a result, it had to pay an additional $1 million to upgrade its technology to handle the overwhelming influx of business.

Like the manias in France, England, and Russia, the riches made by a few early investors encouraged others to find their fortunes. The success of new Internet companies such as Amazon.com and eBay led investors to seek the next hot company. Remarkable first-day gains by IPOs such as VA Software (+698 percent) and Theglobe.com (+606 percent) turned companies with a few million in revenues into companies with multibillion dollar market capitalizations. Cisco Systems, the maker of the switches and routers that enable the Internet to function, became the poster child of the New Economy. As the table in Figure 3-1 shows, Cisco's market cap, just above $541 billion, was approximately the same as the combined market caps of 25 blue-chip stocks, but its earnings and revenue were only a fraction of those of the "Old Economy" stocks. A March 24, 2000 Chart of the Day (a one-page report focusing on a specific topic) featuring the table, states, "... it is clear that the valuation on Cisco (and many other Tech/Net stocks) has already anticipated *years and years* of revenue and sales."

Twenty-four-hour news channels such as CNBC, CNNfn, and Bloomberg News furthered the public's interest through their continuous coverage and constant reminders of the market's ascent. Investment websites such as TheStreet.com and Motley Fool provided investors with real-time

FIGURE 3-1 Investment options comparison.
© *2003 Ned Davis Research, Inc. All rights reserved.*

	INVESTMENT OPTION A					INVESTMENT OPTION B			
Ticker	Company Name	03/23/2000 Market Cap	1999 Revenues	1999 Earnings	Ticker	Company Name	03/23/2000 Market Cap	1999 Revenues	1999 Earnings
F	Ford Motor Co	53.75	162.56	7.22	CSCO	Cisco Sys Inc	541.27	15.00	2.54
TX	Texaco Inc	27.70	35.06	1.15					
MER	Merrill Lynch & Co	39.56	34.88	2.58					
DD	Du Pont (E I) De Nemours & Co	57.36	26.94	7.68					
AET	Aetna Inc	8.24	26.45	0.69					
IP	International Paper Co	16.08	24.58	0.18					
SLE	Sara Lee Corp	16.42	20.15	1.17					
RTN.B	Raytheon Co - Class B	6.34	20.04	0.40					
CAT	Caterpillar Inc	14.19	19.70	0.95					
AMR	AMR Corp	4.71	19.13	0.99					
FDX	Fedex Corp	11.53	17.37	0.63					
MMM	Minnesota Mining & Mfg Co	35.03	15.66	1.76					
MCD	McDonalds Corp	47.64	13.26	1.95					
ADM	Archer-Daniels-Midland Co	6.52	13.21	0.19					
GT	Goodyear Tire & Rubber Co	3.67	12.88	0.24					
JPM	Morgan (JP) & Co Inc	23.80	11.82	2.02					
BUD	Anheuser Busch Cos Inc	28.14	11.70	1.40					
LLY	Lilly (Eli) & Co	70.20	9.91	2.72					
SPLS	Staples Inc	9.74	8.84	0.33					
FOX	FOX Entertainment Group Inc	18.74	7.94	0.18					
ED	Consolidated Edison Hldg Inc	7.02	7.49	0.69					
AAPL	Apple Computer Inc	22.73	6.77	0.63					
MYG	Maytag Corp	2.66	4.32	0.33					
HLT	Hilton Hotels Corp	2.81	2.33	0.17					
DJ	Dow Jones & Co Inc	6.66	2.00	0.27					
	Total	541.24	535.00	36.52		Total	541.27	15.00	2.54
	Price / Sales	1.01				Price / Sales	36.08		
	Price / Earnings	14.82				Price / Earnings	213.10		

NOTE: All numbers in $ Billions

information. Online trading enabled investors to act on this new information and trade faster and cheaper than ever before. Armed with the belief that this time was different, investors flocked to the market, pouring billions of dollars into Technology and Internet stocks.

Nowhere was the mania more evident than in the NASDAQ Composite. The index surged 40 percent in 1998 and 86 percent in 1999, including a 48 percent surge in the fourth quarter. Since the index is capitalization-weighted, the statistics reflected appreciation in only the largest companies. Despite the remarkable rallies in Technology and Internet stocks, most companies were enduring a stealth bear market. Figure 3-2 shows the NASDAQ Composite in the top clip, the NASDAQ Advance/Decline line in the second clip, and the number of NASDAQ stocks making new 52-week highs and lows in the bottom clip. The Advance/Decline line is a cumulative total of the difference between the number of stocks that rise and fall each day. As Figure 3-2 shows, the NASDAQ Composite Advance/Decline line was in a downtrend in the late 1990s even as the price line continued to make record highs. Likewise, the NYSE A/D line peaked in April 1998. Further illustrating the narrow advance, the number of stocks making new 52-week highs peaked at 500 on July 16, 1997. Despite numerous new highs in the NASDAQ over the next 33 months, the number of stocks hitting new highs became entrenched in a downtrend. The mania continued into early

FIGURE 3-2 **NASDAQ Composite Index versus breadth indicators.**

© *2003 Ned Davis Research, Inc. All rights reserved.*

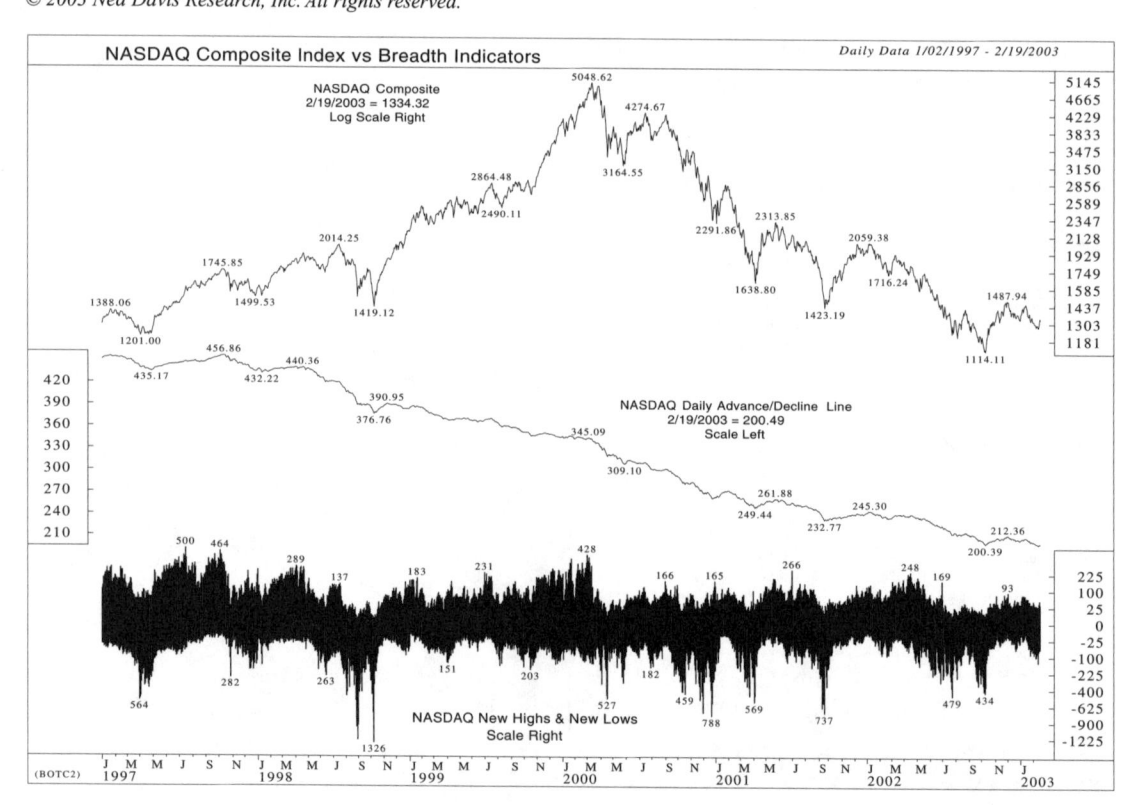

2000. Through March 10 the NASDAQ Composite surged 24 percent to a record high of 5048. But as the Fed took away liquidity by reducing the money supply and raising short-term interest rates, the market began to lose steam. By April 11, just 1 month after hitting its peak, the NASDAQ had given back all its gains for the year. Once the momentum turned negative, there was no going back. Just as investor optimism and greed fed the market's surge, pessimism and fear spurred the decline. The NASDAQ finished year 2000 down 39 percent. The index fell another 21 percent in 2001, and by October 9, 2002, the index had fallen to 1114, a level not seen since August 1996 and 78 percent below its record high.

The stock market decline denied companies' access to much-needed capital. Without the capital, companies burned through cash quickly. Not only did start-up companies such as Pets.com go bankrupt, but more established companies such as Lucent Technologies and Global Crossing faced major difficulties. By late 2002 it became apparent that the new metrics used to value Technology and Internet stocks enabled corporations to mislead investors. Companies such as Enron, WorldCom, and Adelphia Communications had hidden debt, capitalized operating expenses, and overstated revenue, respectively. AOL Time Warner posted a $98.7 billion loss in 2002 as it wrote down the value of assets stemming from America Online's $103.5 billion acquisition of Time Warner in January 2001. Investors worried about missing the gains that the rest of the crowd enjoyed, and so they ignored concerns about accounting practices until after the market crashed.

Economists have coined the terms *endowment effect* and *status quo bias* to explain, at least partially, why investors may have ignored the signs of trouble and even continued to hold NASDAQ stocks after inconsistencies became apparent. As explained by Richard Thaler (1992) in *The Winner's Curse,* the endowment effect asserts that people are generally willing to demand more to sell something they already own or inherit than to buy something they do not own. Pioneered by Richard Zeckhauser and William Samuelson, the status quo bias states that when faced with two or more opportunities, people tend to choose the option that favors the current situation. In the case of the NASDAQ Bubble (and other bubbles as well), the endowment effect and the status quo bias indicate that investors who owned Technology and Internet stocks were inclined to ignore concerns over valuation and accounting methods. As a result, they were less likely to sell until the evidence was overwhelming, at which point stock prices had already dropped considerably.

There are several other examples of manias, such as tulip bulbs in the Netherlands in the 1600s, railroads in the United States and United Kingdom in the 1800s, gold in the United States in the late 1970s and early 1980s, and stocks and real estate in Japan in the 1980s. Figure 3-3, first created by NDR's Larry Winer for a Chart of the Day on January 27, 2000, shows four such bubbles: the Dow Jones Industrial Average from 1924 to 1932, U.S. gold prices from 1979 to 1980, the Nikkei 225 from 1983 to 1992, and the NASDAQ Composite from 1994 to 2003. The text of the Chart of the Day relates the performance of the NASDAQ Composite to the previous three bubbles, stating, "As Alan Greenspan has noted, nobody knows how high is up in a bubble and, in fact, one only knows for sure that it is a bubble several months *after* the top. But what is clear is that most of these bubbles do not end gently. In fact, the aftermath is violent and often retraces a

FIGURE 3-3 Historical market bubbles.
© 2003 Ned Davis Research, Inc. All rights reserved.

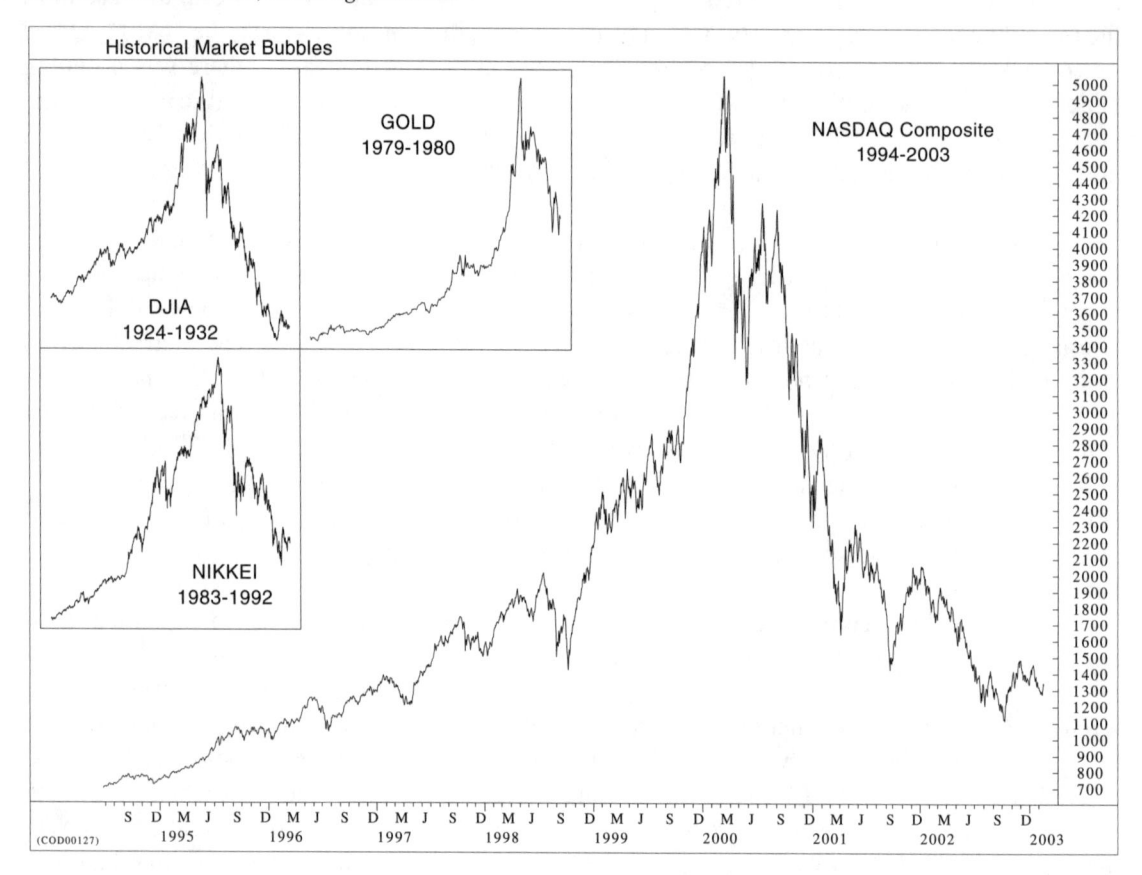

goodly portion of the bubble rise." It does not matter if the bubble occurred 300 years ago or 3 years ago, or if it occurred in Europe, Japan, or America, or if it happened in an emerging market or a developed market—the actions of the crowd are the same. These few examples show that over different time periods, disparate cultures, and various degrees of technological innovation, the powerful forces of crowd psychology have, given the right conditions, repeatedly given rise to manias and their inevitable crashes.

CHAPTER 4

HEADLINES AND COVER STORIES

Some of the best illustrations of extremes in crowd psychology have been provided by magazine and newspaper cover stories. The headlines for these stories, geared to attract attention on the newsstand (and sell magazines to the crowd wrapped up in the headline story), make great contrary opinion indicators and can help identify times to "beware of the crowd at extremes."

The covers of weekly news and business magazines have often served as notable contrary indicators for stock prices. Paul Montgomery, an astute analyst and a friend of NDR, in the early 1980s went back and studied *Time* magazine covers since the 1920s. He found that for about 30 days after a bullish or bearish *Time* cover, the market's performance was usually consistent with the cover. In fact, if you had invested in the stock market for the 30-day period following the cover stories, your investment would have gained at a rate of 30 percent per annum. While the covers have been right for those trailing 30 days, he found that they have been wrong over the subsequent 11-month periods more than 80 percent of the time, thus showing that cover stories have tended to occur near points of maximum momentum on the upside or downside. *By acting contrary to the magazine covers after 30 days, you would have beaten the equivalent buy-and-hold return by about five times over the next 11 months.* The same tendencies have generally held true for *Time* magazine and other major media sources since Montgomery's original findings.

HEADLINES SURROUNDING THE 1929 CRASH

Looking back at 1929, one of the most tumultuous times in U.S. stock market history, we can see how newspaper headlines reflected the mood of the day and mostly acted as contrarian indicators. As shown in Figure 4-1, the headlines in the "newspaper of record," the *New York Times*, prior to and at the start of the market's massive decline reflected optimism and a lack of concern about a possible bubble in stock prices or the possibility of a major drop. One of the leading stock market pundits in 1929 was Yale economist Irving Fisher, who is referenced in the October 16 *Times* headline, saying that stocks were "permanently high." He was a well-known bull at the time and made many of the same arguments justifying the high stock prices of the late 1920s that were echoed 70 years later during the late 1990s bubble period. Other commentators featured in the headlines described the market's rise into mid-1929 as "justified" and proclaimed that stock prices were likely to "stay at high levels for years to come." The *Wall Street Journal* also reflected the bullish enthusiasm just before the peak, and on August 23, 1929, wrote: "According to the Dow theory, this development [the Dow's rise] re-establishes the major upward trend. Reassurance on this score gave fresh stimulus to bullish enthusiasm, and a long list of representative stocks surged upward to new highs. . . . The outlook for the fall months seems brighter than at any time." The Dow's closing high occurred 10 days later on September 3, and was not surpassed for another 25 years.

FIGURE 4-1 DJIA headlines surrounding 1929 crash.
© *2003 Ned Davis Research, Inc. All rights reserved.*

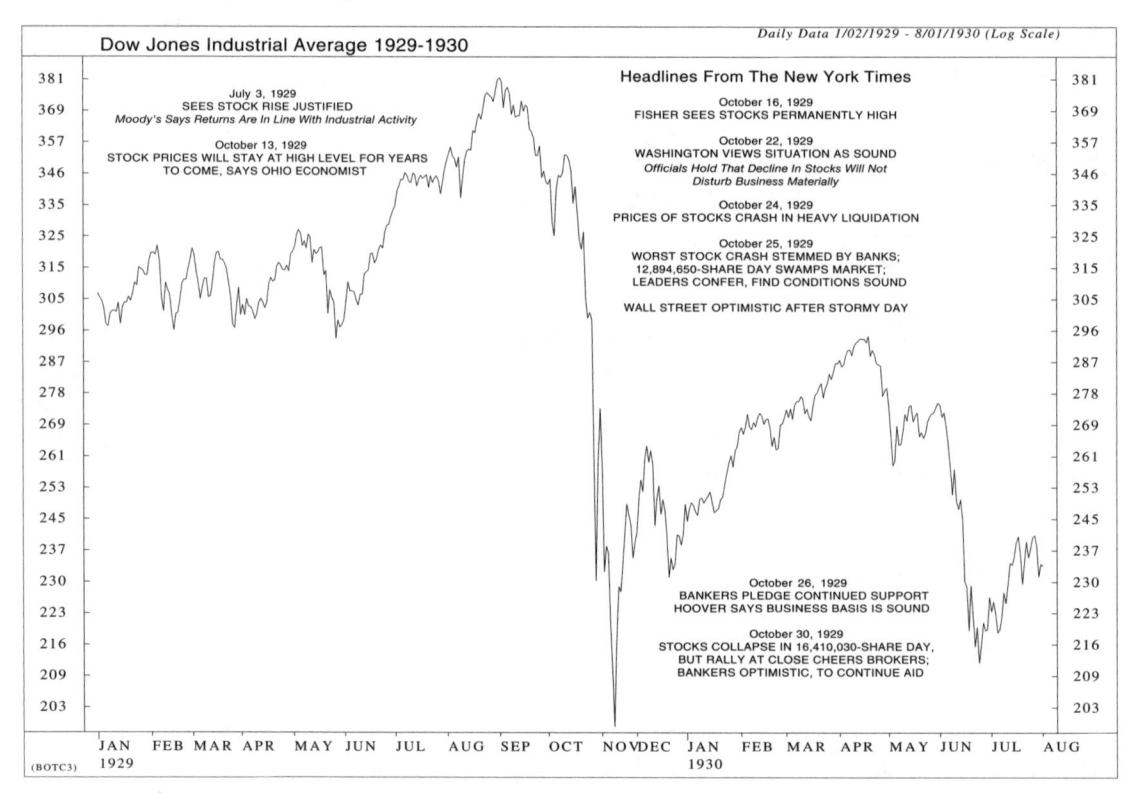

Contrary to the optimistic outlooks featured in the news, after an initial decline and short rally, in a period of approximately 1 month between October 10 and November 13, 1929, the Dow Industrials suffered an enormous 44 percent loss before starting to recover. And even during and after the market crash, the headlines indicated that bankers, business leaders, and President Hoover were still optimistic and saw conditions as "sound." Even the day after the infamous Black Thursday crash on October 24, the *New York Times* headlines said, "Leaders Confer, Find Conditions Sound" and "Wall Street Optimistic after Stormy Day." Such public reassurances from business and political leaders were likely made at least partly with the goal of preventing further panic and pessimism, but they would have been cold comfort to any investor who followed the headlines and held onto his stocks. Despite the massive decline in late 1929, the Dow went on to fall *another* 79 percent from the initial crash low of November 13, 1929, to its ultimate low on July 8, 1932, as the U.S. economy fell into the Great Depression.

COVER STORIES: 1960s–1970s

Turning to more recent times, between 1966 and 1982 stock prices endured another secular bear market like the one that began in 1929, and that saw significant volatility but little or no net gains over the 16-year period. That generally bearish period, however, included several substantial cyclical rallies. Between 1966 and 1982, the Dow Jones Industrial Average saw five rallies and four declines of greater than 30 percent. At or near many of those peaks and troughs were cover stories that, in hindsight, would have been good contrary indicators, as shown in Figure 4-2. For example, on November 2, 1968, *BusinessWeek* featured a story titled "The Boom That Just Won't Stop." The boom did stop, at least in the stock market. One month later, on December 3, 1968, the DJIA peaked at 985. The market proceeded to fall 18.6 percent over the next 7 months on its way to a 35.9 percent total decline over 18 months.

In May 1970, with the Dow in the midst of its deepest bear market in percentage terms since World War II and the longest in duration in over a decade, a May 2, 1970, *Economist* story naturally asked the question, "When Will the Selling Stop?" The article goes on to state that "in the last analysis, there is no floor in equity prices, except that at such a low level that it becomes ludicrous to dwell on it. . . . Once stock prices have begun to roll there is liable to be nothing that will immediately stop the rot." True to Paul Montgomery's analysis, the cover story was correct over the immediate term, with the market tumbling 11.7 percent over the next 3 weeks.

The *Newsweek* of May 25, 1970, also captures the building gloom among investors. The cover is a collage of dismal economic pictures: people selling apples as they come off an unemployment line, houses missing rooftops, stock prices falling off the bottom of a chart, and kettles representing prices and wages about to explode. Three weeks after the *Economist* story and one day after the publishing date of the *Newsweek* cover, the market bottomed on May 26 around 631 and proceeded to climb over the 950 level by April 1971, and in 1972 it burst through the 1000 level for the first time in six years.

FIGURE 4-2 DJIA with headlines from the 1960s and 1970s.

© 2003 Ned Davis Research, Inc. All rights reserved.

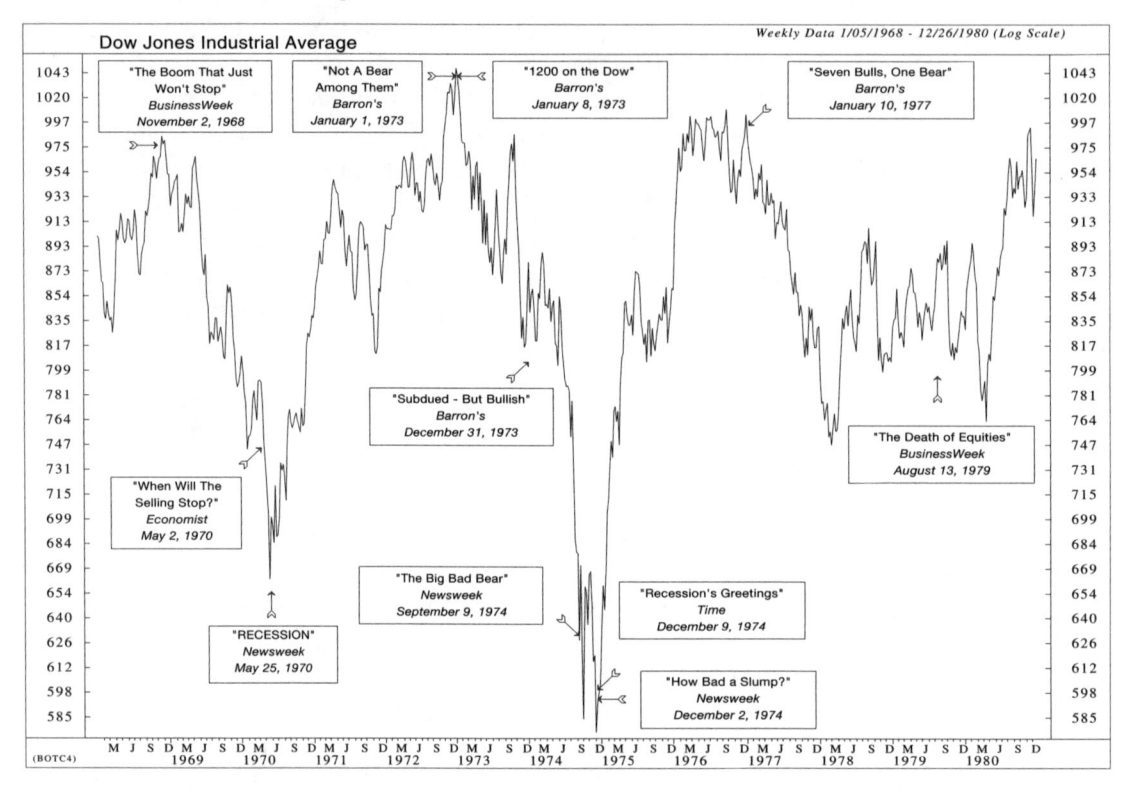

At that point, *Barron's* came out with a classic headline on January 1, 1973, which read "Not a Bear among Them." After bringing the country's best and brightest market professionals to New York for an all-day session on the outlook for the next year, *Barron's* reported that its year-end panel of experts was "bullish on Wall Street, business, the market. Security firms, if not NYSE—will flourish no matter what changes come." In the next week, *Barron's* headline "1200 on the Dow" was deemed "a modest expectation for 1973" by the panel. "With earnings of $74 and a multiple of 18, the Industrials could top 1300." The Dow stood at 1050, and at least 1200 was expected by the best and the brightest of the market's experts. Contrarily, the market slid downhill to a calendar-year low of 788 in early December and continued further down to 577 the following year. What happened that the experts didn't know? There were some random, unpredictable, negative events that occurred. Watergate exploded, and there was a war in the Middle East, which resulted in OPEC pushing up the price of oil. Alone, these events may not have had a prolonged effect on the market. But combined with the low liquidity from all the positive market opinions, they proved to be more than the market could handle. As if someone had yelled "fire" in a crowded theater, the people rushed to get out of stocks, and a lot of people got hurt. Headlines continued to flash the sentiment of "Wall Street" throughout the decline of the 1973–1974 bear market. In December 1973, the *Barron's* year-end panel was "Subdued—But Bullish," while the Dow was reeling from a drop of more than 20 percent over the first 11 months of that year. Following this once again bullish outlook, the market did not oblige and continued downward throughout 1974.

On September 9, 1974, with the Dow down around the 650 level, *Newsweek* came out with an angry bear on the cover. The NYSE pillars were crumbling on either side of the bear, and a sign showed Wall Street as a one-way street heading straight down. The title was "The Big Bad Bear." Stocks did decline for another month into October, consistent with Paul Montgomery's findings stated earlier. The market then rebounded 15 percent from the October low of 584 through early November, before dropping to the ultimate bear market low on December 6, 1974. Sure enough, the December 2, 1974, *Newsweek* cover blared the question "How Bad a Slump?" with a picture of Uncle Sam riding a car down a steep declining price line. *Time,* as Figure 4-3 shows, also shared in the gloom the following week, on December 9, with a sickly

FIGURE 4-3 "Recession's Greetings."
Getty Images.

thin and worn Santa Claus under the holiday message "Recession's Greetings." From that December 6 low the market rose 76 percent in the ensuing bull market.

THE 1980s–EARLY 1990s

The same message continues throughout the subsequent market cycles showing the media's need to sell headlines with the focus on public opinion. The figures in this section show the timing of some of these contrarian-friendly headlines.

As shown in Figure 4-4, the market's plummet in 1987 was no exception to the cover story hype both before and after the significant event. A perfect example was the October 1987 issue of *Fortune* which showed a smiling Greenspan under the headline "Why Greenspan Is Bullish." Note that while the cover date of October 26 was 1 week after the actual market crash, monthly magazines reach newsstands and mailboxes several weeks ahead of their cover date. Just after the crash in October, *Time* flashed in big type on its November 2, 1987, issue, "The Crash—After a wild week on Wall Street, the world is different." This sensational cover, shown in Figure 4-5, certainly set out to capture the doom and gloom sentiment of the day. As it turned out, the Dow Jones Industrial Average had bottomed on October 19 and, after a brief rise and fall into early December, continued on a bull market run gaining 72.5 percent through July 1990.

Not only did the stock market enjoy an extraordinary run during the late 1980s and early

FIGURE 4-4 DJIA and headlines from the 1980s and 1990s.
© 2003 Ned Davis Research, Inc. All rights reserved.

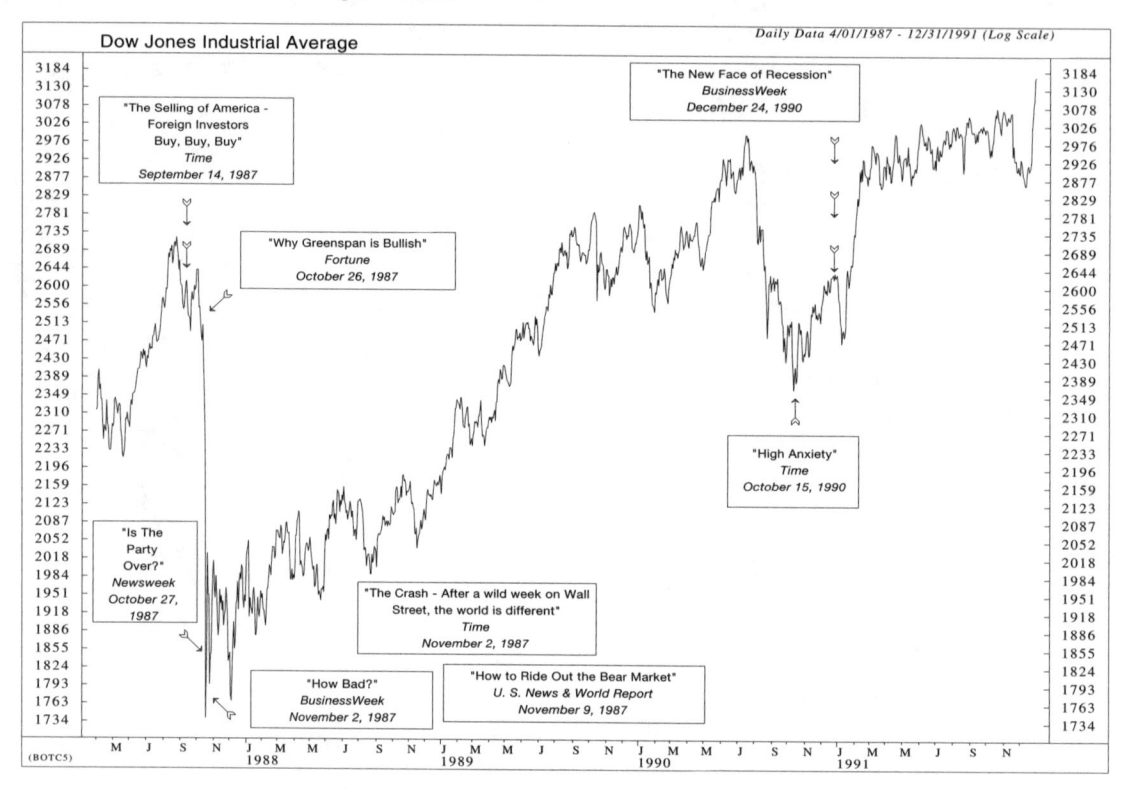

1990s, but the economy was enjoying unprecedented success as well. The United States was in the midst of the longest expansion since the buildup to the Vietnam War. However, the bull market and expansion came to an end in 1990. The Dow Jones Industrial Average peaked in July just shy of 3000, and the economy slipped into recession the same month. By October 11, 1990, the Dow had declined 21.2 percent. Concerns over the stock market and economy were reflected in the *Time* October 15, 1990, cover "High Anxiety." The magazine features a picture of a man hanging from a clock several stories above a busy city street. The subtitle reads, "Looming Recession, government Paralysis, and the threat of War are giving Americans a case of the jitters." While the cover may have accurately reflected the mood of investors, it is often this type of environment in which bull markets begin. On October 11, 1990, the Dow Jones Industrial Average began a 24.1 percent rally through February 15, 1991, on its way to an 8-year bull market, the longest since at least 1900.

On December 24 of the same year, *BusinessWeek* featured a cover titled "The New Face of Recession," depicting uncertainty over the steep losses in white-collar jobs. A subtitle asks the question, "How long will it last?" According to the National Bureau of Economic Research, the

FIGURE 4-5 "The Crash."
Getty Images.

relatively mild recession would end just 3 months later. As for the stock market, the Dow Jones Industrial Average did endure a brief, 2-week, 6.3 percent correction before starting an 18.8 percent surge through mid-February. A year after the cover story, the DJIA was up 16.4 percent and well into the historic bull market.

THE LATE 1990s–EARLY 2000s

Looking to the more recent market swings of the mid- and late 1990s, cover stories can still be found reflecting the exaggerated sentiment of the times as shown in Figure 4-6.

At the beginning of 1994, the Federal Reserve began a series of interest rate increases aimed at limiting potential inflation, and it had the effect of causing a sharp decline of 9 to 10 percent in the major stock indices in February and March of that year. With interest rates rising and stock prices trading near their lowest levels in nearly a year, sentiment had become very bearish. So it is not surprising that *Newsweek's* April 11, 1994, cover featured a grizzly bear tearing through newspaper stock tables with the headline "How to Survive in a Scary Market." But as it turned out, buying when the market looked scariest would have been profitable since the S&P 500 made its low on April 4, 1994, and has never been as low since. A year later, the market was up 15 percent and in the midst of a record-setting bull market. After seeing the Dow surge over 150 percent from the April 1994 lows, the April 27, 1998, *Newsweek* cover showed a cartoon of a bull wearing a wedding dress, with the words "Like It or Not, You're Married to the Market." While the story inside may list the potential risks and rewards of the previous and future market action, this cover shows the exuberant feeling of the crowd and the desire by everyone for the wealth-producing rise to continue. Sure enough, the Dow topped on July 17, 1998, and proceeded into the first bear market period in an extremely long time.

After the bear market bottomed on August 31, 1998, there were expected feelings of worry and fear that this was a sign of the future. *Newsweek's* cover for October 12, 1998, reads "The Crash of '99?" with a subtitle of "It doesn't have to happen—but here's why it might." To the contrarian, this was a bullish sign.

Contrary to all the gloom in the fall of 1998, the major indices embarked on a dramatic surge from the 1998 lows to their all-time peaks in early 2000, and optimism again pervaded. A widely noted (and subsequently derided) example of excessive optimism prior to the market's peak in early 2000 was the cover of the September 1999 issue of *The Atlantic Monthly* titled "DOW 36,000: The Right Price for Stocks" (see Figure 4-7). The article and a book of the same name made the case that the stock market was severely undervalued and that the Dow, then trading around 10,000, would be fairly valued at 36,000. The authors' reasoning was determined to be

FIGURE 4-6 DJIA with headlines from early 1990s to late 2002.
© 2003 Ned Davis Research, Inc. All rights reserved.

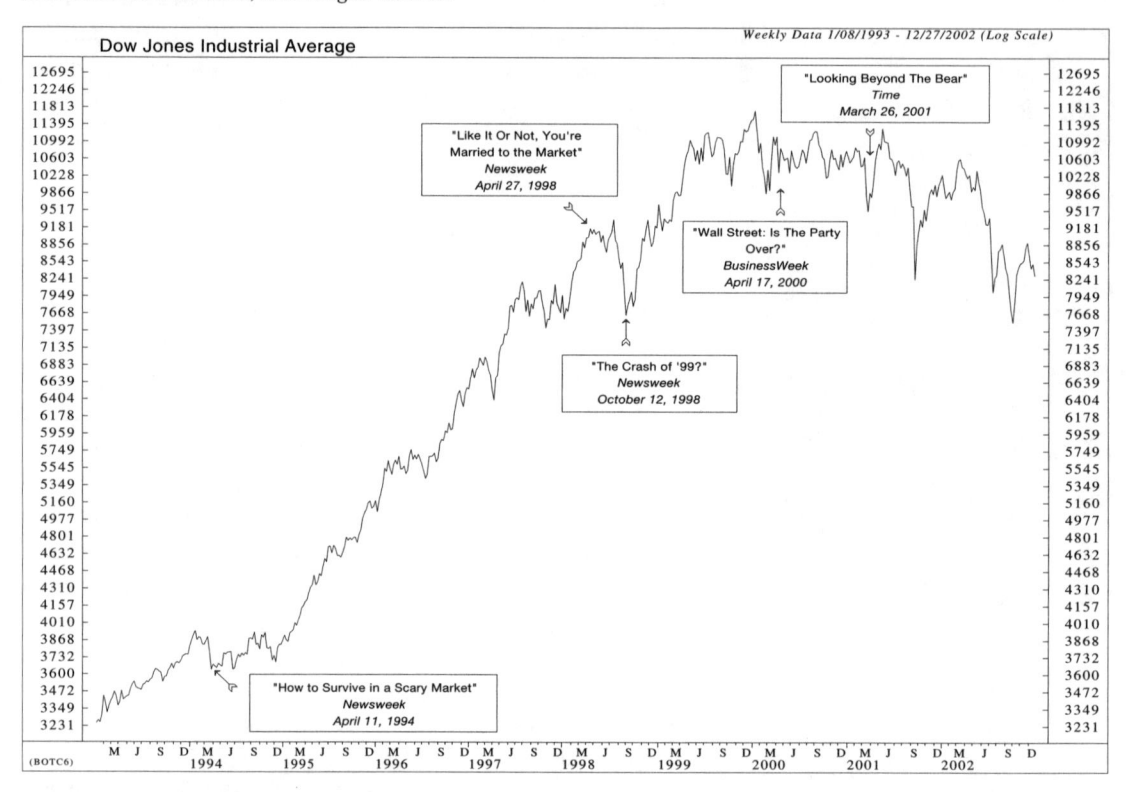

based on incorrect financial formulas and on the controversial assumption that stocks are less risky than bonds. So even though few investors are likely to have really believed that the Dow would suddenly triple in value, the article's appearance on the cover of a general-interest literary magazine was a clear example of how far optimism about the market had spread at that time. It also reflects how even analysis based on quantitative data and financial theories can be distorted by excessive optimism.

After the market's initial decline from the March peaks in the NASDAQ and S&P 500, *BusinessWeek's* April 17, 2000, cover asked "Wall Street: Is The Party Over?" The subheading answered the question and reflected the general lack of concern about the market's high valuations and recent correction: "High-tech stocks are undergoing a much-needed correction. But relax, the overall market probably won't tank. What we're seeing looks more like a healthy flight to quality." This outlook turned out to be another contrarian sign, since after a short summer rally, the broad market did in fact continue to "tank," led by a continued collapse in technology-related stocks.

And about a year later, *Time* magazine had a growling grizzly bear (accessorized in Wall Street style with a briefcase, cell phone, tie, and hat—see Figure 4-8) on its March 26, 2001, cover with the words "Looking beyond the Bear. Yes, it's scary out there, but a recession isn't a sure

Figure 4-7 "Dow 36,000."
Christoph Niemann (artist); Atlantic Monthly, *September 1999.*

thing. Here's why." As fate would have it, the National Bureau of Economic Research, the official arbiter of recessions and expansions, would later declare the first recession in over a decade to have in fact begun that very month of March 2001. And *Time's* reassurance about "looking beyond the bear" was also a contrarian sign since the market was soon falling again even before the terrorist attacks of that September.

Perhaps an even more dramatic illustration of the ability of magazine covers to "call the top" is again found in *Time* magazine, but in this case for a particular company or industry's stock prices. The editors of *Time* bestow the title of Person of the Year on the individual who most influenced the events of that year. Reflecting the dominance of the Internet on the stock market and economy, the 1999 Person of the Year was none other than Jeff Bezos, CEO of Amazon.com, the leading Internet-based retailer. The subtitle reads, "E-Commerce is changing the way the world shops." The choice of Bezos reflects how the optimism over the Internet had pervaded not only Wall Street but Main Street as well. Despite the fact that the company had never been profitable, Amazon.com was an investor favorite and bellwether for the technology sector. Amazon soared 42.2 percent in 1999 to bring its total appreciation since its May 1997 IPO to over 5300 percent. But once again, by the time the story of Amazon's growth was big enough for *Time* to make its CEO Person of the Year, Amazon's stock had seen its peak: The all-time record high for Amazon.com occurred on December 10, 1999, just about the time the magazine hit the newsstands, and by September 2001 had fallen as much as 94 percent from that level. Other Internet-related companies saw similar declines in their stock prices as the Internet bubble burst and reality set in.

In summary, media covers serve the contrarian well as both a reflection of extreme sentiment and a purveyor of the same. Observing this extreme sentiment and realizing its effect on liquidity only helped clarify when the turning points would occur. So while media headlines and cover stories cannot be used alone as the basis for investment decisions, they can provide a valuable real-time picture of popular sentiment and can serve as anecdotal support for other measures of stock market psychology.

FIGURE 4-8 "Looking beyond the Bear."
Getty Images.

POLITICALLY MOTIVATED QUOTES

Just as the media headlines abound with reflections of public hype, speech makers also provide their version of extreme sentiment. Often this is the result of their research on the feelings of the public they serve. Douglas Casey (1995) claims, in *Media, Mania & the Markets,* that during Clinton's first presidential campaign, the candidate received 120 pages of faxes per day summarizing what the media were saying about the political candidates and the election. All this information was used to help his team of speechwriters determine what should be said and promoted. While *reflecting* public sentiment, public speakers have the ability to *influence* crowd opinion with their words as well. Either way, the stronger the sentiment, the greater the absorption. In the 1890s, Gustave Le Bon wrote in his book *The Crowd: A Study of the Popular Mind* (republished in 1982), "Given to exaggeration in its feeling, *a crowd is only impressed by excessive sentiments.* An orator wishing to move a crowd must make an abusive use of violent affirmations." This follows the contrary opinion theory that if the crowd's opinion is too strong, investors should be prepared to look the other way.

Looking back to the early part of the twentieth century, Calvin Coolidge provided his opportunity to share the extreme optimism of the day. On December 4, 1928, his State of the Union address included these words: "No Congress of the United States ever assembled, on surveying the state of the union, has met with a more pleasing prospect than that which appears at the present time. In the domestic field there is tranquility and contentment . . . and the highest record of years of prosperity." As you can see in Figure 4-9, he was speaking before the biggest period of economic despair in the country's modern history. Perhaps his words both reflected and inspired the people's extreme optimism that led to the topping of the market.

Another example occurred during the tumultuous time of the Vietnam War. Lyndon Johnson had to deal with the economics of war on top of all the other factors. His State of the Union address at the beginning of 1966 came at a time when the market was peaking and recession had not been seen since 1961. He spoke of the state of national prosperity with the words "I can report to you tonight what you have seen for yourselves already—in every city and countryside. This Nation is flourishing." Following that note of optimism, the market peaked on February 9, 1966, before heading into a recession later in the same year. The peak level of 995 was not reached again until November 1972.

In the period between, the market rallied from the 1966 lows around 744 to a top (lower than the 1966 peak) in December 1968. Following Richard Nixon's 1968 election, in January 1969, President Johnson, in his farewell State of the Union address, showed a renewed positive sentiment, as he had 3 years earlier. He stated, "I think all Americans know that our prosperity is broad and it is deep, and it has brought record profits, the highest in our history, and record wages." Once again, the politicians and the crowd were too enthusiastic about the future, creating an extreme in sentiment that ended the market's climb. The Dow Industrials dropped by over 35 percent over the next year and a half.

Just prior to Richard Nixon's January 1973 State of the Union address, the Dow Industrials had a spectacular recovery from the May 1970 low of 631 to climb over the 1000 mark for the first

FIGURE 4-9 Presidential sentiment.

© 2003 Ned Davis Research, Inc. All rights reserved.

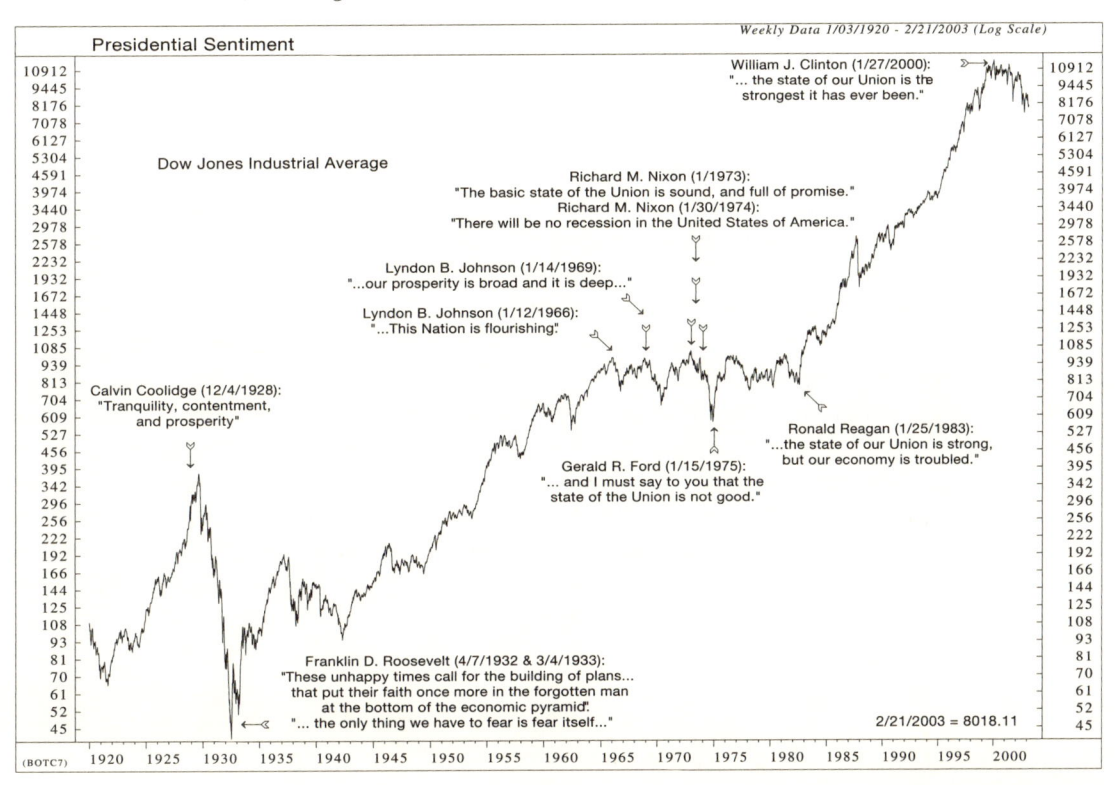

time ever. With the wind behind his sails, the President proclaimed, "The basic state of the Union today is sound, and full of promise. We enter 1973 economically strong, militarily secure, and most important of all, at peace after a long and trying war." This was a grand display of optimism for all to hear. As is now evident, the 1973–1974 bear market ensued from that month onward, culminating in a drop of 45 percent from the January 1973 highs.

Ignoring the results of the previous year, and perhaps telling his constituents what they wanted to hear, in his January 1974 State of the Union address, Nixon promised, "There will be no recession in the United States of America." Little did he know, the recession had *already begun,* and it became evident in the months to come. By the end of the year, the market was hitting its lows. The GDP growth rate (year-to-year percentage change) dropped almost 3 percent from the last quarter of 1973 to the first quarter of 1974.

After Gerald Ford took over for Nixon, he presented a classic contrarian quote when he delivered his address in January 1975. He ended his opening remarks with "and I must say to you *that the State of the Union is not good.*" From that point of maximum pessimism, with the President of the United States reflecting the financial woes of the people, the market *roared* into a new bull market.

A similar note of economic pessimism can be found in Ronald Reagan's address in January 1983 when he said "the state of our Union is strong, but our economy is troubled." While the economy certainly did appear troubled at the time, the stock market had made its major low in the preceding August of 1982 and was in the early stages of a new secular bull market phase. So by the time the economic worry was great enough to make it into the President's speeches, all the nervous investors had sold, and the market was already looking ahead to the next phase of the cycle.

Finally, during his last State of the Union address, President Clinton spoke on January 27, 2000, and showed his enthusiasm with the positive statement, "the state of our Union is the strongest it has ever been." Surely, he was sharing the positive feelings expressed by the previous year's low unemployment rate, high investor inflows, and surging stock market indices. What he was not referencing was the dangerous lack of liquidity from all those inflows and high consumer debt. The Dow's all-time peak occurred on January 14, 2000, and since then the index has fallen as much as 37 percent from that peak.

These are just a handful of examples, all taken from the words of U.S. presidents. More can be found throughout history, from various leaders and "experts" who are followed by the masses. The important thing to understand is that when listening to someone speak, try to determine the motivation for the comments, see how it fits into the picture of public sentiment, and look for possible contrary outcomes for the future. Once again, *beware of the crowd at extremes,* for they will *create* the turning points that can be most profitable.

CHAPTER 5

INDICATORS OF CROWD PSYCHOLOGY

BECAUSE CROWD SENTIMENT IS SUCH A POWERFUL force on stock prices, it is natural to look for ways to quantify and analyze sentiment to use it as a tool for making investment decisions. This is particularly true when we realize that in many cases, price movements cannot be satisfactorily explained by changes in underlying economic fundamentals. Much of the observed volatility in stock prices, particularly in the short run, must therefore be attributed to changes in investor perceptions or psychology. So tracking investor psychology on an ongoing basis is one of our primary goals at Ned Davis Research, and we have developed various methods of monitoring sentiment and using it for investment decision making. In fact, one of the long-standing tenets of NDR's research efforts is "beware of the crowd at extremes," and the indicators in this chapter are examples of the quantitative methods we use to identify when the crowd may be at an extreme.

But it quickly becomes apparent that accurately tracking and quantifying the perceptions and emotions of thousands or millions of investors over time is a tall order. Even if precise measurements of crowd sentiment were available, we would still be faced with the more daunting problem of *how do we know for sure when sentiment has gone "too far" and will reverse?* While government agencies and investment firms impose certain regulations on activities like short selling, program trading, or borrowing money to buy stocks, there are few true constraints on how bullish or bearish investors can become. This is evident by looking at the history of manias, bubbles, and crashes discussed earlier in this book. So if poll data or other data show that, say, 70 percent of investors are bullish and 30 percent are bearish, how do we know if that represents excessive bullishness and signals an imminent market reversal or if investors will become even more bullish and reach 80 or 90 percent bulls before a reversal occurs?

The answer is that we cannot know for certain at a given moment if we have reached a sentiment extreme. We can only know for certain in hindsight. But we have found that it is not necessary to know the exact moment of a sentiment peak as it occurs. *If we wait for readings that have indicated extremes in the past, and then see signs of a reversal occurring, we can still make money by taking a contrary position.* The indicators discussed in this chapter show some of the ways we incorporate sentiment data into our market outlook.

INDICATORS BASED ON SURVEYS AND MARKET DATA

Figure 5-1 shows a relatively straightforward example of tracking sentiment and the market's tendency to perform contrary to the majority opinion. The line plotted in the top section of the chart is the weekly closing value of the S&P 500 Index. The solid line plotted in the bottom section is based on a weekly survey of members of the American Association of Individual Investors (AAII), who are asked to indicate their opinion about the direction of the stock market over the

FIGURE 5-1   S&P 500 versus American Association of Individual Investors.
Source: Copyright © 2003, Standard & Poor's, a division of The McGraw-Hill Companies, Inc.
© 2003 Ned Davis Research, Inc. All rights reserved.

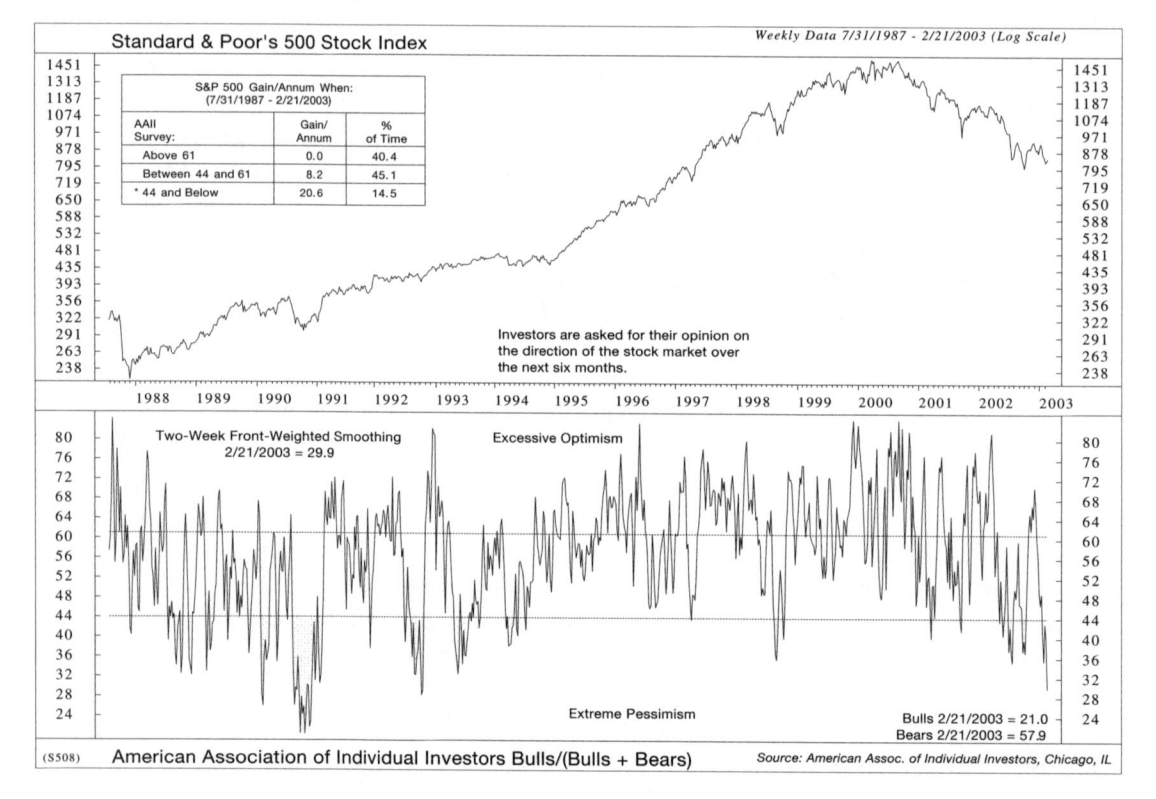

next 6 months. Responses are classified as bullish (optimistic), neutral, or bearish (pessimistic). For this indicator, we take the percentage of bullish responses and divide by the sum of the bullish plus the bearish responses to get the percentage of all those with a definite opinion who are bullish each week (the neutral responses are not included). The line shown in the Figure is a 2-week average of the weekly calculation to reduce the indicator's volatility.

Our historical analysis indicates that readings below 44 percent bulls reflect extreme pessimism among individual investors, while readings above 61 percent reflect potentially excessive optimism. The box in the upper left-hand corner of the figure shows the S&P 500's historical performance based on the indicator's reading at any given time. When the AAII bullish percentage has been below 44 percent, the S&P has confounded the bearish majority and risen at a rate well above average. But when the indicator has been above 61 percent, the S&P has frustrated the bullish majority and shown almost no net gain on average. And when the indicator has been between those two extremes, the market has shown an annualized gain in line with the market's long-run average return. Thus we can see in Figure 5-1 quantifiable evidence of how the market tends to perform contrary to the crowd when too many people are on the same side of the fence.

There are similar data based on the market outlook expressed by professional market newsletter writers, which are determined each week by Investors Intelligence, Inc. Investors Intelligence classifies the advice given by a wide variety of stock market advisory services as bullish, bearish, or basically bullish but expecting a "correction" or near-term decline and thus on the fence. As we did with Figure 5-1, we construct an indicator by taking the percentage of bulls and dividing by the sum of the bulls plus the bears (again, ignoring the "correction" or neutral opinions).

But as noted above, it can be difficult to find levels that consistently indicate extreme bullishness or bearishness over the longer-term history of these data. We find that the levels that represent extremes in advisory sentiment can shift over time, and that these shifts can be explained to a large degree by considering the fundamental backdrop reflected in the monetary (interest rate) conditions of the U.S. economy. So when monetary conditions are favorable for stocks (i.e., when short-term interest rates are falling), there is fundamental justification for people being bullish, and we require more extreme bullish readings and less extreme bearish readings to generate a contrary signal. Conversely, when interest rate conditions are unfavorable for stocks (rising rates), it does not take as much bullishness to signify extreme optimism, and more bearishness is required to signal a pessimistic extreme.

In Figure 5-2, we use the current trend in short-term bond prices to alter the levels that signify excessive bullishness or bearishness dynamically. That is, when rates are falling, excessive bullishness is indicated by readings of more than 81 percent bulls, and extreme pessimism is indicated by readings below 51 percent. When rates are rising, it only requires a reading of 58 percent bulls to indicate an extreme in optimism, while a reading of 31 percent is needed for a pessimistic extreme. The results shown in the figure indicate that the hypothetical historical results of a strategy of buying when extreme pessimism is signaled ("B" arrows in the figure) and selling stocks and switching to cash (commercial paper) when extreme optimism is signaled ("S" arrows) would have seen no losing trades, and the strategy's return would be significantly higher than the buy-and-hold return of the S&P 500 over the period shown. And by being safely in cash for a signifi-

FIGURE 5-2 S&P versus bulls/ (bulls + bears)—dynamic brackets.
Source: Copyright © 2003, Standard & Poor's, a division of The McGraw-Hill Companies, Inc.
© 2003 Ned Davis Research, Inc. All rights reserved.

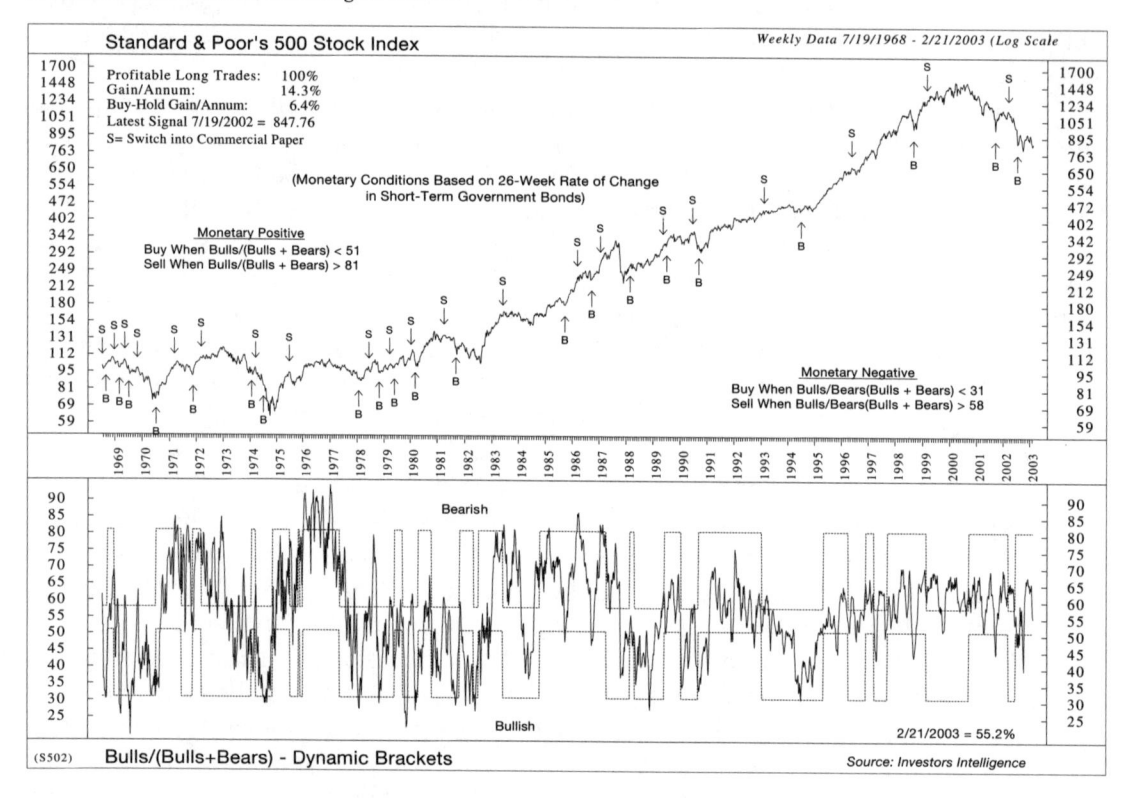

cant part of the time, an investor's overall risk level would be lower than it would be if it were exposed to stocks all the time.

There are other indicators based not on surveys but on the actual flows of money into various financial instruments that indicate whether investors are becoming more bullish or bearish. An example of an indicator based on what people are actually doing with their money (rather than what they say) is shown in Figure 5-3. It is based on the amount of money invested in certain Rydex mutual funds that are designed to track, either directly (long) or inversely (short), certain market indices like the S&P 500 and NASDAQ-100. We combine the assets held in all the funds designed to be "long" the market (the "bull" funds), some of which use leverage to magnify returns, and divide by the total assets held in both bull and bear funds (bear funds provide returns equivalent to being short the underlying index, and some also use leverage). This again shows us the percentage of assets invested in bullish funds relative to bullish plus bearish funds. As shown in the box in the figure, when Rydex fund investors have more than 82.5 percent of their total assets in bull funds, it indicates excessive optimism, and the S&P 500 has declined substantially on average under those conditions. When bull fund assets make up less than 51 percent of the

FIGURE 5-3 S&P 500 versus Rydex bull funds/Rydex bull + bear funds.
Source: Copyright © 2003, Standard & Poor's, a division of The McGraw-Hill Companies, Inc.
© 2003 Ned Davis Research, Inc. All rights reserved.

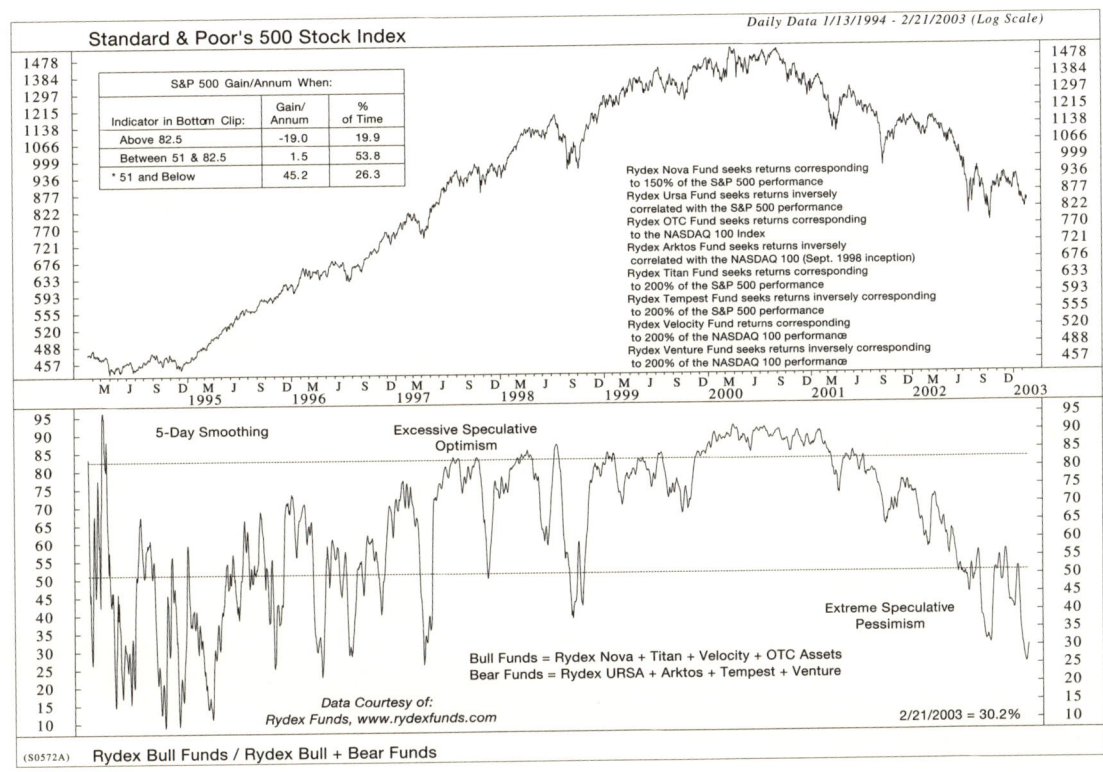

total, signaling extreme bearishness, the S&P has shown much better than average gains. While the amount of historical data is limited, indicators like this help tell us what investors are doing rather than what they are saying, and confirm that it generally pays to move contrary to the position of the crowd.

Another way of looking at what traders are actually doing with their money is to track the positions of futures traders who buy and sell contracts on the benchmark S&P 500 stock index. As part of its regulation of U.S. futures markets, the Commodity Futures Trading Commission (CFTC) collects data weekly from U.S. futures brokers on the positions of different categories of traders. It divides traders into categories based on the type of trading they do and the size of their positions. The first distinction is between commercial traders and noncommercial traders, with commercial traders being those who regularly deal in the asset underlying a futures contract (in this case the stocks in the S&P 500 Index) and who register as such with the CFTC. These traders are also called "hedgers" since they often are using futures to hedge or offset exposure to the underlying asset. Noncommercial traders are all other traders, and are generally assumed to be taking positions in futures on a speculative basis. Noncommercial traders are also divided into large and small speculators based on the size of the positions they hold.

Because the speculative trader historically has tended to be more influenced by sentiment and is most often on the wrong side of the market at extremes, NDR has used the data on noncommercial futures traders to construct an indicator of their current positions (shown in the bottom clip of Figure 5-4). The indicator represents the net aggregate position (sum of the number of contracts held long minus those held short) of noncommercial traders as a percentage of the highest and lowest net position over the last 78 weeks (18 months). Thus it shows speculators' positions relative to the range of their recent history. Heavy net long positions relative to recent history (high indicator readings) indicate high optimism among speculators in the S&P 500; heavy net short positions (low readings) reflect high pessimism. The results in the figure's box show that readings below 40 percent (high pessimism) have been associated with the S&P 500 rising strongly, while readings above 60 percent (high optimism) have been associated with the S&P 500 losing ground on average. So again we find that when speculators in the S&P 500 ("the crowd") are leaning heavily to

FIGURE 5-4 S&P 500 Index futures versus Speculator COT Index.
Perpetual Contract®. Perpetual Contract® is a registered trademark of CSI® (Commodity Systems, Inc.)
Source: Copyright © 2003, Standard & Poor's, a division of The McGraw-Hill Companies, Inc.
© 2003 Ned Davis Research, Inc. All rights reserved.

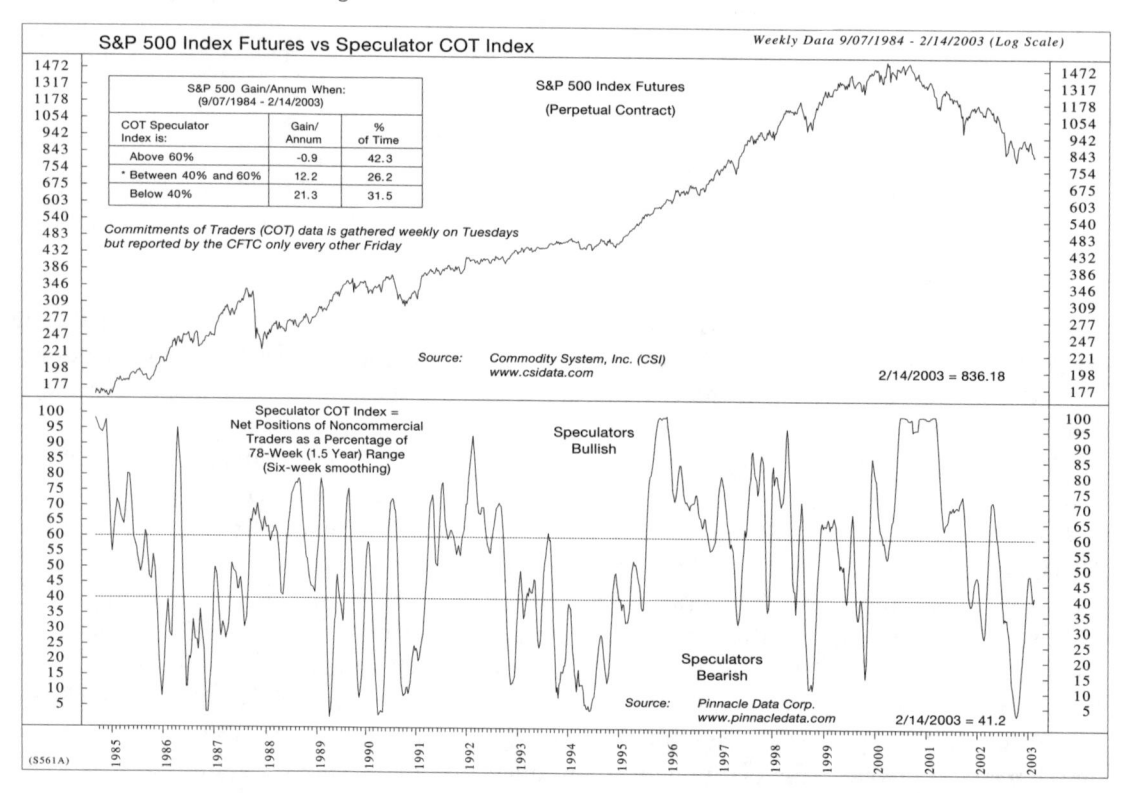

INDICATORS OF CROWD PSYCHOLOGY

one side (with commercial traders holding the opposite positions, since every futures contract must represent a long and a short), the market has tended to move contrary to the crowd's position.

Lest it seem that references to "the crowd" or "the public" are meant to include only nonprofessional investors and exclude Wall Street professionals, Figure 5-5 shows an indicator reflecting the bullishness or bearishness of Wall Street market strategists. High readings in the data in the figure's lower clip indicate that market strategists at major Wall Street investment firms are bullish and recommending higher allocations to stocks. Low readings reflect caution by the strategists and lower recommended stock allocations. Despite the fact that these are experienced professional stock market analysts, when they are excessively bullish as a group, the market has tended to perform poorly, while extreme pessimism among the strategists has tended to occur near market lows and be associated with better-than-average returns in the S&P 500. So even supposedly savvy professionals, who are paid handsomely to advise their firms' clients about the stock market, are often wrong when they become excessively bullish or bearish as a group.

Figure 5-6 shows a composite short-term sentiment indicator that NDR has constructed (the NDR crowd sentiment poll) that combines the readings of seven different sentiment indicators like

FIGURE 5-5 **S&P 500 stock index versus Wall Street strategist sentiment.**
Source: Copyright © 2003, Standard & Poor's, a division of The McGraw-Hill Companies, Inc.
© 2003 Ned Davis Research, Inc. All rights reserved.

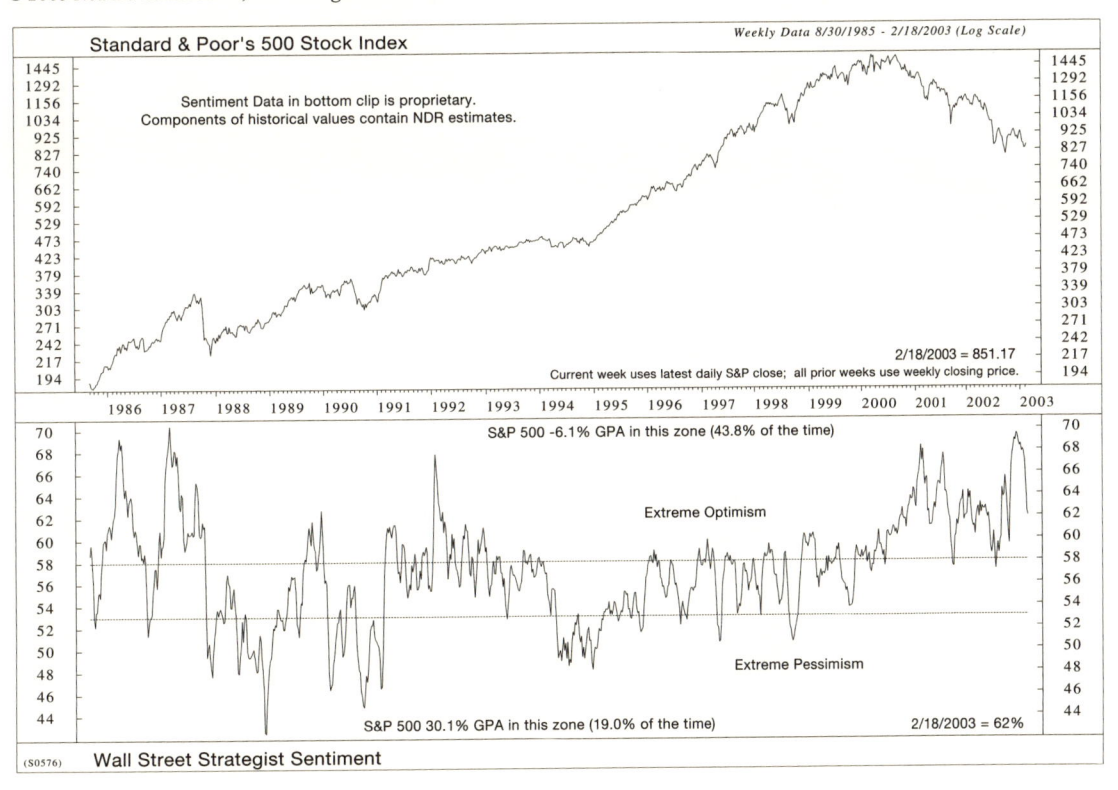

the ones described above. By incorporating measures of sentiment based on different types of investors or traders (e.g., newsletter writers, individual investors, option traders), we can get a more comprehensive picture of market sentiment. Like the other indicators, the one plotted in the lower clip represents the percentage of investors who are bullish at any given time, while the upper clip plots the S&P 500 Index.

And while the available data history is again relatively limited, we have used these data to identify peaks and troughs in sentiment to give us a better idea of where sentiment peaks and troughs are likely to occur in the future. The arrows shown in the figure are not "buy" or "sell" trading signals that could have been followed in real time; they are placed in the figure only in hindsight to indicate the points of extreme optimism and pessimism at past market turning points. By doing this we see, for instance, that the average reading at optimistic extremes has been 66.9 percent bulls, while the average reading at pessimistic extremes has been 47.1 percent bulls. So we can use these levels as a frame of reference for assessing sentiment going forward. The box in the figure also indicates the S&P 500's annualized returns based on the level of the indicator. Read-

FIGURE 5-6 S&P 500 Composite Index versus NDR crowd sentiment poll.
Source: Copyright © 2003, Standard & Poor's, a division of The McGraw-Hill Companies, Inc.
© 2003 Ned Davis Research, Inc. All rights reserved.

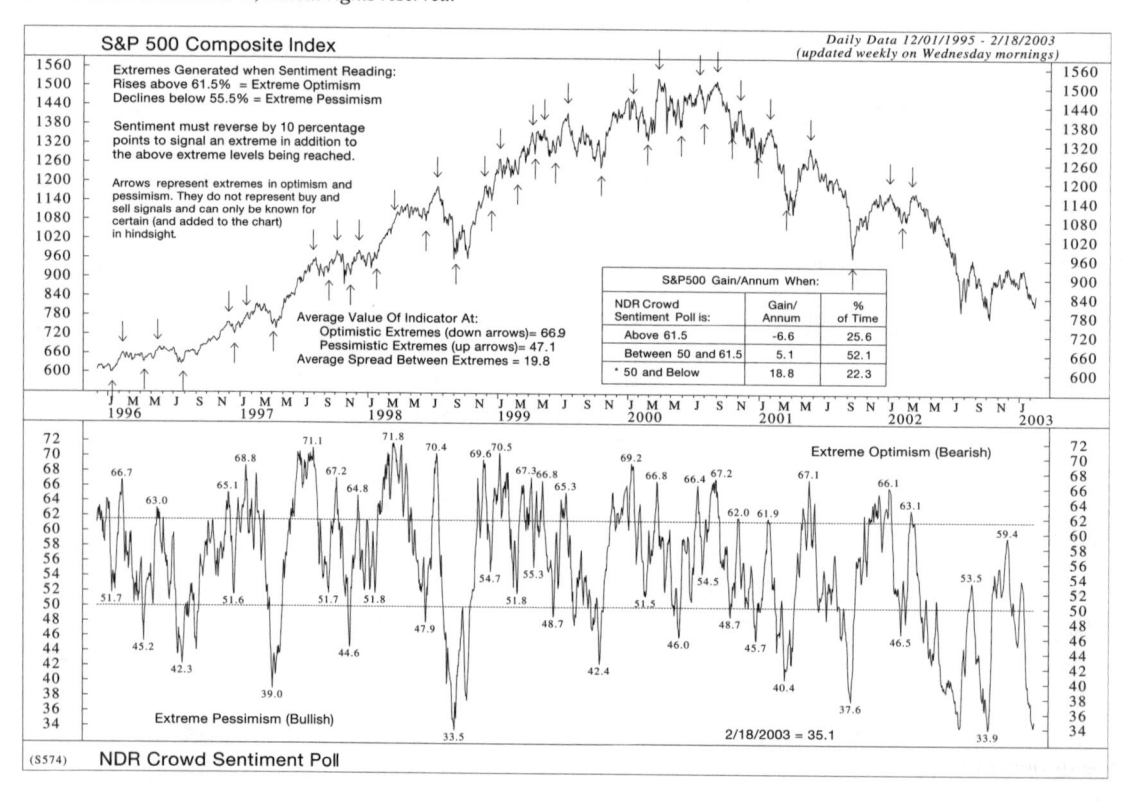

ings below 50 percent have been associated with higher average returns in the S&P 500, while readings above 61.5 percent have been associated with negative S&P returns.

For an even more dramatic example of how following the crowd can be dangerous, Figure 5-7 shows the historical record of what would have happened if an investor had bought the S&P 500 at the points of extreme optimism and reversed position (sold short) at the points of extreme pessimism. *In every case, the market moved contrary to the crowd,* and such a strategy would have resulted in huge losses. Again, the peaks and troughs in sentiment were determined in hindsight, so it would have been impossible to actually follow such a trading strategy (or its profitable reverse) in reality. But using the parameters and perspective drawn from this hypothetical demonstration can provide us with a powerful tool for judging the crowd's psychology and the market's likely direction going forward.

NONTRADITIONAL SENTIMENT INDICATORS

One of the ways that Ned Davis Research differs from other analysts is that we often use indicators that are not traditionally considered sentiment indicators to gauge investor psychology, particularly for longer-term perspective. For example, the price-earnings ratio of the S&P 500 (see Figure 5-8) is generally considered a valuation indicator, but we frequently use valuation as a measure of investor expectations and sentiment. Any measure that reflects what investors are willing to pay for stocks relative to their current underlying sales, earnings, dividends, or other fundamental factors can be useful for assessing the mood of investors. That is, an investor willing to pay 20 times a company's yearly earnings can be assumed to be more optimistic about the company's prospects than an investor who is only willing to pay 10 times earnings. So when investors as a group are willing to pay very high prices for each dollar of underlying revenue, earnings, dividends, or assets, it implies high expectations and high optimism. When investors will only buy stocks at low valuations, it reflects low expectations and pessimism. And the same principle used with other sentiment indicators can be applied: When investor sentiment or expectations become extreme, the market tends to react by moving in the opposite direction.

While valuation measures can be very useful in gauging sentiment and expectations, they tend to be longer term in nature and thus can be more difficult to use for tactical market timing than the indicators discussed earlier in this chapter. For more intermediate-term indicators, we often use relative valuation measures, typically comparing stock valuations with bond yields to see if investors have become excessively optimistic or pessimistic about either of those two competing asset classes. Figure 5-9 shows an indicator representing the ratio of the yield on the 10-year Treasury note to the earnings yield of the S&P 500 Index (the earnings yield is the reciprocal of the P/E ratio shown in Figure 5-8). High readings indicate investors are becoming excessively optimistic about stocks relative to bonds, while low readings indicate excessive enthusiasm for bonds over stocks. Again, we find that extreme readings in this ratio are a warning and that the asset that has attracted the most enthusiasm has tended to underperform the other as investors reallocate into the undervalued asset.

FIGURE 5-7 Crowd sentiment poll based on Figure 5-6.
Source: Copyright © 2003, Standard & Poor's, a division of The McGraw-Hill Companies, Inc.
© 2003 Ned Davis Research, Inc. All rights reserved.

DATE	EXTREME PESSIMISM	EXTREME OPTIMISM	S&P 500	POINT P/L	CROWD RIGHT	CROWD WRONG
01/15/96	51.732		600	-62		x
02/12/96		66.748	662	-25		x
04/12/96	45.241		637	-32		x
05/17/96		63.026	669	-38		x
07/29/96	42.258		631	-126		x
11/29/96		65.101	757	-36		x
12/16/96	51.556		721	-56		x
01/20/97		68.753	777	-19		x
040/4/97	39.008		758	-194		x
07/30/97		71.140	952	-33		x
09/15/97	51.726		920	-63		x
10/07/97		67.153	983	-77		x
11/12/97	44.570		906	-78		x
12/05/97		64.805	984	-27		x
01/26/98	51.800		957	-122		x
03/16/98		71.791	1079	-2		x
06/15/98	47.853		1077	-107		x
07/16/98		70.440	1184	-210		x
09/04/98	33.536		974	-214		x
11/23/98		69.614	1188	-47		x
12/14/98	54.665		1141	-134		x
01/08/99		70.528	1275	-50		x
03/02/99	51.762		1226	-124		x
04/13/99		67.262	1350	-44		x
04/20/99	55.281		1306	-61		x
05/13/99		66.787	1368	-74		x
06/14/99	48.672		1294	-125		x
07/16/99		65.275	1419	-165		x
10/18/99	42.412		1254	-196		x
01/13/00		69.209	1450	-96		x
02/24/00	51.473		1353	-174		x
03/24/00		66.828	1528	-146		x
05/25/00	45.997		1382	-129		x
07/17/00		66.361	1511	-91		x
07/28/00	54.507		1420	-101		x
09/01/00		67.152	1521	-147		x
10/13/00	48.721		1374	-58		x
11/06/00		62.020	1432	-117		x
12/26/00	45.653		1315	-59		x
01/30/01		61.922	1374	-223		x
03/16/01	40.412		1151	-158		x
05/22/01		67.121	1309	-343		x
09/21/01	37.581		966	-207		x
01/04/02		66.079	1173	-76		x
02/08/02	46.501		1096	-68		x
03/08/02		63.082	1164	-327		x
02/20/03	33.857?		837	?		x?
AVERAGE	47.08	66.88	TOTAL	-5059		

INDICATORS OF CROWD PSYCHOLOGY

FIGURE 5-8 S&P 500 stock index versus S&P 500 price-earnings ratio.
Source: Copyright © 2003, Standard & Poor's, a division of The McGraw-Hill Companies, Inc.
© 2003 Ned Davis Research, Inc. All rights reserved.

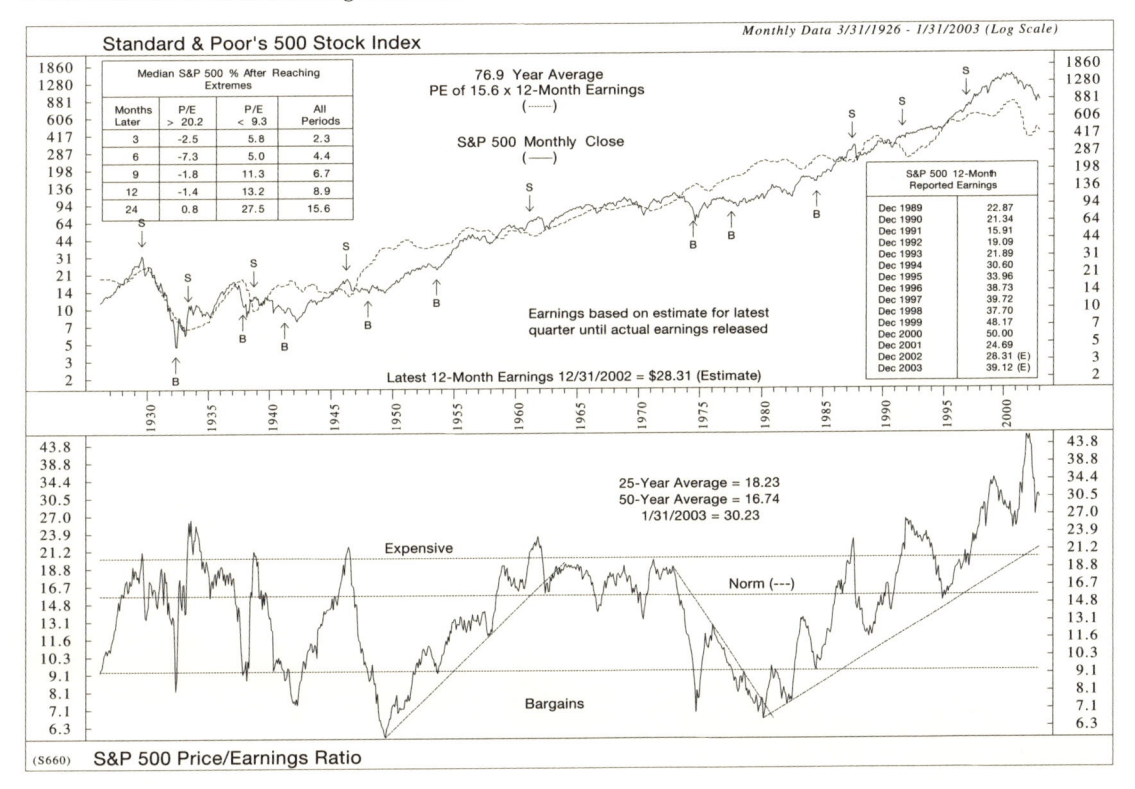

An even longer-term perspective on investor psychology and expectations can be seen by monitoring the percentage of all financial assets held in stocks. Investors' decisions about what fraction of their investable assets to put into stocks reflect their long-term expectations and risk assessments. High stock holdings indicate high optimism about the long-term returns for stocks, while low readings indicate low expectations and potentially excessive bearishness. Again, we look for extremes in perceptions and sentiment to be followed by reversals contrary to the majority.

Figure 5-10 shows the percentage of household financial assets held in stocks over time, based on data collected by the Federal Reserve. Because this percentage is based on the market values of stocks and other assets, changes in this percentage can be caused either by changes in stock prices relative to other assets (bonds, etc.) or by investors shifting money between stocks and other assets. To get perspective on current investor sentiment, we can compare the current percentage of household assets held in stocks with the long-term norms shown in the figure and with the extreme readings found at past major market peaks and troughs. Extreme readings tell us to be on alert for potentially significant long-term reversals in the stock market.

FIGURE 5-9 S&P 500 total return/Lehman Bros. long-term bond total return.
Source: Copyright © 2003, Standard & Poor's, a division of The McGraw-Hill Companies, Inc.
© 2003 Ned Davis Research, Inc. All rights reserved.

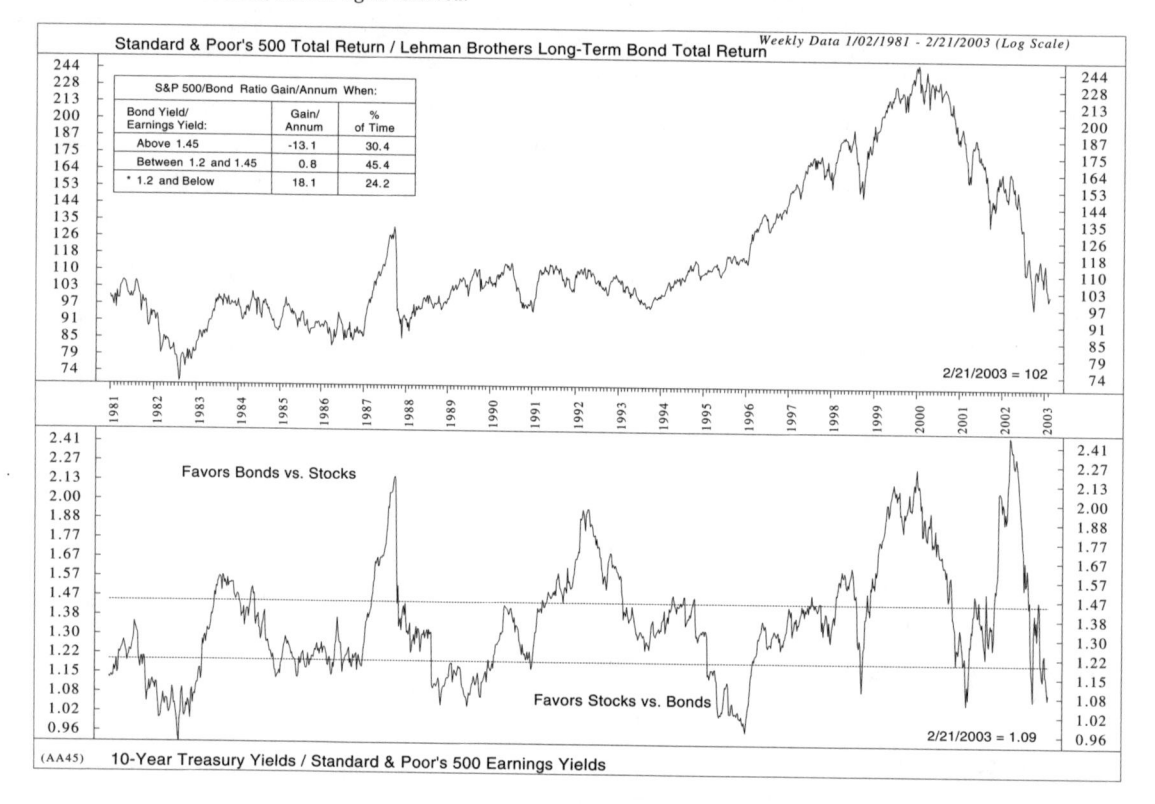

S&P 500/Bond Ratio Gain/Annum When:		
Bond Yield/ Earnings Yield:	Gain/ Annum	% of Time
Above 1.45	-13.1	30.4
Between 1.2 and 1.45	0.8	45.4
* 1.2 and Below	18.1	24.2

Finally, a more anecdotal but intuitive way of tracking the enthusiasm of individual investors for stocks on a longer-term basis is to monitor the number of active investment clubs in the United States. Based on data from the National Association of Investors Corporation, the number of domestic investment clubs can be an indication of the public's interest in the stock market. During periods of drawn-out market weakness, like 1981–1982, public investors have little need for an investment club since they're not even exposed to the market (note in Figure 5-11 the low investment club totals during that period). But when the market enters prolonged periods of strength, as was the case after the 1990 bottom, public investors find themselves plunging into the stock market but needing help in deciding which stocks to buy. As with the explosive interest in mutual fund buying during the 1990s, the rise in the number of investment clubs reflected widespread public demand for stocks.

While public demand helps power the market upward, it's important to recognize that once extremely high levels have been reached, the implication is that the market is very overbought—and vulnerable as a result. When public demand is extremely weak, the implication is that the worst news has already been seen, that the market is very oversold, and that a new advance lies ahead.

FIGURE 5-10 Stocks as a percentage of financial assets—households and personal trusts.
© 2003 Ned Davis Research, Inc. All rights reserved.

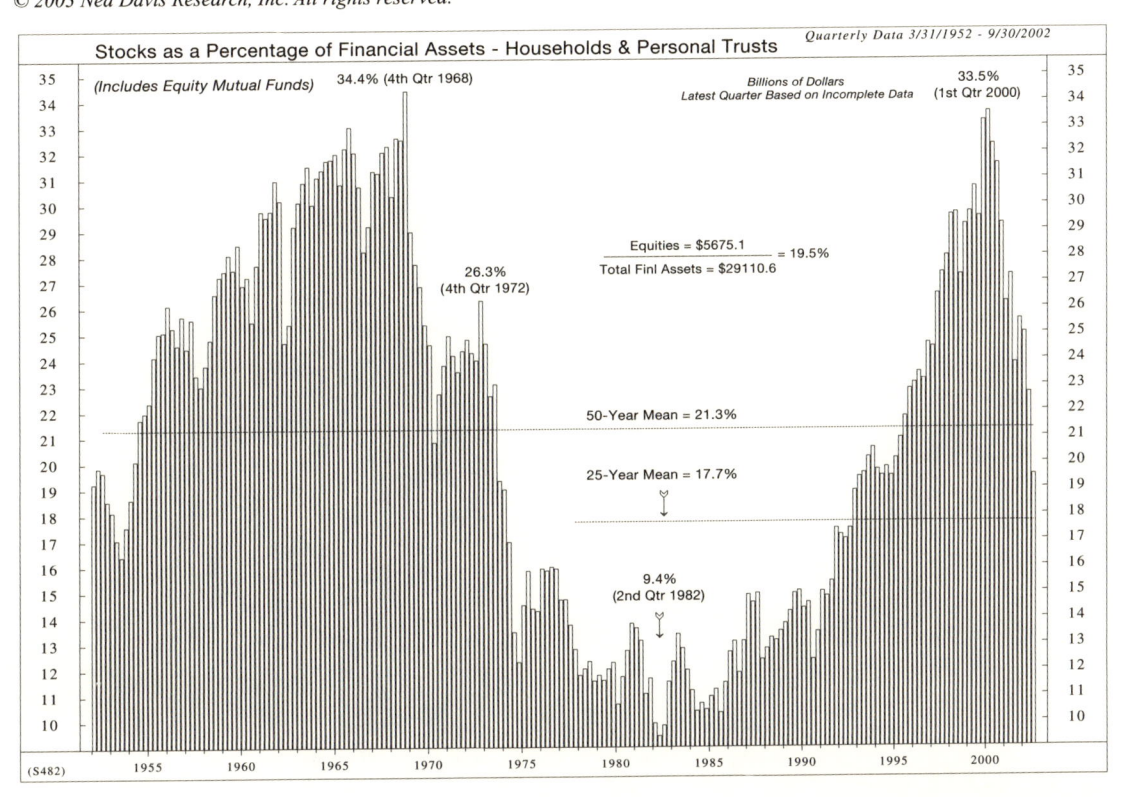

In conclusion, it appears that most investors and analysts would agree that it is all but impossible to satisfactorily explain the movements in stock (or other asset) prices based strictly on changes in underlying economic fundamentals. Because stock prices are determined in an open market by humans making decisions based on incomplete information, it is inevitable that the emotional and psychological tendencies and biases that affect all humans will be reflected in the behavior of stock prices. And there is ample evidence both within and outside the history of financial markets that people behave differently when they are a part of a group or crowd than they would if acting alone.

Consequently, at Ned Davis Research we have focused considerable effort over the years on developing ways to track the psychological state and crowd behavior of investors as a means of improving our ability to avoid our own psychological biases and the well-documented pitfalls of following the crowd. The indicators discussed in this chapter are examples of the quantitative data that we have found useful in objectively analyzing the sentiment of investors as a group. And by being willing to view indicators that are not normally considered "sentiment" indicators from the perspective of looking for signs of extremes in investor psychology, we can construct a more diverse array of tools to use in market analysis. Those interested in further details about stock

FIGURE 5-11 DJIA versus number of investment clubs.
© 2003 Ned Davis Research, Inc. All rights reserved.

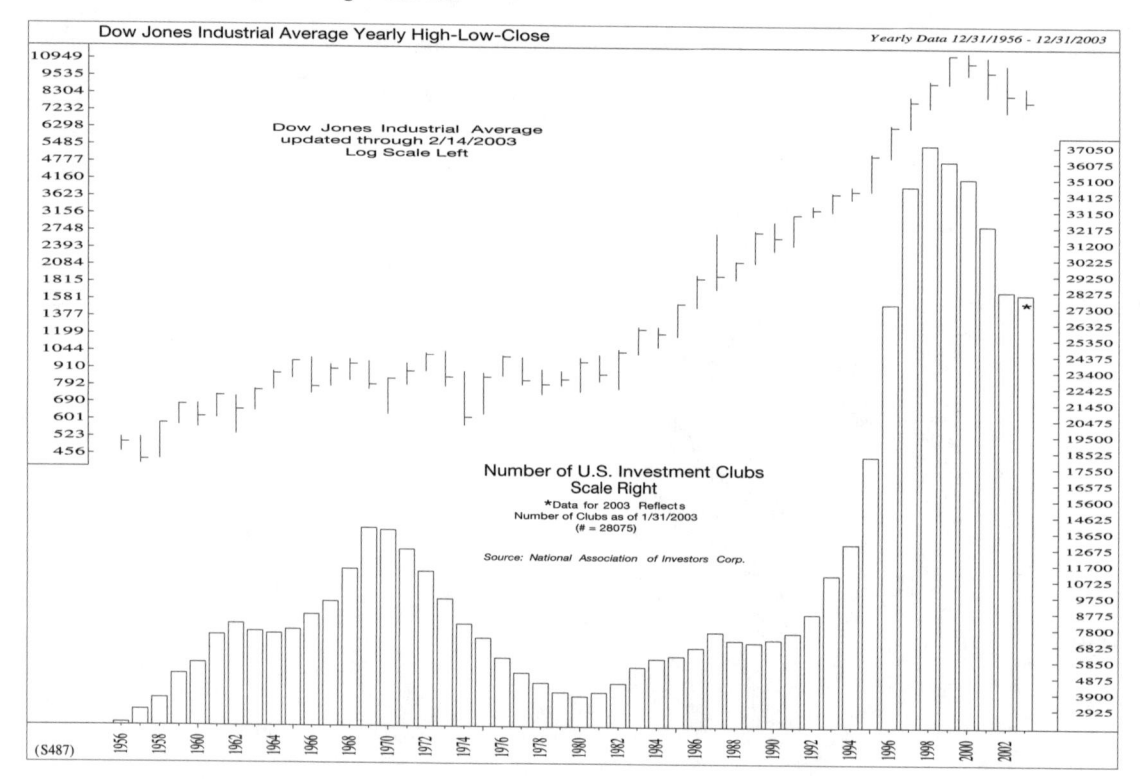

market sentiment indicators should also refer to the information in Chapters 6 and 7 of *The Research Driven Investor*, a comprehensive guide to investment timing indicators written by NDR's Global Equity Strategist Tim Hayes (2000). So while economic fundamentals tend to be reflected in financial asset prices *eventually*, we believe the magnitude of the nonfundamentally driven changes in stock prices over time makes analysis of investor psychology and crowd behavior essential for risk management and return enhancement.

CHAPTER 6

POSTSCRIPT

THIS POSTSCRIPT HAS NOTHING TO DO WITH investing. It is rather my "two-cents-worth" opinion on taking the "road less traveled" in one's personal life.

I first started thinking about all this as a freshman in high school when I heard a speech about "the grave dangers of conformity." Since that time, I have watched too many teenagers and college students fall victim to conformity as they attempted to ingratiate themselves with the "in crowd"—the popular group. I saw their passion for "being accepted" and "fitting in" lead to crowd madness, including binge drinking, taking drugs, cheating on tests, becoming anorexic, or really destroying their lives by reacting to crowd rejection with suicides, depression, or even Columbine-type anger. It made me see how good, rational individuals were really changed by *peer pressure,* which is incredibly powerful in making the individual conform to the group.

It is not just individual lives being destroyed that bothers me. I had a quote in my introductory chapter about "how evil is probably a lot closer to the surface than we like to think." I believe that people have free will to do good or evil. But the most unspeakable evil throughout history has come when evil infects a mob (or a dictator leading a mob), sometimes even in the name of religion.

So when I went to college, I was determined to be an individual rather than a member of a popular fraternity or group. I was attracted by thoughts from diverse writers that celebrated the individual—from the "right" by libertarians like Ayn Rand, who extolled rugged individualism and freedom, saying "civilization is the process of setting man free from men" (*The Fountainhead,* quoted in Bartlett, 1992) and from the "left" by Jean Paul Sartre, who in *Huis Clos (No Exit)* stated that "Hell is seeing yourself through other people's eyes" (Bartlett, 1992). Of course, that gives others control over who you are. I want to be respectful of others' feelings, and I want to listen to criticism because there may be something I can learn. But I decided that the one person I really had to live with 24 hours every day was myself, so I mostly try to see myself through my eyes.

Later I remember being stirred by a Paul Anka song that Frank Sinatra made famous. It says,

> I've lived a life that's full, I traveled
> each and every highway, and more,
> much more than this, I did it my way.

In my business endeavors I have also been mindful of these words by J. Paul Getty in 1983 (the Bill Gates and Warren Buffett of my youth—note also his book was originally published by *Playboy*) that I read as I started my career:

> The resourceful and aggressive man who wants to get rich will find the field wide open, provided he is willing to heed and act upon his imagination, relying on his own abilities and judgment rather than conforming to patterns and practices established by others.
>
> The nonconformist—the leader and originator—has an excellent chance to make his fortune in the business world. He can wear a green toga instead of a gray-flannel suit, drink yak's milk rather than martinis, drive a Kibitka instead of a Cadillac and vote the straight Vegetarian Ticket—and none of it will make the slightest difference. Ability and achievement are bona fides no one dares question, no matter how unconventional the man who presents them.
>
> It has always been my contention that an individual who can be relied upon to be himself and to be honest unto himself can be relied upon in every other way.

I want to summarize my thoughts thus far by quoting Ralph Waldo Emerson:

> Society everywhere is in conspiracy against the manhood of every one of its members. . . . The virtue in most request is conformity. Self-reliance is its aversion. It loves not realities and creators, but names and customs.
>
> Whoso would be a man must be a nonconformist.
>
> It is easy in the world to live after the world's opinion; it is easy in solitude to live after our own; but the great man is he who in the midst of the crowd keeps with perfect sweetness the independence of solitude.
>
> A foolish consistency is the hobgoblin of little minds, adored by little statesmen and philosophers and divines. With consistency a great soul has simply nothing to do.
>
> Nothing can bring you peace but yourself.
>
> (*Self Reliance,* quoted in Bartlett, 1992).

After 9/11 my focus changed somewhat from my own goals and philosophy to a profound thankfulness that I grew up in a nation that, in my opinion, allows freedom and individualism to flourish. Yes, we are a democracy where, by definition, the majority (crowd) rules. And that in itself is a historic gift, but *only* when guided by laws and principles to protect the individual. So the fathers and framers of this country inserted into the Constitution a series of checks and balances to make certain that we could not have tyranny either from the masses (crowd) or from the rulers. Note that the Declaration of Independence first talks of *individuals* being endowed by their creator with certain unalienable rights—"that among these are life, liberty and the pursuit of happiness" and it is only *after that* it states that "to secure these rights, governments are instituted."

Then nine of the first ten Amendments to the Constitution, which compose the bulk of the Bill of Rights, are all about protecting individuals' *freedom to be different* with freedom of religion, freedom of speech, the freedom of the press, the freedom to assemble and protest, etc. All of the first nine amendments were designed to protect individual liberties from being trampled by the crowd.

It is my view that this country is not great because of the incredible multitude of goods and services we have been able to produce in a free enterprise system, nor do I believe this is a great country because we are the main superpower with unbelievable military might. Rather, I think this is a great country because the Constitution, and especially the Bill of Rights, set up a framework where we *spiritually nourished* those free individuals who wanted to take the road less traveled. And these contrarians, nonconformists, creative originators, etc., brought forth inventors from Thomas Jefferson, Thomas Edison, Henry Ford, Ben Franklin, George Washington Carver, Wilbur and Orville Wright, Eli Whitney, Isaac Singer, Albert Einstein, Robert Fulton, Robert Jarvik, Samuel Morse, Alexander Graham Bell, Jonas Salk, Bill Gates, etc., who have created inventions, wiped out disease, and by their spirit and individualism helped the human condition as much as any other people.

Lord Acton said in 1887 that "power tends to corrupt and absolute power corrupts absolutely" (letter to Bishop Mandell Creighton, quoted in Bartlett, 1992). I agree with this observation, and I tend to distrust any entity (person, government, business, etc.) that might try to wield absolute power. So I am grateful for the extensive system of restraints on absolute power that we have—and the resulting freedom that it affords us as citizens. Thus, we have three branches of government—executive, legislative, and judicial—that share power.

This is a country that celebrates individual freedom and achievement, and there is no doubt in my mind that the Bill of Rights and the separation of power have nourished an independent entrepreneurial spirit to explore the road less traveled. That is the very reason we have had so many achievements that have benefited the entire world.

Sometimes taking the road less traveled is lonely, and you must be willing to ignore a lot of people pressuring you to take the popular road and conform to the majority. But in my stock market career, in my country, and in my life—for me the road less traveled makes all the difference. The final word on following kings or crowds goes to Rudyard Kipling (from the poem "A Charm," quoted in Bartlett, 1992):

> If you can talk with crowds and keep your virtue,
> Or walk with Kings—nor lose the common touch.
> Yours is the Earth and everything that's in it.
> And—which is more—you'll be a Man, my son!

Addendum

SENTIMENT ON INDIVIDUAL STOCKS

THE PRECEDING CHAPTERS OF THIS BOOK have primarily focused on sentiment and psychology as they relate to the overall stock market or other categories of assets. And while sentiment indicators for the overall market are critical, many investors own only particular stocks rather than the entire market. Thus *there is a need for an analysis of sentiment indicators for individual stocks.* Like the valuation-oriented sentiment indicators for the market discussed in Chapter 5, at NDR we find that we can use indicators based on the fundamental variables of an individual company as measures of crowd sentiment and psychology toward that stock. Such indicators are typically based on *a comparison of a company's current stock price to some measure of the company's underlying value, such as its assets, earnings, revenues, or dividends.* The charts shown in the figures on the following pages represent our analysis of a number of representative stocks using fundamental variables to assess investor sentiment.

Regardless of which of the various variables is chosen, though, the same principle applies: When investors are willing to pay a high price for a company's assets, earnings, etc., they are most likely very optimistic about the company's future and potentially overconfident, and investors who will pay only a low price for a stock relative to its fundamentals are likely to be relatively pessimistic and potentially overly fearful. So we can see what the "crowd" is thinking about a stock's prospects by looking at how much investors are willing to pay for each dollar of underlying assets, earnings, etc. *When we see crowd sentiment toward a stock reaching extreme levels, we look for an opportunity to take a contrary position to that of the crowd.*

Differences among companies and industries can cause the range of values that constitutes "high" or "low" valuations, and thus extreme crowd sentiment, to vary significantly among stocks and industries. *So we look at a stock's valuation measure in the context of its own historical range,* and make the determination of valuation-optimism being high or low based on the historical relationship of each stock's current valuation to its own long-term norms.

One challenge we face, though, is determining which of the innumerable pieces of data on a company's underlying fundamentals to use as the basis for analyzing market sentiment for a particular stock. Because there is such a wide variety of companies and industries represented in the stock market, one particular fundamental variable (such as earnings) may not be appropriate or the most useful for all companies. A given variable may be more relevant than another for particular companies or industries due to variations in accounting practices, corporate structures, regulatory influences, or simply what investors or analysts have chosen to focus on.

Consequently, we have analyzed each of the stocks shown on the following pages by testing seven different fundamental variables to see which one has been most useful in identifying extremes in investor sentiment for each stock. Those variables include trailing four-quarter per share values for:

1. Cash dividends
2. Sales—total top-line revenues
3. Earnings—bottom-line net income according to generally accepted accounting principles
4. Cashflow—earnings adjusted for non-cash accounting figures such as depreciation
5. A 20-quarter average of earnings
6. A 20-quarter average of cashflow
7. Book value (shareholder's equity)—corporate assets minus liabilities

We included the 20-quarter (5-year) averages of earnings and cashflow as variables in order to smooth out the earnings and cashflow (both of which can be negative) for certain companies that have had very volatile earnings and would otherwise be difficult to analyze.

For each variable, we also tested a range of threshold values to determine what level of the variable's reading has best indicated an extreme relative to the stock's historical norms. For example, if we are considering sales as the fundamental variable, we use the ratio of the stock's price per share to sales per share and test a range of different price-sales ratios to see what levels would have best signaled excessive optimism and pessimism historically. We might find, for instance, that a ratio of 1.5 times sales has indicated excessive euphoria by investors, while a ratio of 0.7 times sales has indicated excessive pessimism. The same process is used to test each of the seven variables listed above, and the best results from that process are used in the charts shown in the figures.

Each stock charted in the figures on the following pages thus has dashed lines plotted alongside the historical prices in the bottom section of the figure that reflect *the levels we have found to have indicated excessive bullishness or bearishness among investors in that stock,* based on one of the seven fundamental variables. By using these levels as a frame of reference, we can get a clearer view of the impact of crowd psychology on individual stock prices. And we can use these charts going forward to tell us when sentiment toward a particular stock is likely to be excessively bullish or bearish and thus when we should be watching for an opportunity to buy (if investors are overly fearful) or sell (if investors are overly optimistic). Readers can use the parameters shown in the figures in the following pages and apply them to the most current fundamental data to gauge investor sentiment for those stocks in the future. It should be kept in mind, however, that all of the analysis shown on the following pages was developed with the benefit of hindsight, and therefore the results shown are hypothetical. Their primary purpose is to give a "big-picture" perspective on crowd sentiment on individual stocks, rather than to serve as the basis for a trading system.

Nonetheless, the parameters shown in the figures that follow can be used as guides for assessing the stocks going forward. For example, if a figure for a particular stock shows that 1.5 times sales represents excessive optimism and 0.7 times sales represents excessive pessimism, one could simply look up the company's most recent four-quarter sales per share figure (generally available at no cost from various financial websites) and calculate the current price-sales ratio and see if it falls outside the range of 0.7 to 1.5.

And while the readings generated through this type of valuation-based analysis are very useful, trying to use them by themselves can be difficult. Stocks can be undervalued and out of favor, or overvalued and excessively popular, for frustratingly long periods of time in some cases. This means that buying as soon as a stock first falls to a level indicating excessive pessimism can mean having to hold through further declines or sideways periods before sentiment starts to reverse and a new sustainable uptrend takes hold. The reverse is true when selling stocks that show excessive optimism. Also note that in many cases a stock may have spent perhaps 60 percent of the time in the optimism or pessimism zones (i.e., outside the two dashed lines in the figure), and so the zones are not meant to be targets to act on themselves, but rather buy or sell "alerts." In addition, while it is generally the case that the further back in time a stock's historical data go, the more valuable the valuation-sentiment perspective is, companies can in some cases change their underlying business or behavior enough to make comparisons with the past less relevant. For these reasons, investors should incorporate other indicators based on a stock's price trend and relative strength to fine-tune entry and exit points. *By using technical (price momentum–based) indicators alongside sentiment-based indicators, investors can improve their odds of outperforming and significantly reduce downside risk.* One example of such a trend indicator is shown in the top section of each figure, which is a 39-week moving average of the weekly closing price. When the price is above the moving average, the trend is positive; and when the moving average itself is also rising, the uptrend is considered stronger. So, for example, if we see a stock showing excessive bearish sentiment (in the lower section of the figure), we would watch for the price to then cross above its 39-week moving average (in the figure's upper section) to identify a low-risk entry point. Potential sale candidates would be identified using the reverse process: Watch for stocks showing excessive optimism and then falling below the moving average. Regardless of any quantitative readings, though, further research is always advised before taking any action based on the information in these figures.

In conclusion, the figures shown in this addendum present examples of how the impact of crowd psychology can be monitored for individual stocks using a combination of the stock's price and fundamental variables related to the company. This sort of sentiment analysis is most effectively used in conjunction with price trend indicators to help fine-tune the timing of buys and sells. The same principle of crowd psychology that applies to asset classes can be applied to individual stocks: Beware of the crowd at extremes, and look for opportunities to take positions *contrary to the crowd* after it reaches an extreme in sentiment.

FIGURE A-1 3M Company (MMM).
© 2003 Ned Davis Research, Inc. All rights reserved.

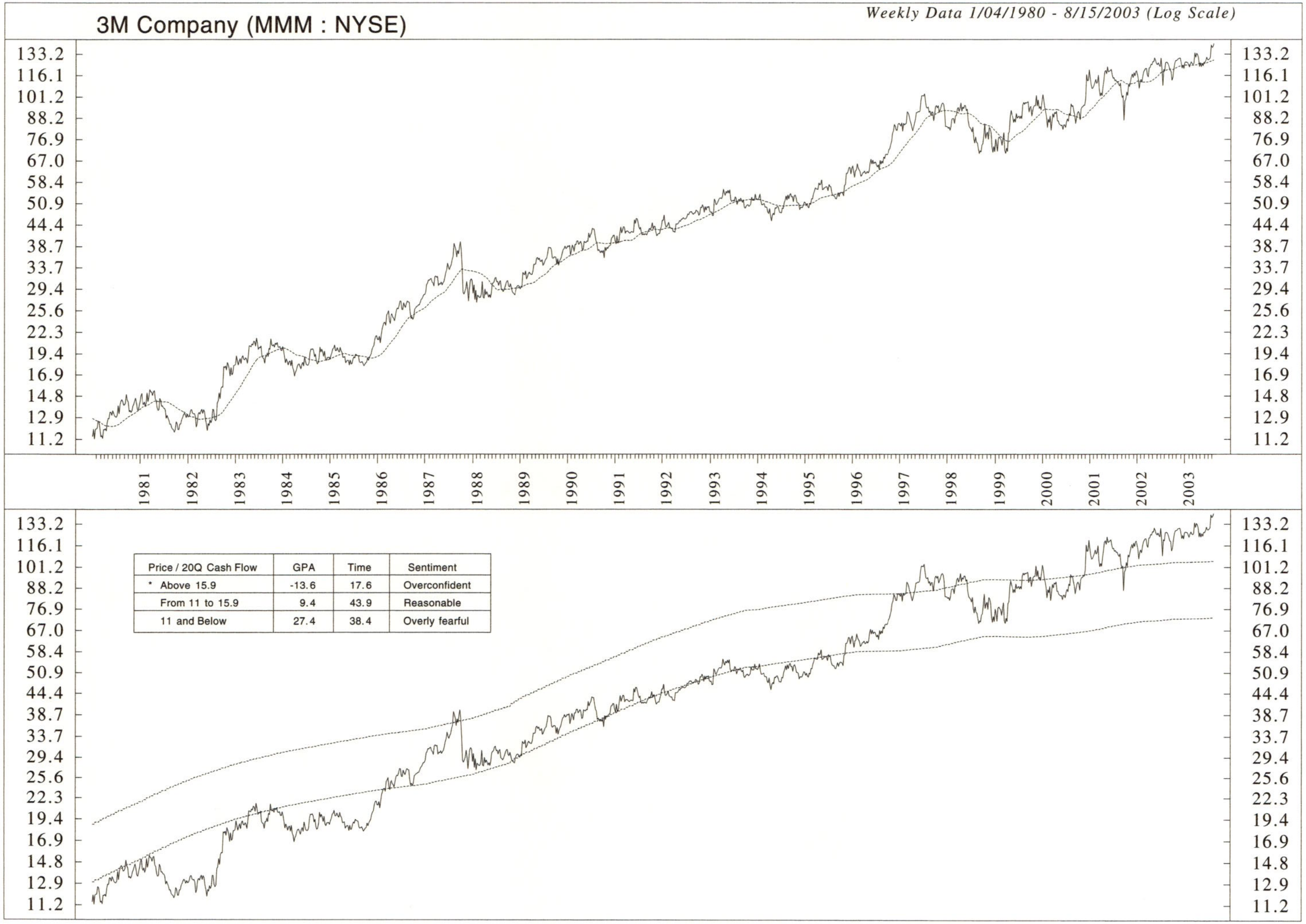

FIGURE A-2 Abbott Laboratories (ABT).

© 2003 Ned Davis Research, Inc. All rights reserved.

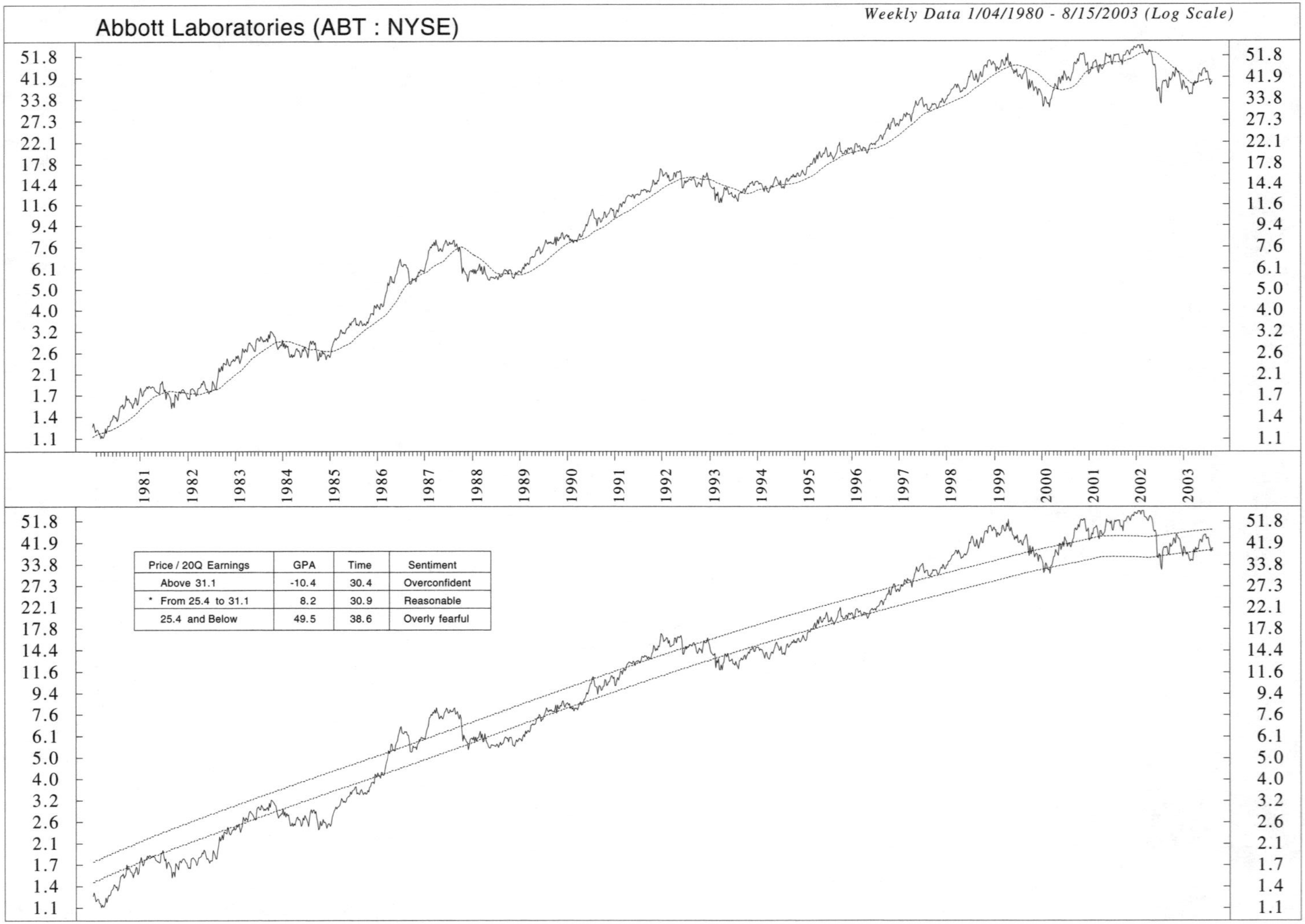

Abbott Laboratories (ABT : NYSE) — Weekly Data 1/04/1980 - 8/15/2003 (Log Scale)

Price / 20Q Earnings	GPA	Time	Sentiment
Above 31.1	-10.4	30.4	Overconfident
• From 25.4 to 31.1	8.2	30.9	Reasonable
25.4 and Below	49.5	38.6	Overly fearful

FIGURE A-3 Advanced Micro Devices, Inc. (AMD).
© 2003 Ned Davis Research, Inc. All rights reserved.

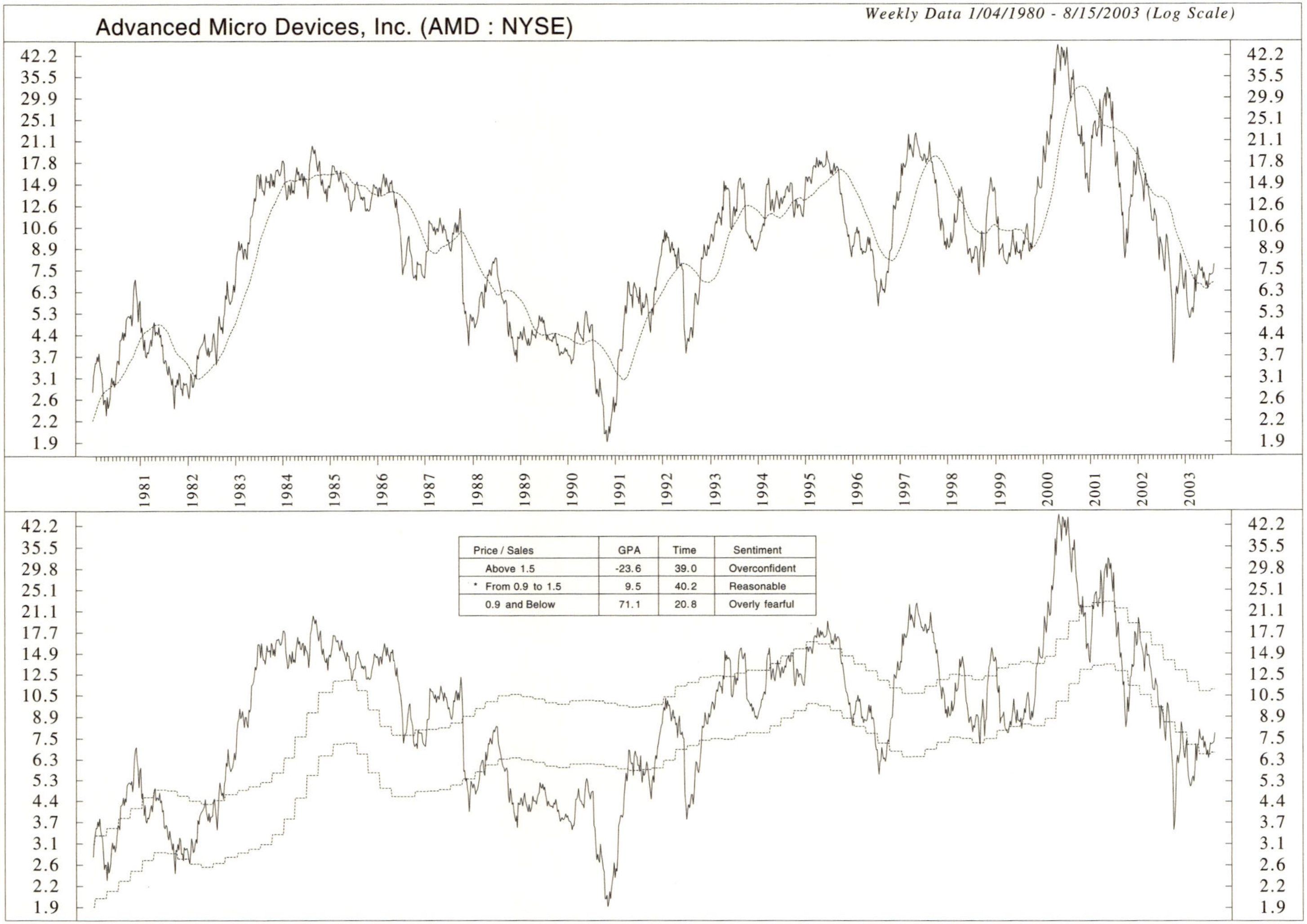

FIGURE A-4 Affiliated Computer Services, Inc. (ACS).
© 2003 Ned Davis Research, Inc. All rights reserved.

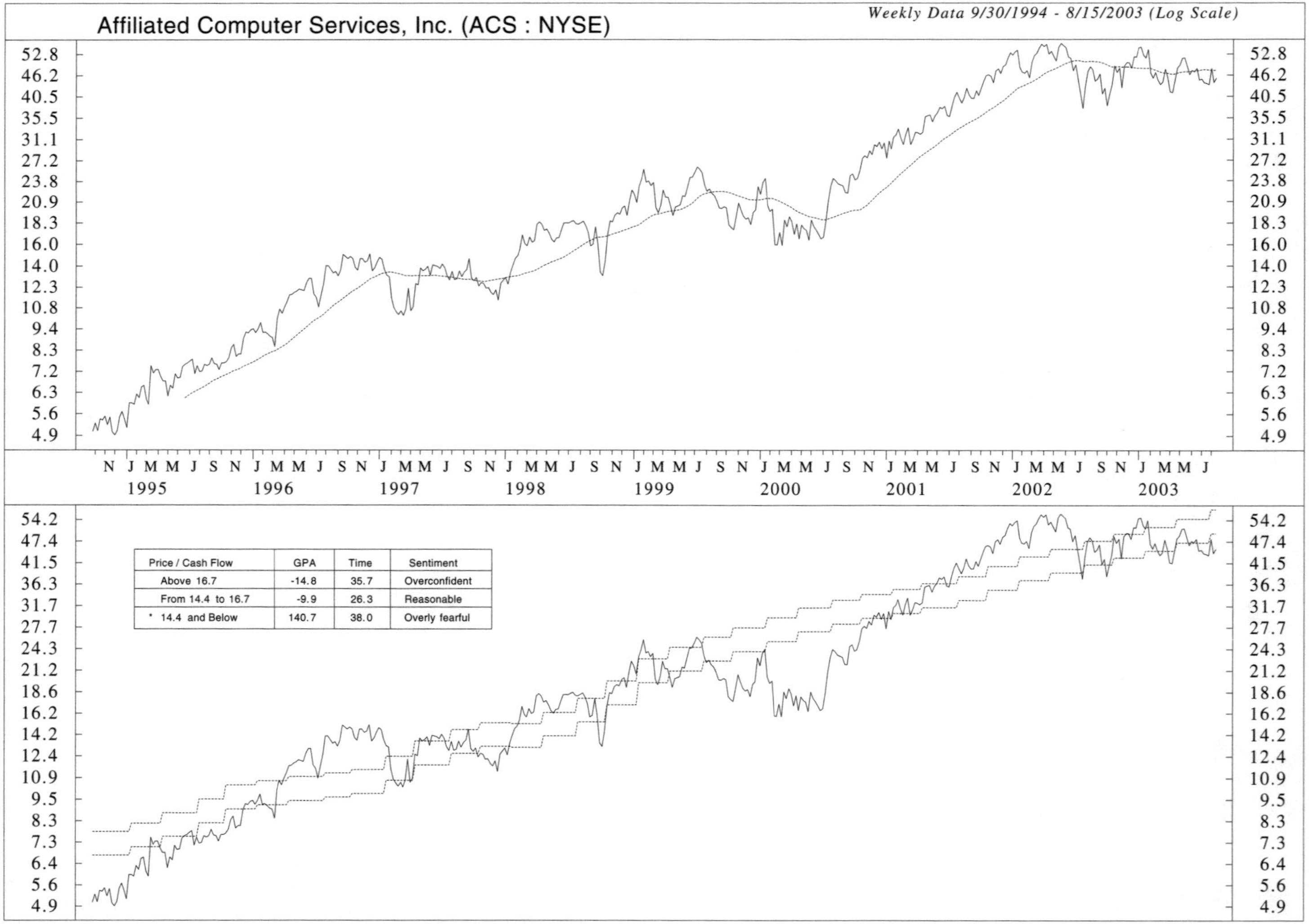

FIGURE A-5 Air Products and Chemicals, Inc. (APD).
© 2003 Ned Davis Research, Inc. All rights reserved.

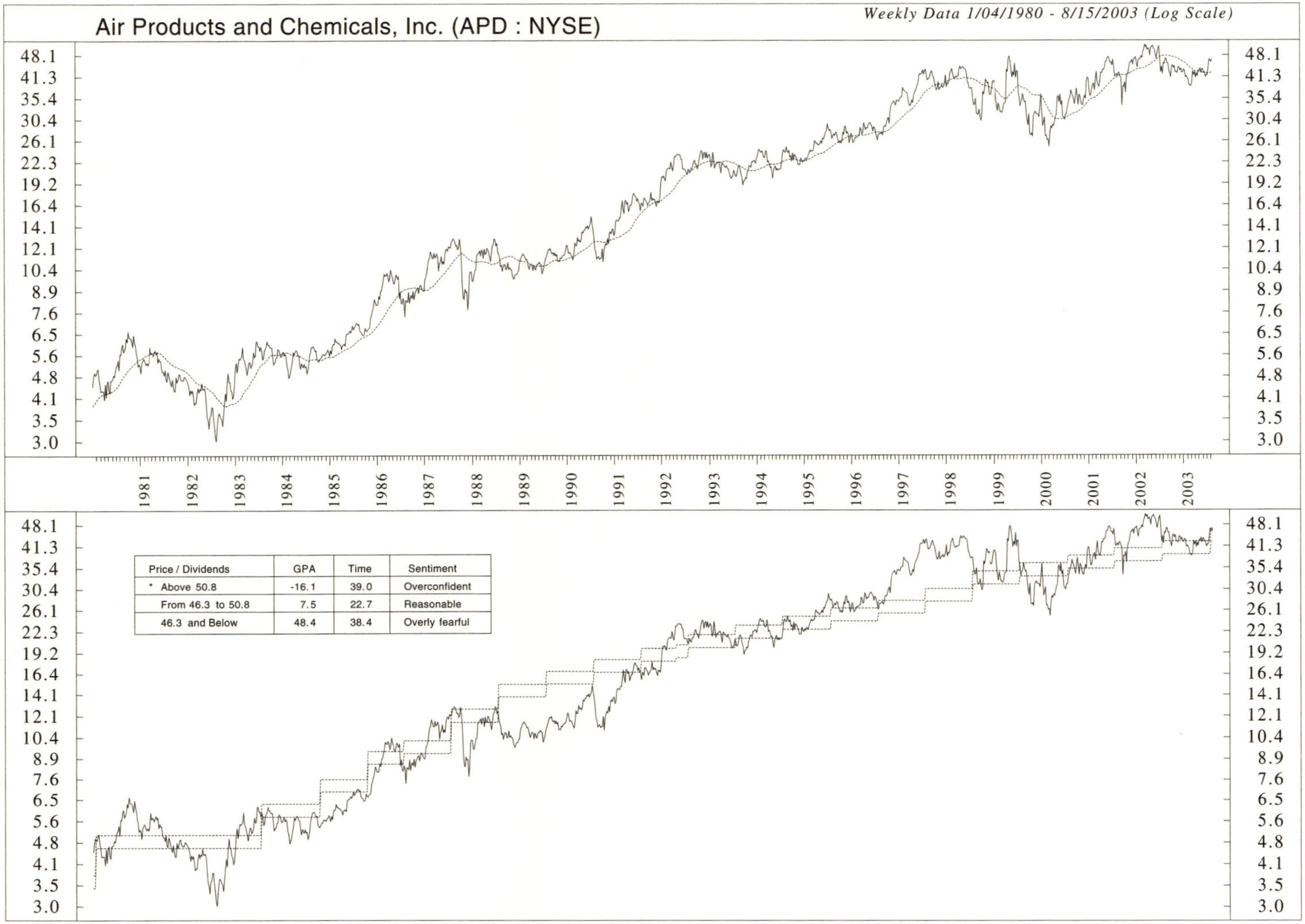

FIGURE A-6 Alberto-Culver Company (ACV).
© 2003 Ned Davis Research, Inc. All rights reserved.

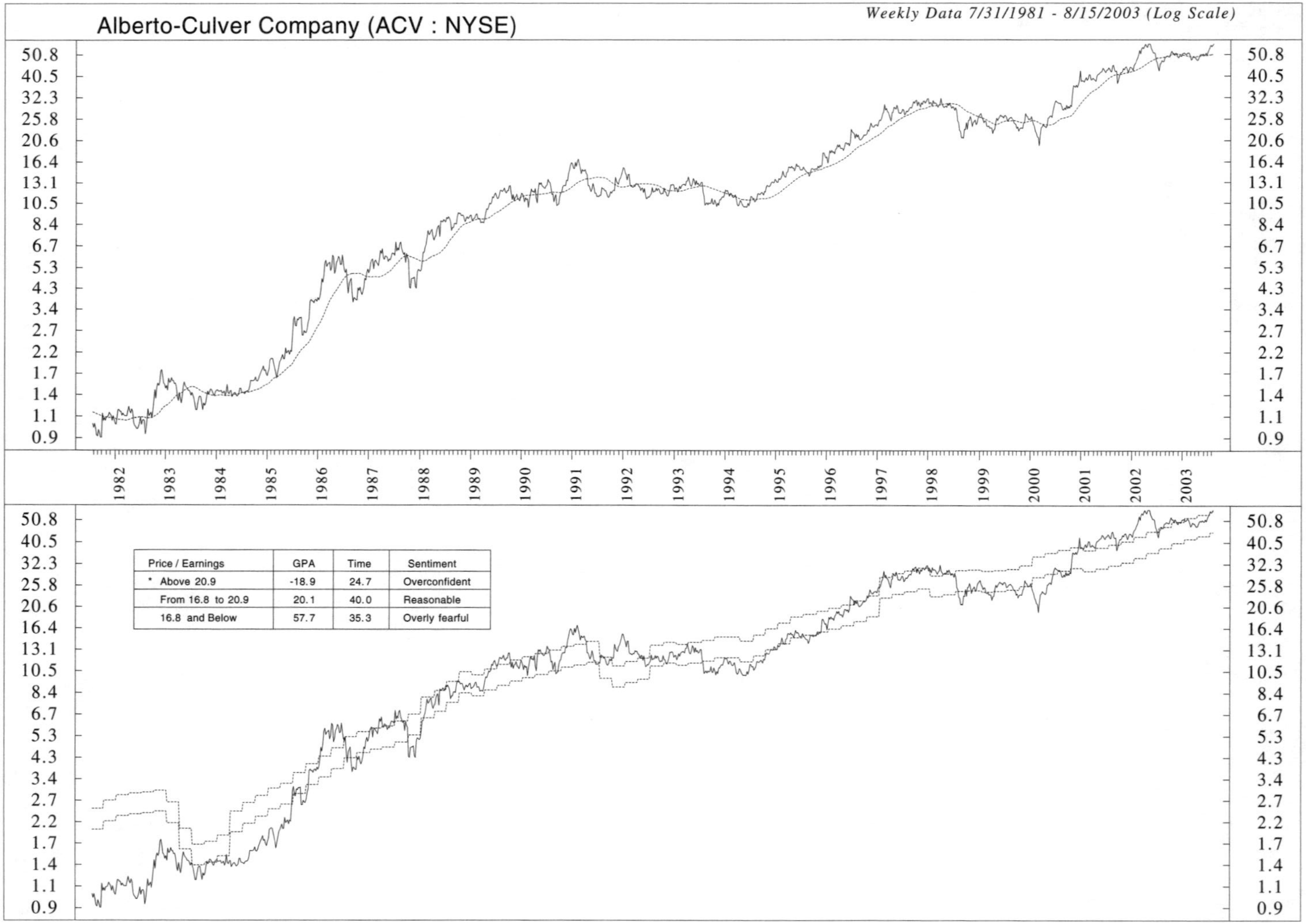

FIGURE A-7 Alcan, Inc. (AL).
© 2003 Ned Davis Research, Inc. All rights reserved.

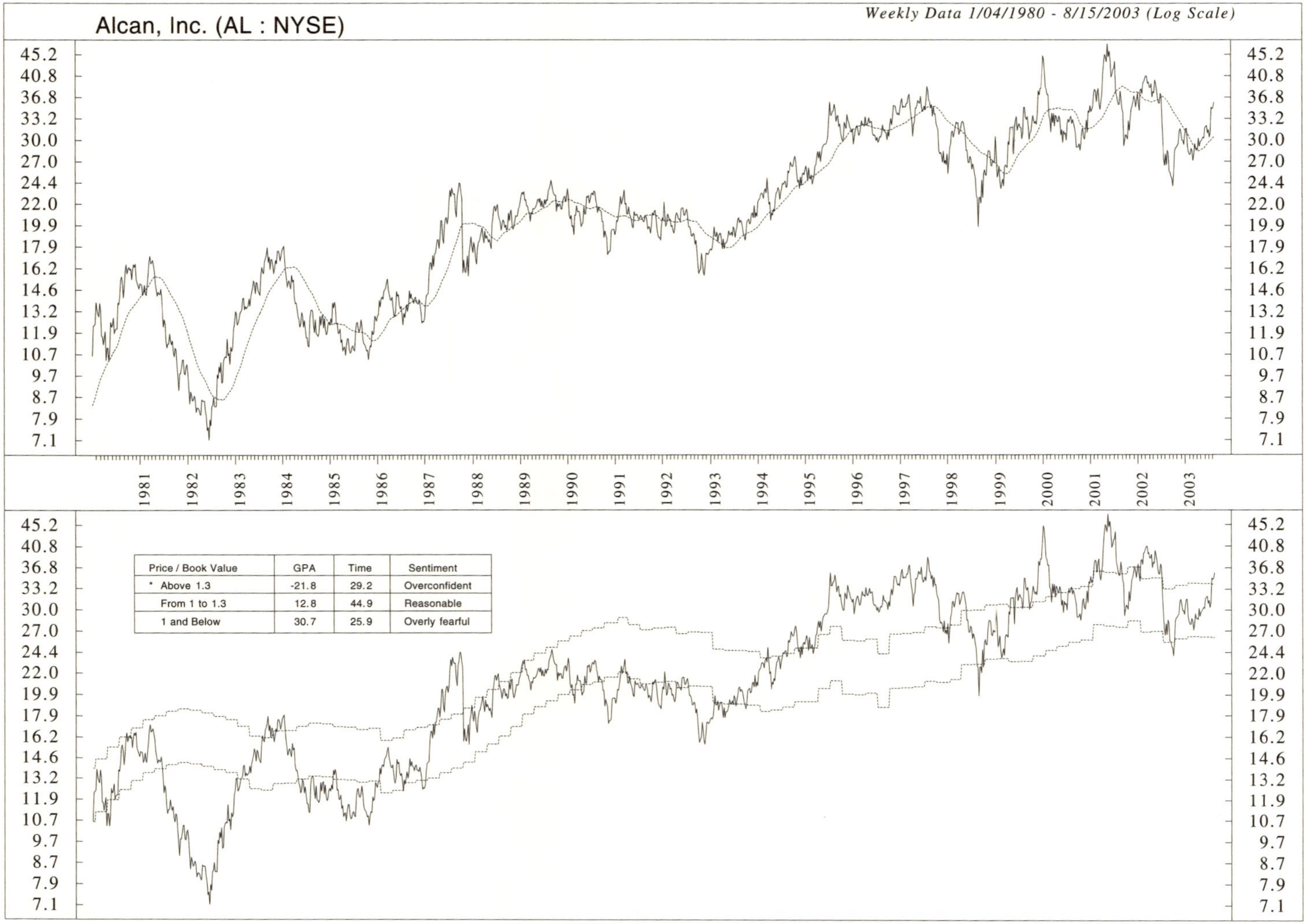

FIGURE A-8 Alcoa, Inc. (AA).
© 2003 Ned Davis Research, Inc. All rights reserved.

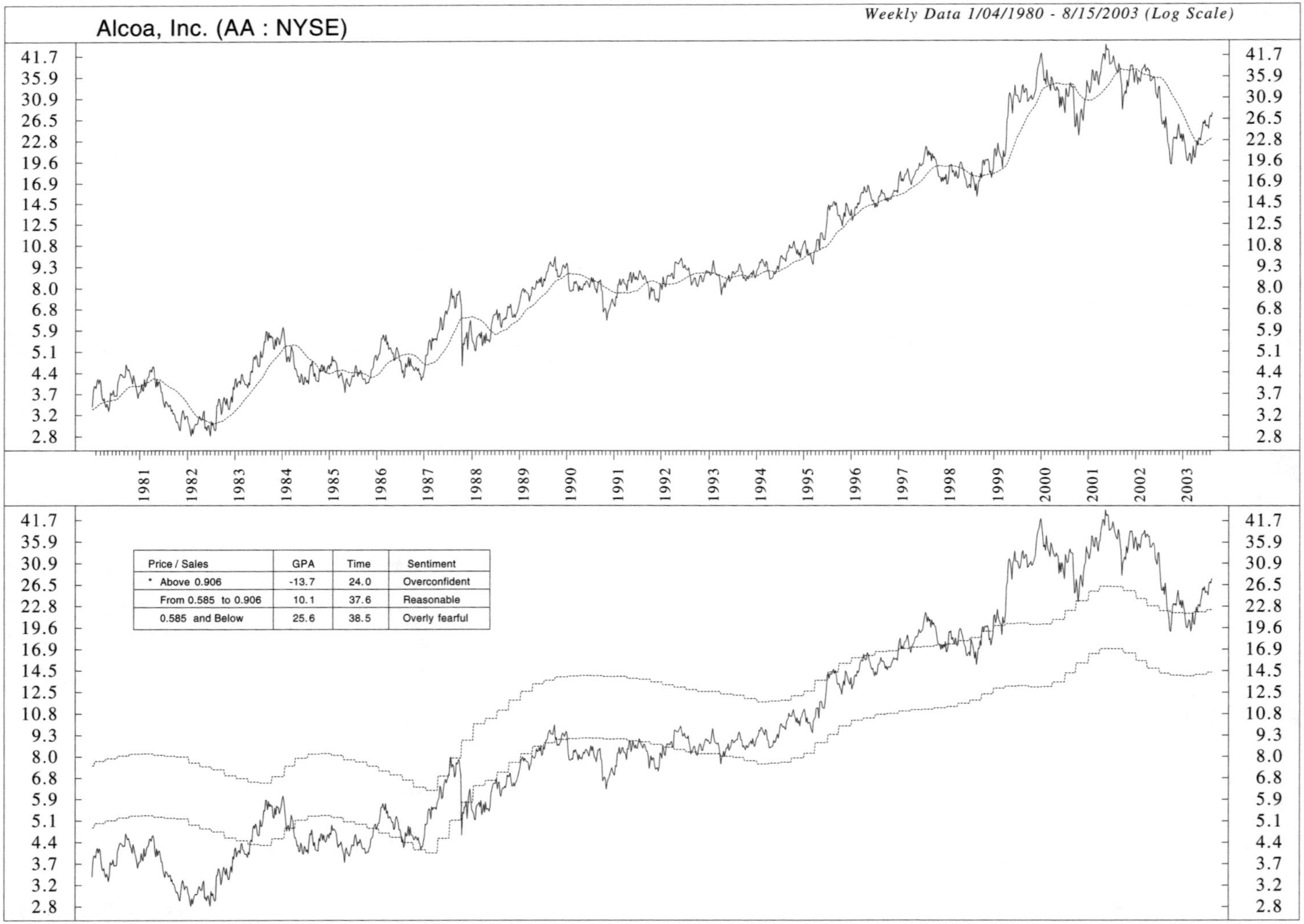

FIGURE A-9 Altria Group, Inc. (MO).
© 2003 Ned Davis Research, Inc. All rights reserved.

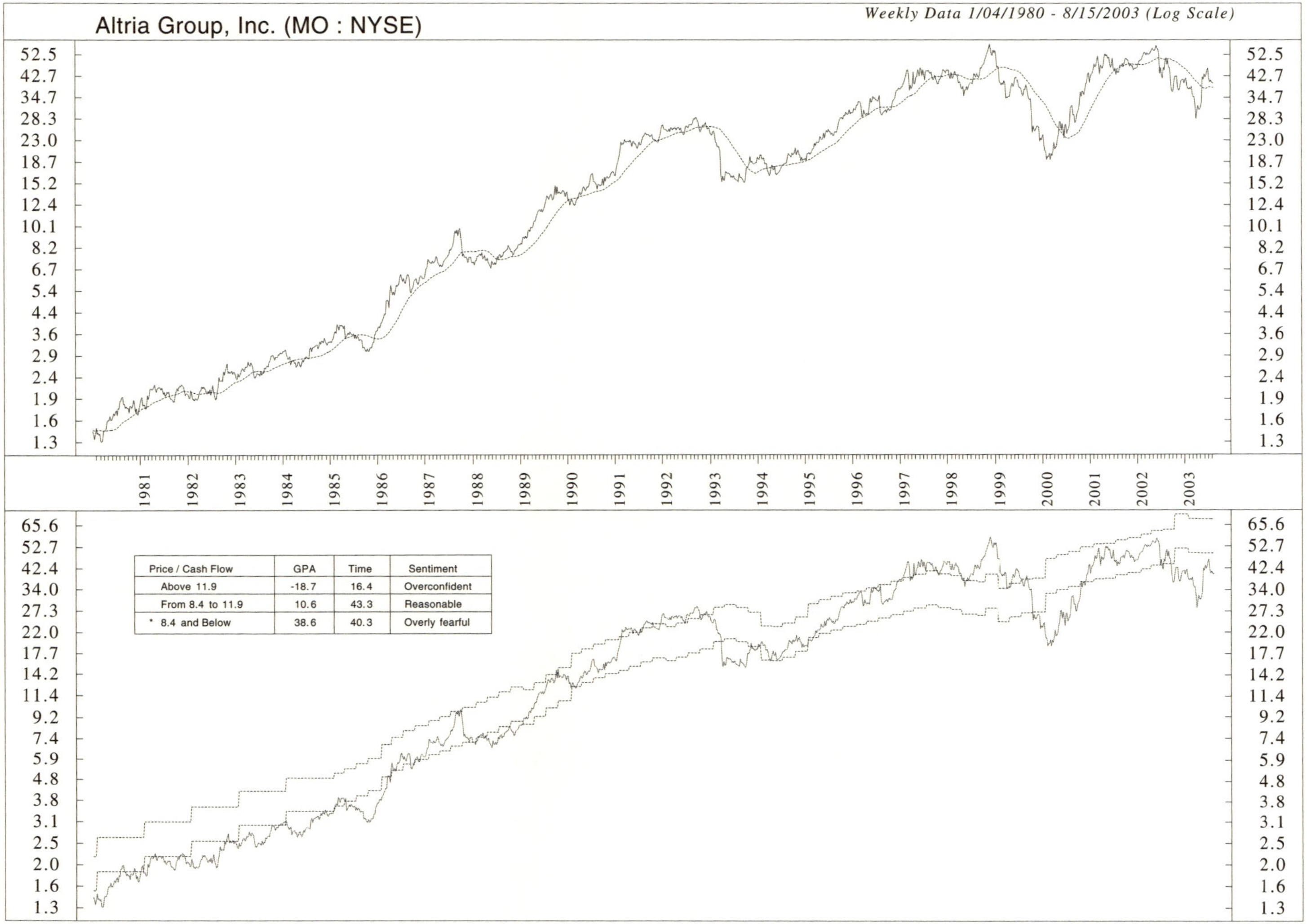

Altria Group, Inc. (MO : NYSE)   Weekly Data 1/04/1980 - 8/15/2003 (Log Scale)

Price / Cash Flow	GPA	Time	Sentiment
Above 11.9	-18.7	16.4	Overconfident
From 8.4 to 11.9	10.6	43.3	Reasonable
* 8.4 and Below	38.6	40.3	Overly fearful

FIGURE A-10 American Express Company (AXP).

© 2003 Ned Davis Research, Inc. All rights reserved.

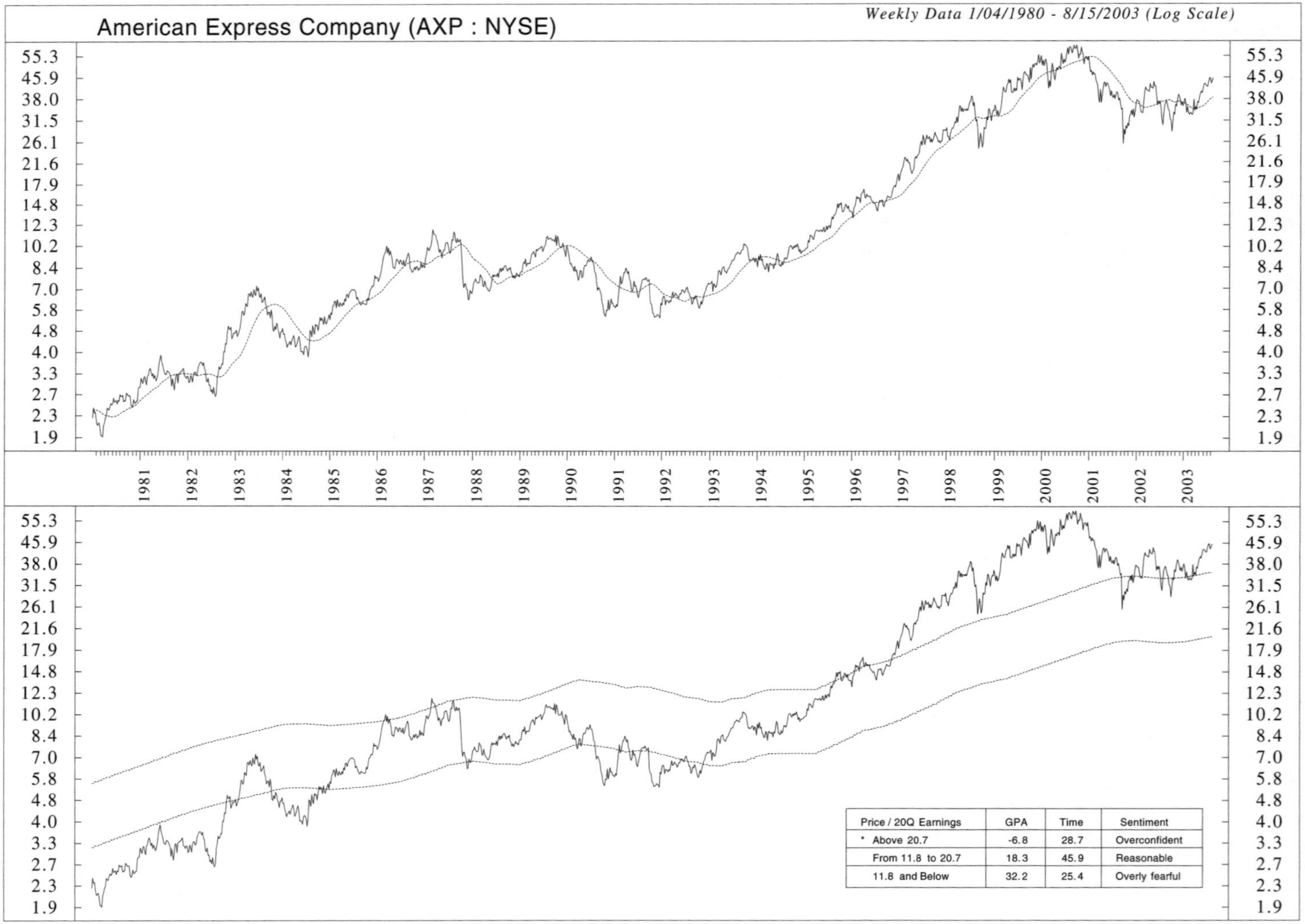

FIGURE A-11 Amgen, Inc. (AMGN).
© 2003 Ned Davis Research, Inc. All rights reserved.

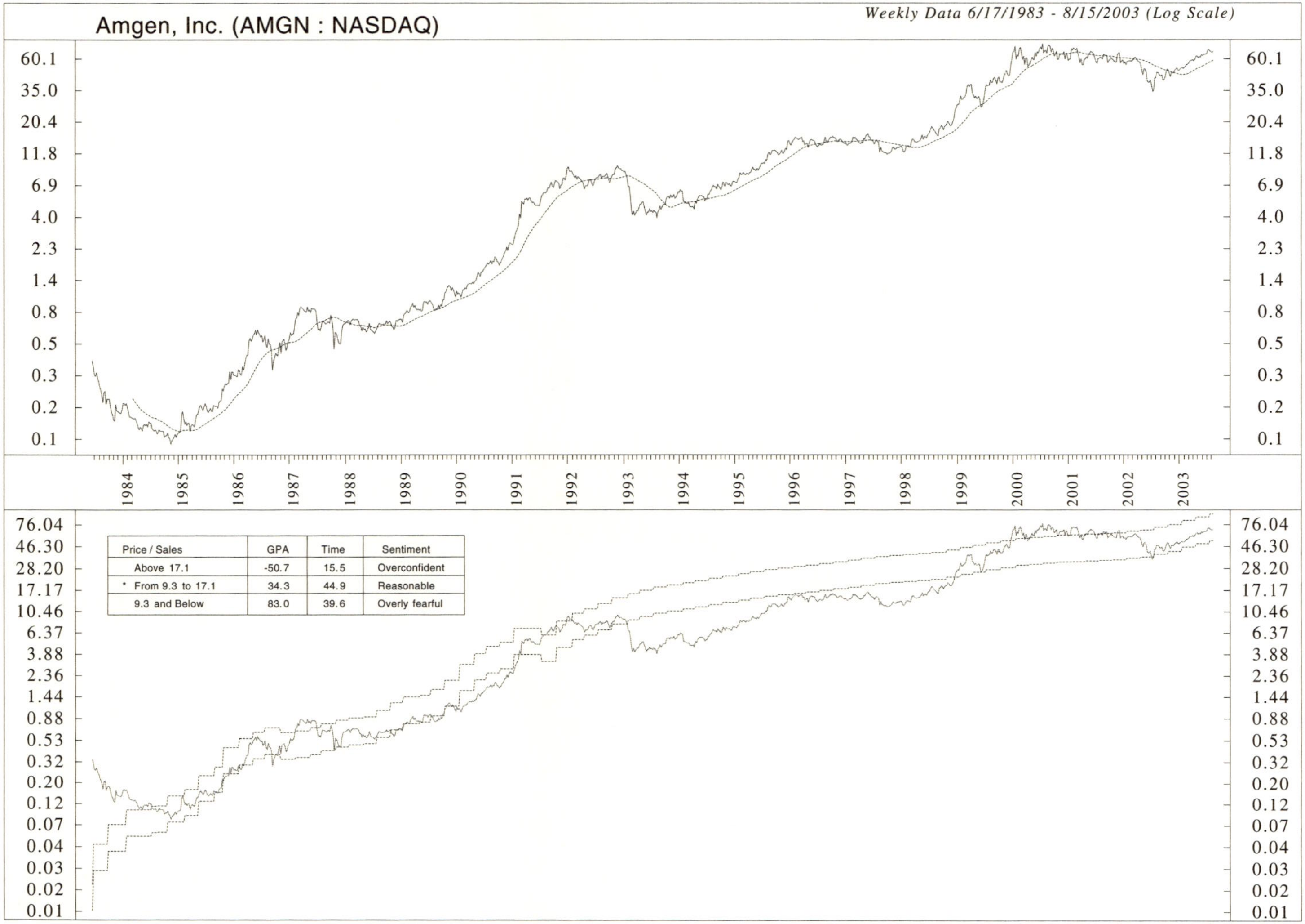

Amgen, Inc. (AMGN : NASDAQ) Weekly Data 6/17/1983 - 8/15/2003 (Log Scale)

Price / Sales	GPA	Time	Sentiment
Above 17.1	-50.7	15.5	Overconfident
From 9.3 to 17.1	34.3	44.9	Reasonable
9.3 and Below	83.0	39.6	Overly fearful

FIGURE A-12 Analog Devices, Inc. (ADI).
© 2003 Ned Davis Research, Inc. All rights reserved.

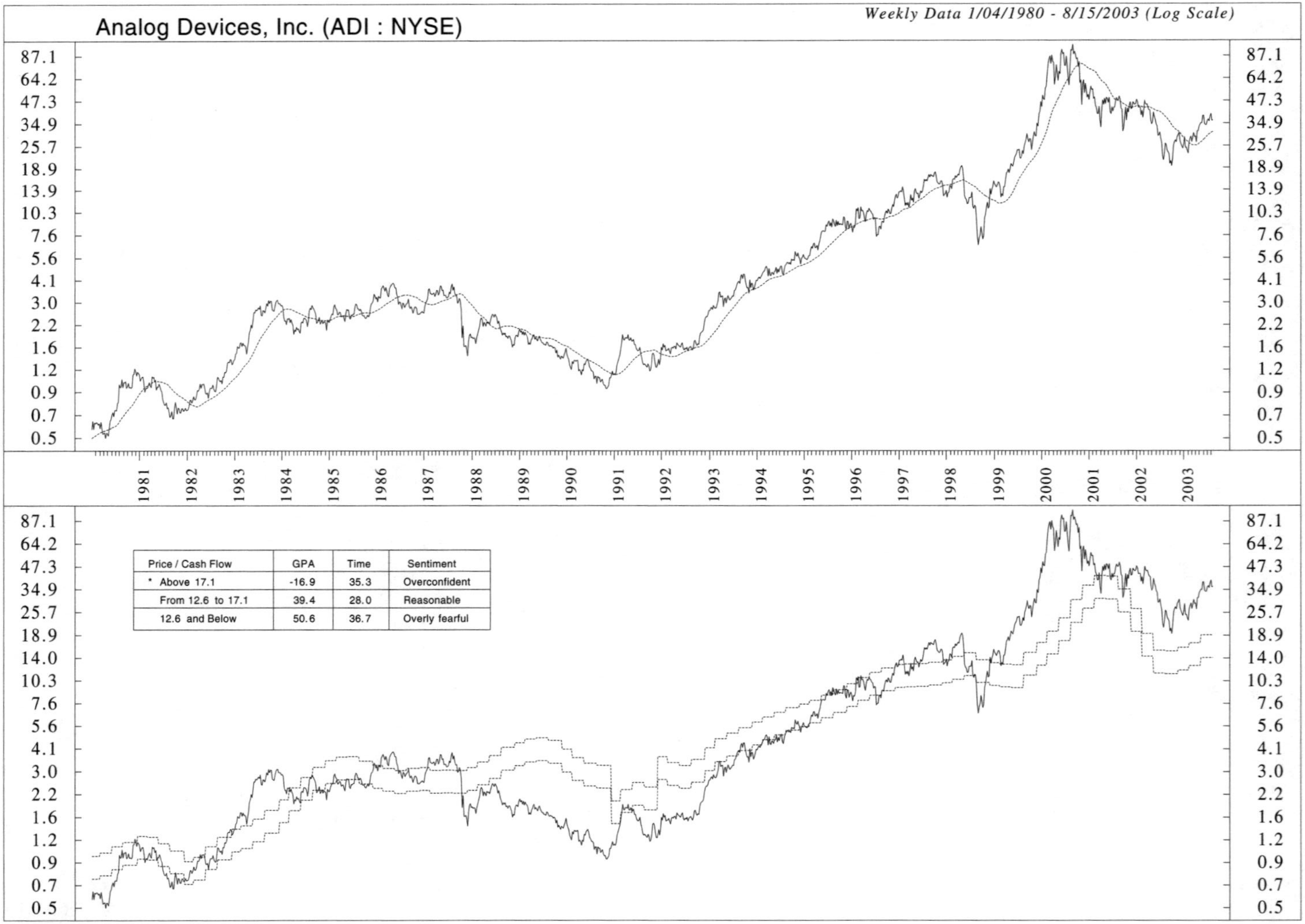

FIGURE A-13 Anheuser-Busch Companies, Inc. (BUD).

© 2003 Ned Davis Research, Inc. All rights reserved.

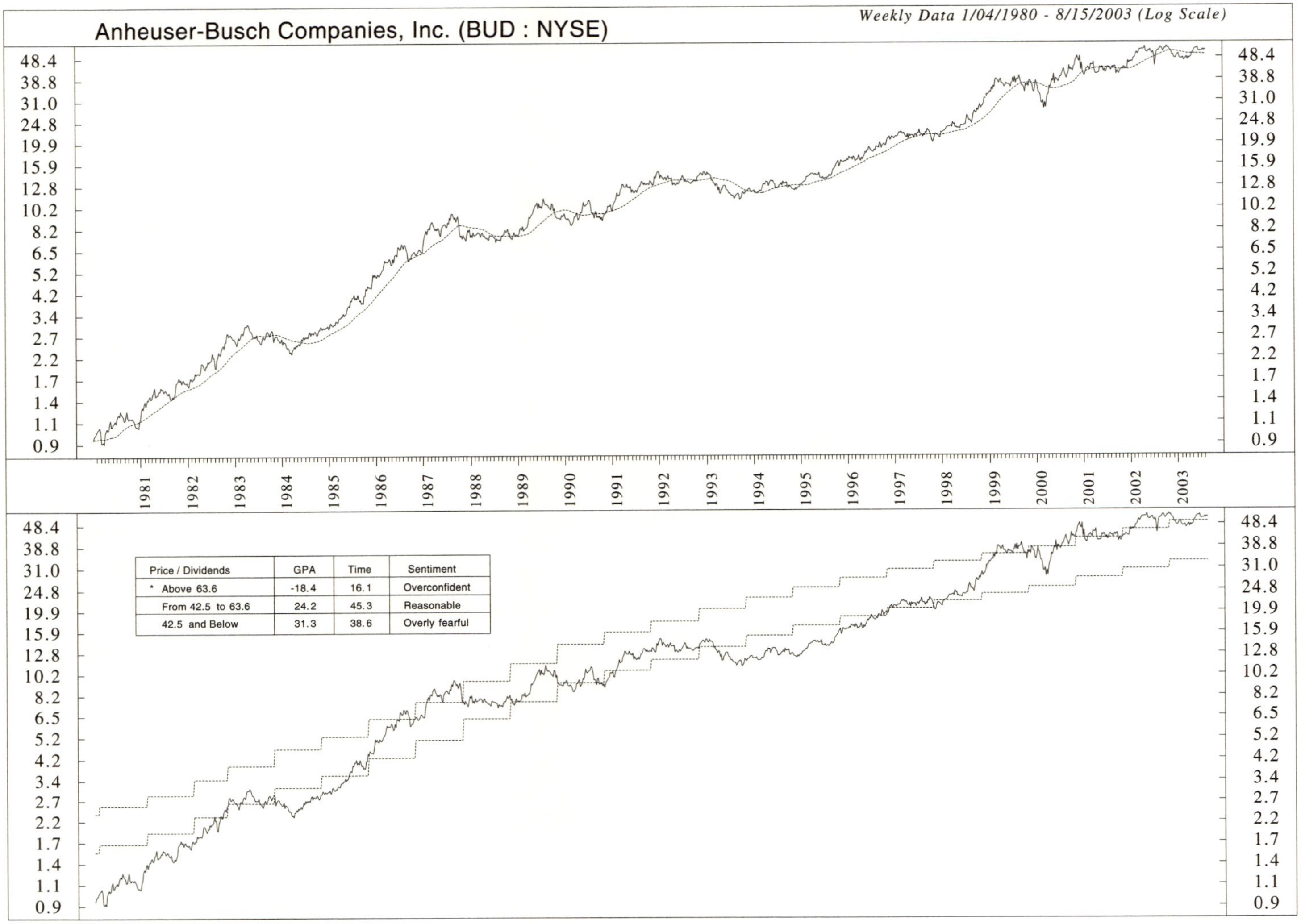

Price / Dividends	GPA	Time	Sentiment
* Above 63.6	-18.4	16.1	Overconfident
From 42.5 to 63.6	24.2	45.3	Reasonable
42.5 and Below	31.3	38.6	Overly fearful

FIGURE A-14 Archer-Daniels-Midland Company (ADM).
© 2003 Ned Davis Research, Inc. All rights reserved.

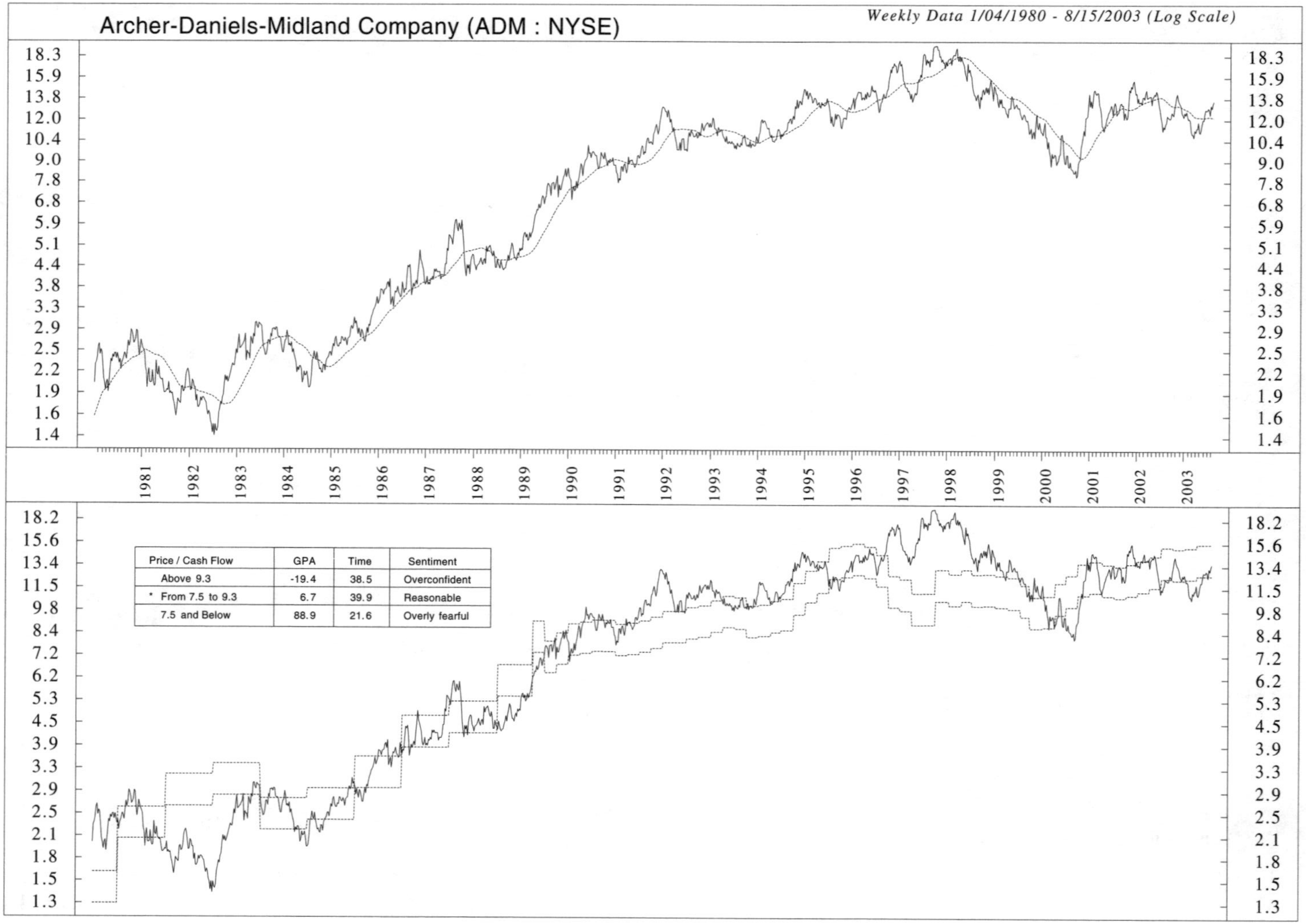

FIGURE A-15   Bank of America Corporation (BAC).
© 2003 Ned Davis Research, Inc. All rights reserved.

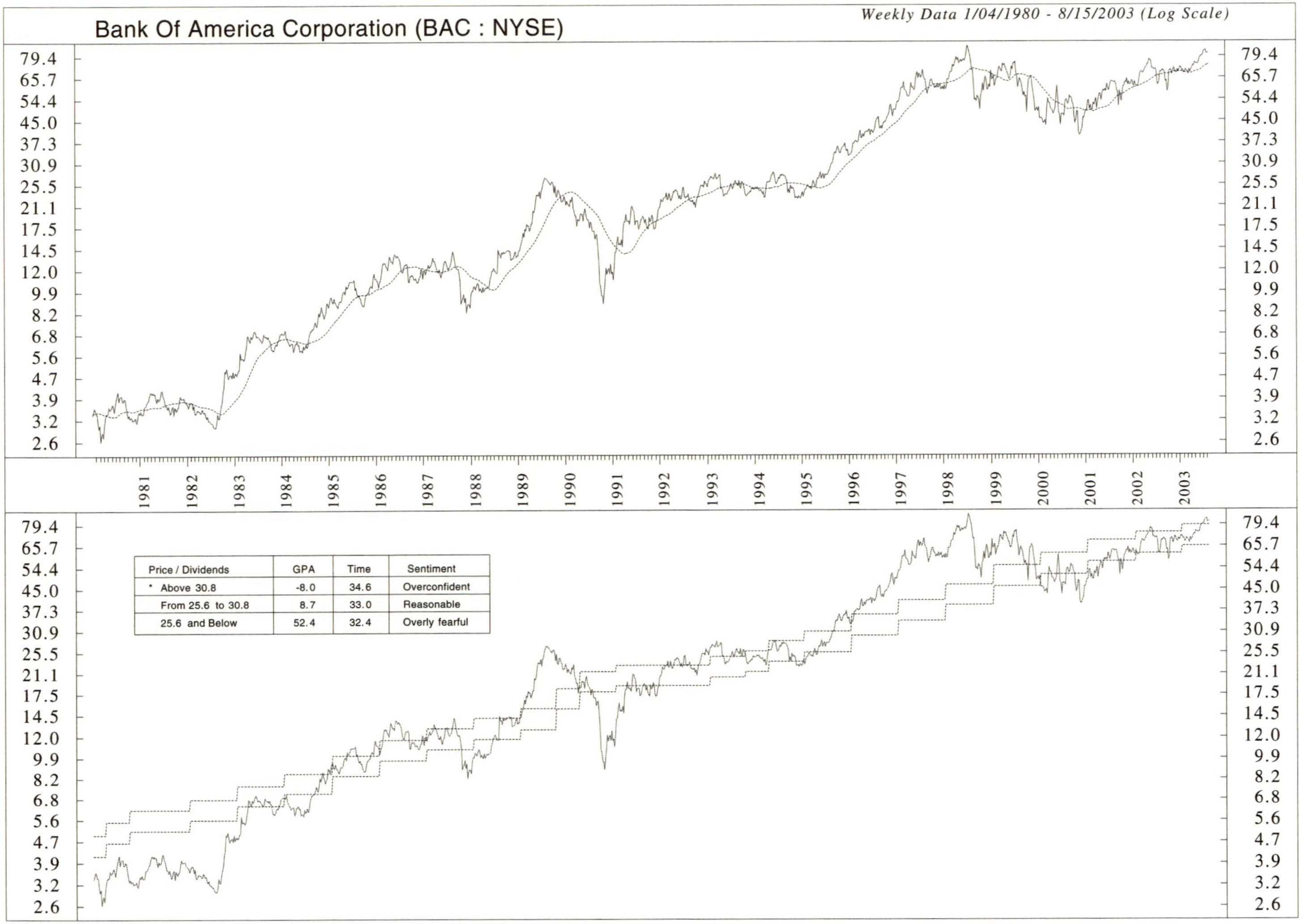

FIGURE A-16 Bank One Corporation (ONE).
© 2003 Ned Davis Research, Inc. All rights reserved.

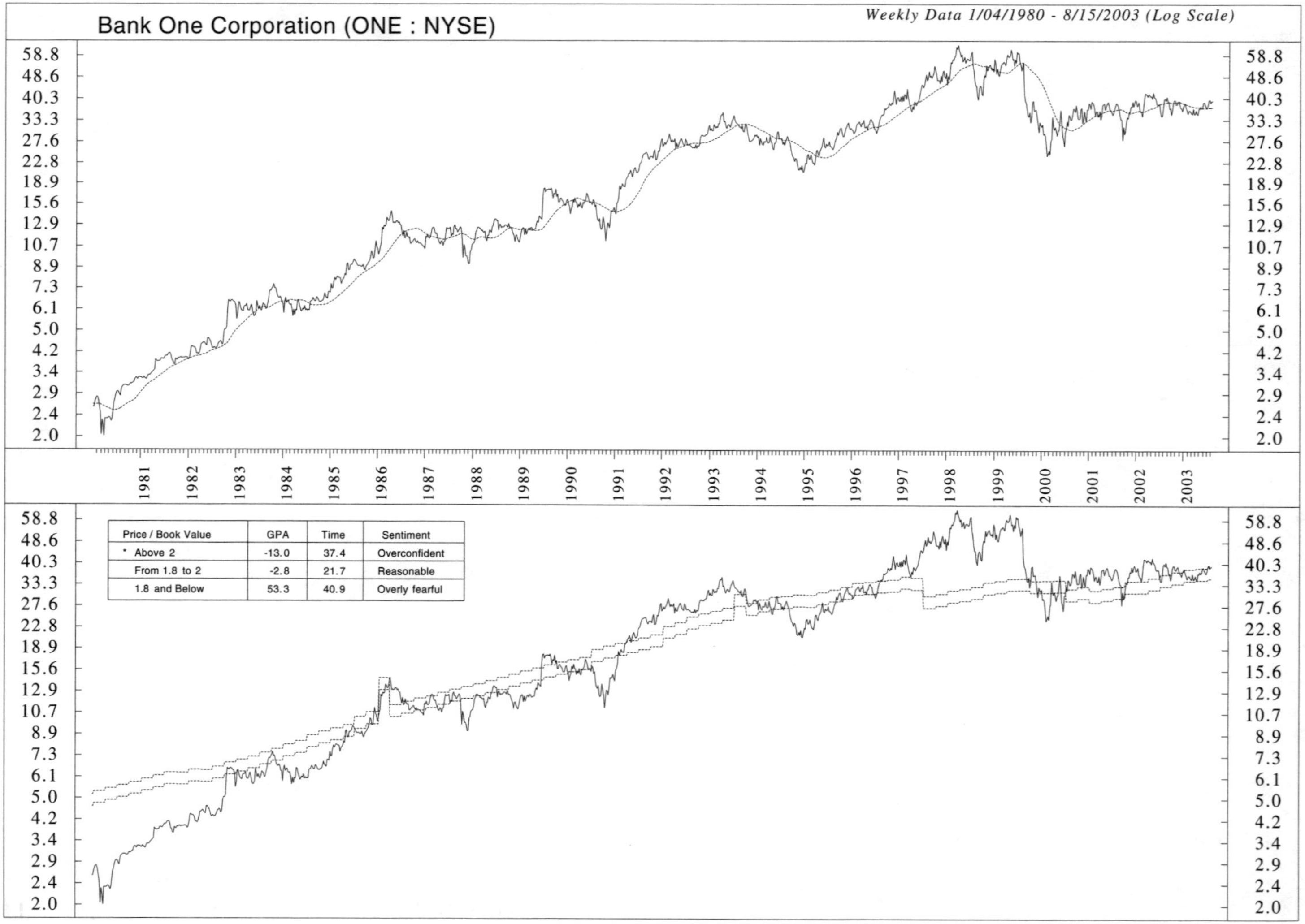

FIGURE A-17 Baxter International, Inc. (BAX).
© 2003 Ned Davis Research, Inc. All rights reserved.

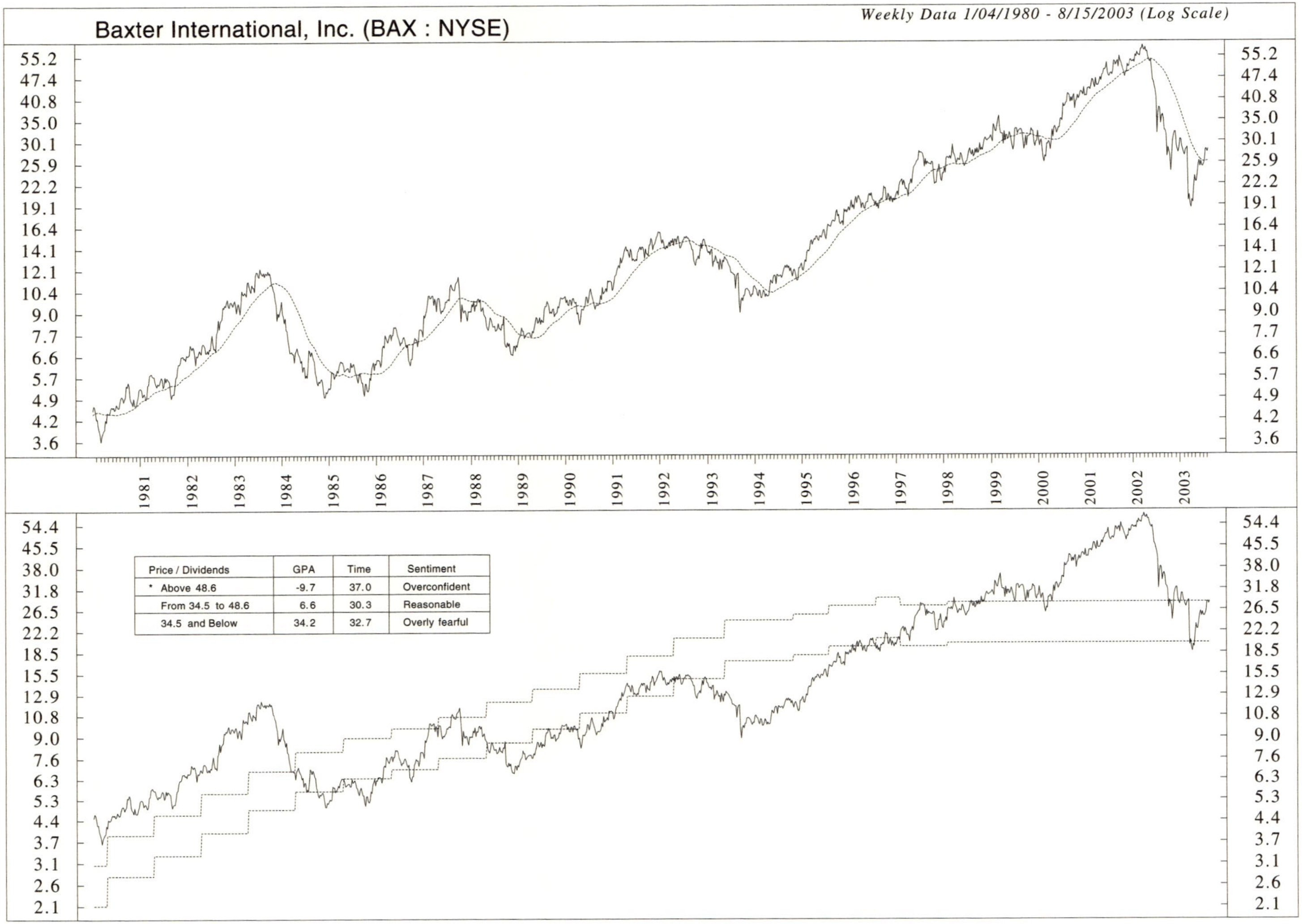

Baxter International, Inc. (BAX : NYSE)

Weekly Data 1/04/1980 - 8/15/2003 (Log Scale)

Price / Dividends	GPA	Time	Sentiment
* Above 48.6	-9.7	37.0	Overconfident
From 34.5 to 48.6	6.6	30.3	Reasonable
34.5 and Below	34.2	32.7	Overly fearful

FIGURE A-18 Boeing Company, The (BA).
© 2003 Ned Davis Research, Inc. All rights reserved.

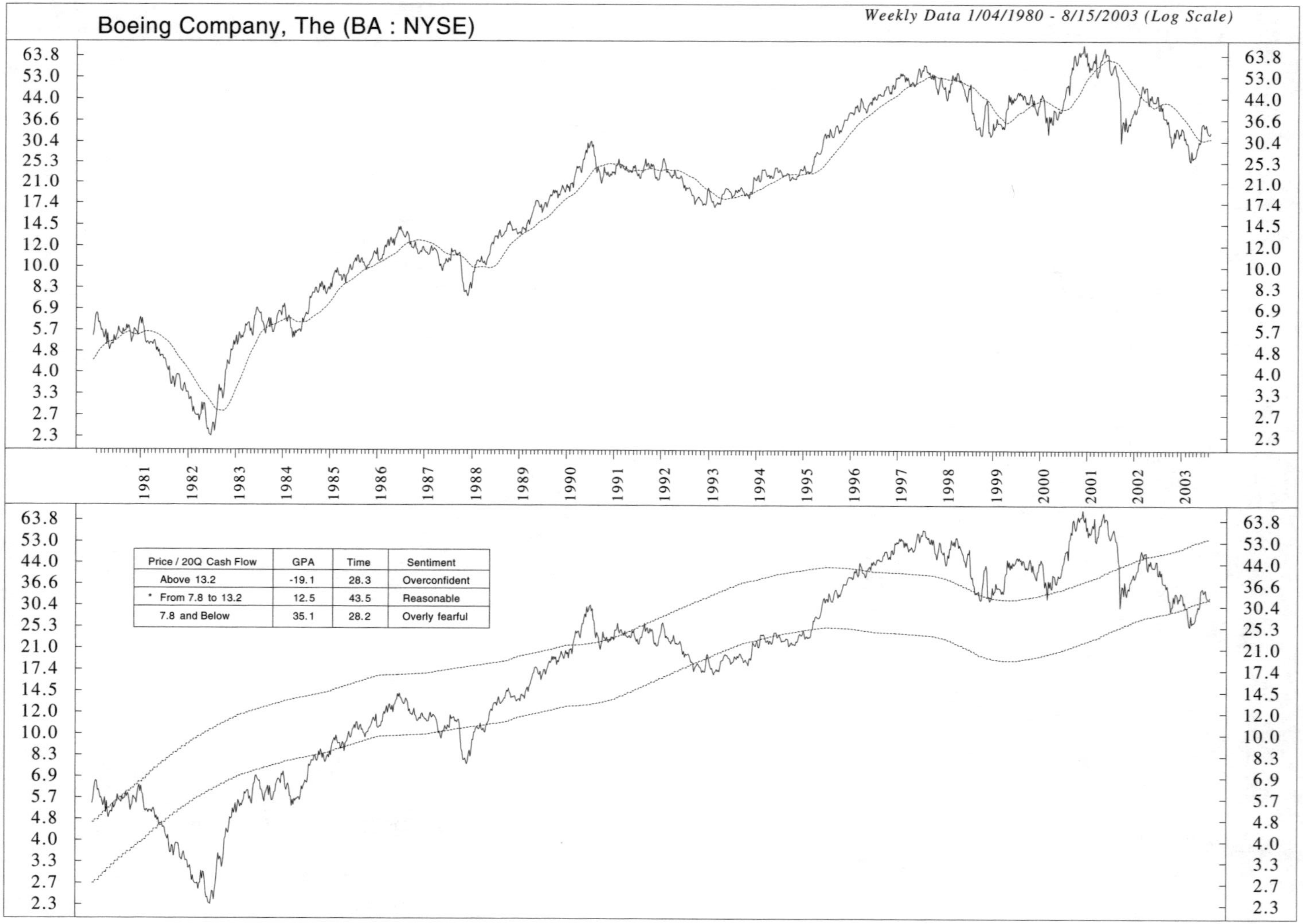

FIGURE A-19 Boise Cascade Corporation (BCC).
© 2003 Ned Davis Research, Inc. All rights reserved.

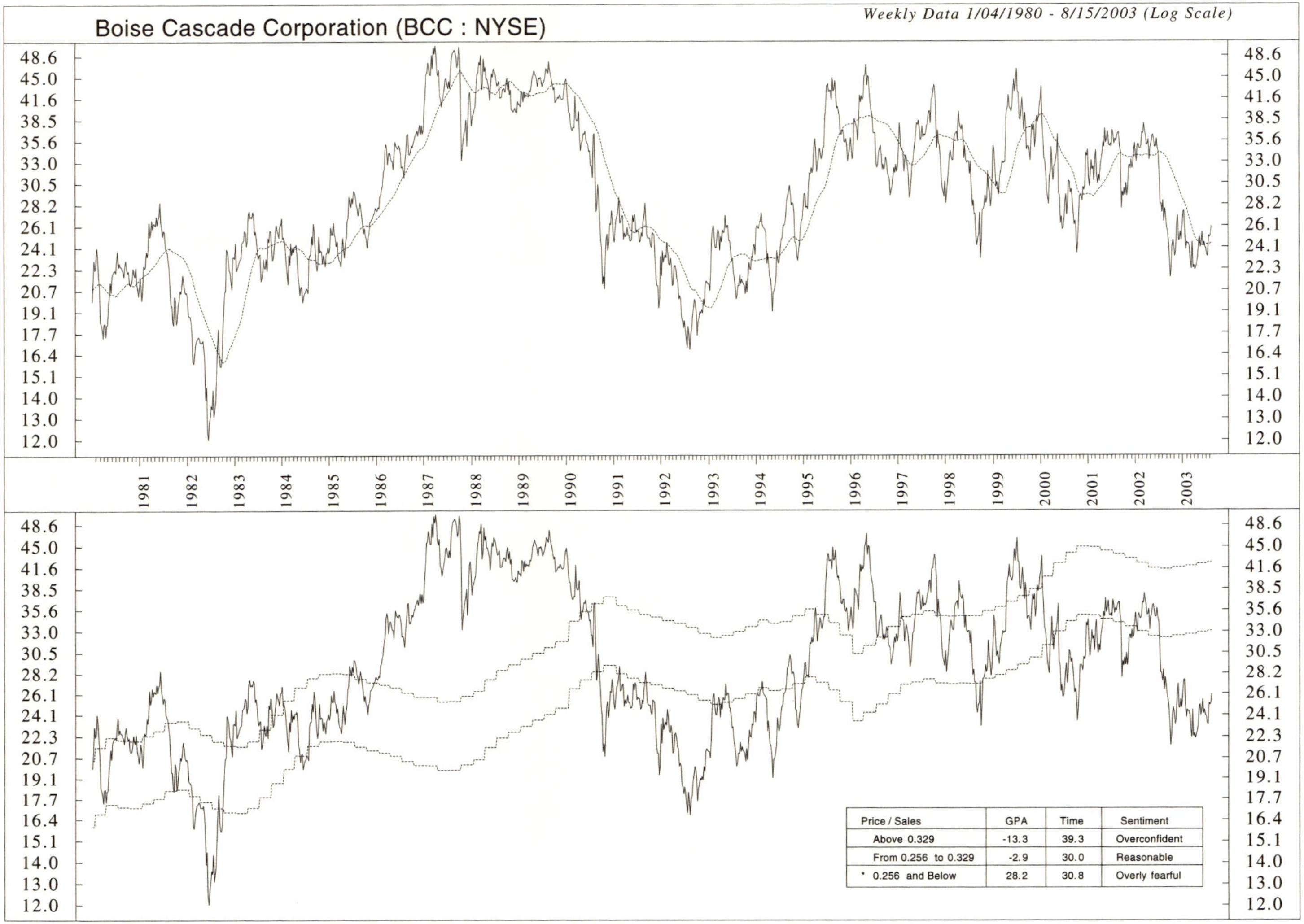

FIGURE A-20 Campbell Soup Company (CPB).
© 2003 Ned Davis Research, Inc. All rights reserved.

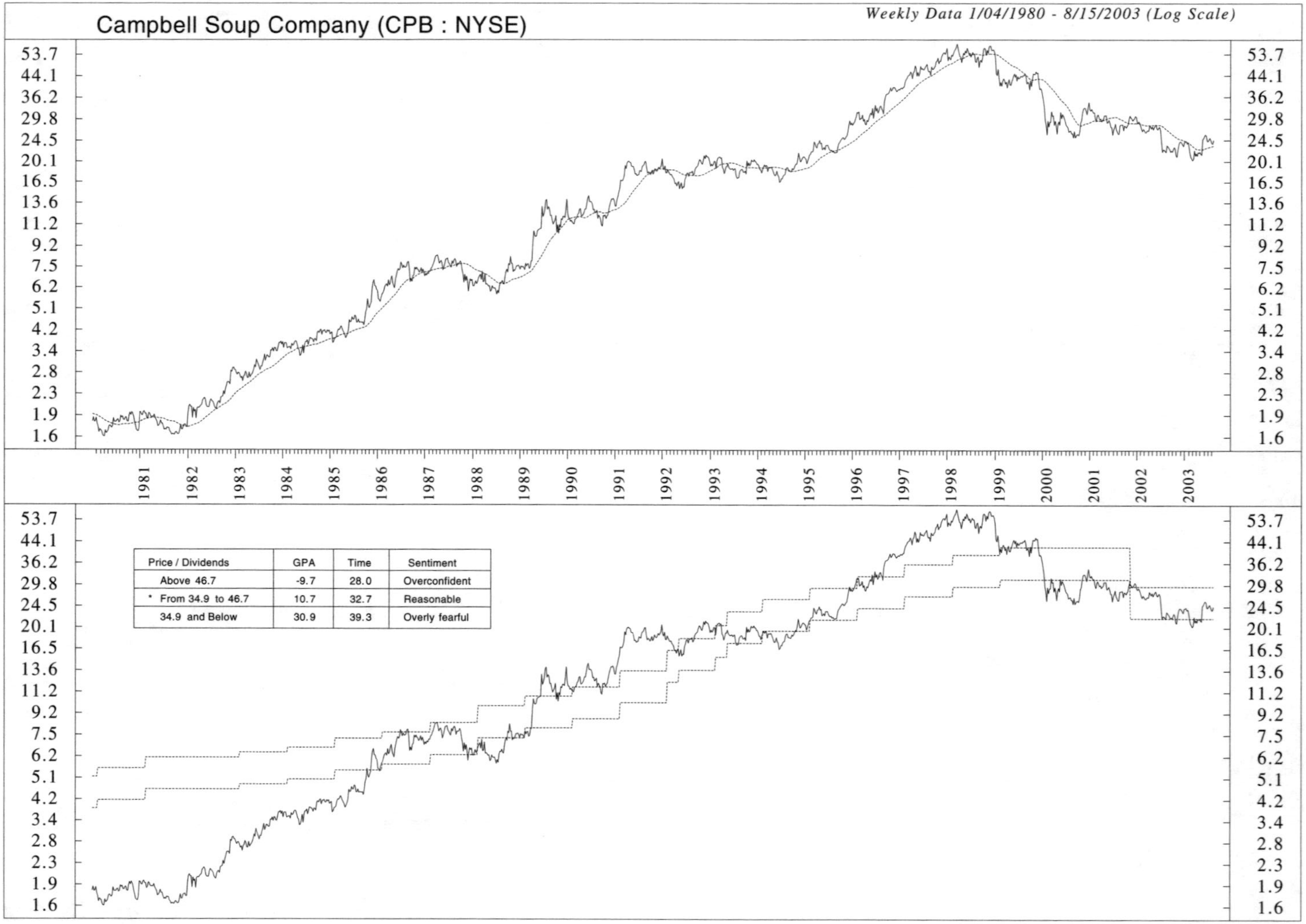

Price / Dividends	GPA	Time	Sentiment
Above 46.7	-9.7	28.0	Overconfident
* From 34.9 to 46.7	10.7	32.7	Reasonable
34.9 and Below	30.9	39.3	Overly fearful

FIGURE A-21   Chubb Corporation (CB).
© 2003 Ned Davis Research, Inc. All rights reserved.

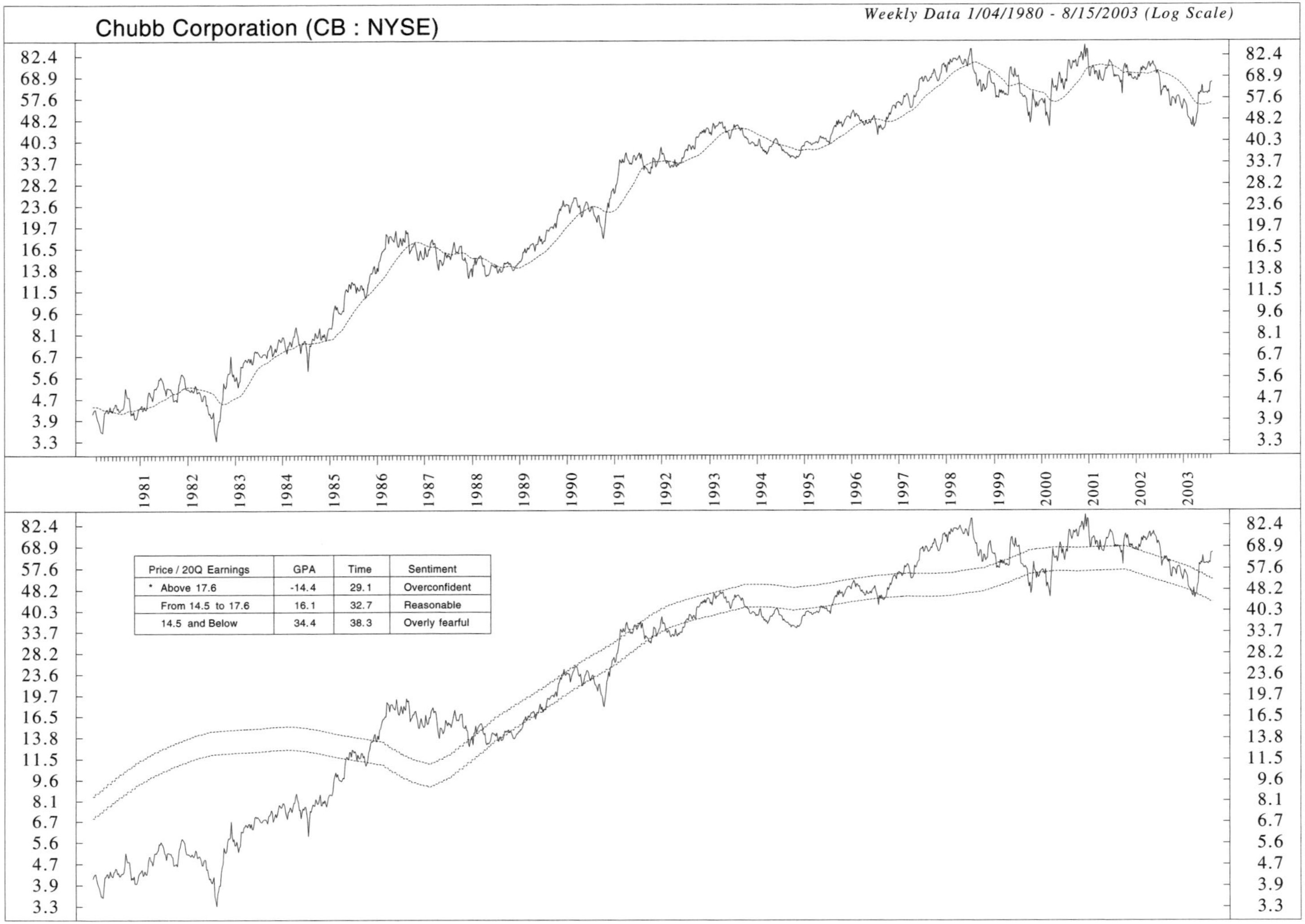

Price / 20Q Earnings	GPA	Time	Sentiment
* Above 17.6	-14.4	29.1	Overconfident
From 14.5 to 17.6	16.1	32.7	Reasonable
14.5 and Below	34.4	38.3	Overly fearful

FIGURE A-22 Cisco Systems, Inc. (CSCO).
© 2003 Ned Davis Research, Inc. All rights reserved.

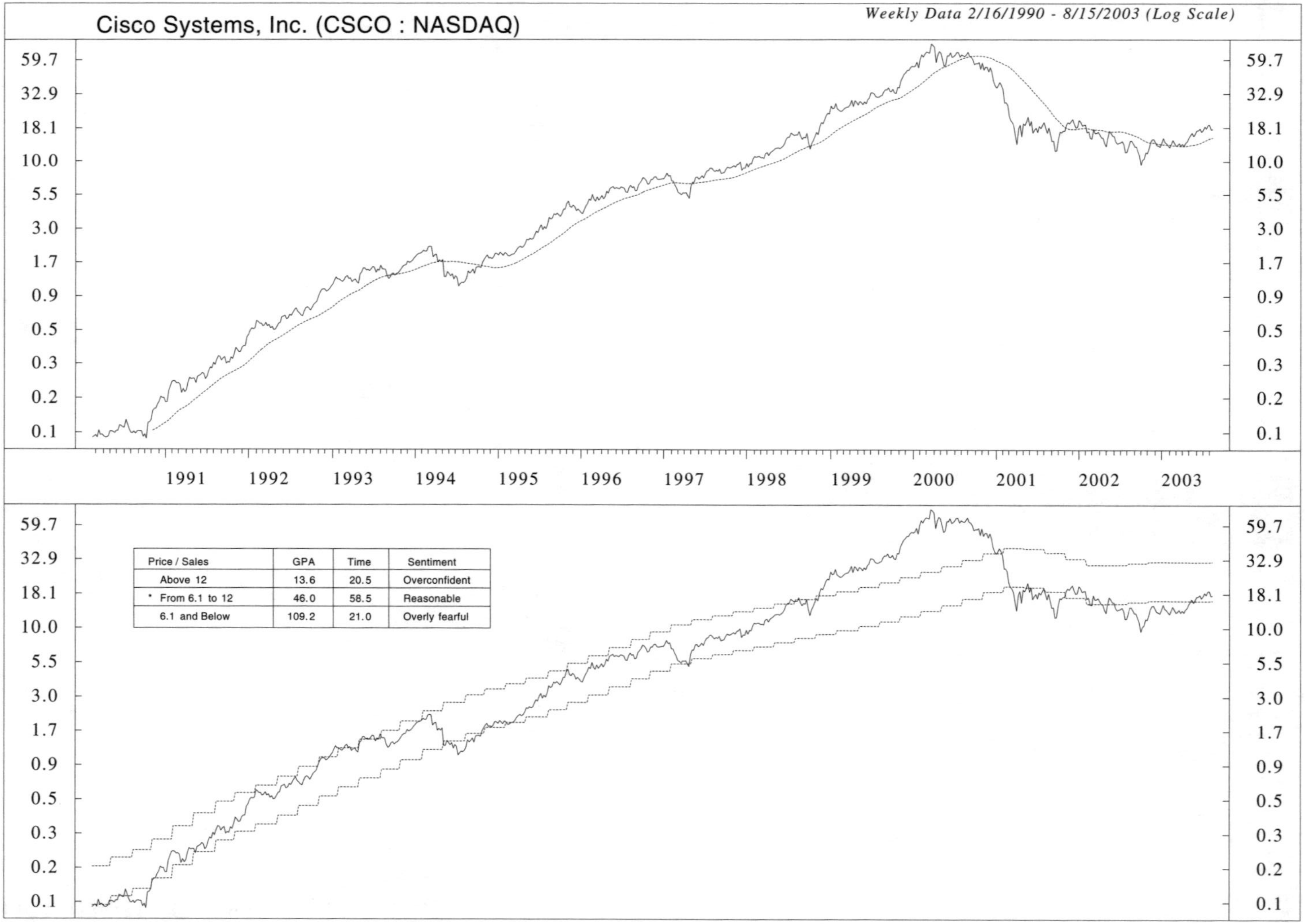

Cisco Systems, Inc. (CSCO : NASDAQ) — Weekly Data 2/16/1990 - 8/15/2003 (Log Scale)

Price / Sales	GPA	Time	Sentiment
Above 12	13.6	20.5	Overconfident
• From 6.1 to 12	46.0	58.5	Reasonable
6.1 and Below	109.2	21.0	Overly fearful

FIGURE A-23 Citigroup, Inc. (C).
© 2003 Ned Davis Research, Inc. All rights reserved.

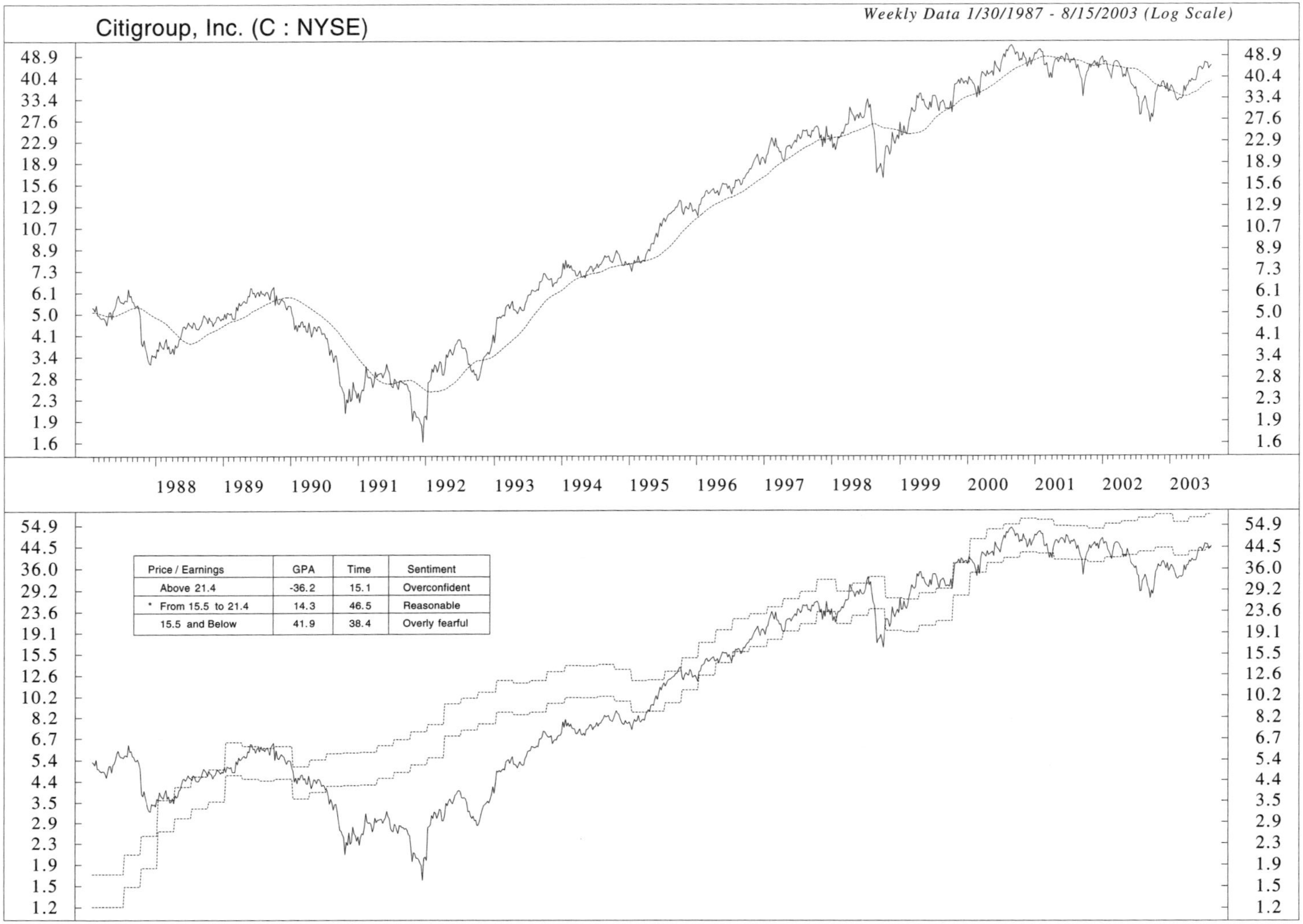

Citigroup, Inc. (C : NYSE) — Weekly Data 1/30/1987 - 8/15/2003 (Log Scale)

Price / Earnings	GPA	Time	Sentiment
Above 21.4	-36.2	15.1	Overconfident
* From 15.5 to 21.4	14.3	46.5	Reasonable
15.5 and Below	41.9	38.4	Overly fearful

93

FIGURE A-24 Comcast Corporation—Class A (CMCSA).

© 2003 Ned Davis Research, Inc. All rights reserved.

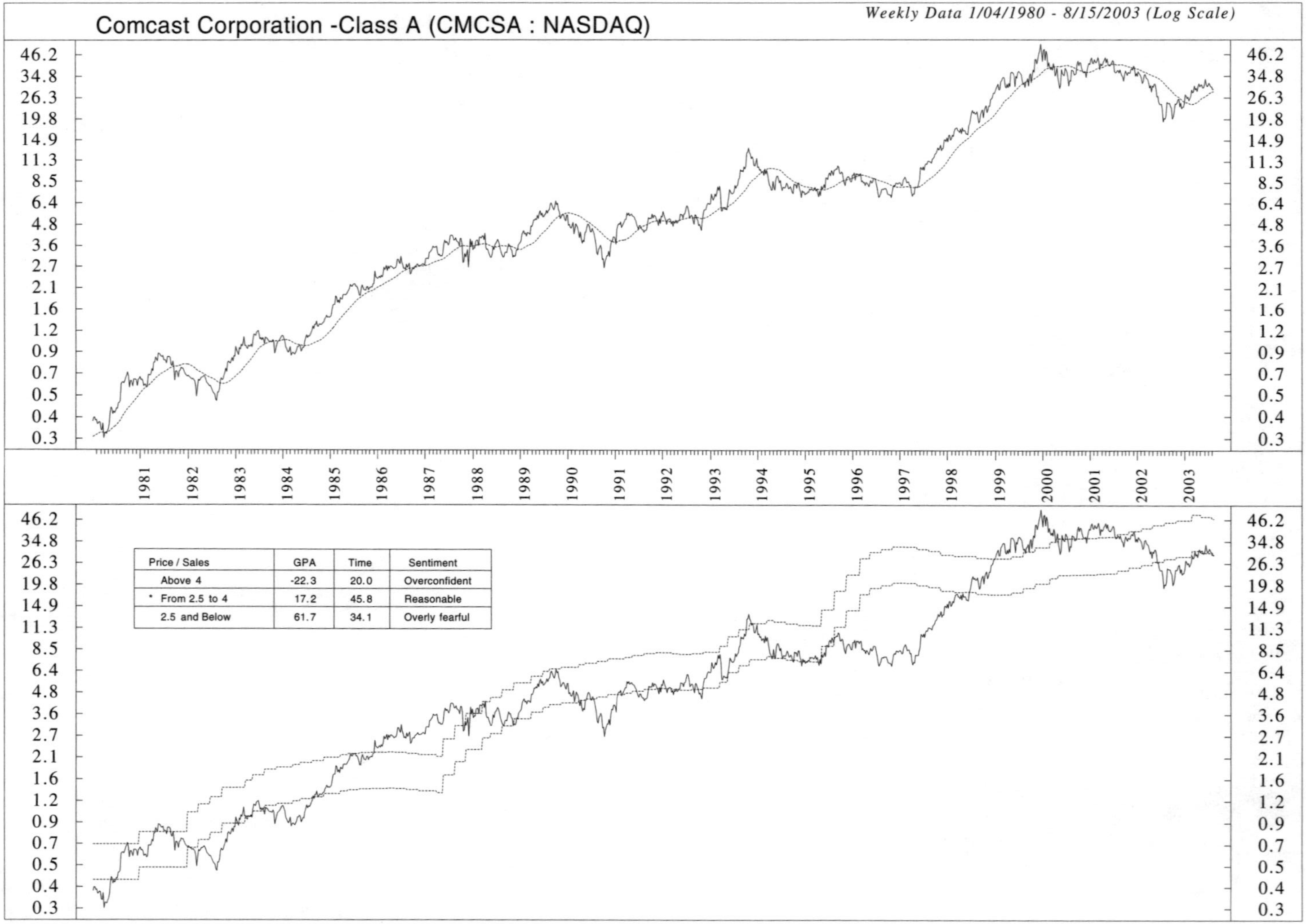

FIGURE A-25 Computer Sciences Corporation (CSC).
© 2003 Ned Davis Research, Inc. All rights reserved.

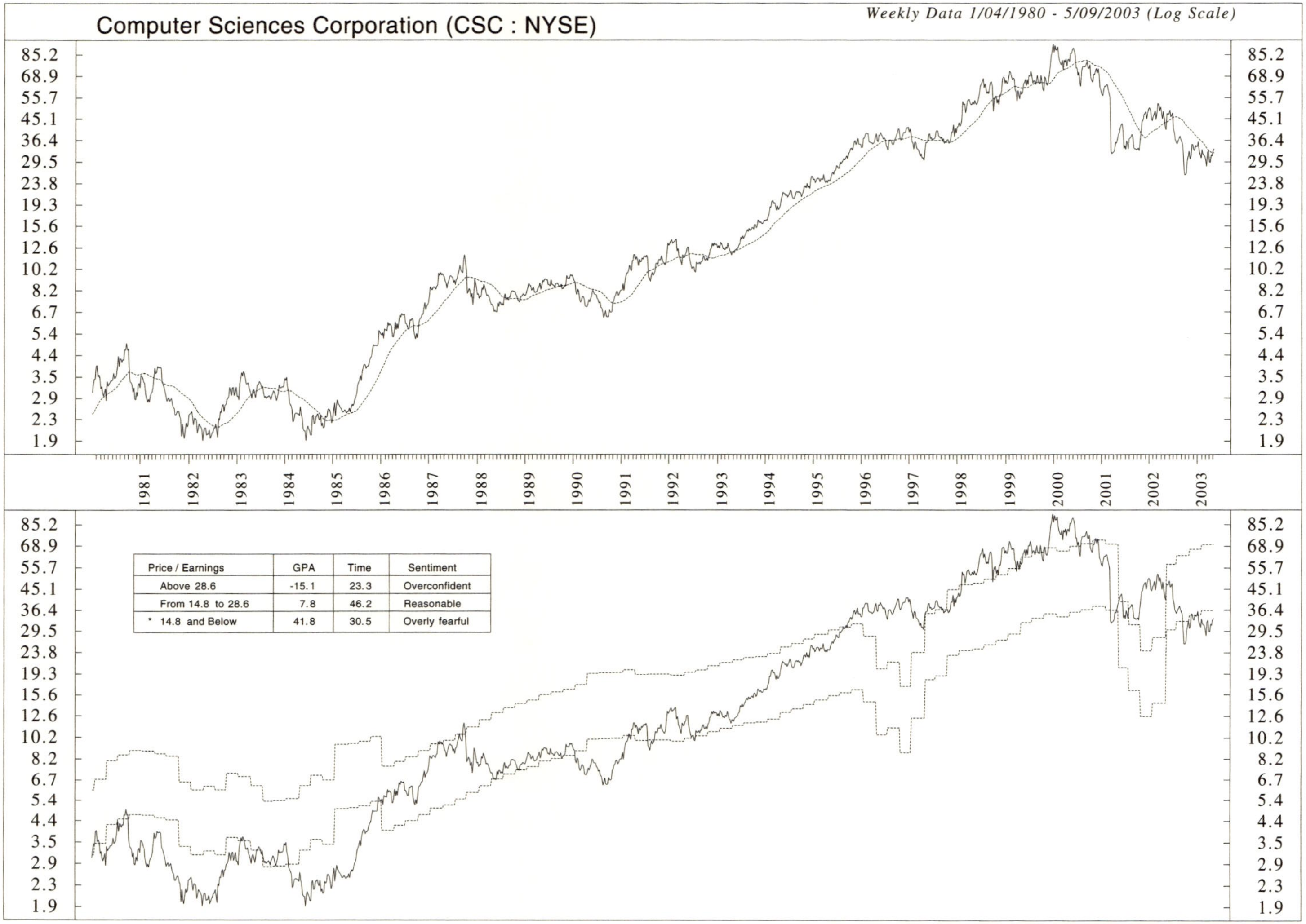

FIGURE A-26 ConAgra Foods, Inc. (CAG).

© 2003 Ned Davis Research, Inc. All rights reserved.

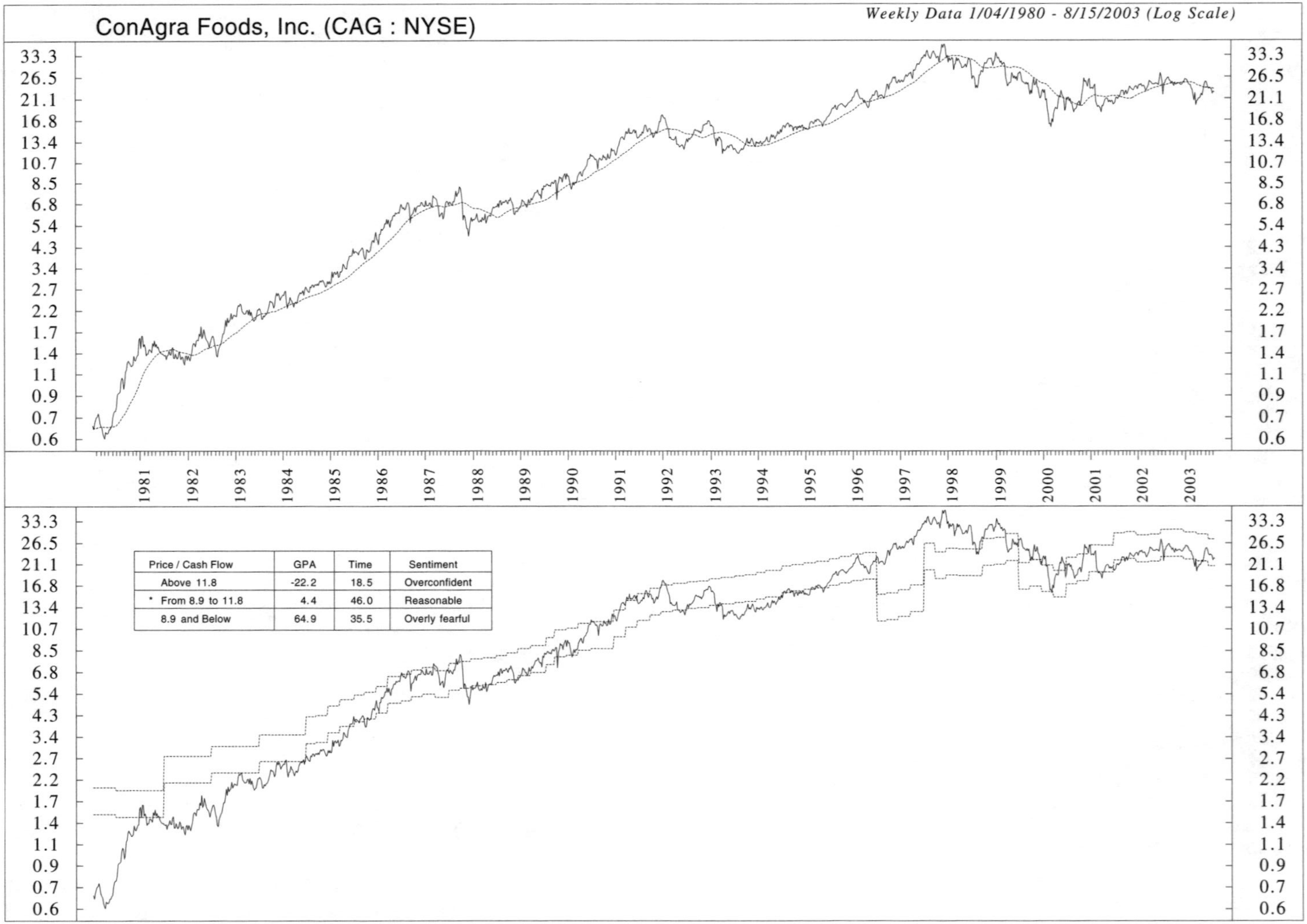

FIGURE A-27 Diagnostic Products Corporation (DP).
© *2003 Ned Davis Research, Inc. All rights reserved.*

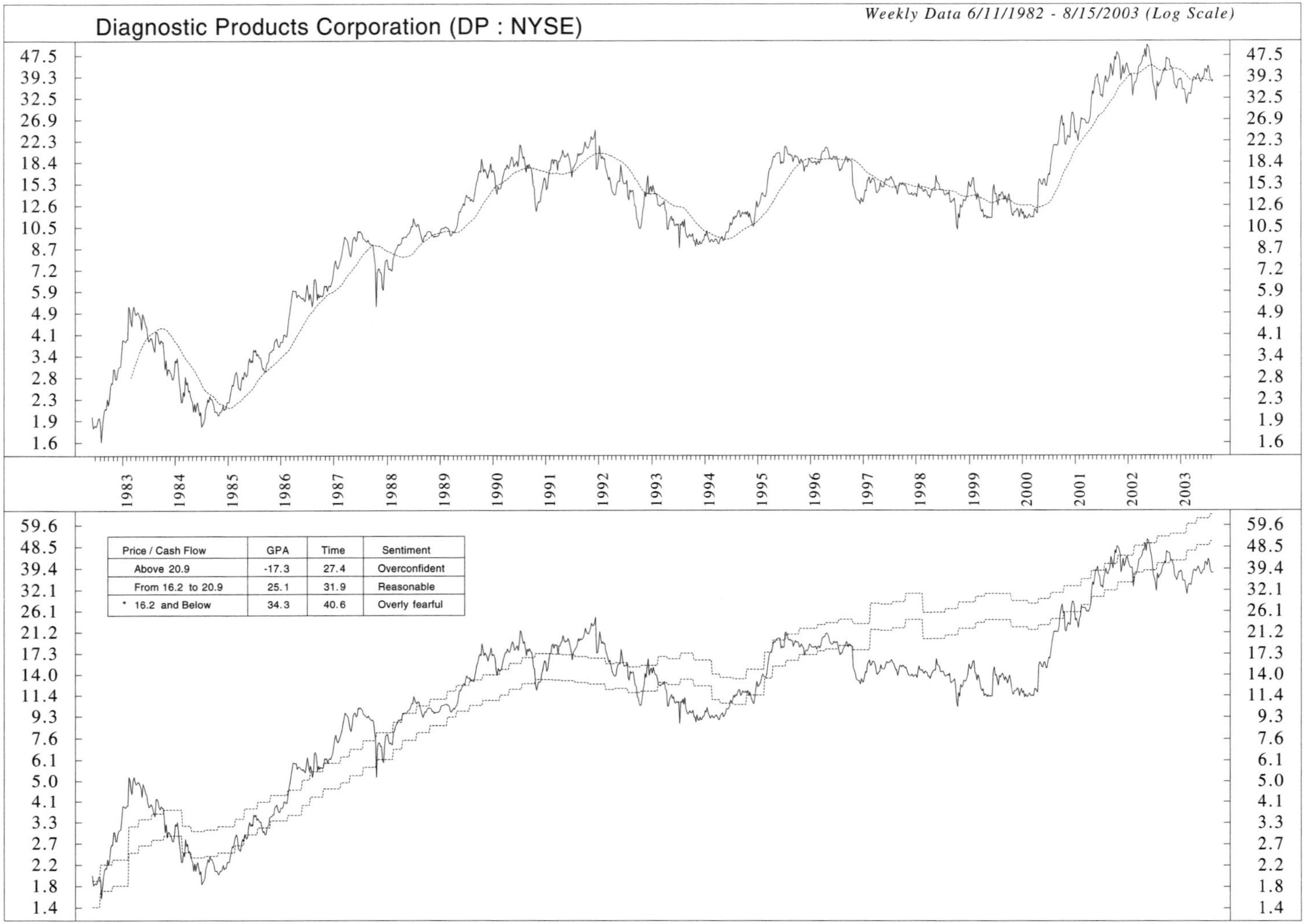

Price / Cash Flow	GPA	Time	Sentiment
Above 20.9	-17.3	27.4	Overconfident
From 16.2 to 20.9	25.1	31.9	Reasonable
* 16.2 and Below	34.3	40.6	Overly fearful

FIGURE A-28 Dow Chemical Company, The (DOW).
© 2003 Ned Davis Research, Inc. All rights reserved.

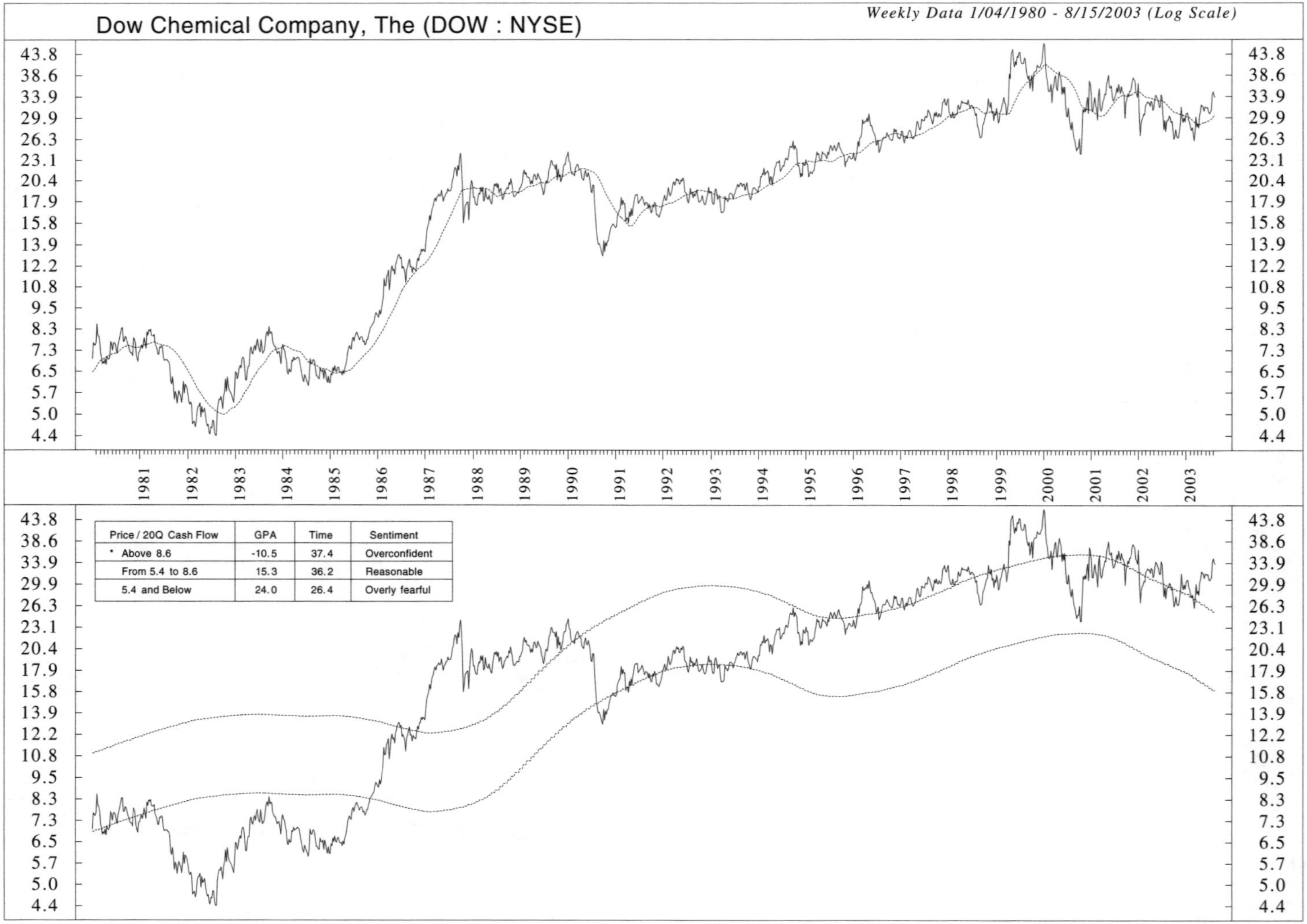

FIGURE A-29 EMC Corporation (EMC).
© 2003 Ned Davis Research, Inc. All rights reserved.

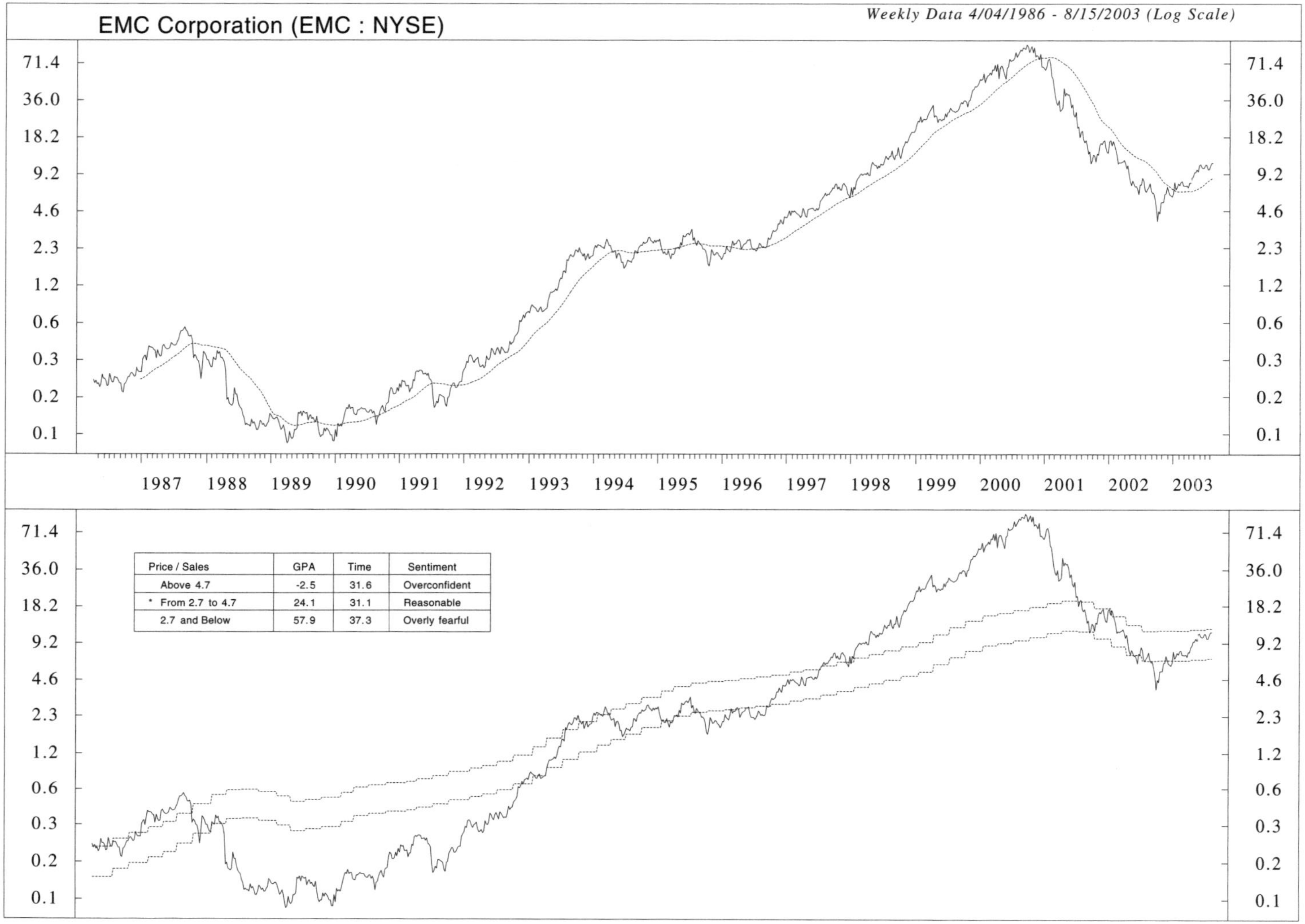

Weekly Data 4/04/1986 - 8/15/2003 (Log Scale)

EMC Corporation (EMC : NYSE)

Price / Sales	GPA	Time	Sentiment
Above 4.7	-2.5	31.6	Overconfident
From 2.7 to 4.7	24.1	31.1	Reasonable
2.7 and Below	57.9	37.3	Overly fearful

FIGURE A-30 Eastman Kodak Company (EK).
© 2003 Ned Davis Research, Inc. All rights reserved.

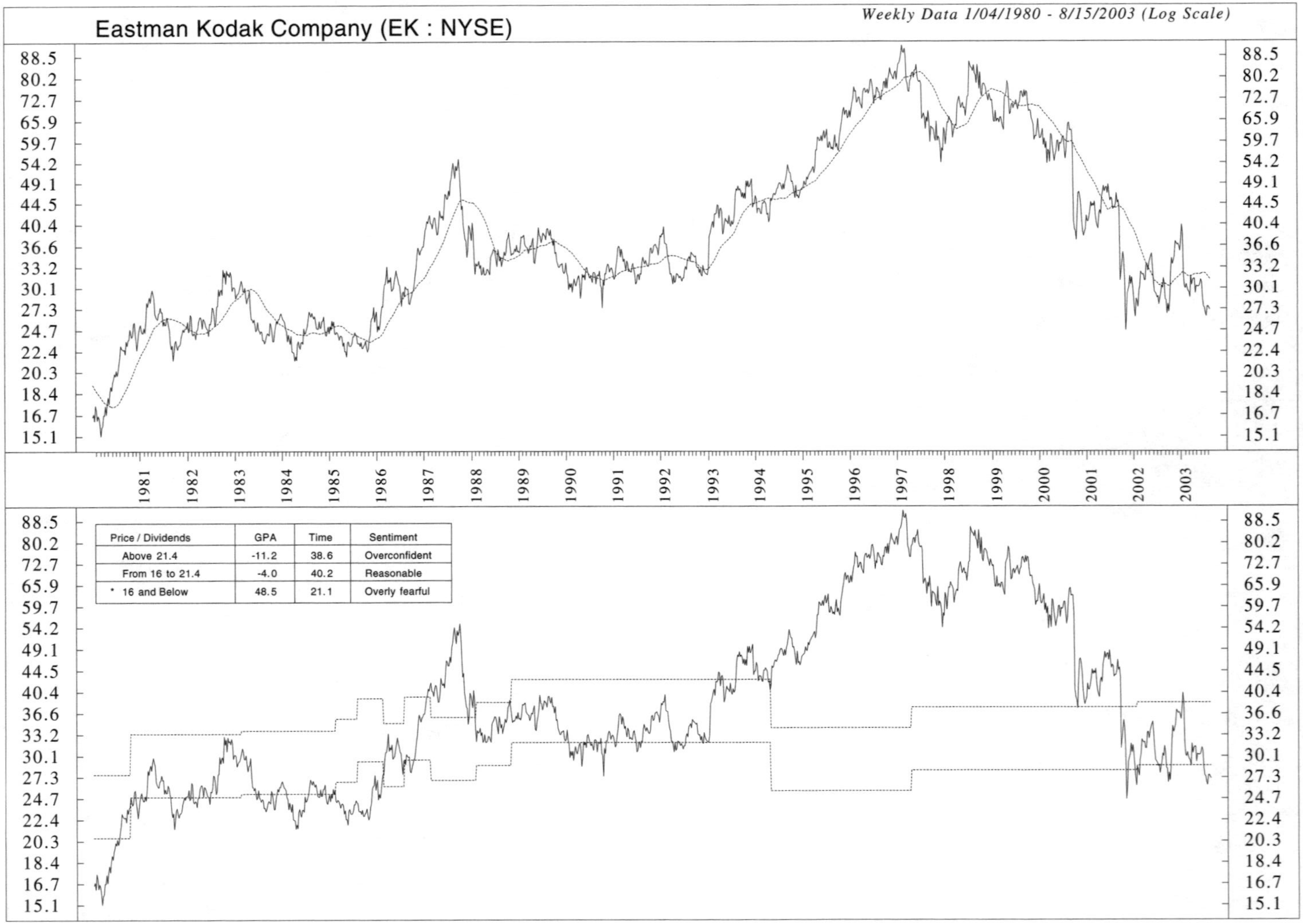

FIGURE A-31 Emerson Electric Company (EMR).
© 2003 Ned Davis Research, Inc. All rights reserved.

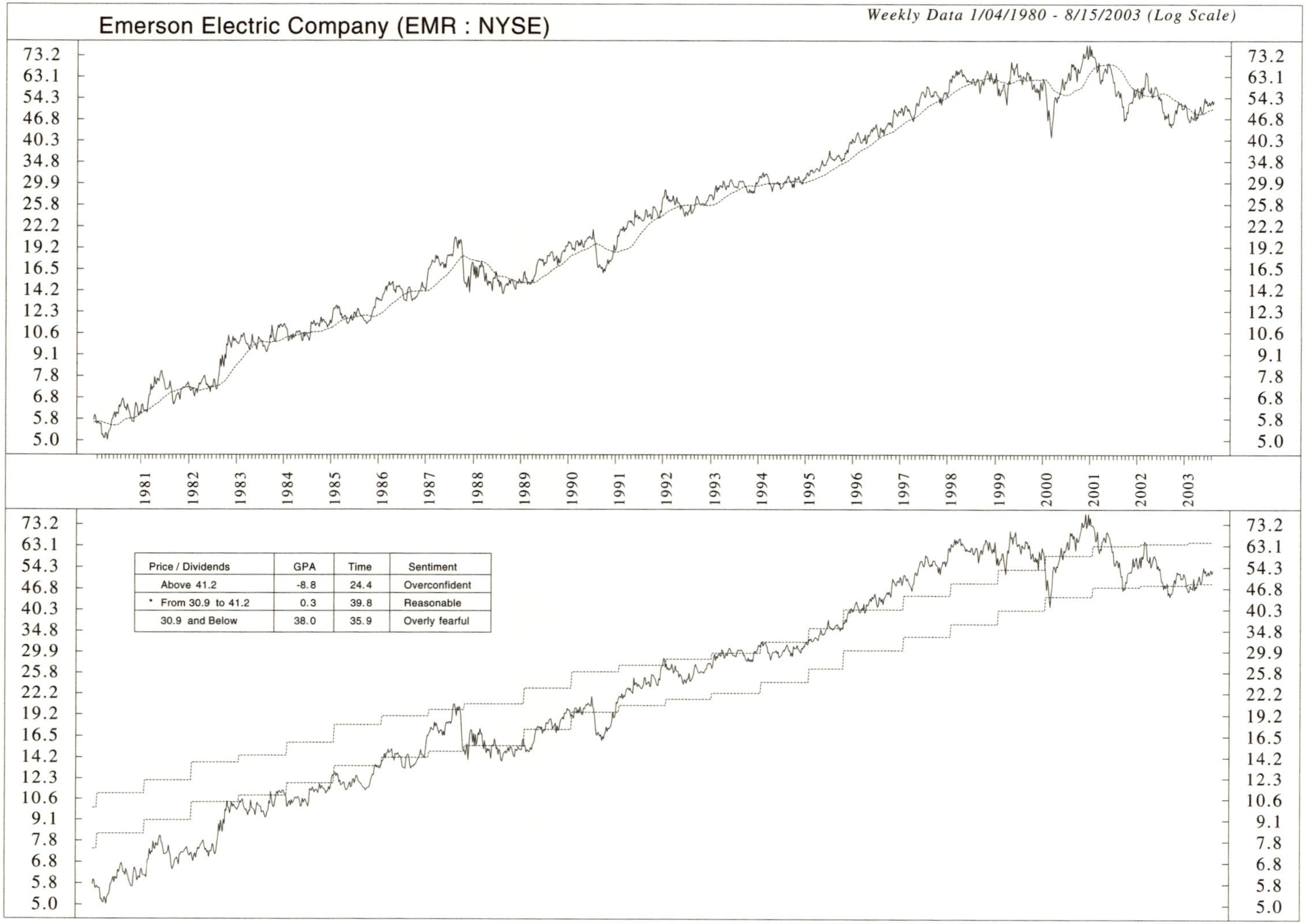

FIGURE A-32 FactSet Research Systems, Inc. (FDS).
© 2003 Ned Davis Research, Inc. All rights reserved.

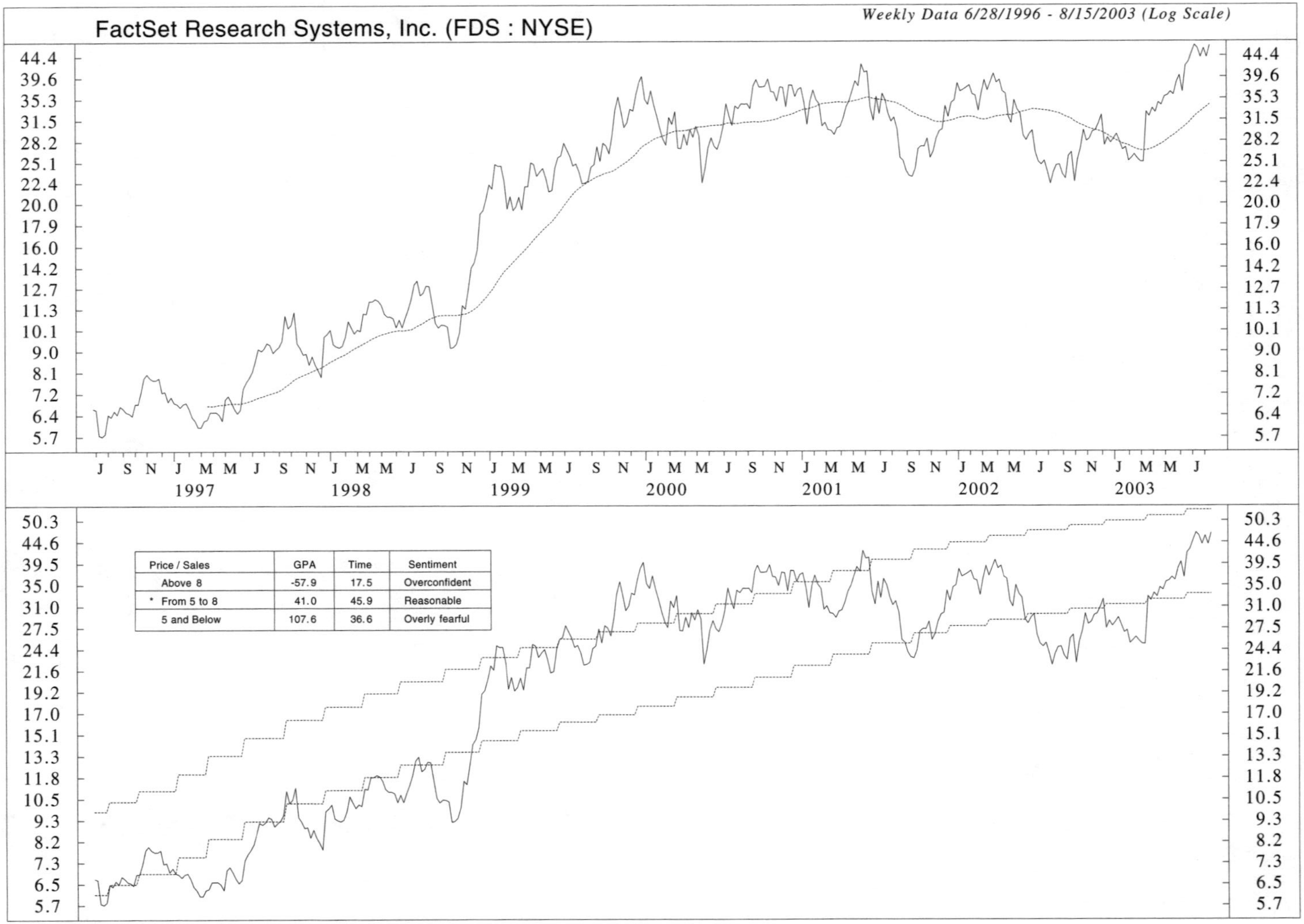

FactSet Research Systems, Inc. (FDS : NYSE) Weekly Data 6/28/1996 - 8/15/2003 (Log Scale)

Price / Sales	GPA	Time	Sentiment
Above 8	-57.9	17.5	Overconfident
* From 5 to 8	41.0	45.9	Reasonable
5 and Below	107.6	36.6	Overly fearful

FIGURE A-33 First Data Corporation (FDC).
© 2003 Ned Davis Research, Inc. All rights reserved.

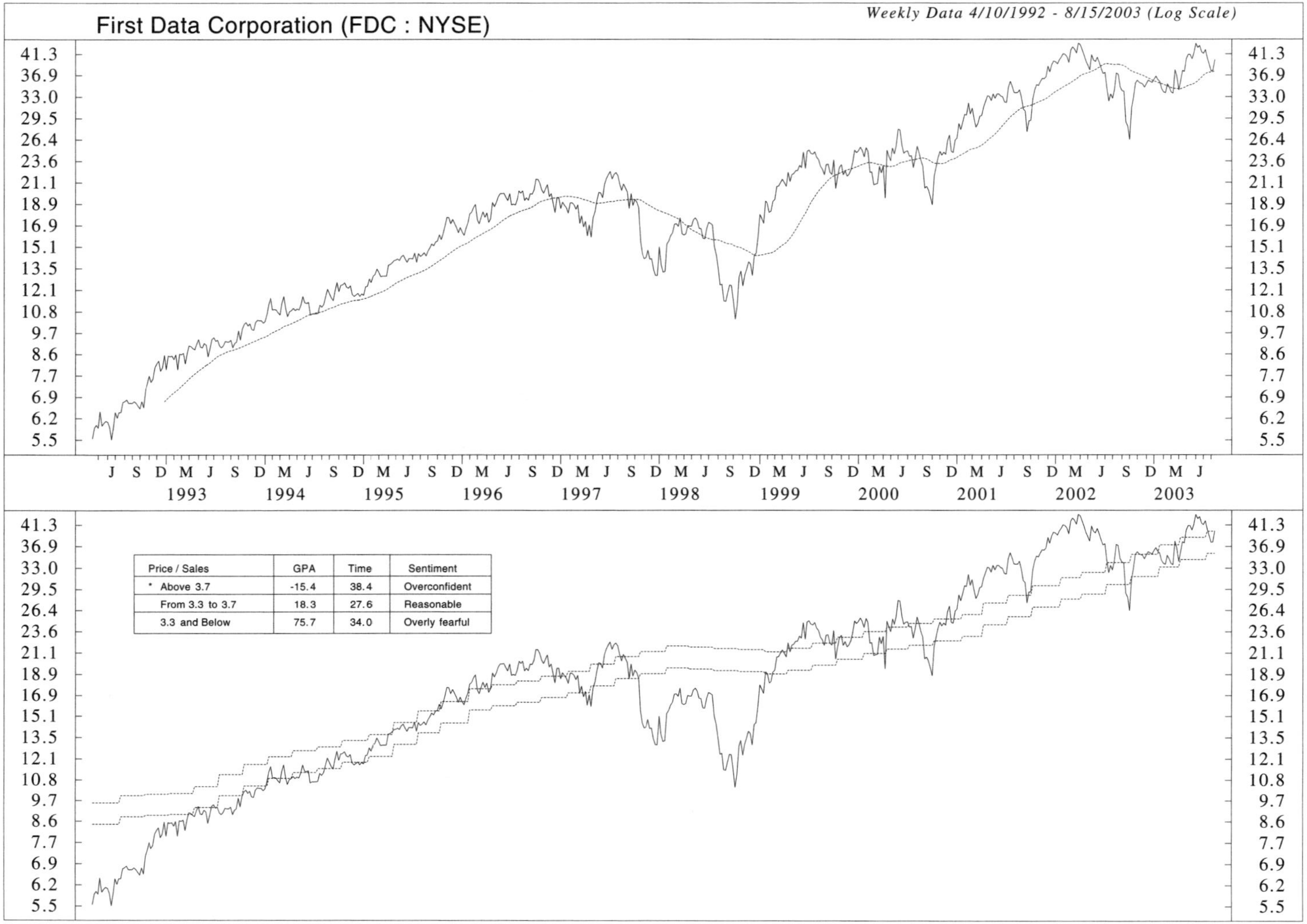

First Data Corporation (FDC : NYSE) — Weekly Data 4/10/1992 - 8/15/2003 (Log Scale)

Price / Sales	GPA	Time	Sentiment
* Above 3.7	-15.4	38.4	Overconfident
From 3.3 to 3.7	18.3	27.6	Reasonable
3.3 and Below	75.7	34.0	Overly fearful

103

FIGURE A-34 Ford Motor Company (F).

© 2003 Ned Davis Research, Inc. All rights reserved.

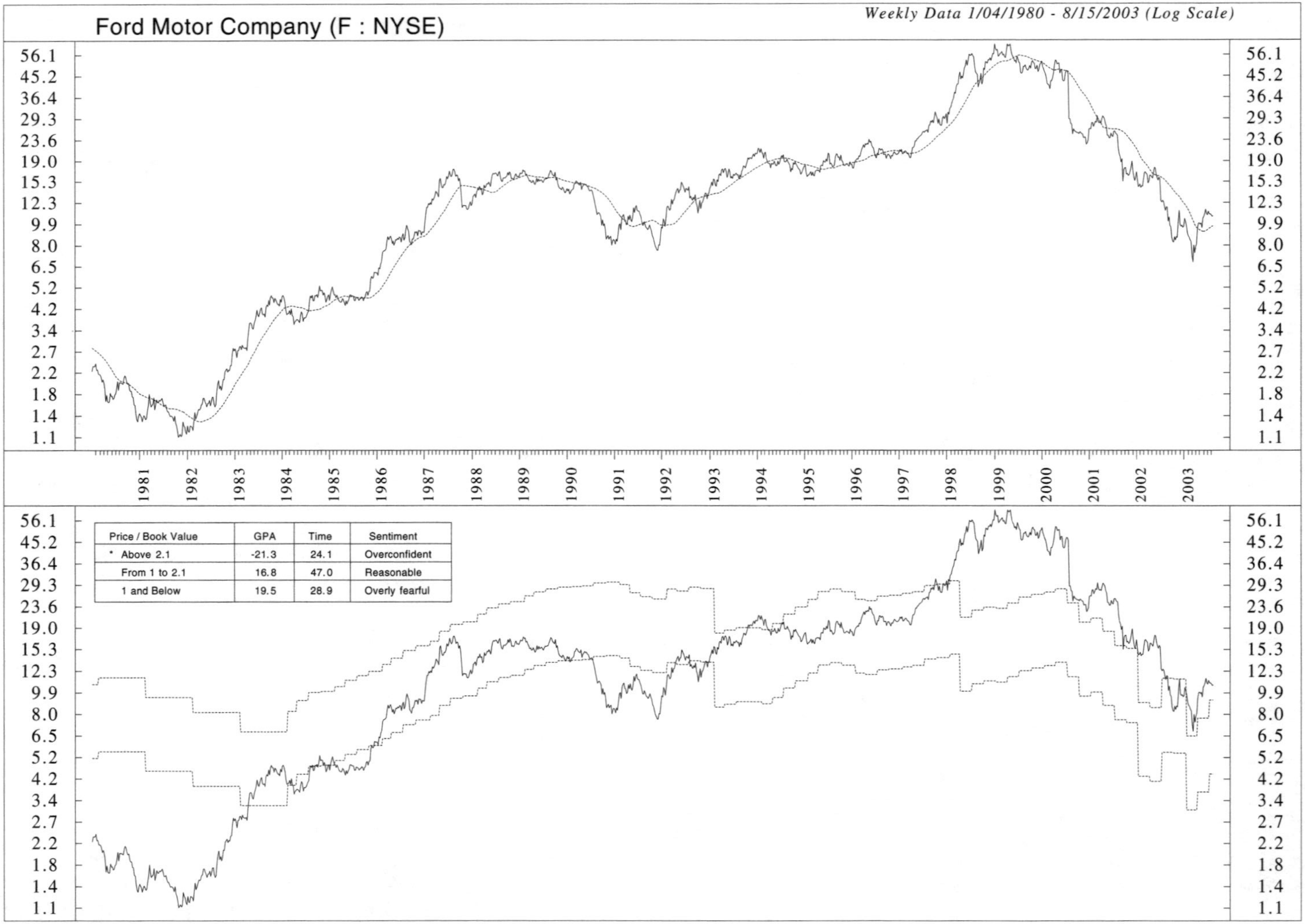

Price / Book Value	GPA	Time	Sentiment
* Above 2.1	-21.3	24.1	Overconfident
From 1 to 2.1	16.8	47.0	Reasonable
1 and Below	19.5	28.9	Overly fearful

FIGURE A-35 Forest Laboratories, Inc. (FRX).
© 2003 Ned Davis Research, Inc. All rights reserved.

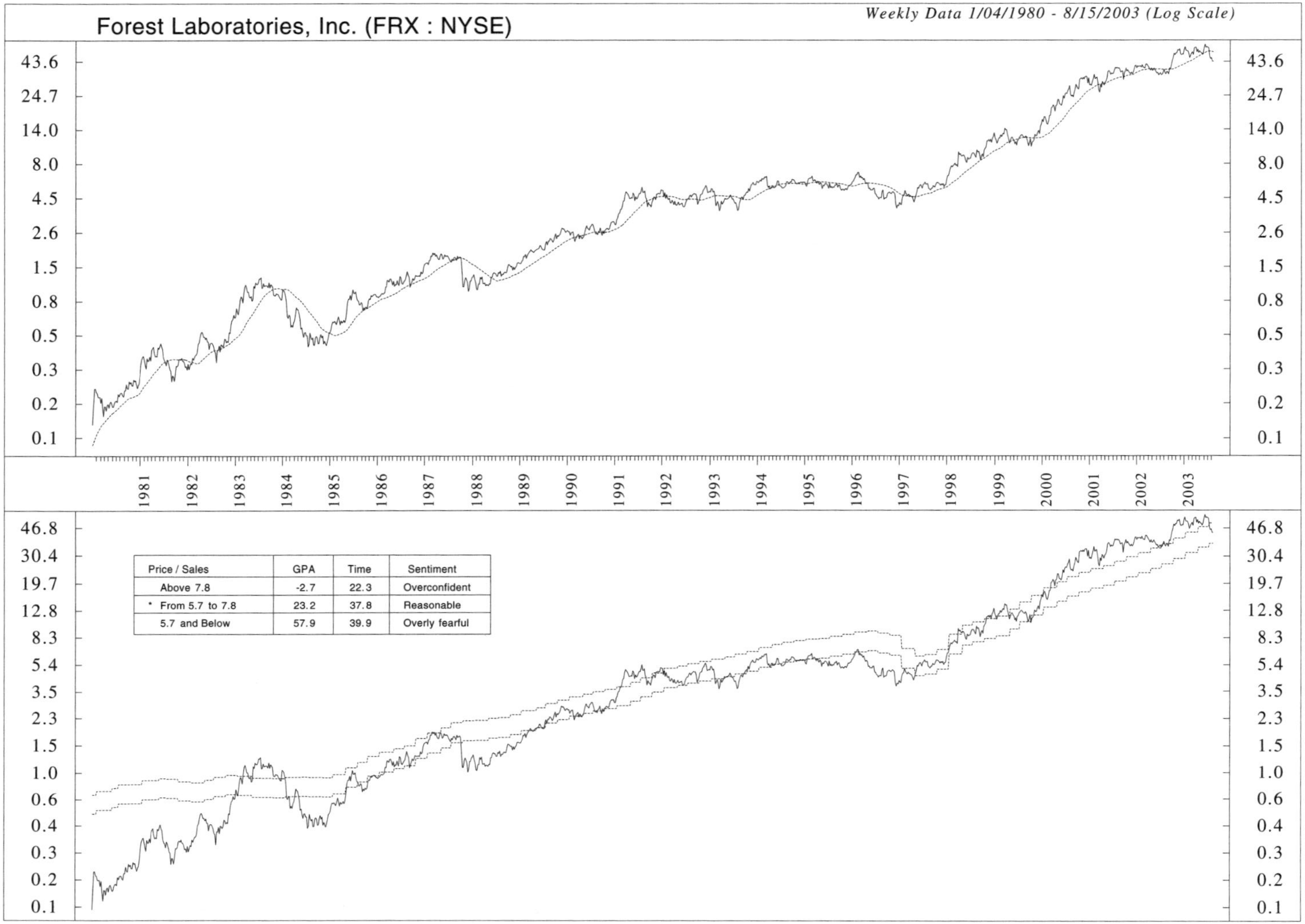

Price / Sales	GPA	Time	Sentiment
Above 7.8	-2.7	22.3	Overconfident
* From 5.7 to 7.8	23.2	37.8	Reasonable
5.7 and Below	57.9	39.9	Overly fearful

FIGURE A-36 General Dynamics Corporation (GD).

© 2003 Ned Davis Research, Inc. All rights reserved.

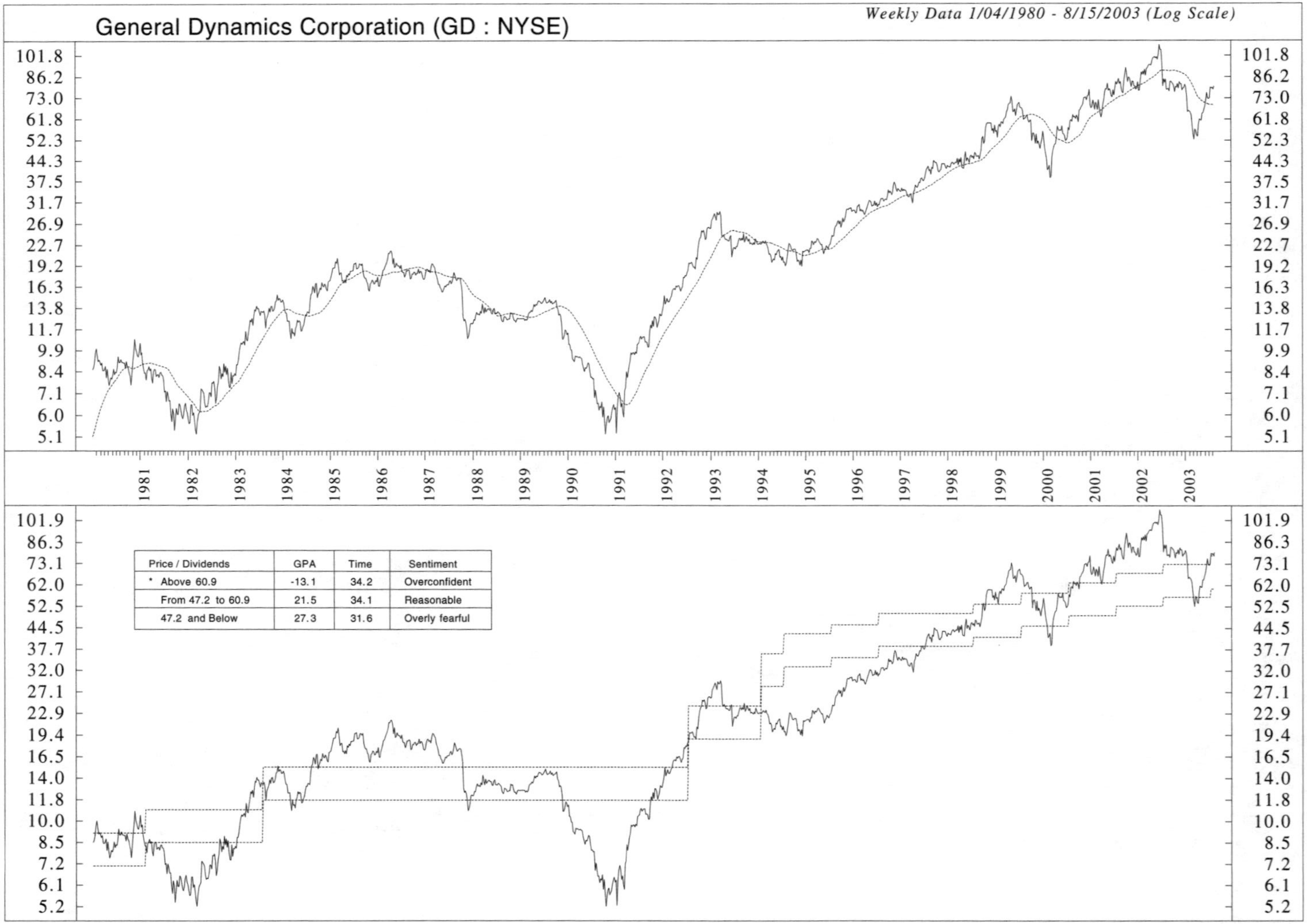

FIGURE A-37 General Electric Company (GE).
© 2003 Ned Davis Research, Inc. All rights reserved.

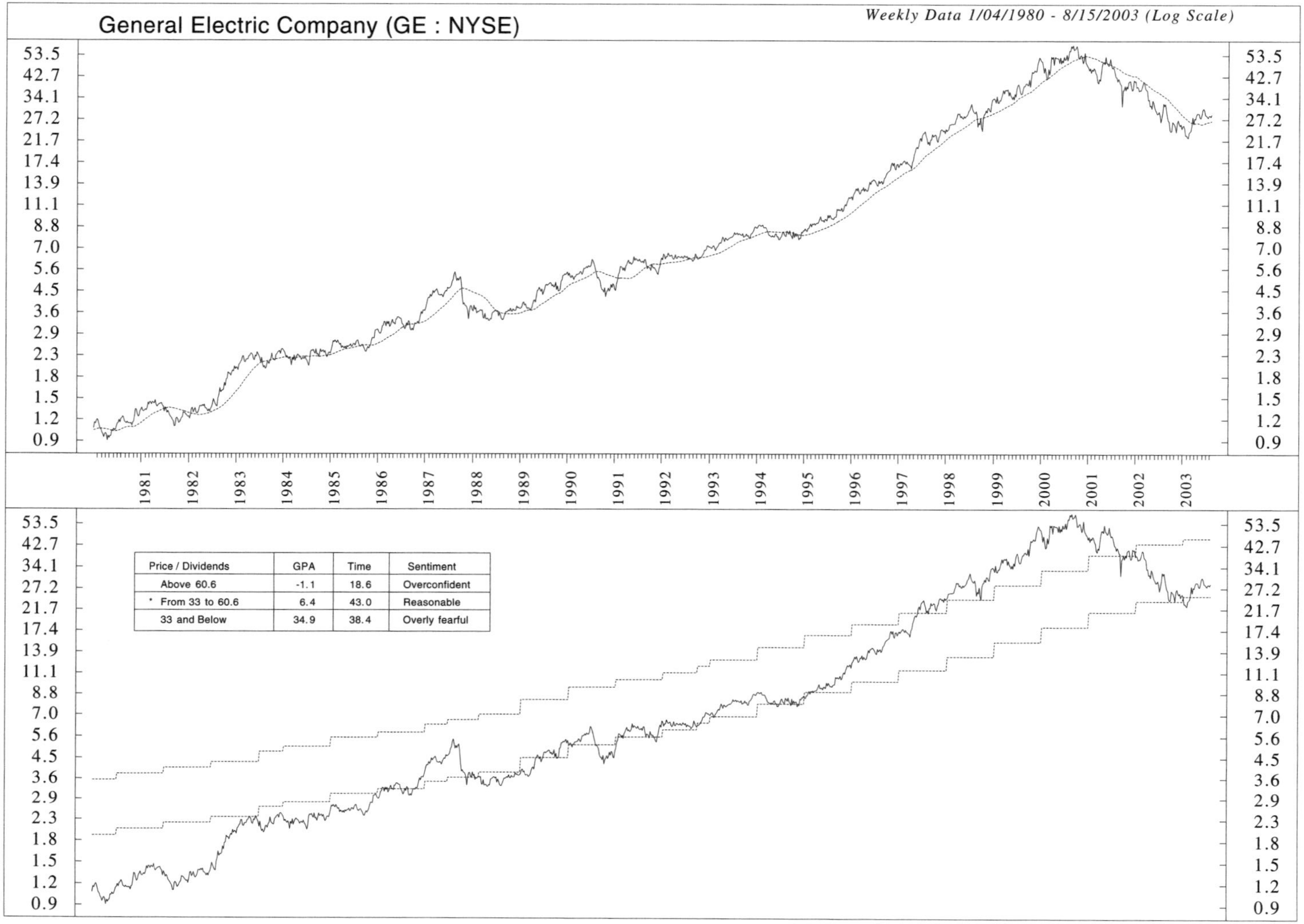

FIGURE A-38 General Motors Corporation (GM).
© 2003 Ned Davis Research, Inc. All rights reserved.

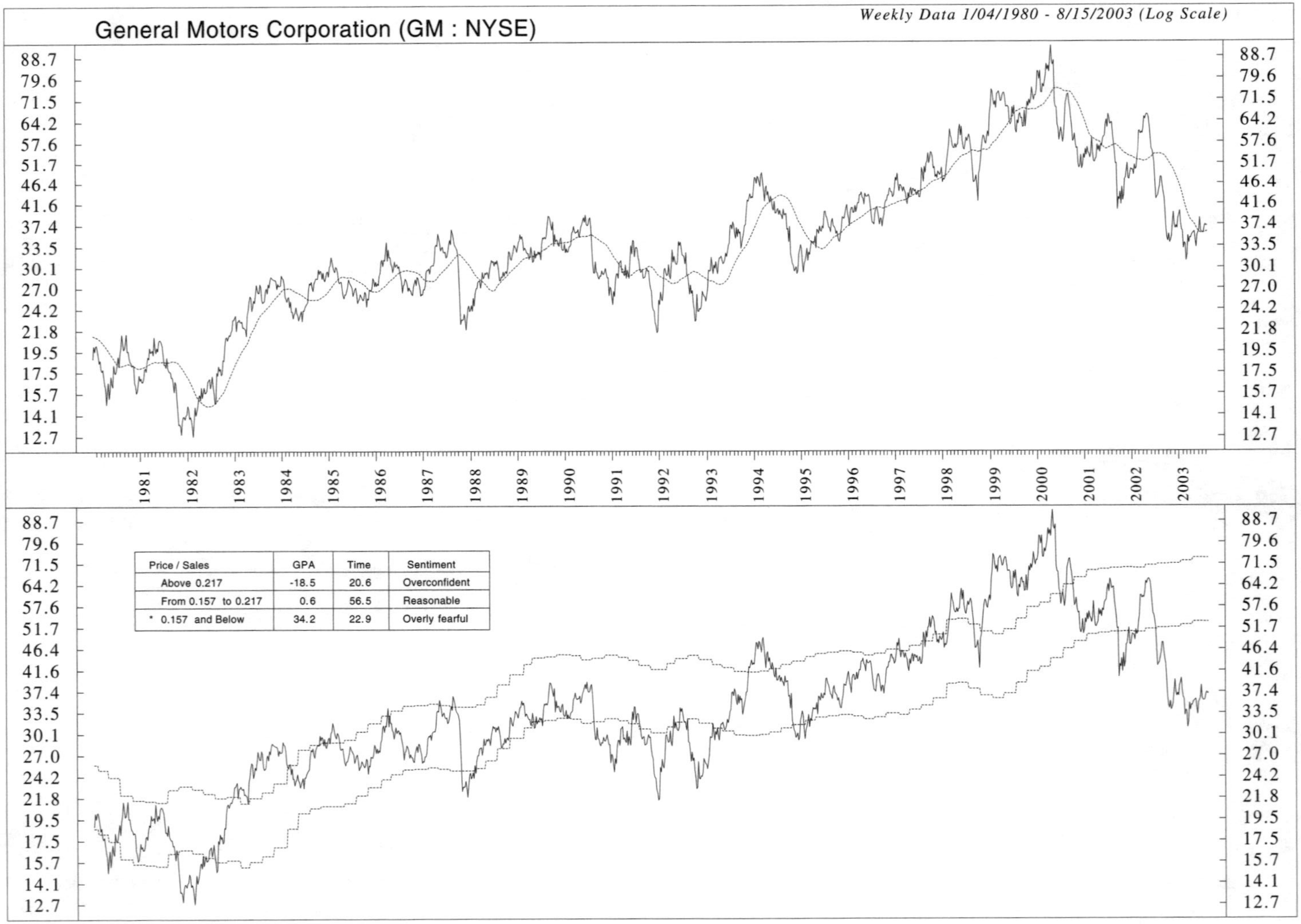

Price / Sales	GPA	Time	Sentiment
Above 0.217	-18.5	20.6	Overconfident
From 0.157 to 0.217	0.6	56.5	Reasonable
* 0.157 and Below	34.2	22.9	Overly fearful

FIGURE A-39 Genuine Parts Company (GPC).
© *2003 Ned Davis Research, Inc. All rights reserved.*

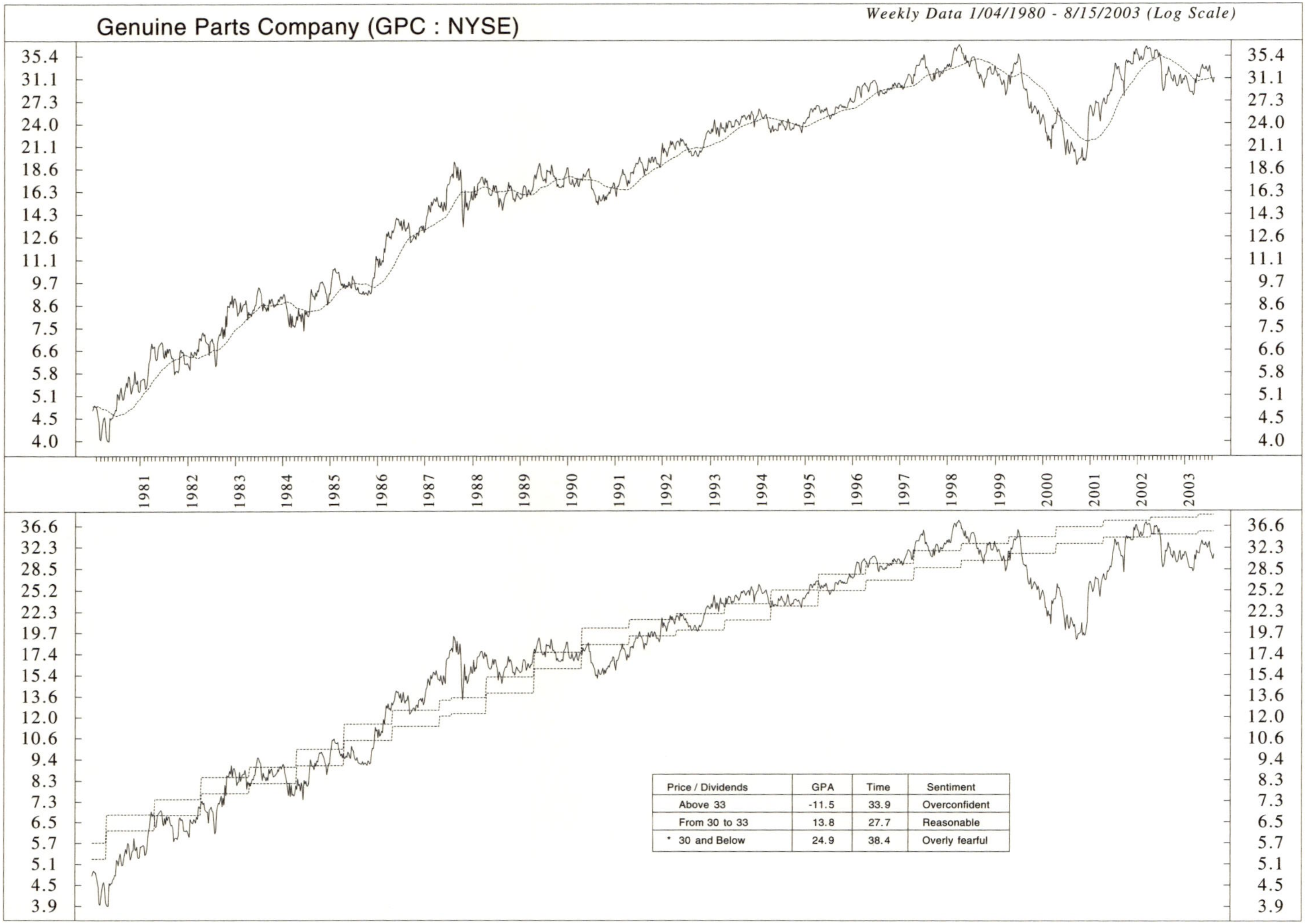

Price / Dividends	GPA	Time	Sentiment
Above 33	-11.5	33.9	Overconfident
From 30 to 33	13.8	27.7	Reasonable
• 30 and Below	24.9	38.4	Overly fearful

FIGURE A-40 Georgia-Pacific Corporation (GP).
© 2003 Ned Davis Research, Inc. All rights reserved.

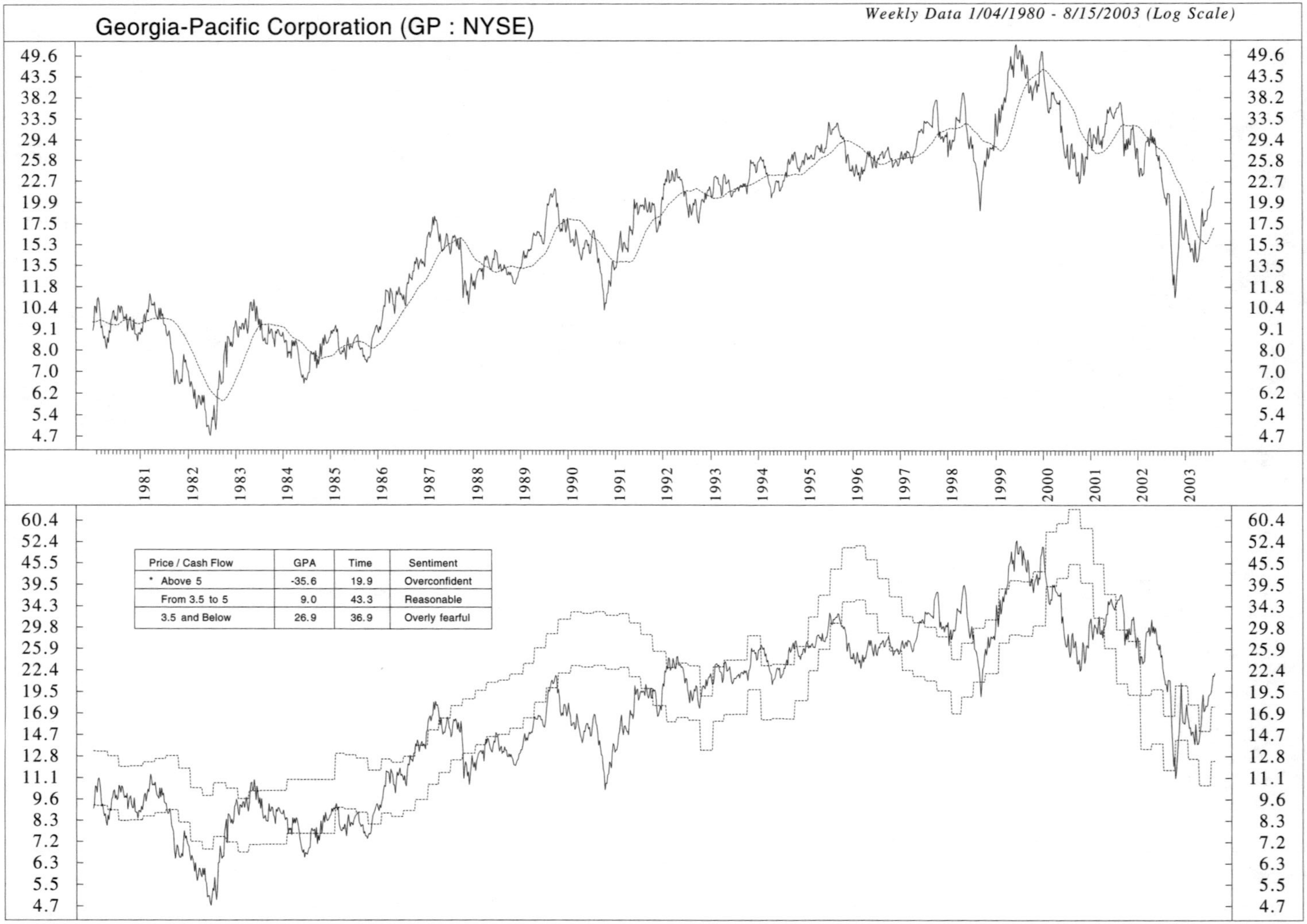

Price / Cash Flow	GPA	Time	Sentiment
Above 5	-35.6	19.9	Overconfident
From 3.5 to 5	9.0	43.3	Reasonable
3.5 and Below	26.9	36.9	Overly fearful

110

FIGURE A-41 Gillette Company, The (G).
© 2003 Ned Davis Research, Inc. All rights reserved.

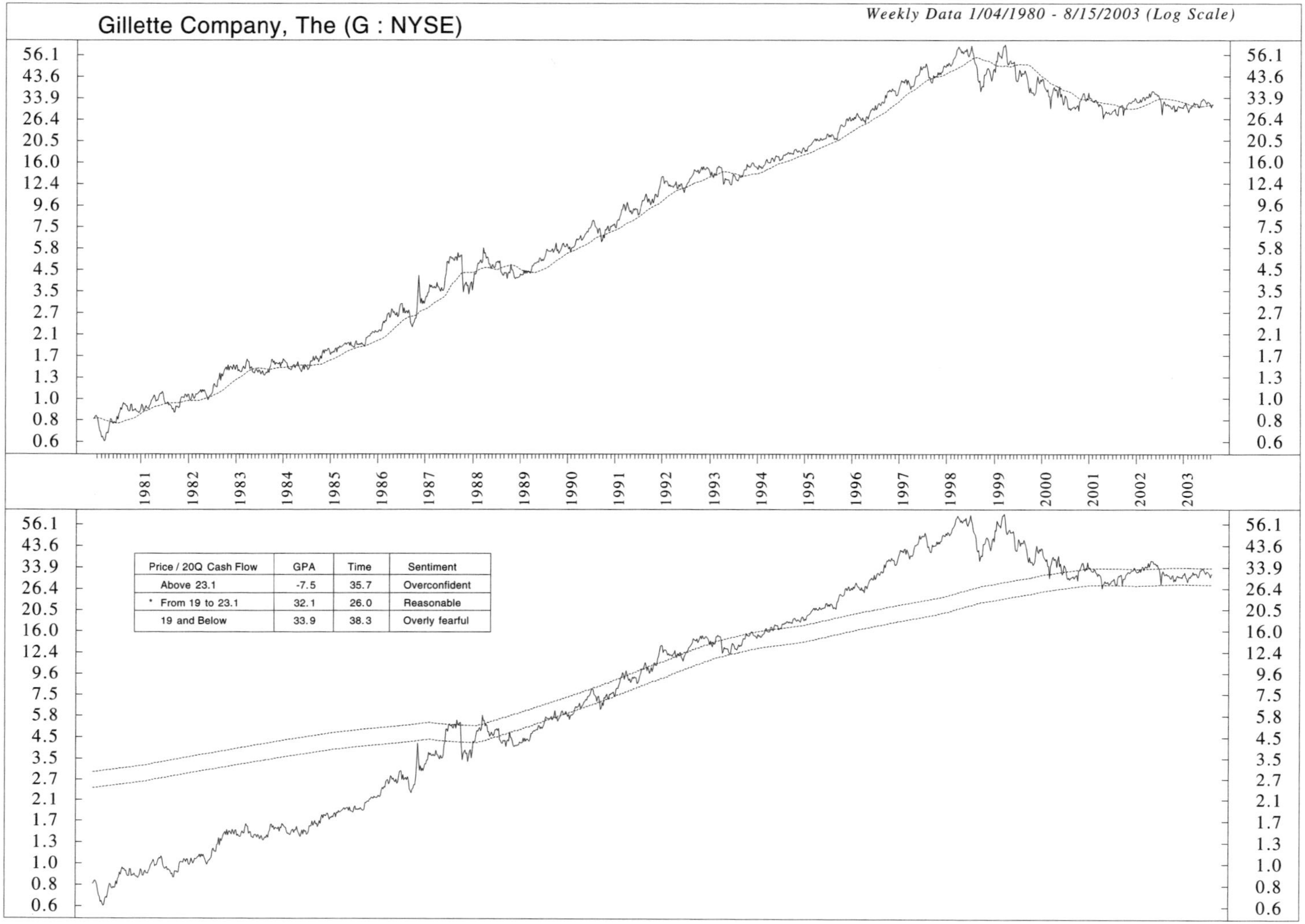

Price / 20Q Cash Flow	GPA	Time	Sentiment
Above 23.1	-7.5	35.7	Overconfident
* From 19 to 23.1	32.1	26.0	Reasonable
19 and Below	33.9	38.3	Overly fearful

FIGURE A-42 GlaxoSmithKline plc (GSK).
© 2003 Ned Davis Research, Inc. All rights reserved.

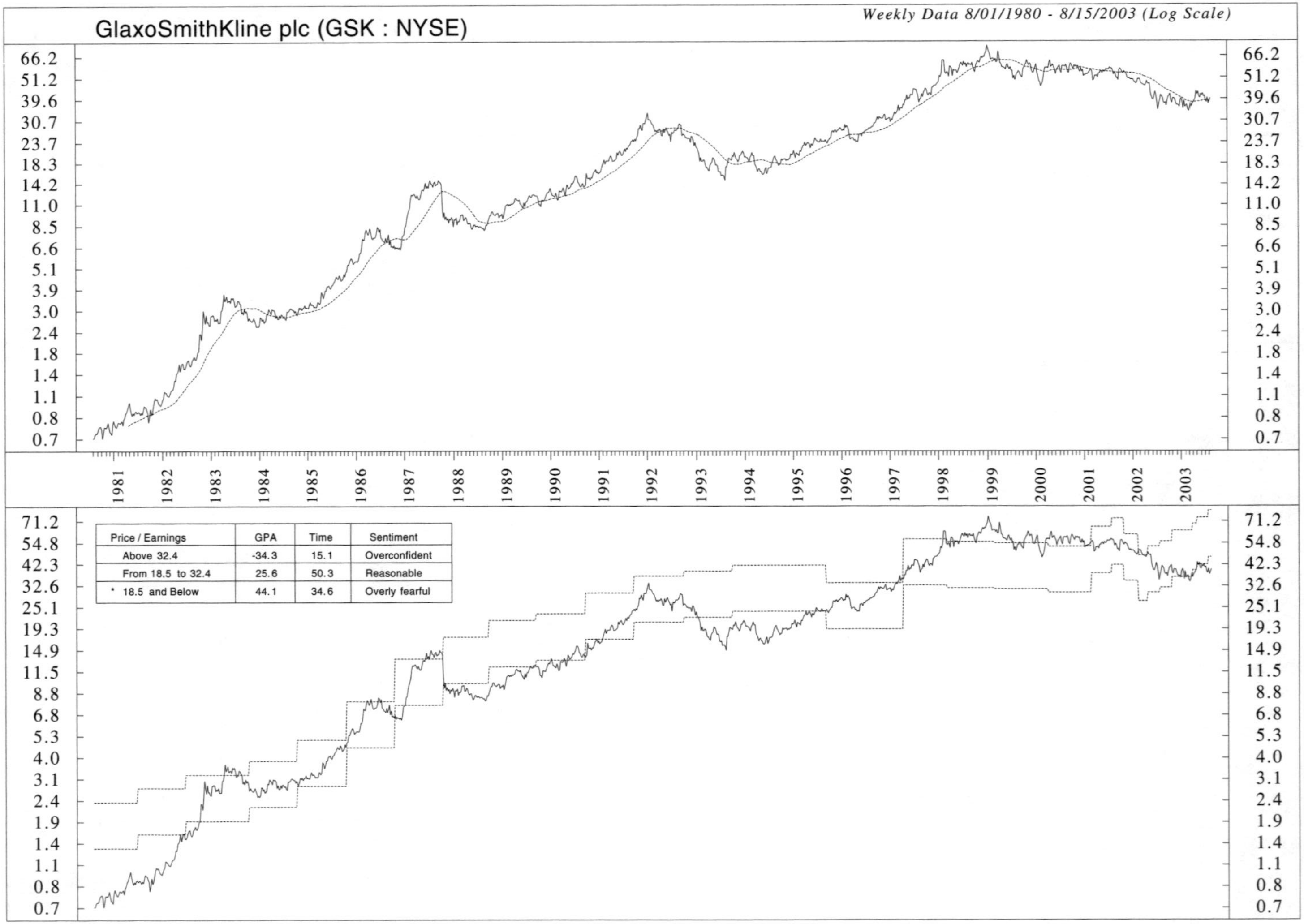

112

FIGURE A-43 H.J. Heinz Company (HNZ).
© 2003 Ned Davis Research, Inc. All rights reserved.

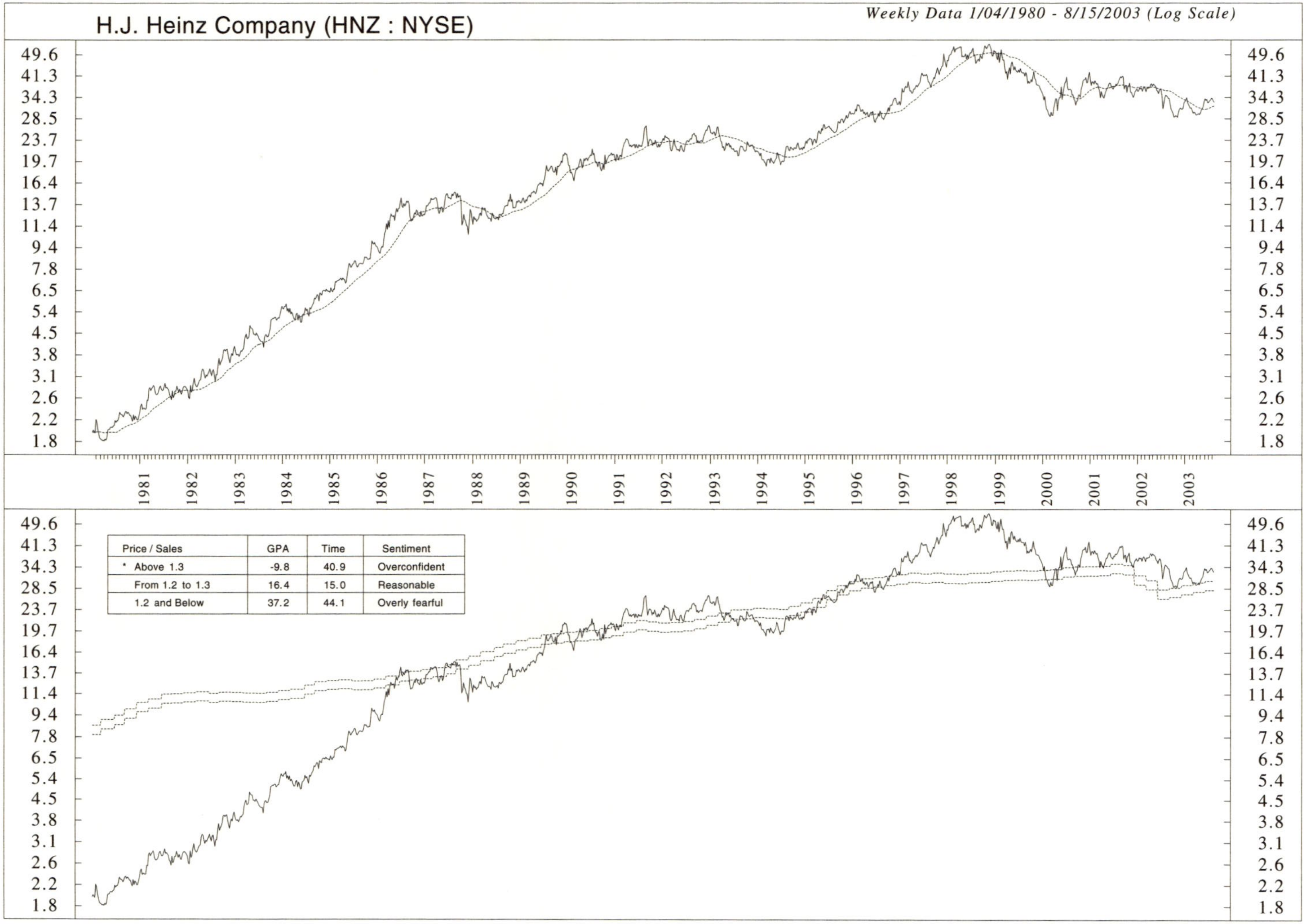

FIGURE A-44 HON Industries, Inc. (HNI).
© 2003 Ned Davis Research, Inc. All rights reserved.

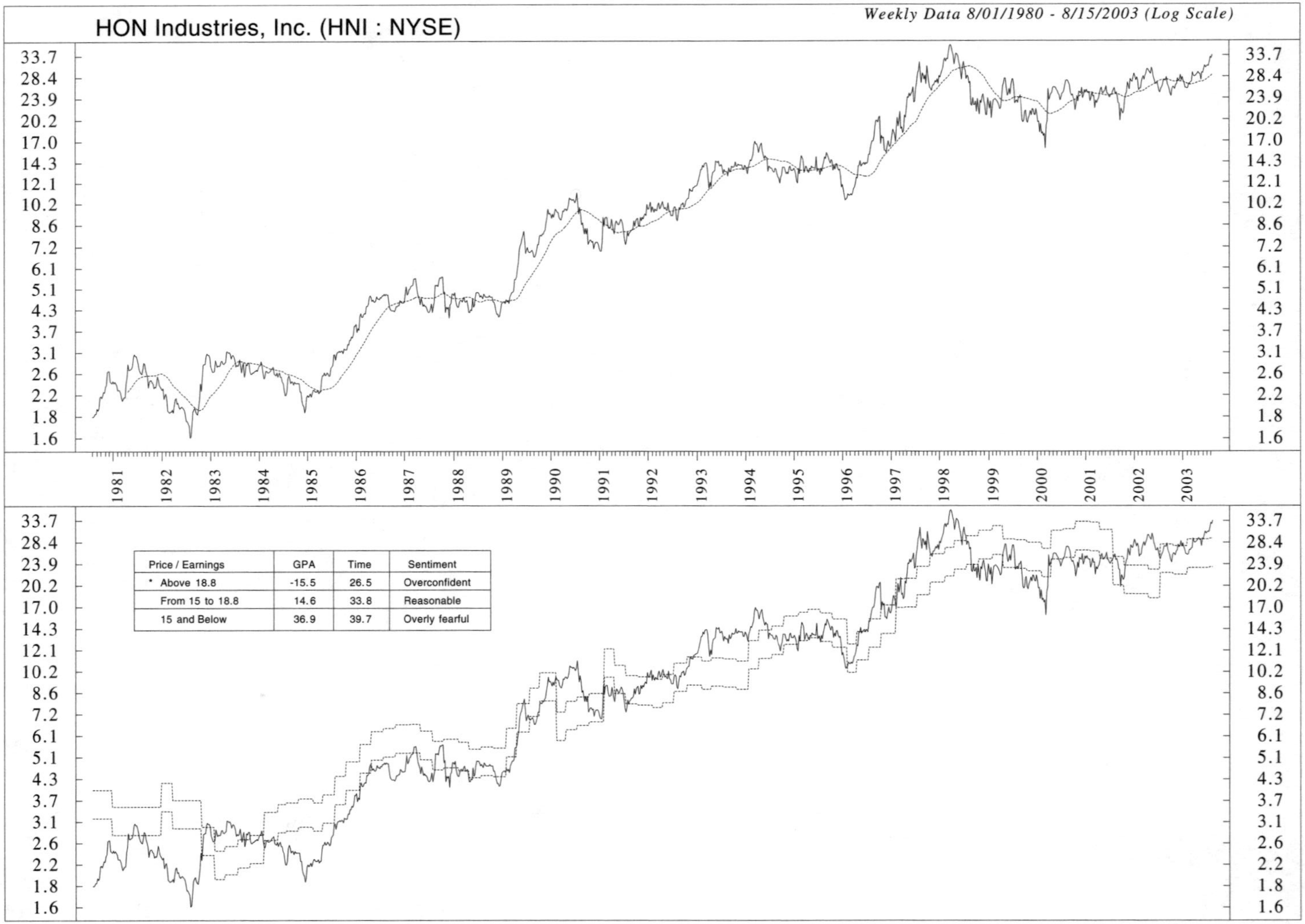

Price / Earnings	GPA	Time	Sentiment
* Above 18.8	-15.5	26.5	Overconfident
From 15 to 18.8	14.6	33.8	Reasonable
15 and Below	36.9	39.7	Overly fearful

FIGURE A-45 Halliburton Company (HAL).
© 2003 Ned Davis Research, Inc. All rights reserved.

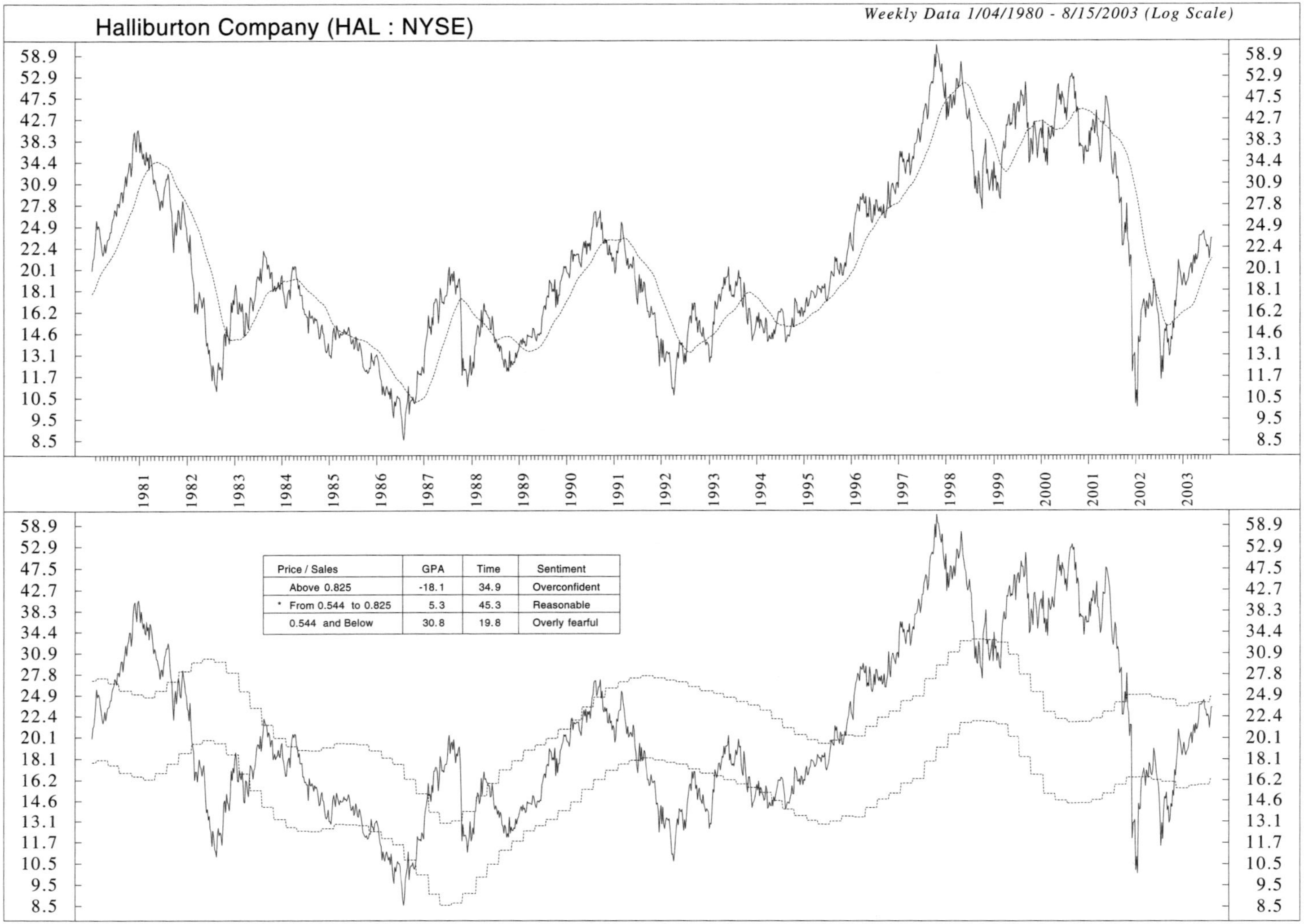

115

FIGURE A-46 Harrah's Entertainment, Inc. (HET).

© 2003 Ned Davis Research, Inc. All rights reserved.

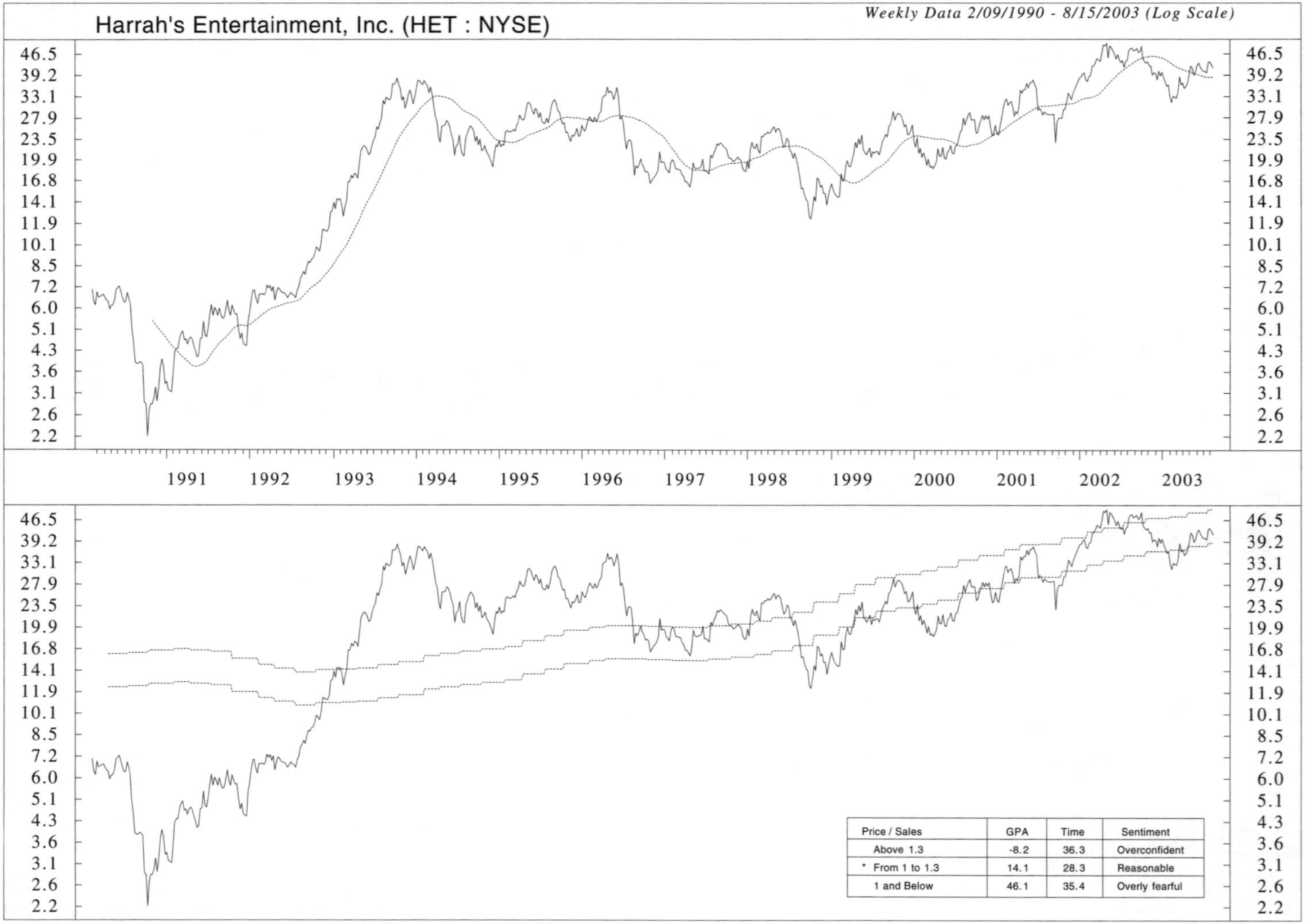

FIGURE A-47 Harsco Corporation (HSC).
© 2003 Ned Davis Research, Inc. All rights reserved.

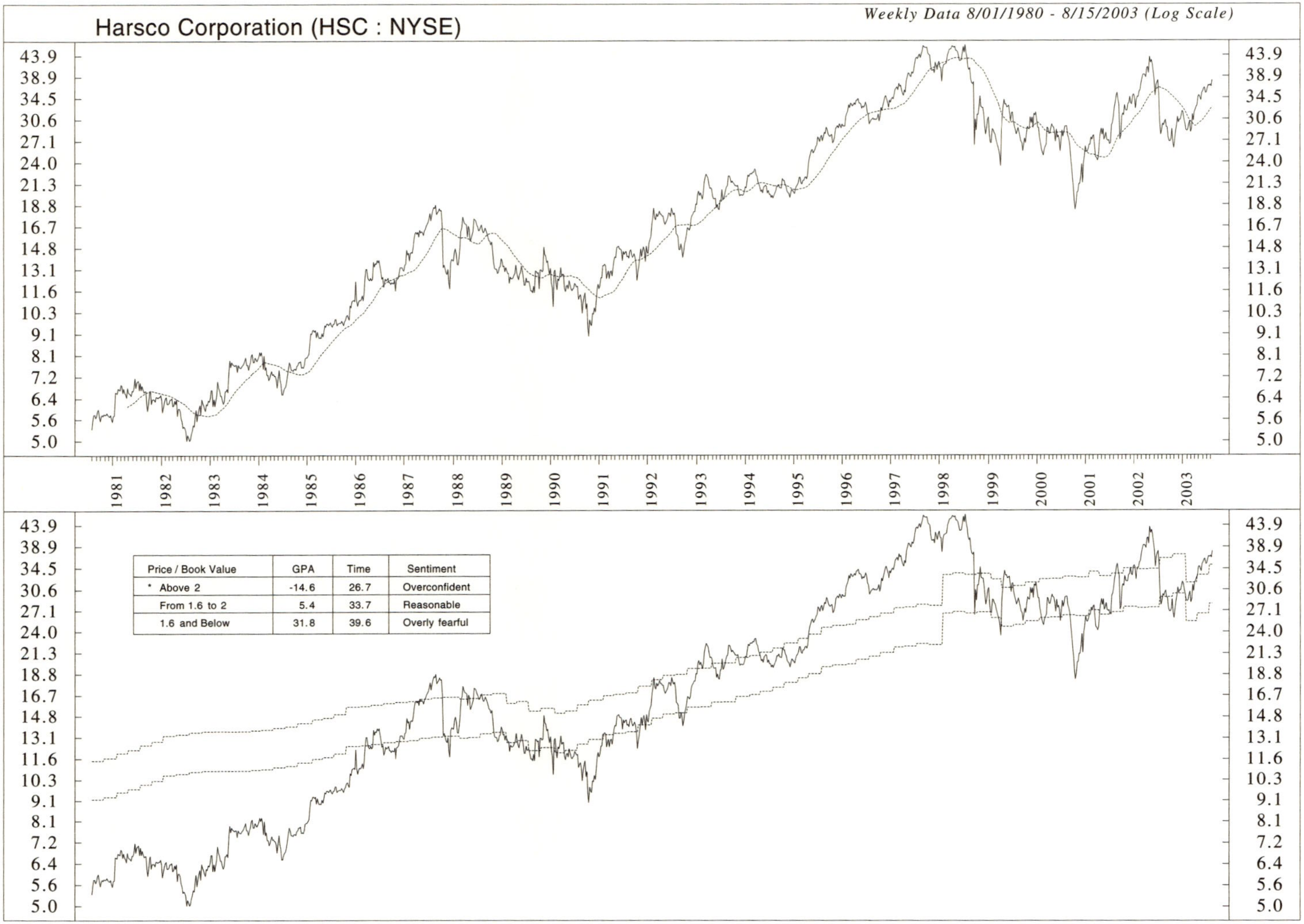

FIGURE A-48 Hewlett-Packard Company (HPQ).

© 2003 Ned Davis Research, Inc. All rights reserved.

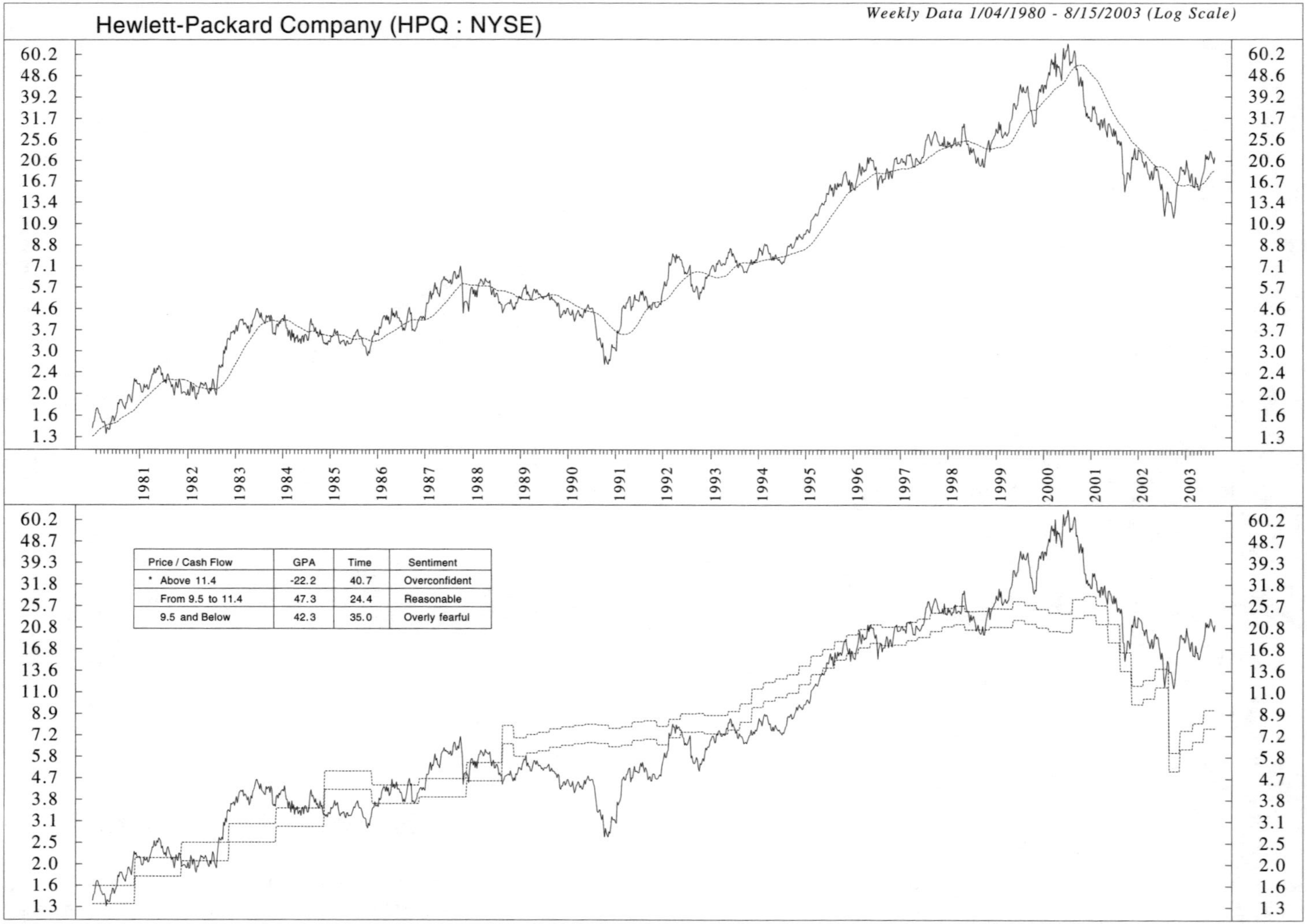

FIGURE A-49 Hilton Hotels Corporation (HLT).
© 2003 Ned Davis Research, Inc. All rights reserved.

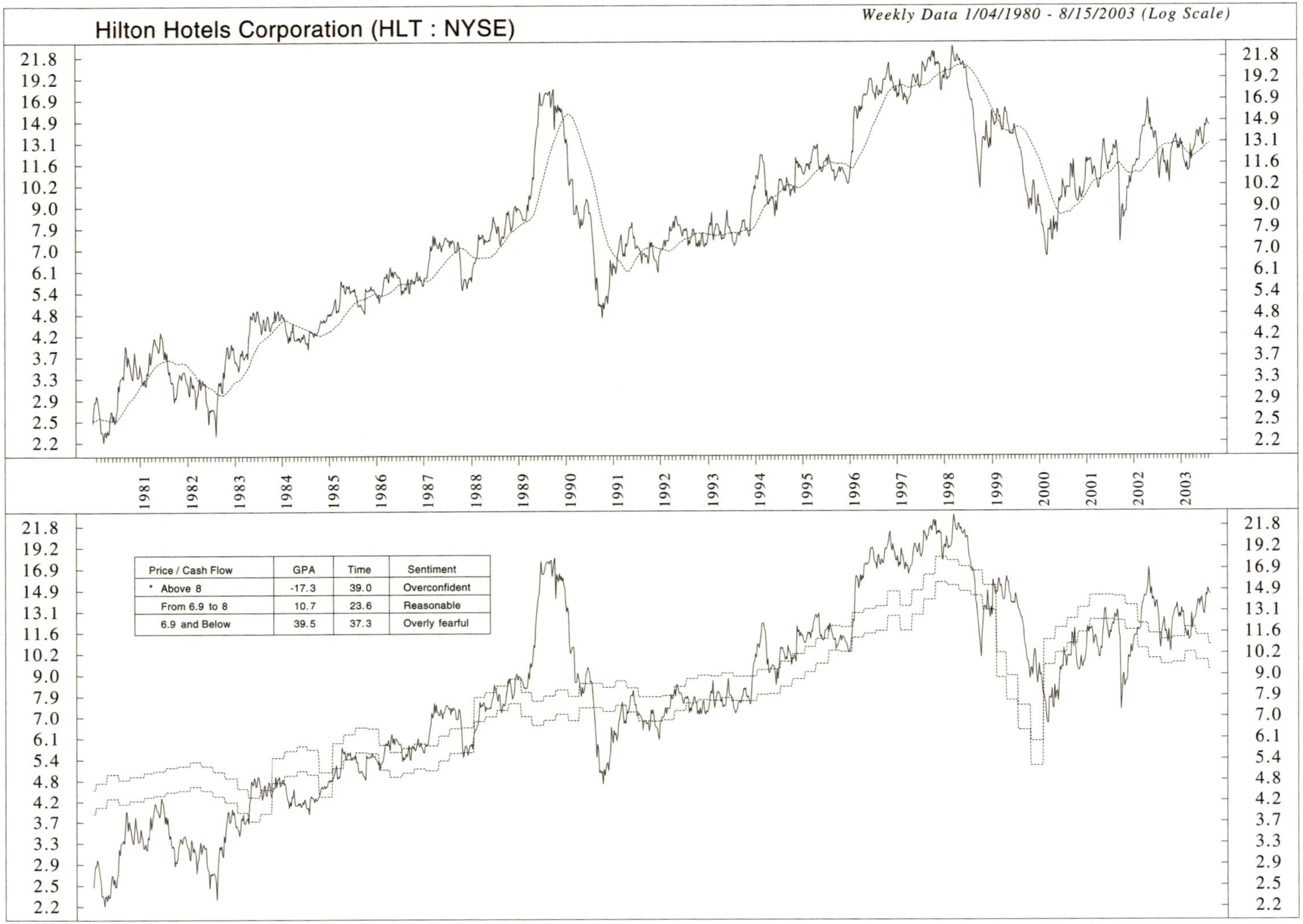

FIGURE A-50 Home Depot, Inc., The (HD).
© 2003 Ned Davis Research, Inc. All rights reserved.

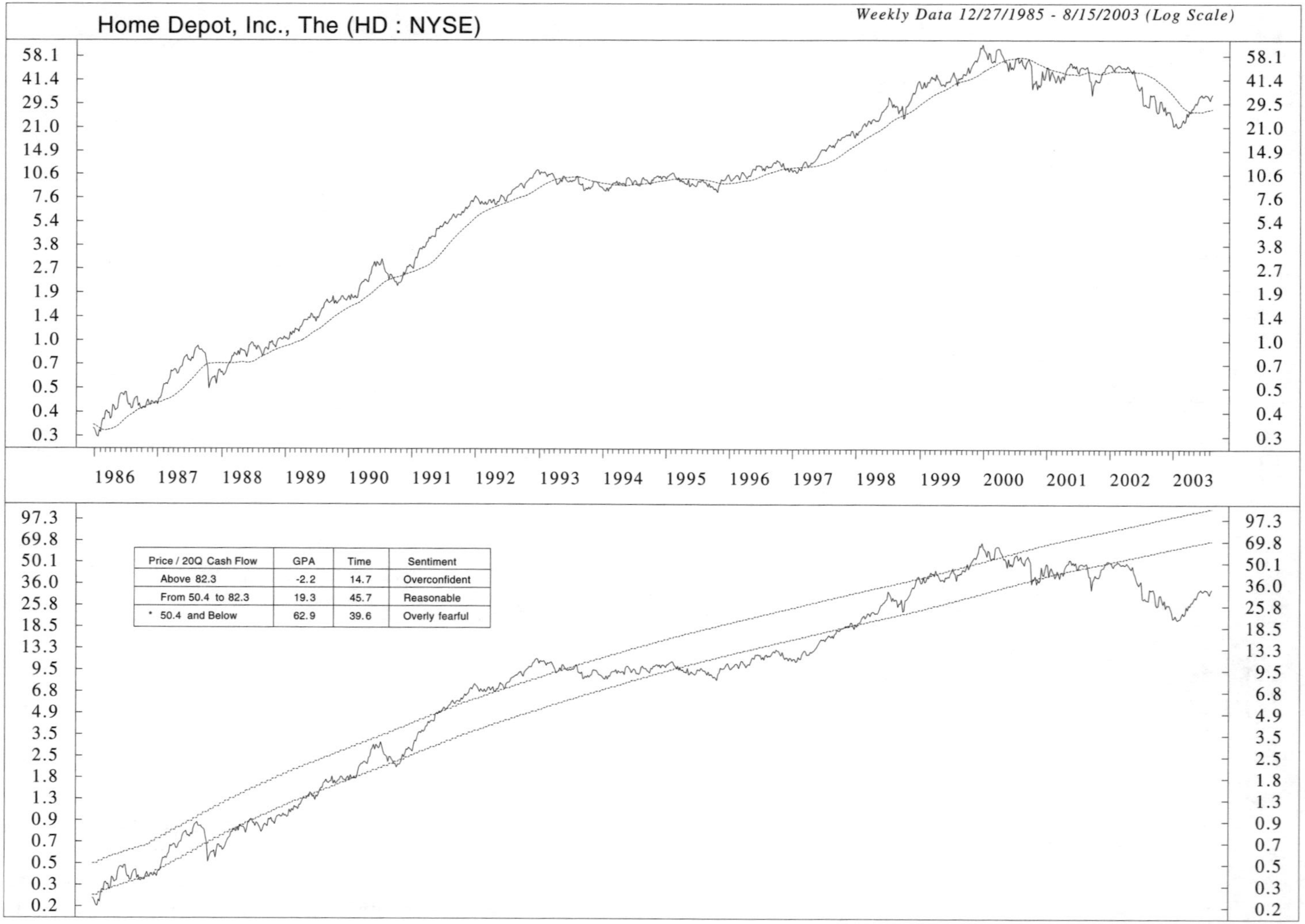

Home Depot, Inc., The (HD : NYSE)

Weekly Data 12/27/1985 - 8/15/2003 (Log Scale)

Price / 20Q Cash Flow	GPA	Time	Sentiment
Above 82.3	-2.2	14.7	Overconfident
From 50.4 to 82.3	19.3	45.7	Reasonable
50.4 and Below	62.9	39.6	Overly fearful

FIGURE A-51 Honda Motor Co., Ltd. (HMC).
© 2003 Ned Davis Research, Inc. All rights reserved.

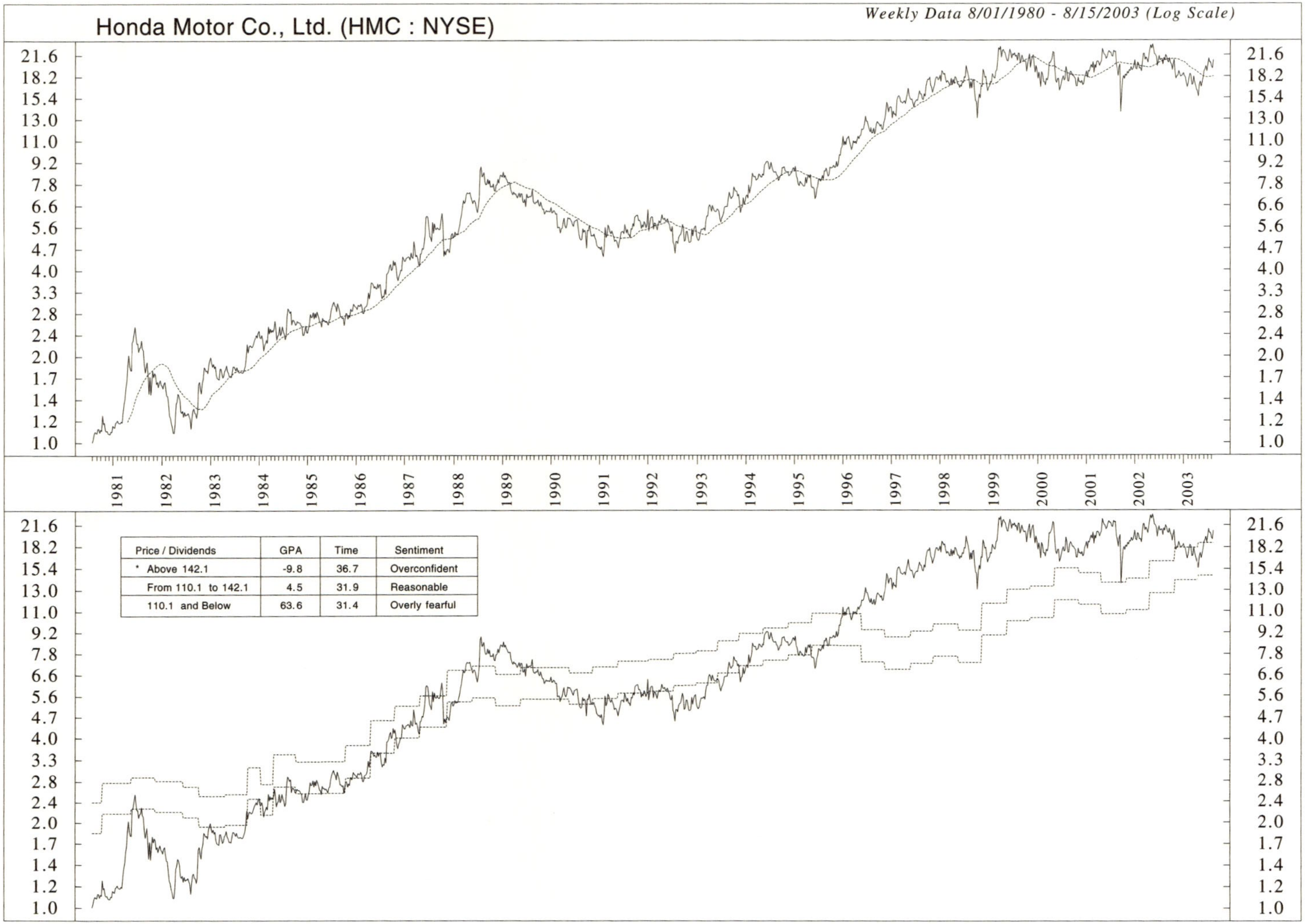

FIGURE A-52 Illinois Tool Works, Inc. (ITW).

© 2003 Ned Davis Research, Inc. All rights reserved.

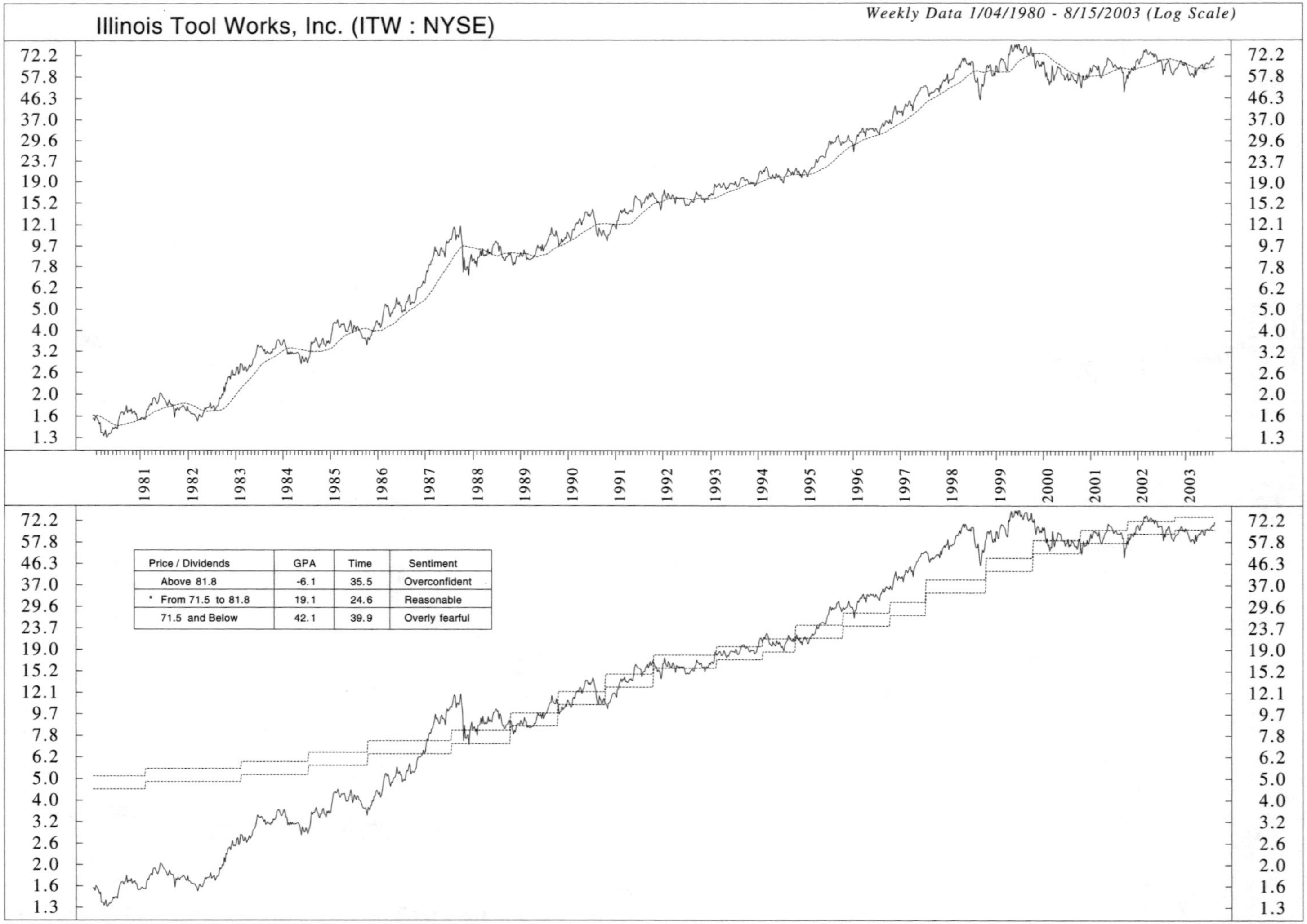

FIGURE A-53 Ingersoll-Rand Company Limited (IR).
© 2003 Ned Davis Research, Inc. All rights reserved.

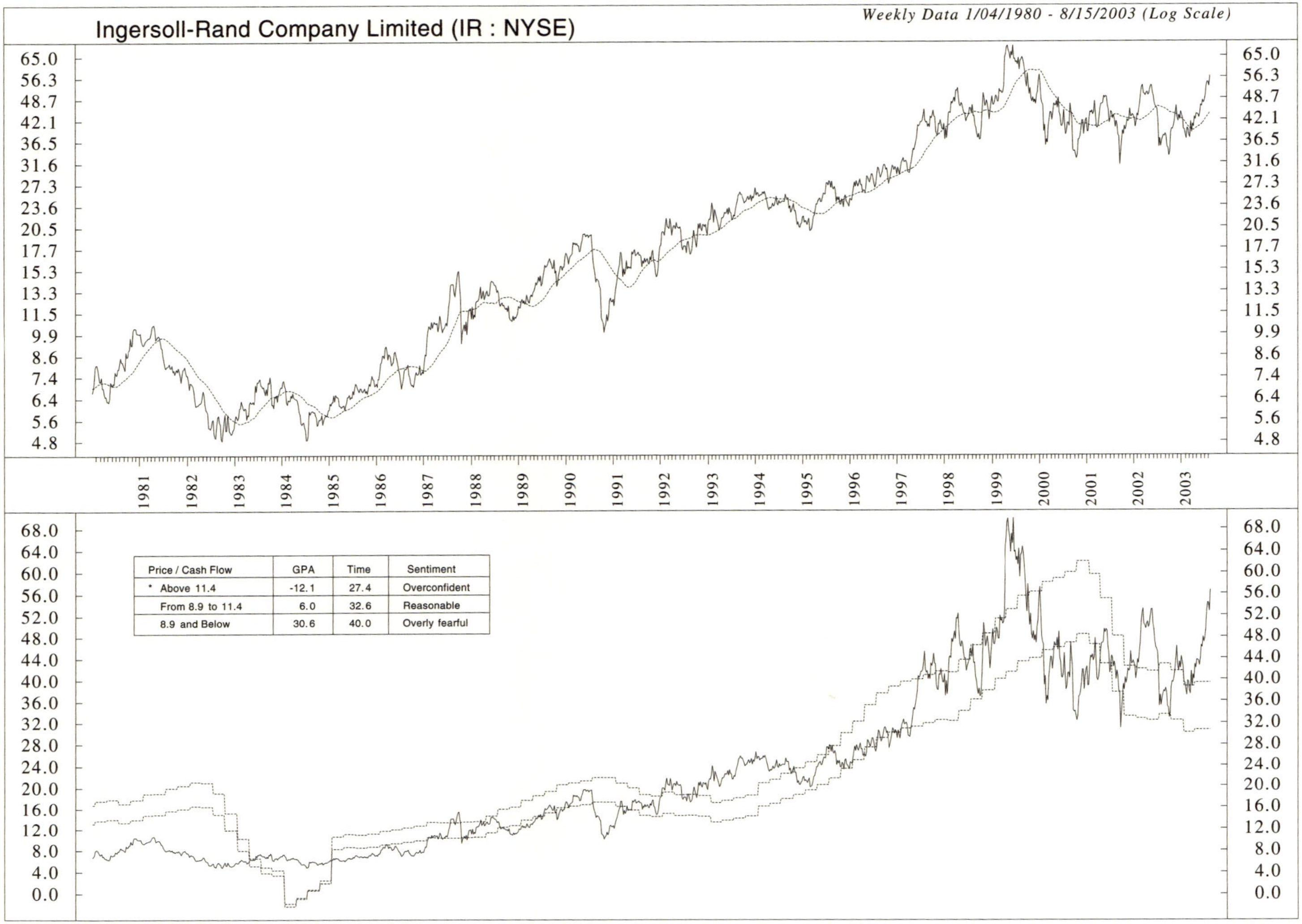

Ingersoll-Rand Company Limited (IR : NYSE) — Weekly Data 1/04/1980 - 8/15/2003 (Log Scale)

Price / Cash Flow	GPA	Time	Sentiment
* Above 11.4	-12.1	27.4	Overconfident
From 8.9 to 11.4	6.0	32.6	Reasonable
8.9 and Below	30.6	40.0	Overly fearful

FIGURE A-54 Integrated Device Technology, Inc. (IDTI).
© 2003 Ned Davis Research, Inc. All rights reserved.

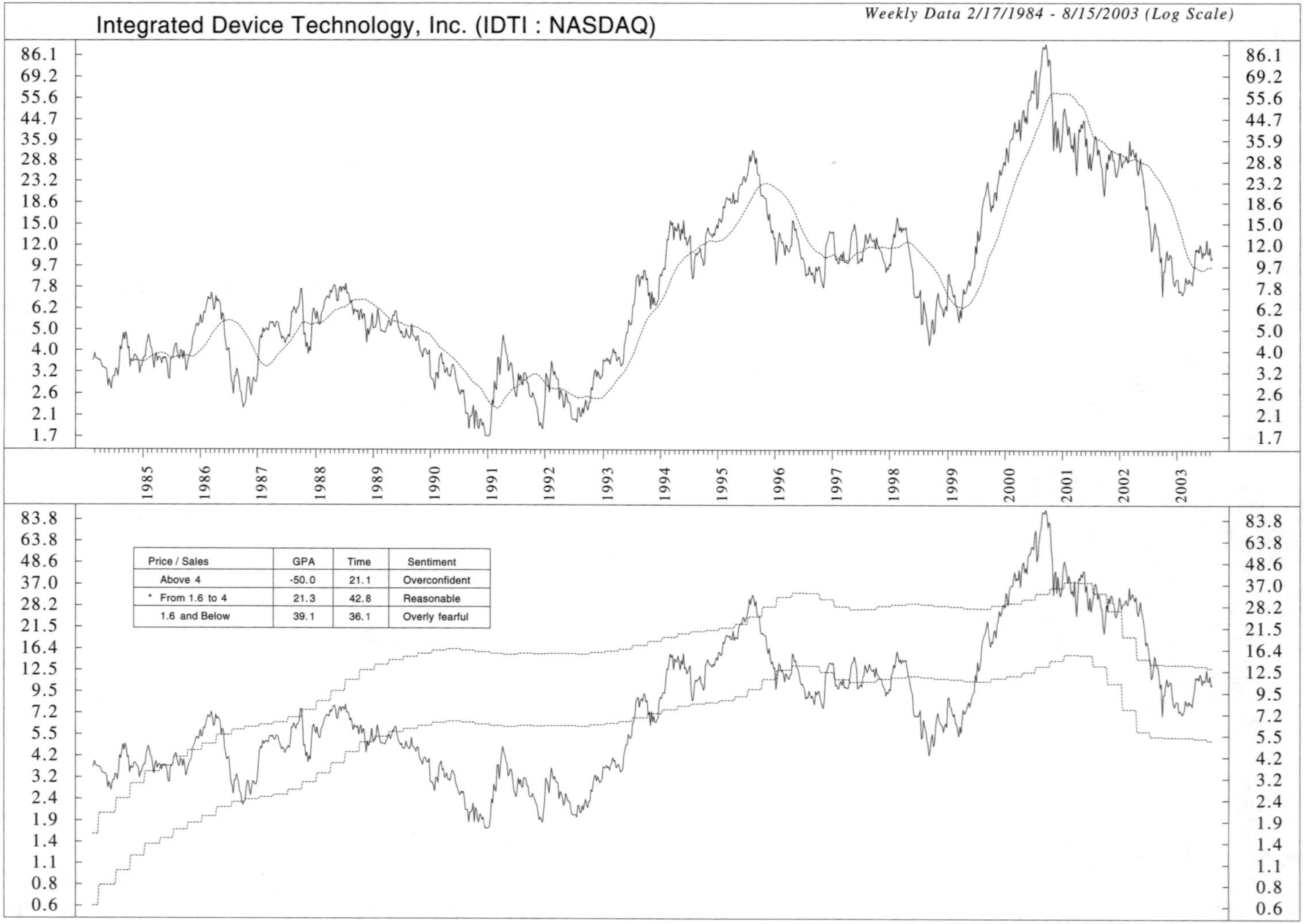

FIGURE A-55 Intel Corporation (INTC).
© 2003 Ned Davis Research, Inc. All rights reserved.

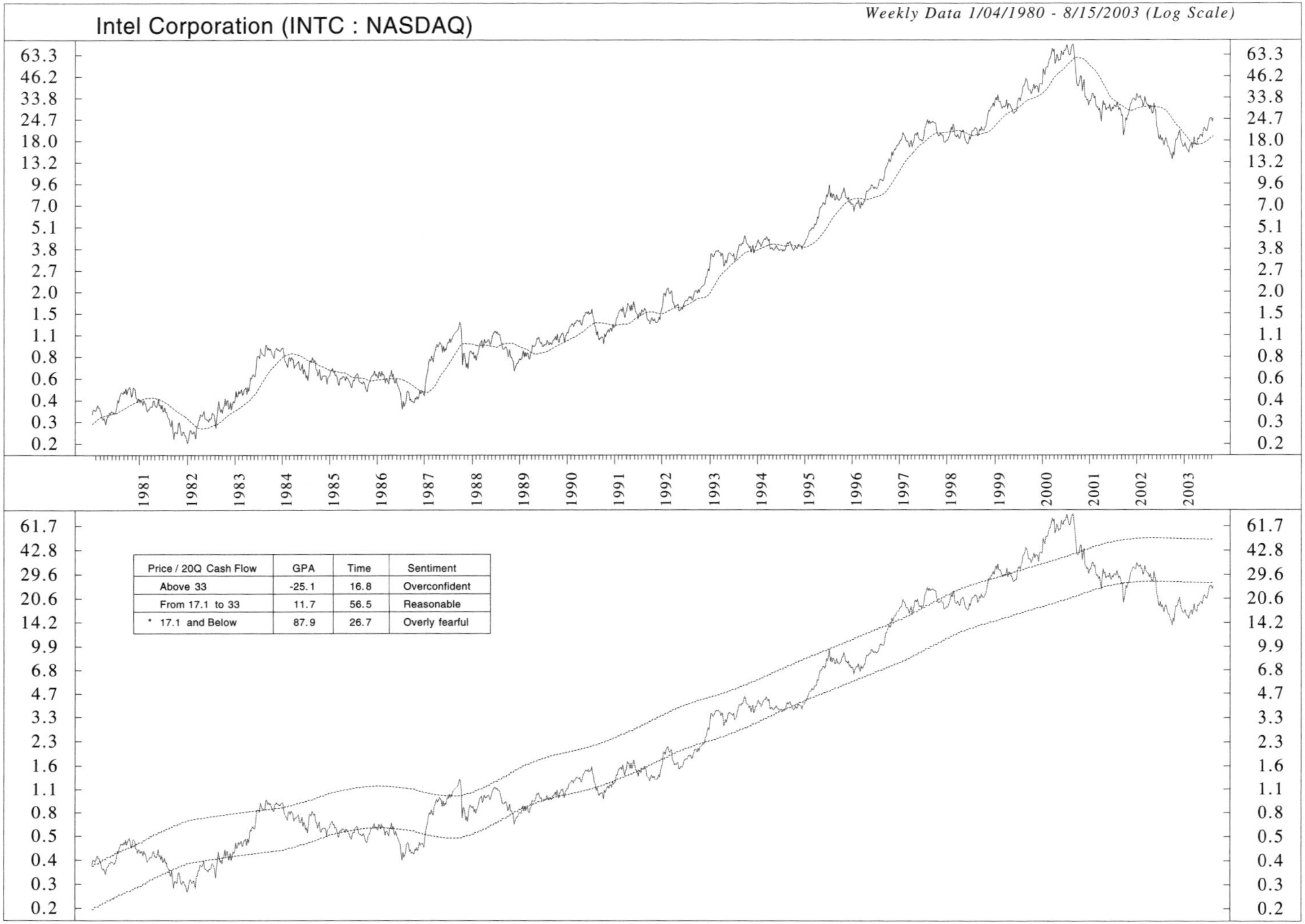

Intel Corporation (INTC : NASDAQ)

Weekly Data 1/04/1980 - 8/15/2003 (Log Scale)

Price / 20Q Cash Flow	GPA	Time	Sentiment
Above 33	-25.1	16.8	Overconfident
From 17.1 to 33	11.7	56.5	Reasonable
* 17.1 and Below	87.9	26.7	Overly fearful

FIGURE A-56 International Business Machines Corporation (IBM).
© 2003 Ned Davis Research, Inc. All rights reserved.

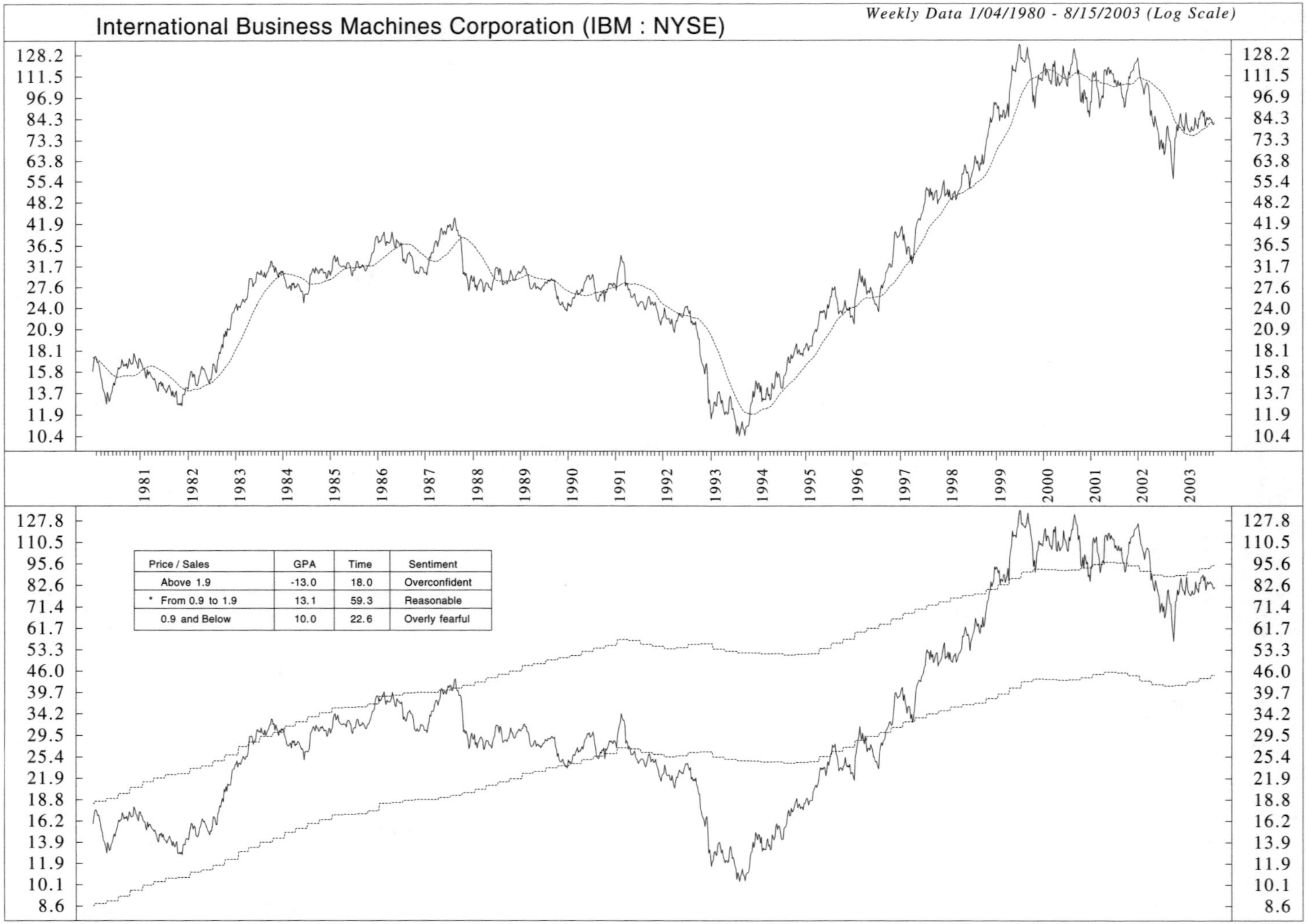

FIGURE A-57 International Paper Company (IP).
© 2003 Ned Davis Research, Inc. All rights reserved.

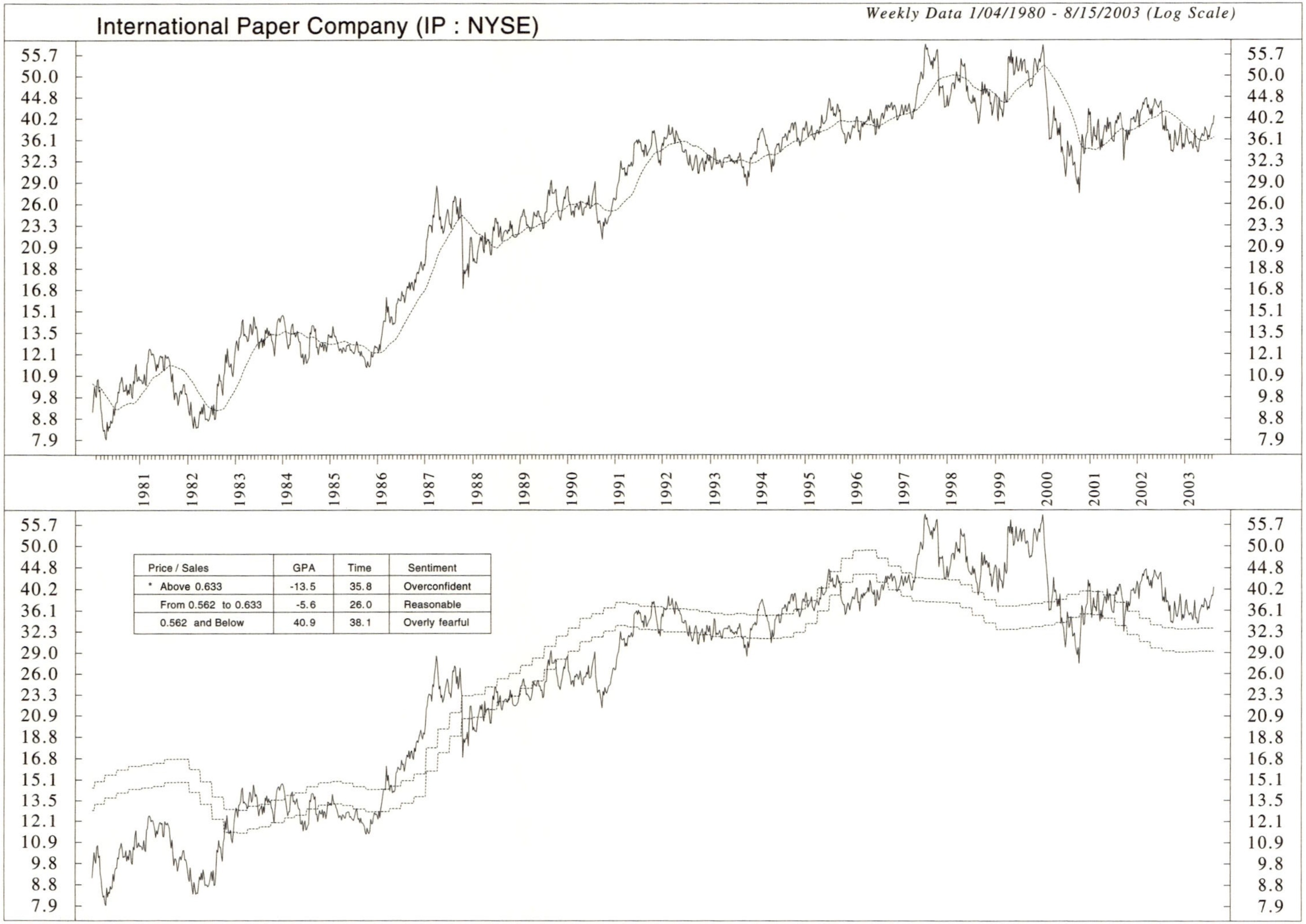

FIGURE A-58 Intuit, Inc. (INTU).
© 2003 Ned Davis Research, Inc. All rights reserved.

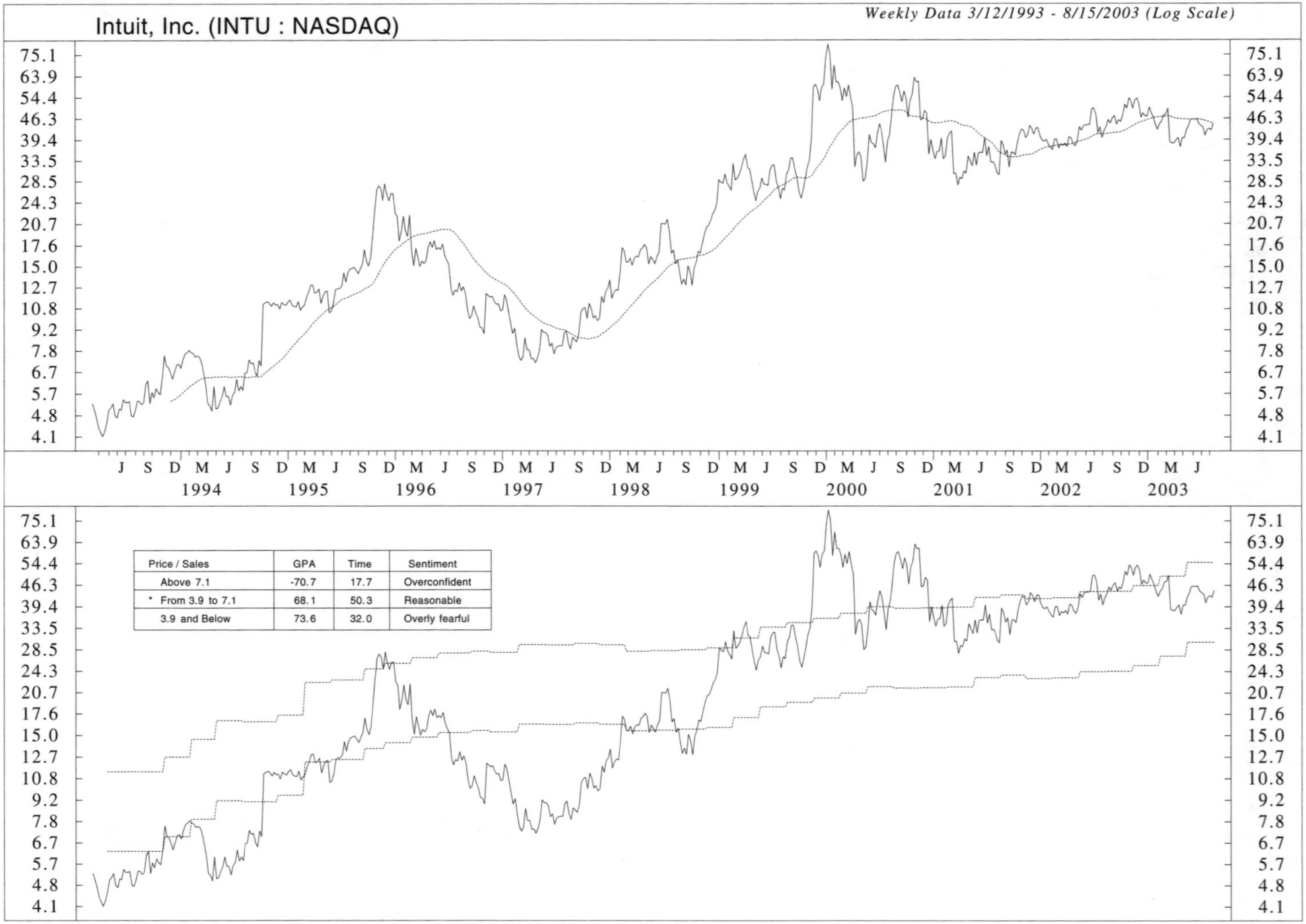

Intuit, Inc. (INTU : NASDAQ)

Weekly Data 3/12/1993 - 8/15/2003 (Log Scale)

Price / Sales	GPA	Time	Sentiment
Above 7.1	-70.7	17.7	Overconfident
* From 3.9 to 7.1	68.1	50.3	Reasonable
3.9 and Below	73.6	32.0	Overly fearful

FIGURE A-59 Jabil Circuit, Inc. (JBL).
© 2003 Ned Davis Research, Inc. All rights reserved.

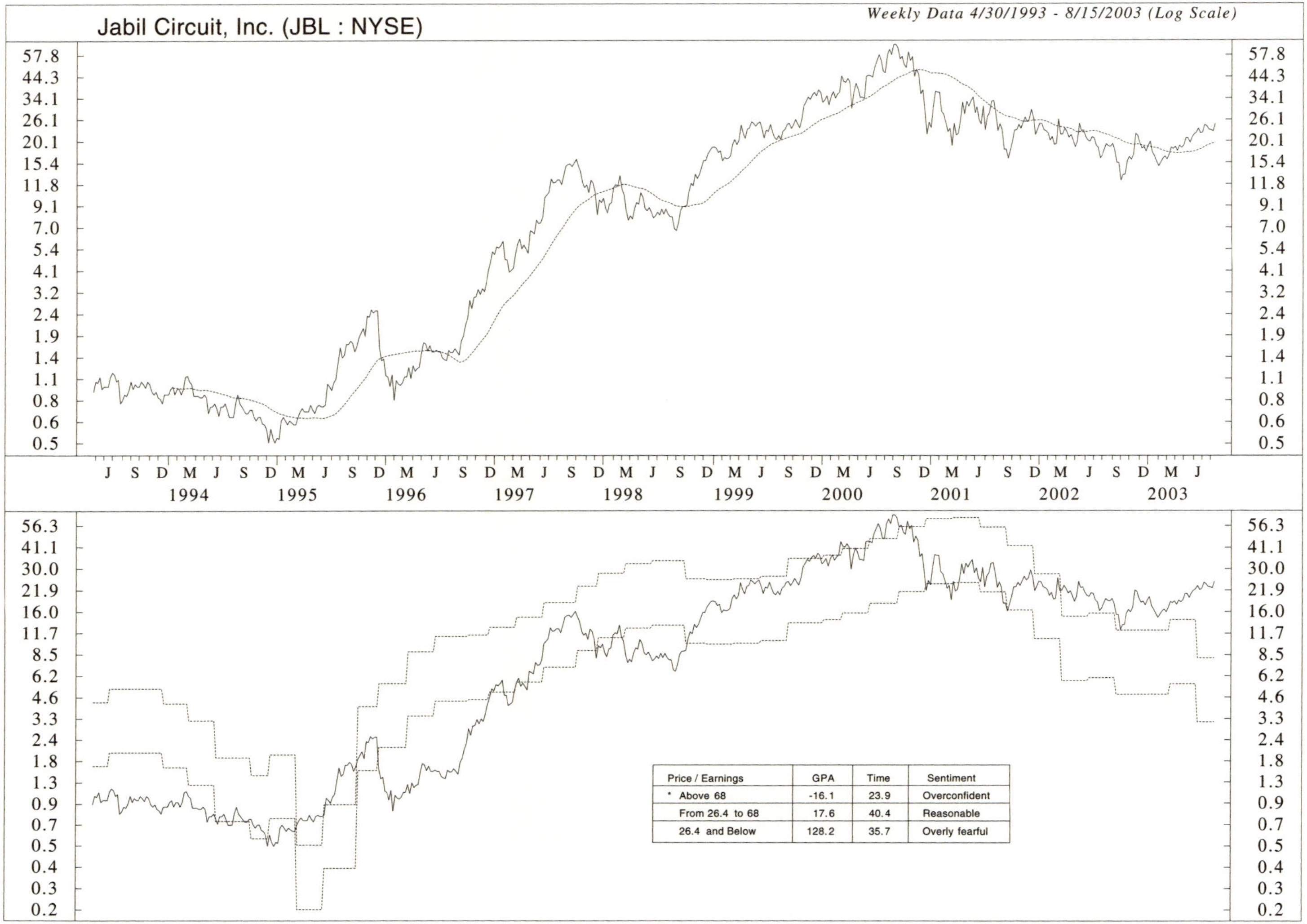

FIGURE A-60 Jefferson-Pilot Corporation (JP).

© 2003 Ned Davis Research, Inc. All rights reserved.

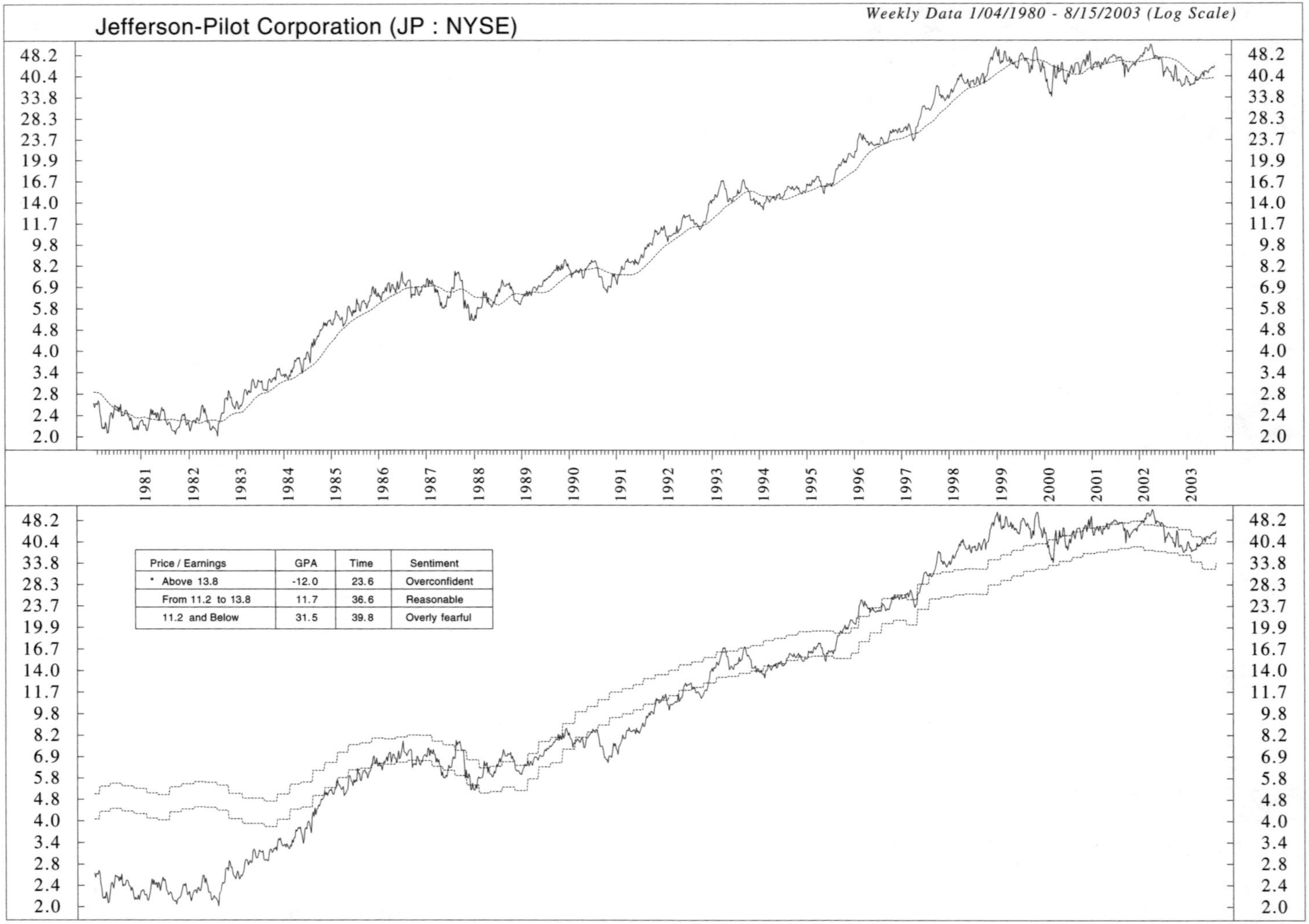

FIGURE A-61 Johnson Controls, Inc. (JCI).
© 2003 Ned Davis Research, Inc. All rights reserved.

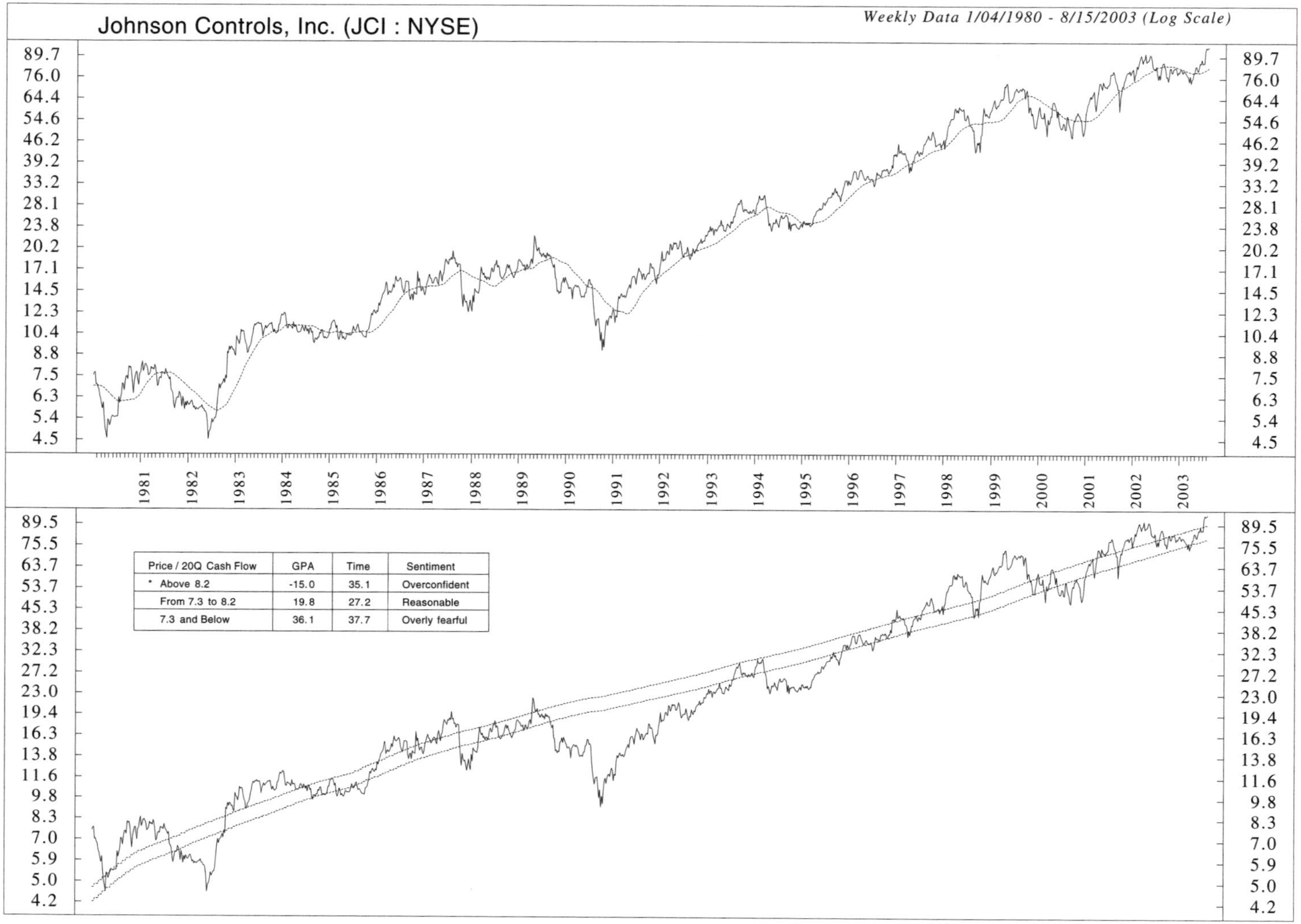

Johnson Controls, Inc. (JCI : NYSE)   Weekly Data 1/04/1980 - 8/15/2003 (Log Scale)

Price / 20Q Cash Flow	GPA	Time	Sentiment
* Above 8.2	-15.0	35.1	Overconfident
From 7.3 to 8.2	19.8	27.2	Reasonable
7.3 and Below	36.1	37.7	Overly fearful

FIGURE A-62 Johnson and Johnson (JNJ).
© 2003 Ned Davis Research, Inc. All rights reserved.

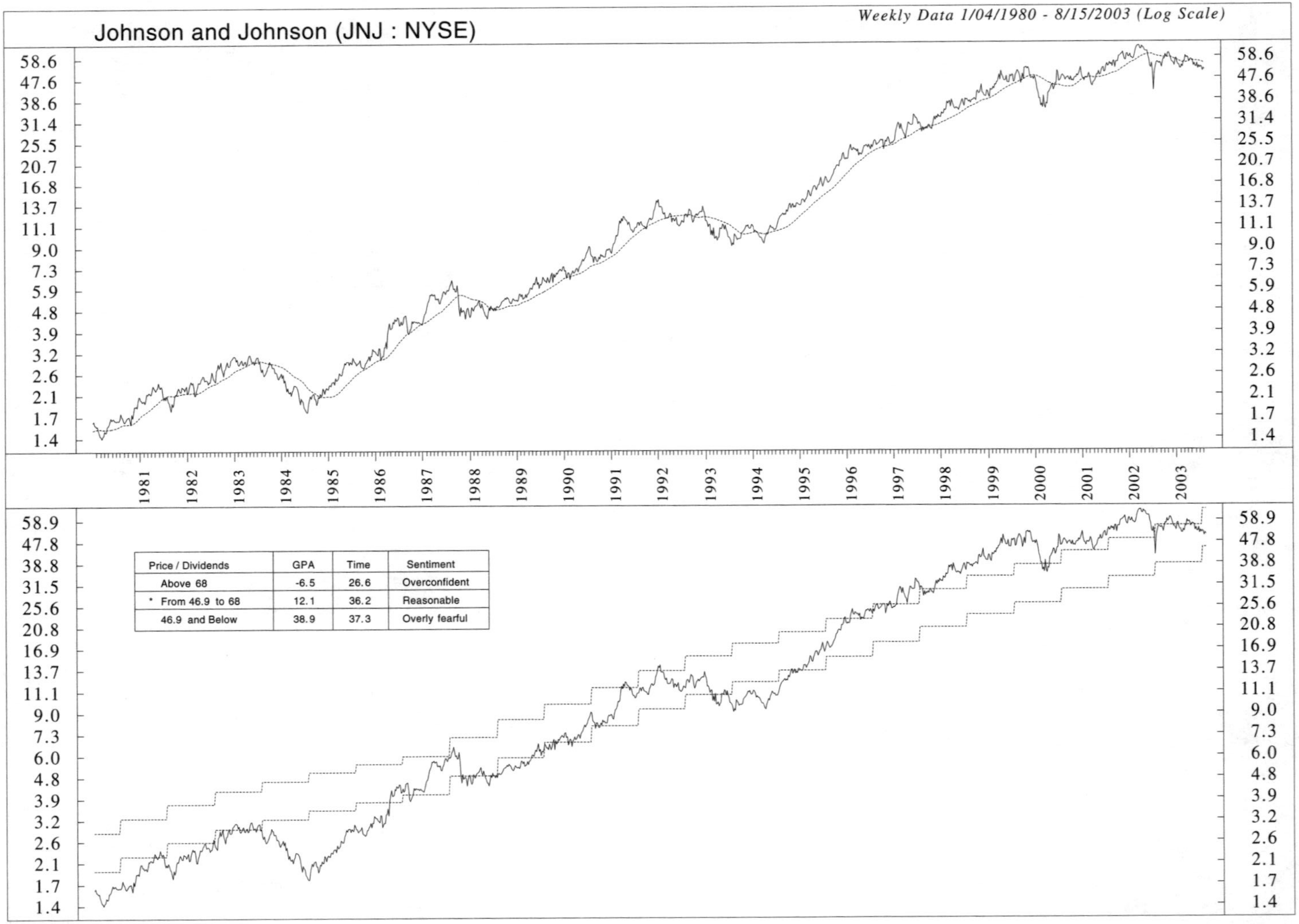

FIGURE A-63   Jones Apparel Group, Inc. (JNY).
© 2003 Ned Davis Research, Inc. All rights reserved.

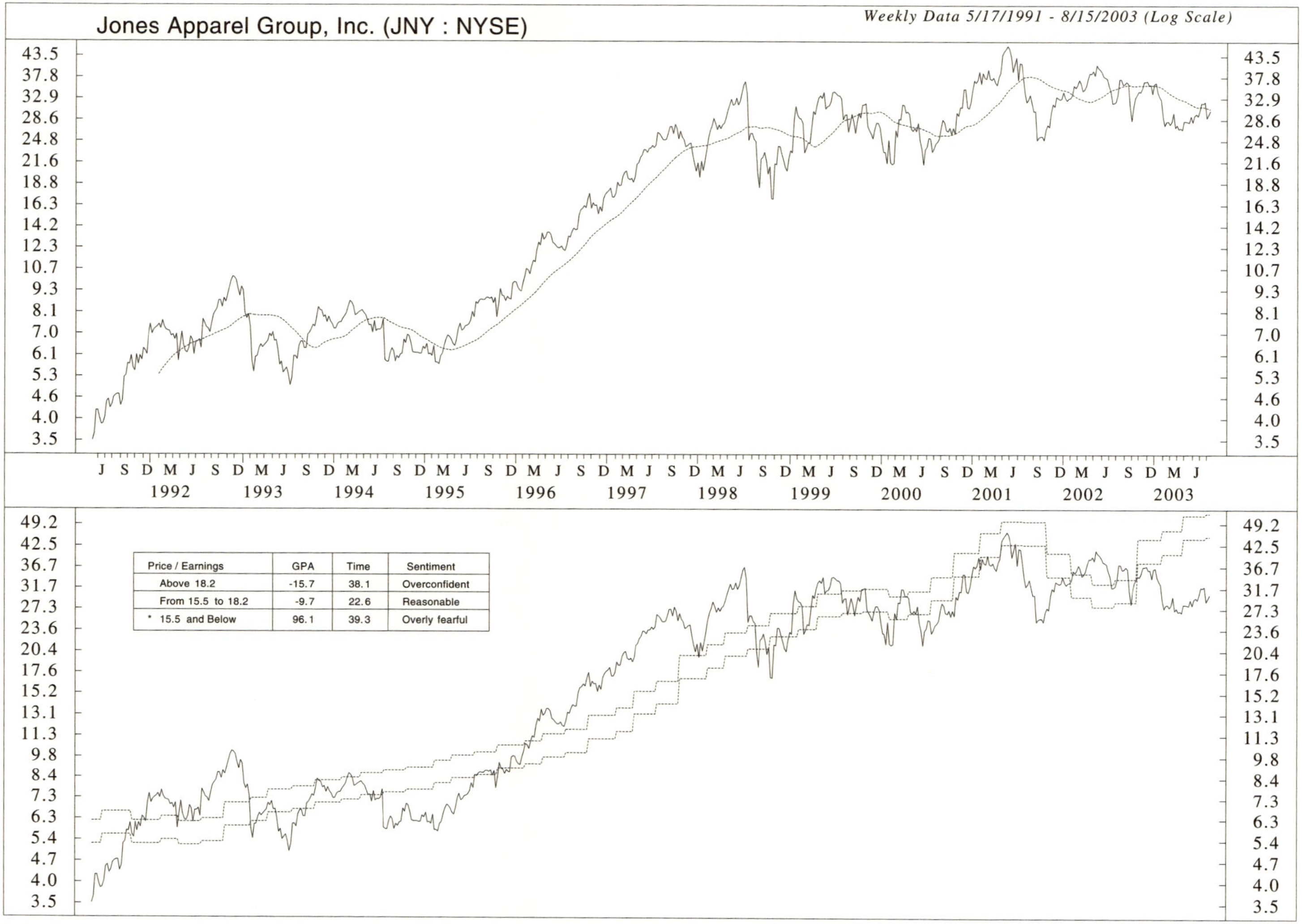

Jones Apparel Group, Inc. (JNY : NYSE)   *Weekly Data 5/17/1991 - 8/15/2003 (Log Scale)*

Price / Earnings	GPA	Time	Sentiment
Above 18.2	-15.7	38.1	Overconfident
From 15.5 to 18.2	-9.7	22.6	Reasonable
* 15.5 and Below	96.1	39.3	Overly fearful

FIGURE A-64 KLA-Tencor Corporation (KLAC).
© 2003 Ned Davis Research, Inc. All rights reserved.

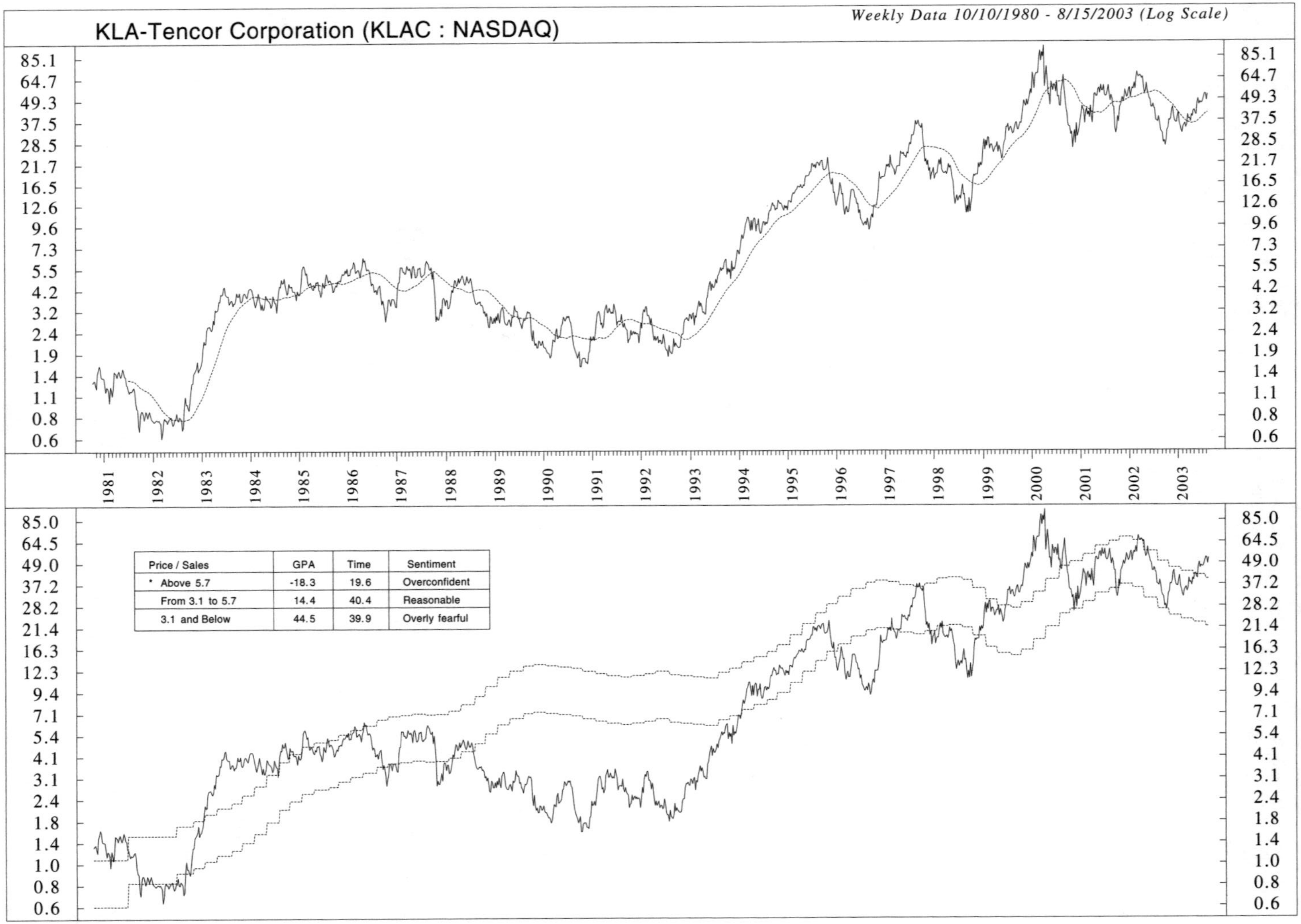

FIGURE A-65 Kellogg Company (K).
© 2003 Ned Davis Research, Inc. All rights reserved.

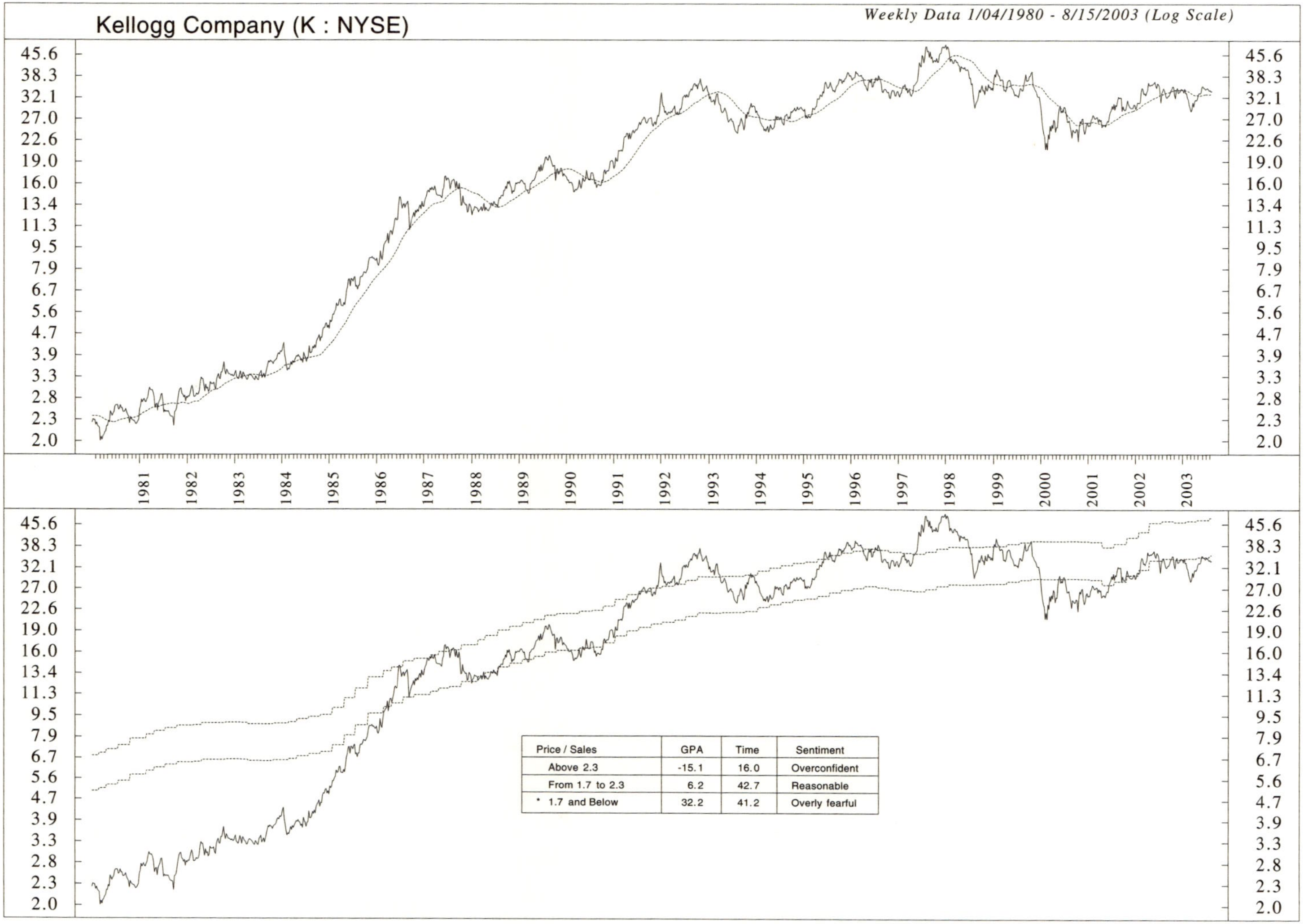

FIGURE A-66 Knight-Ridder, Inc. (KRI).
© 2003 Ned Davis Research, Inc. All rights reserved.

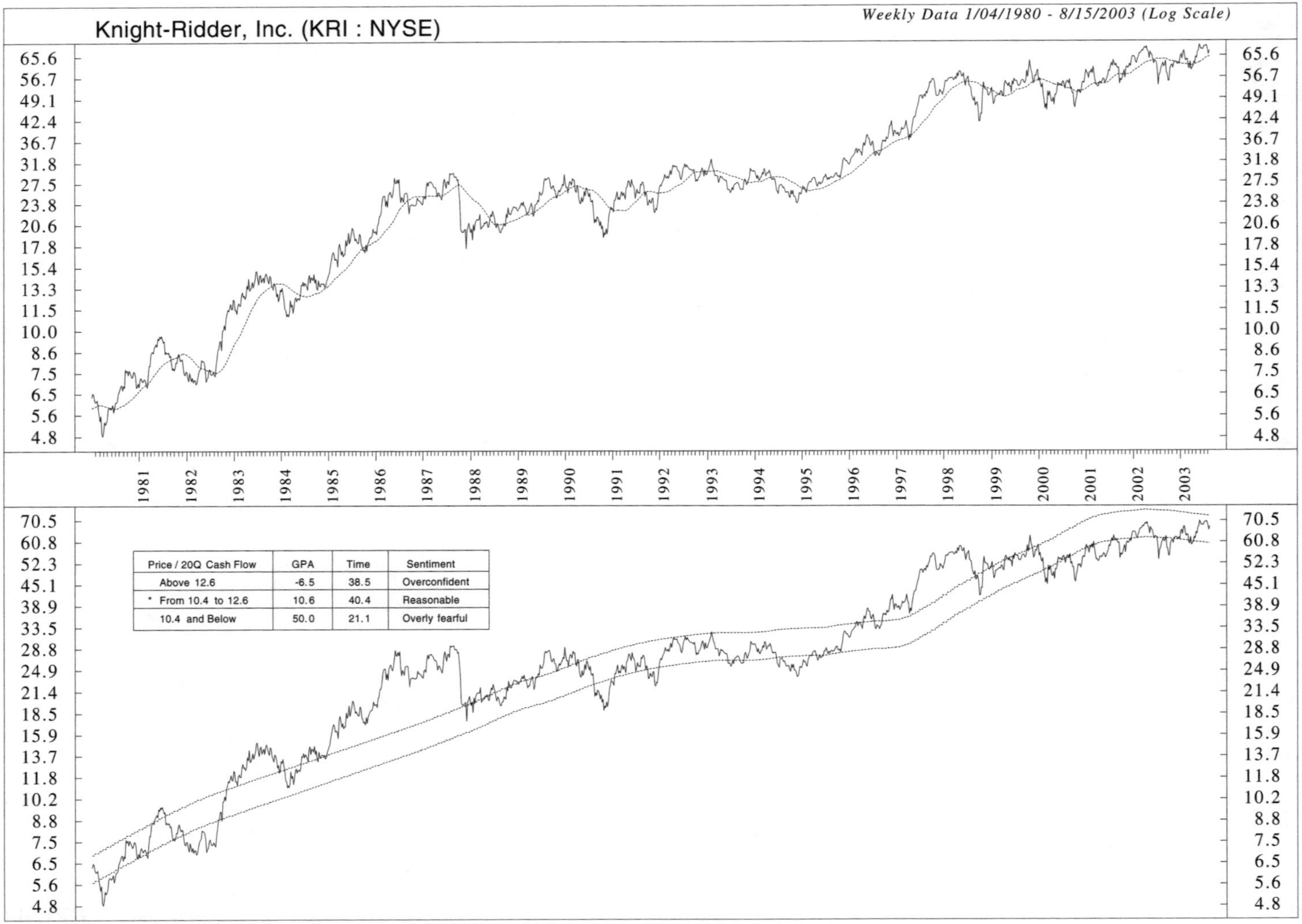

FIGURE A-67 Lehman Brothers Holding, Inc. (LEH).

© 2003 Ned Davis Research, Inc. All rights reserved.

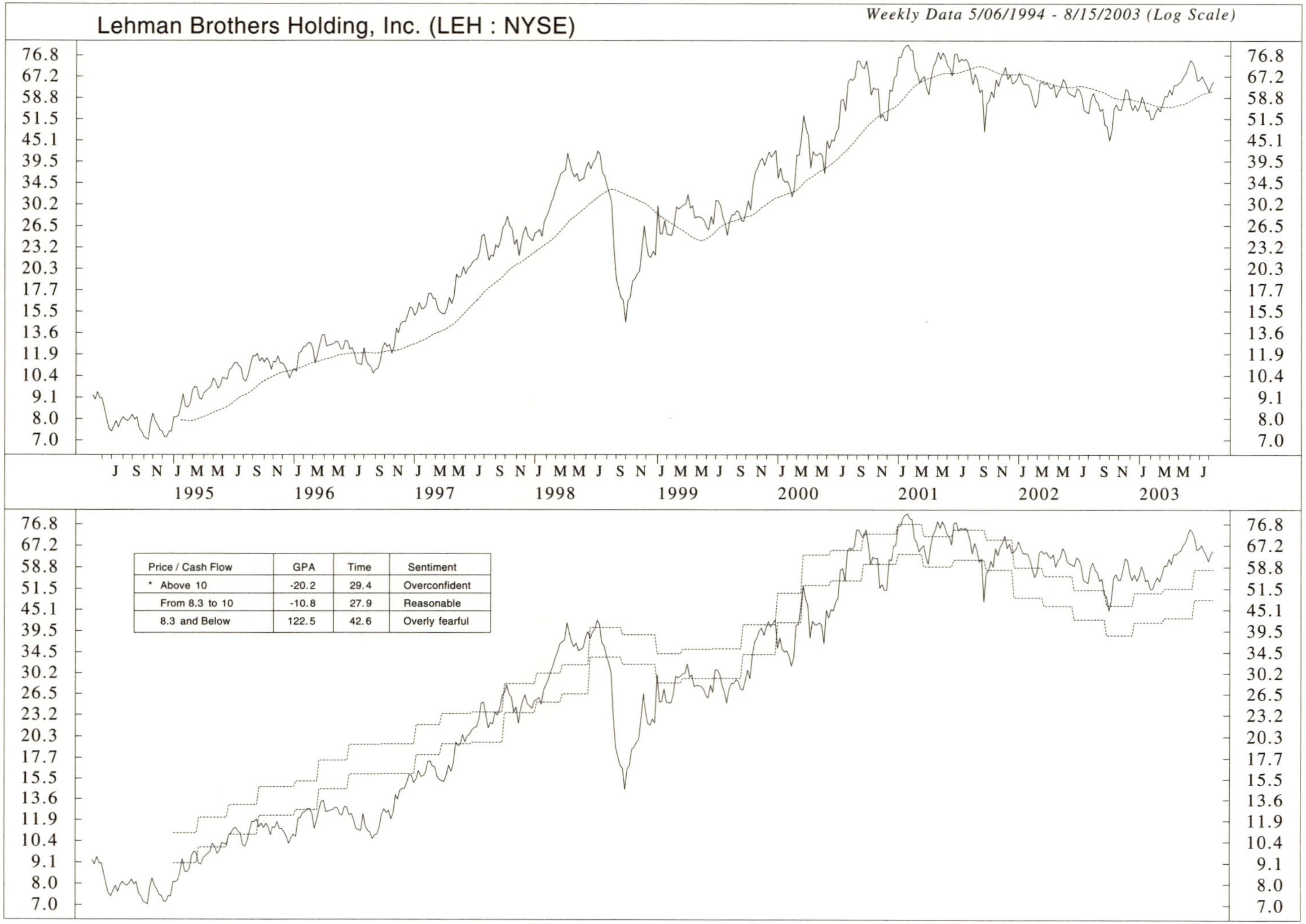

Lehman Brothers Holding, Inc. (LEH : NYSE) Weekly Data 5/06/1994 - 8/15/2003 (Log Scale)

Price / Cash Flow	GPA	Time	Sentiment
* Above 10	-20.2	29.4	Overconfident
From 8.3 to 10	-10.8	27.9	Reasonable
8.3 and Below	122.5	42.6	Overly fearful

137

FIGURE A-68 Limited Brands, Inc. (LTD).
© 2003 Ned Davis Research, Inc. All rights reserved.

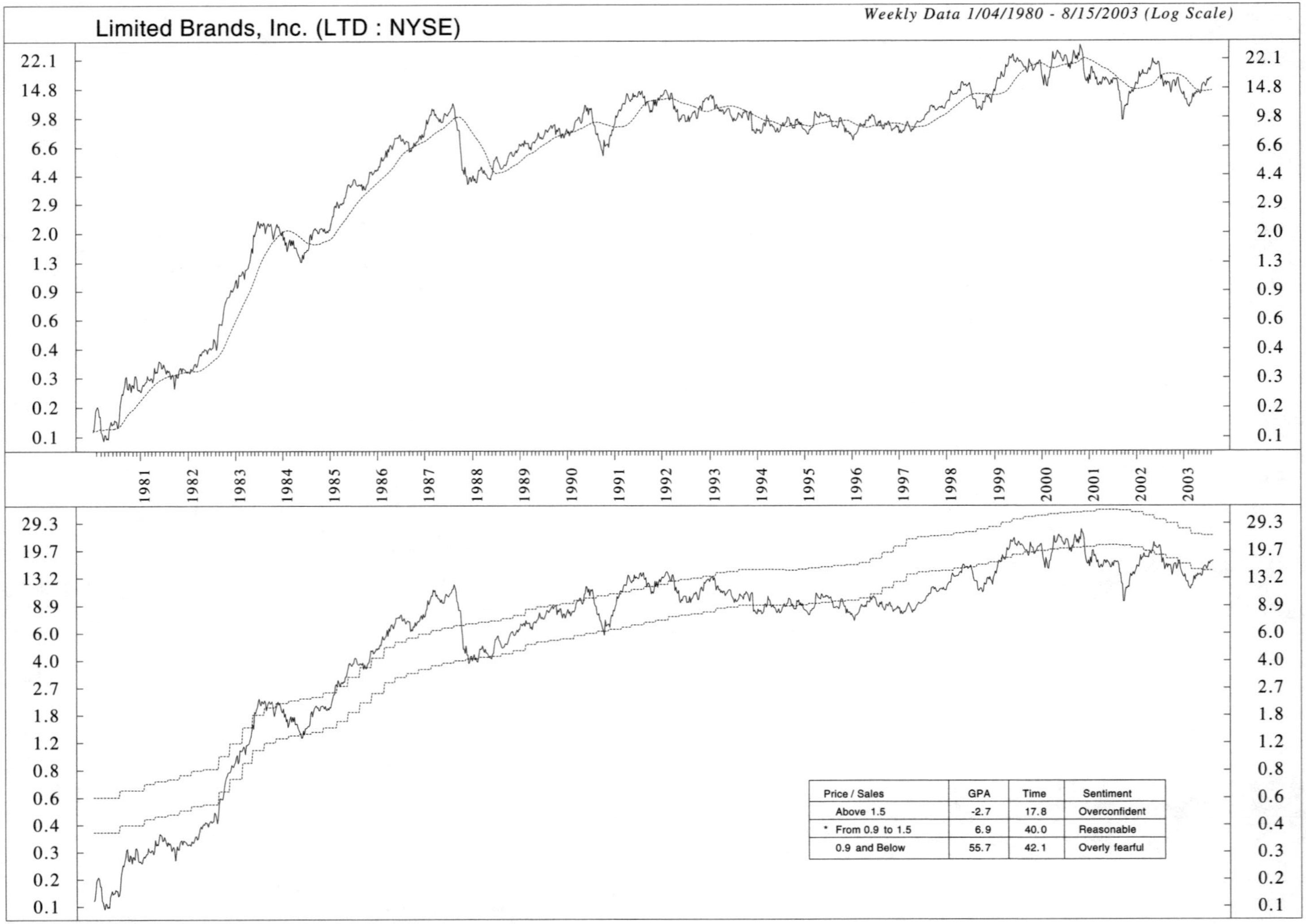

FIGURE A-69 Lowe's Companies, Inc. (LOW).
© 2003 Ned Davis Research, Inc. All rights reserved.

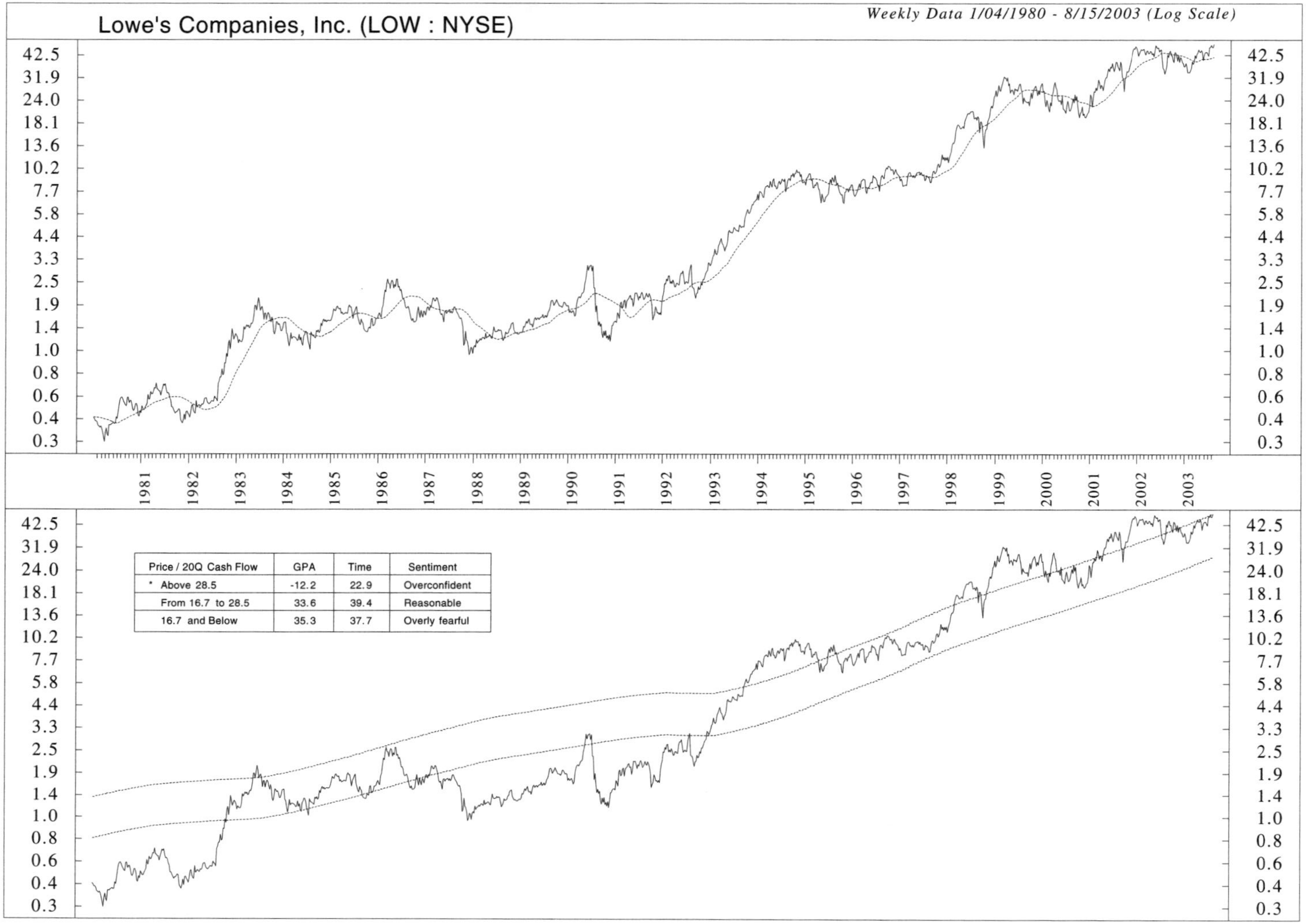

Price / 20Q Cash Flow	GPA	Time	Sentiment
* Above 28.5	-12.2	22.9	Overconfident
From 16.7 to 28.5	33.6	39.4	Reasonable
16.7 and Below	35.3	37.7	Overly fearful

FIGURE A-70 May Department Stores Company (MAY).
© 2003 Ned Davis Research, Inc. All rights reserved.

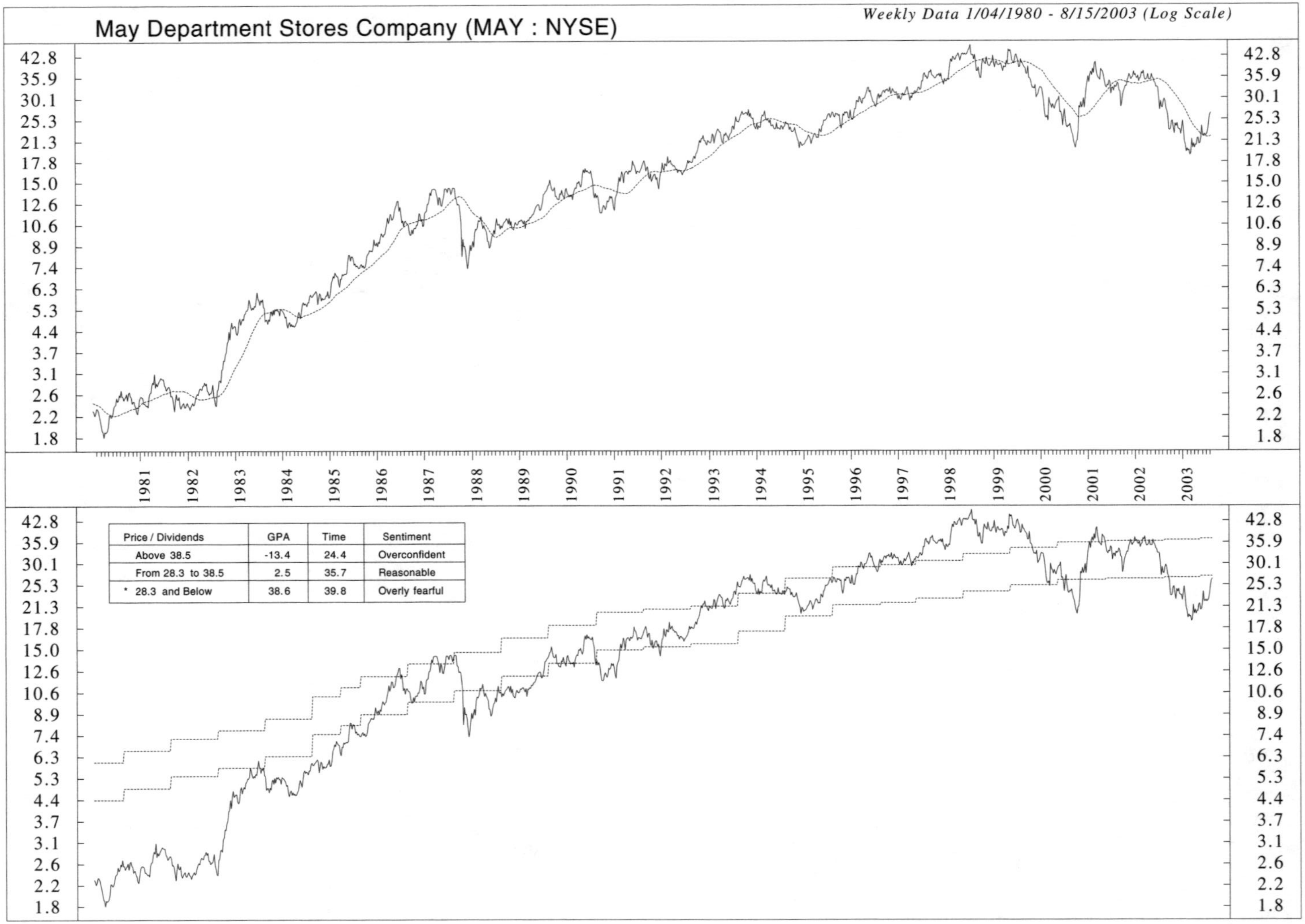

May Department Stores Company (MAY : NYSE)

Weekly Data 1/04/1980 - 8/15/2003 (Log Scale)

Price / Dividends	GPA	Time	Sentiment
Above 38.5	-13.4	24.4	Overconfident
From 28.3 to 38.5	2.5	35.7	Reasonable
* 28.3 and Below	38.6	39.8	Overly fearful

FIGURE A-71 McDonald's Corporation (MCD).
© 2003 Ned Davis Research, Inc. All rights reserved.

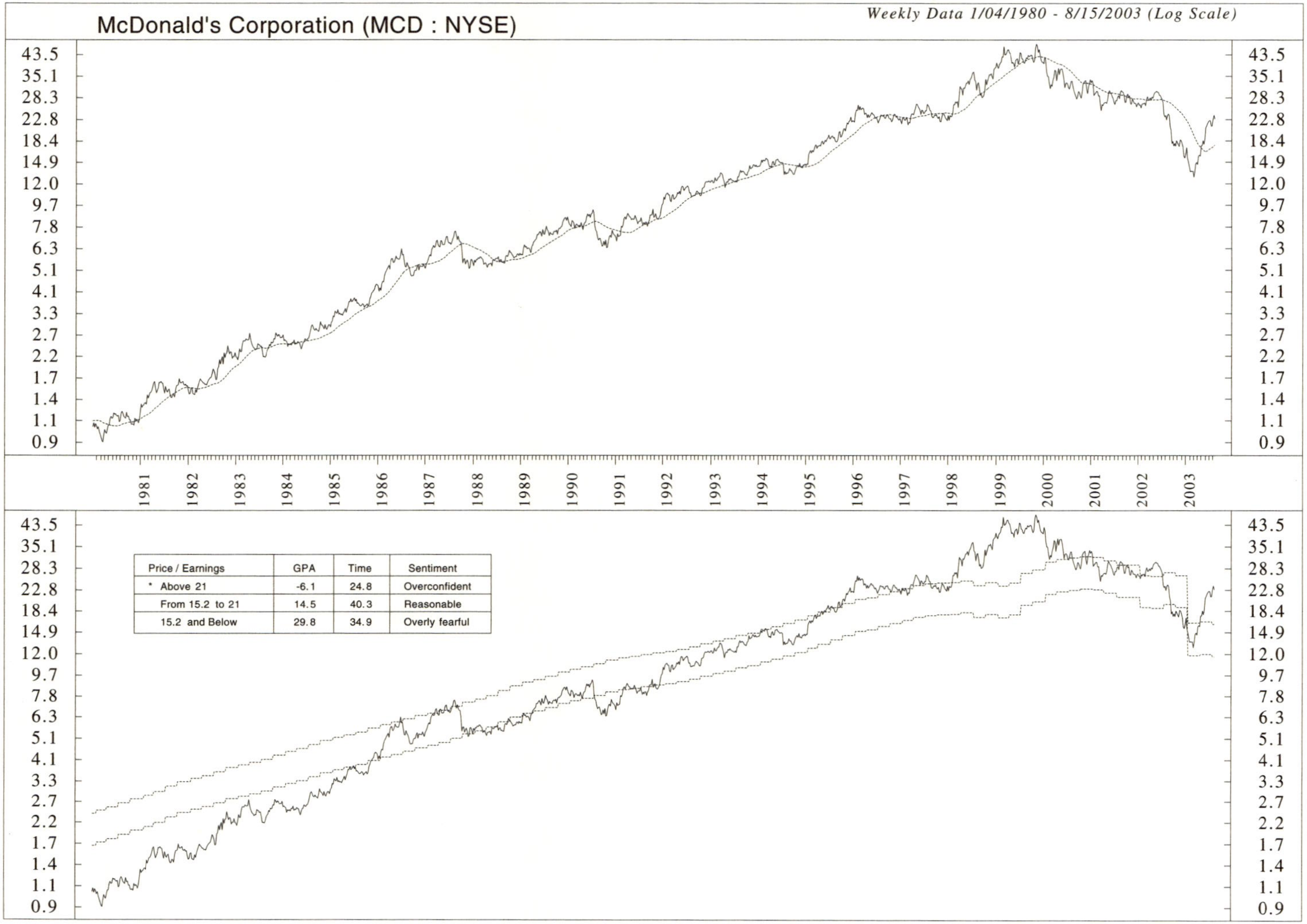

McDonald's Corporation (MCD : NYSE) — Weekly Data 1/04/1980 - 8/15/2003 (Log Scale)

Price / Earnings	GPA	Time	Sentiment
* Above 21	-6.1	24.8	Overconfident
From 15.2 to 21	14.5	40.3	Reasonable
15.2 and Below	29.8	34.9	Overly fearful

FIGURE A-72 McGraw-Hill Companies, Inc. (MHP).
© 2003 Ned Davis Research, Inc. All rights reserved.

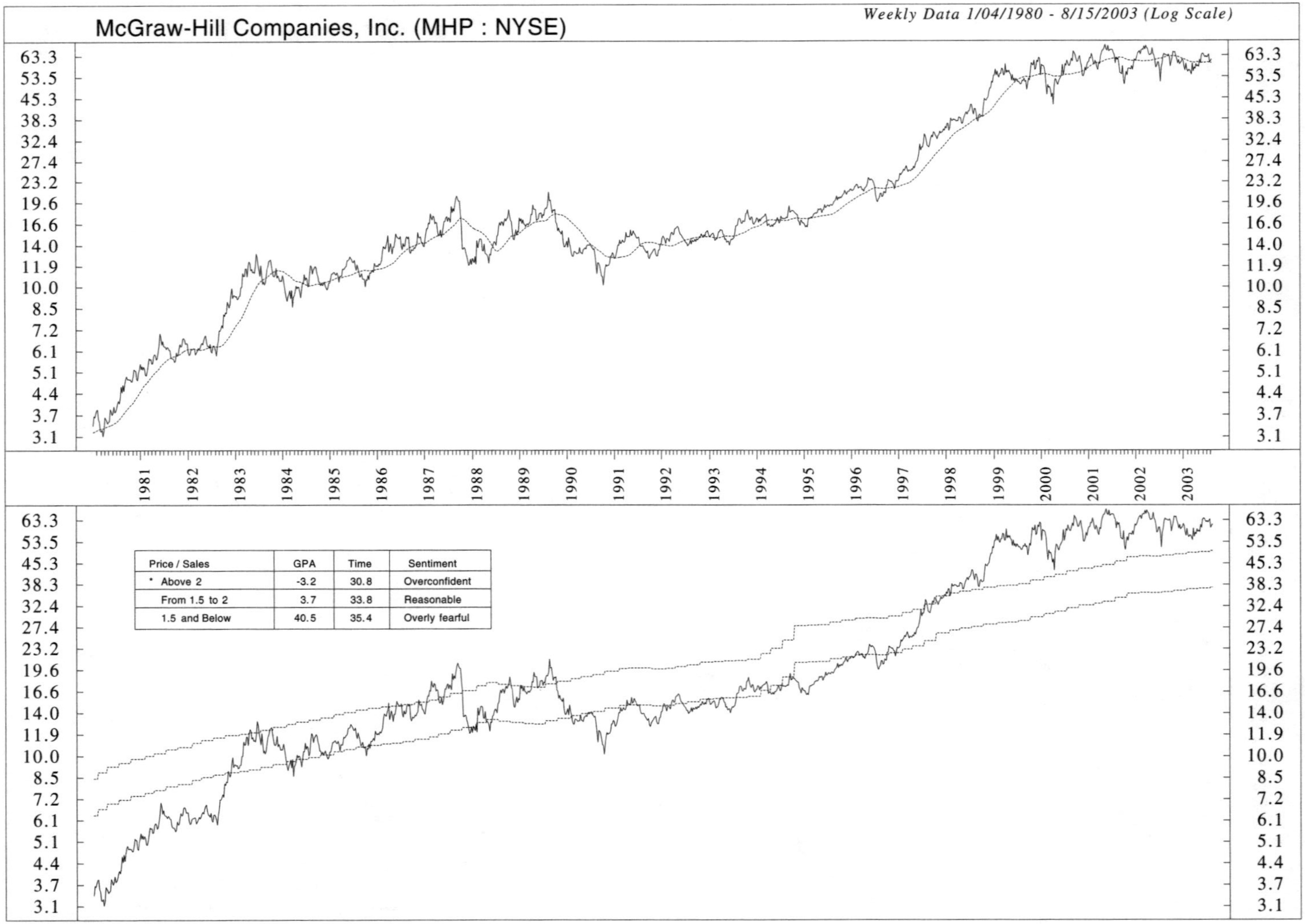

Price / Sales	GPA	Time	Sentiment
* Above 2	-3.2	30.8	Overconfident
From 1.5 to 2	3.7	33.8	Reasonable
1.5 and Below	40.5	35.4	Overly fearful

FIGURE A-73 MedImmune, Inc. (MEDI).
© 2003 Ned Davis Research, Inc. All rights reserved.

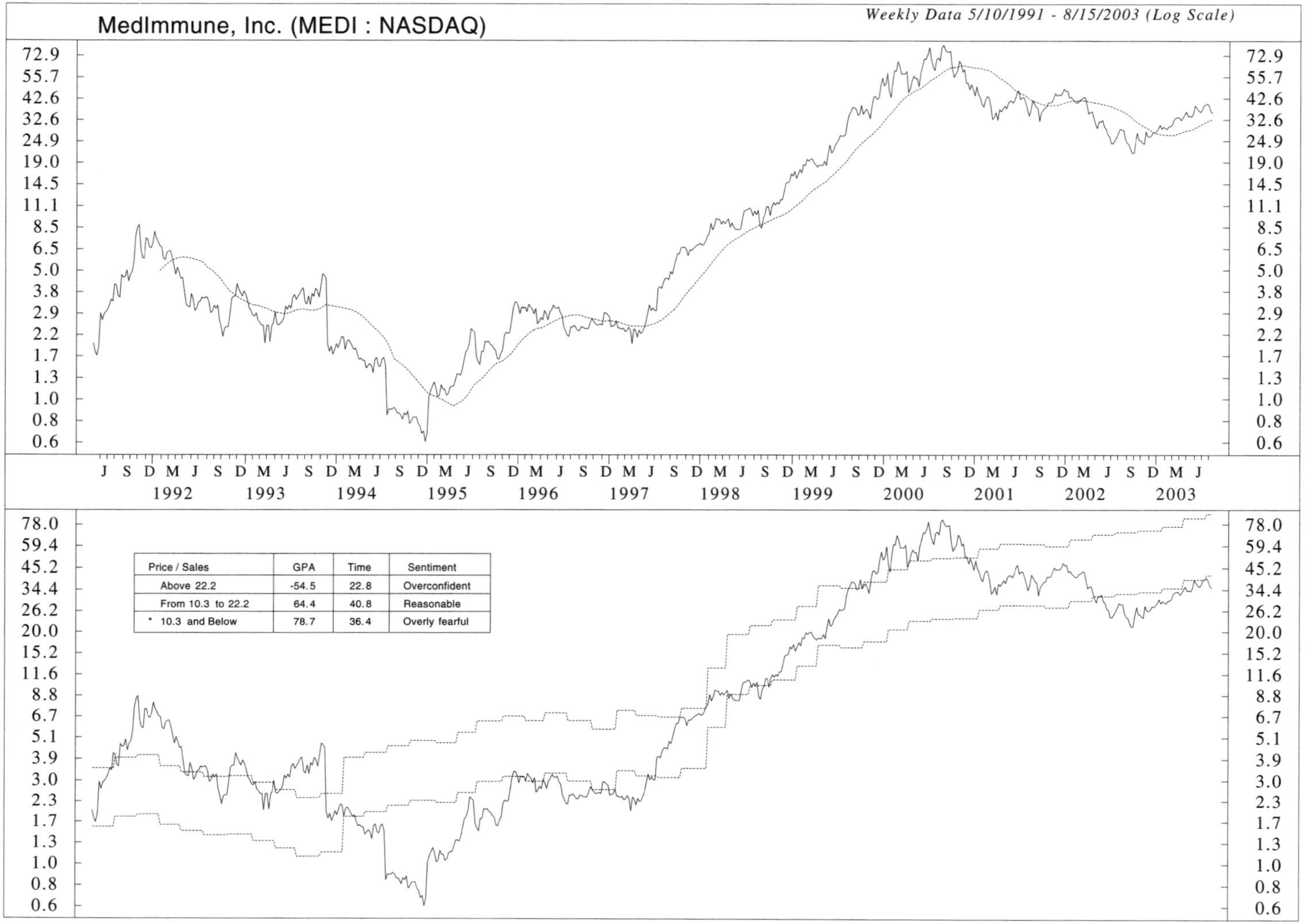

MedImmune, Inc. (MEDI : NASDAQ)

Weekly Data 5/10/1991 - 8/15/2003 (Log Scale)

Price / Sales	GPA	Time	Sentiment
Above 22.2	-54.5	22.8	Overconfident
From 10.3 to 22.2	64.4	40.8	Reasonable
* 10.3 and Below	78.7	36.4	Overly fearful

FIGURE A-74 Merck and Company, Inc. (MRK).
© 2003 Ned Davis Research, Inc. All rights reserved.

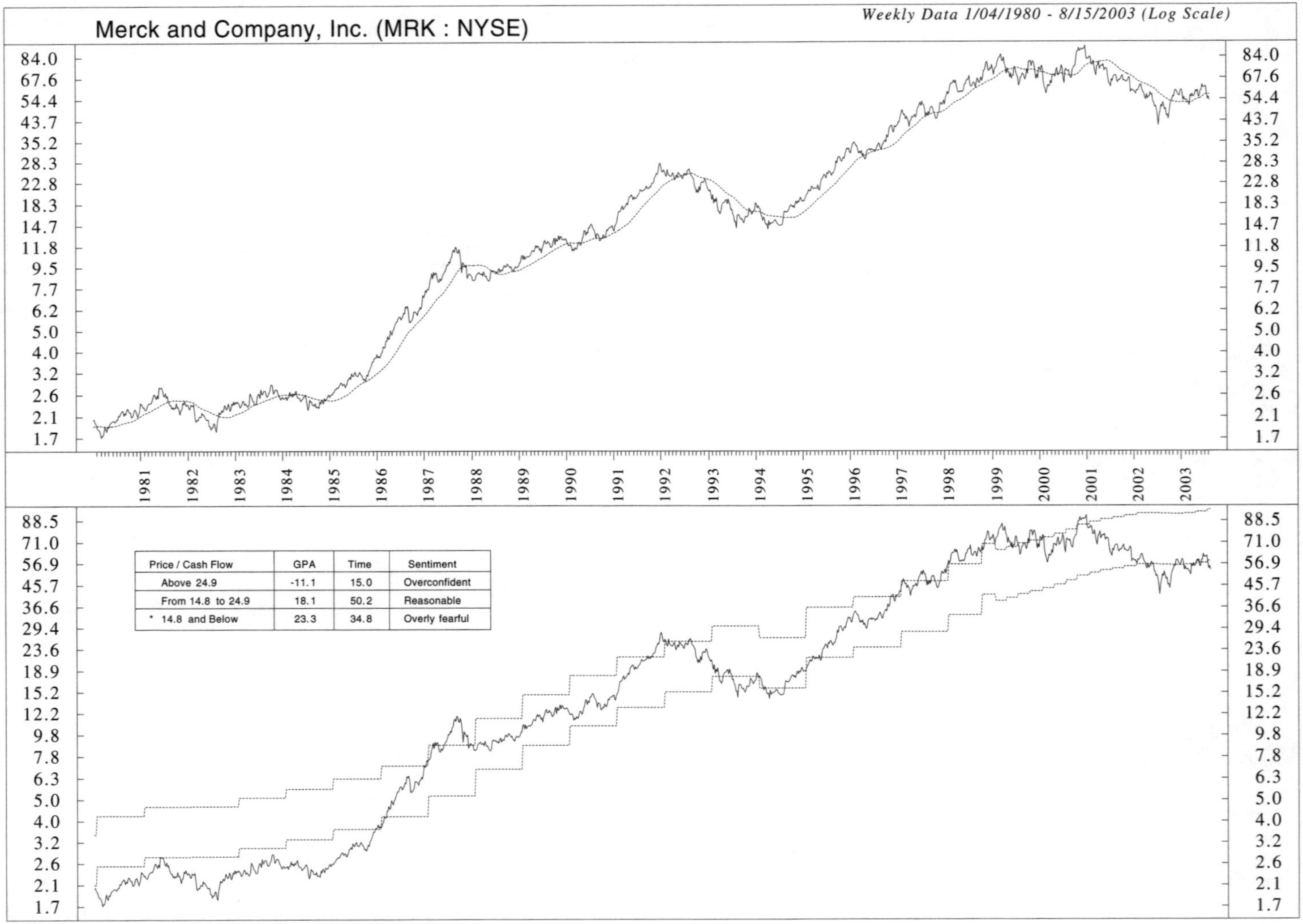

Price / Cash Flow	GPA	Time	Sentiment
Above 24.9	-11.1	15.0	Overconfident
From 14.8 to 24.9	18.1	50.2	Reasonable
* 14.8 and Below	23.3	34.8	Overly fearful

FIGURE A-75 Merrill Lynch and Company (MER).
© 2003 Ned Davis Research, Inc. All rights reserved.

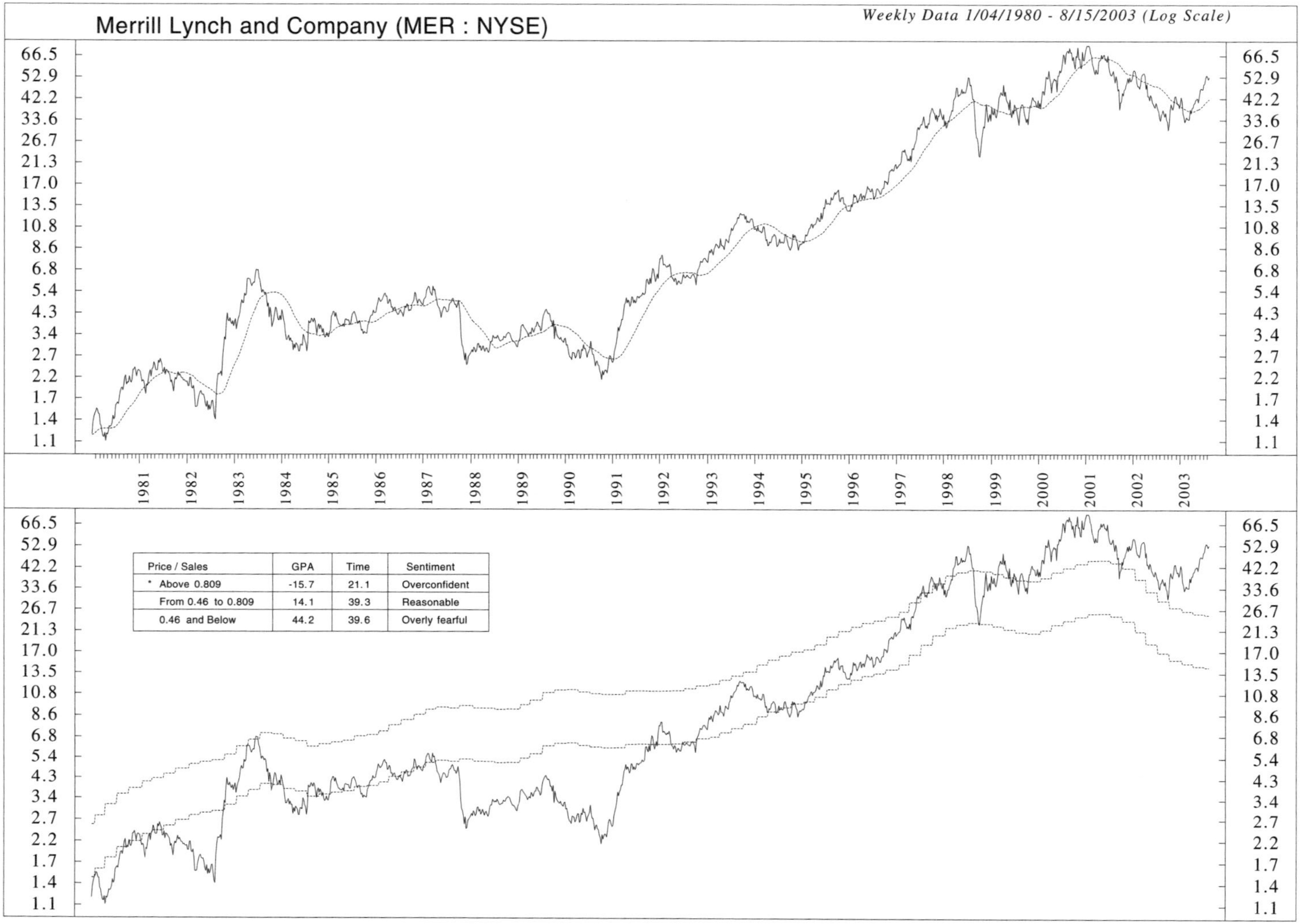

145

FIGURE A-76 Microsoft Corporation (MSFT).
© 2003 Ned Davis Research, Inc. All rights reserved.

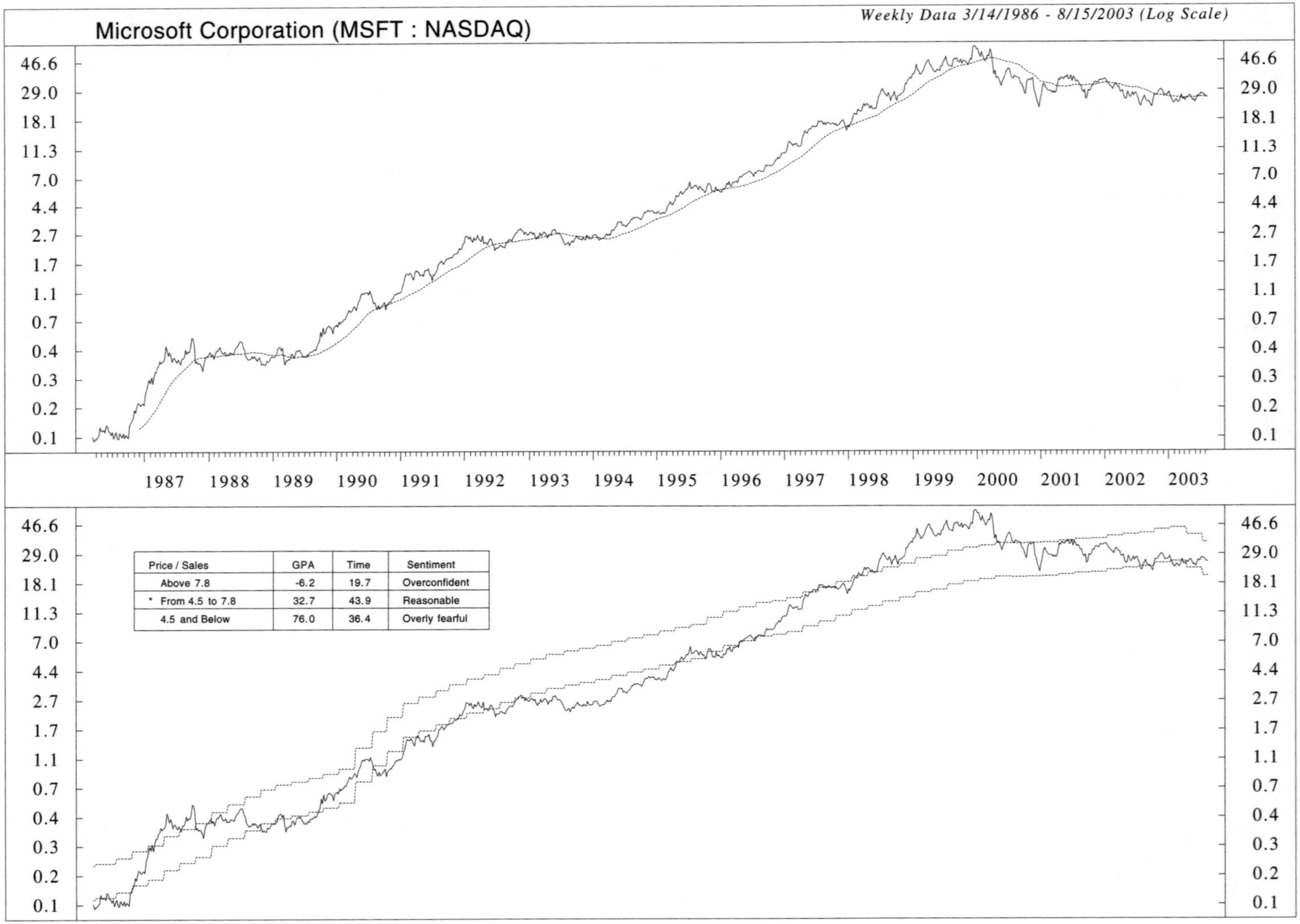

Price / Sales	GPA	Time	Sentiment
Above 7.8	-6.2	19.7	Overconfident
From 4.5 to 7.8	32.7	43.9	Reasonable
4.5 and Below	76.0	36.4	Overly fearful

FIGURE A-77 Motorola, Inc. (MOT).
© 2003 Ned Davis Research, Inc. All rights reserved.

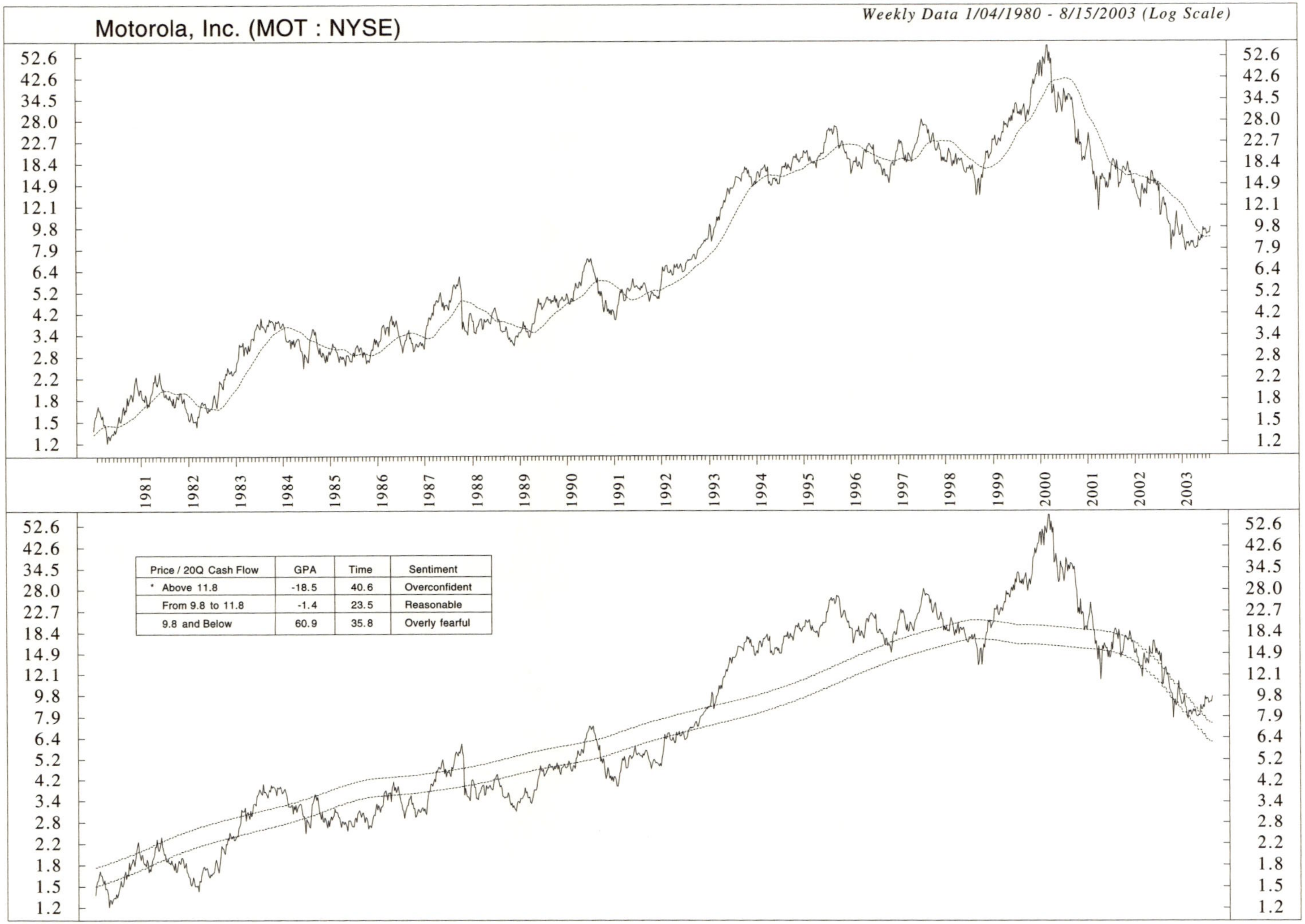

FIGURE A-78 National Semiconductor Corporation (NSM).

© 2003 Ned Davis Research, Inc. All rights reserved.

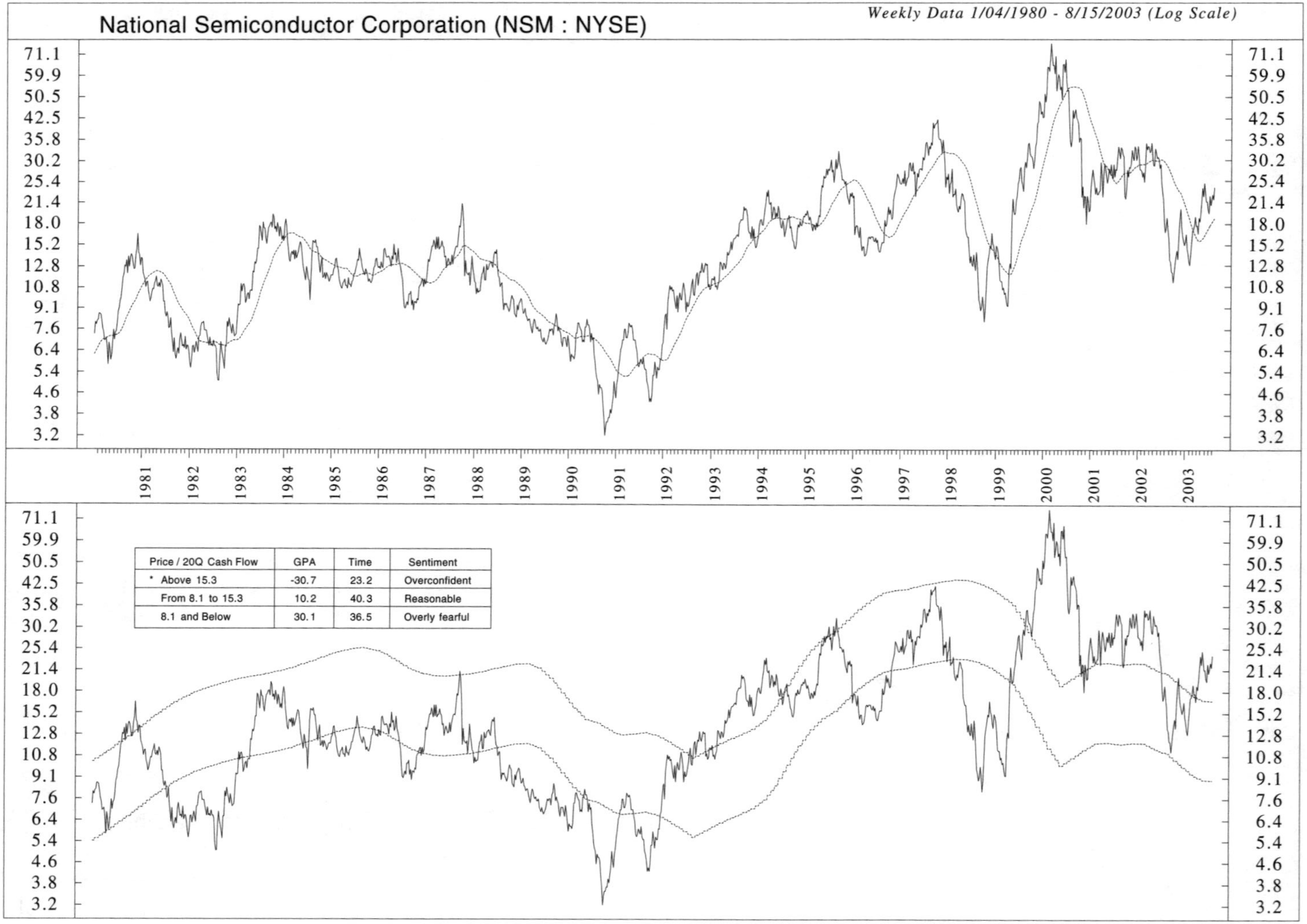

FIGURE A-79 Newell Rubbermaid, Inc. (NWL).
© 2003 Ned Davis Research, Inc. All rights reserved.

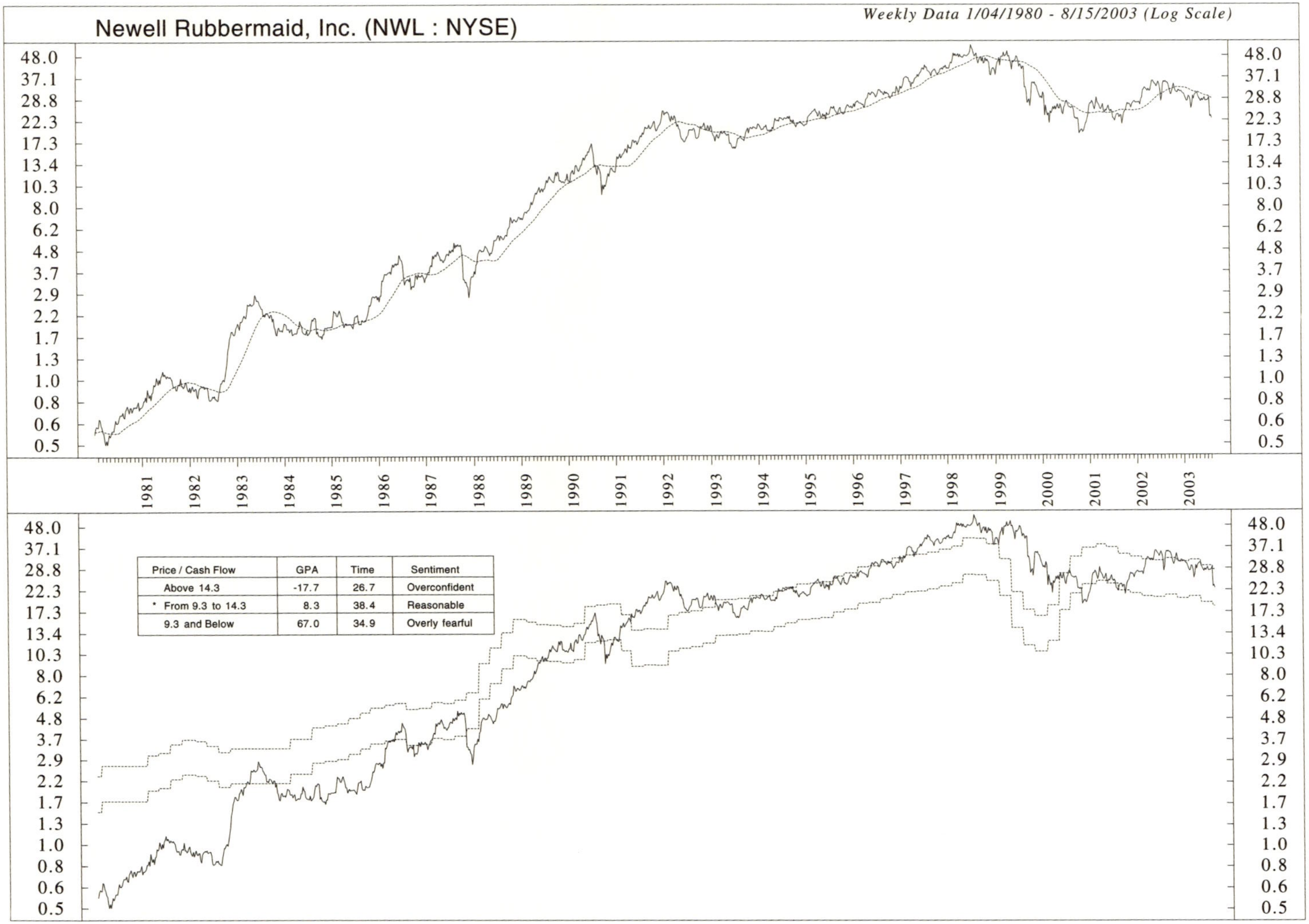

FIGURE A-80 Oracle Corporation (ORCL).
© 2003 Ned Davis Research, Inc. All rights reserved.

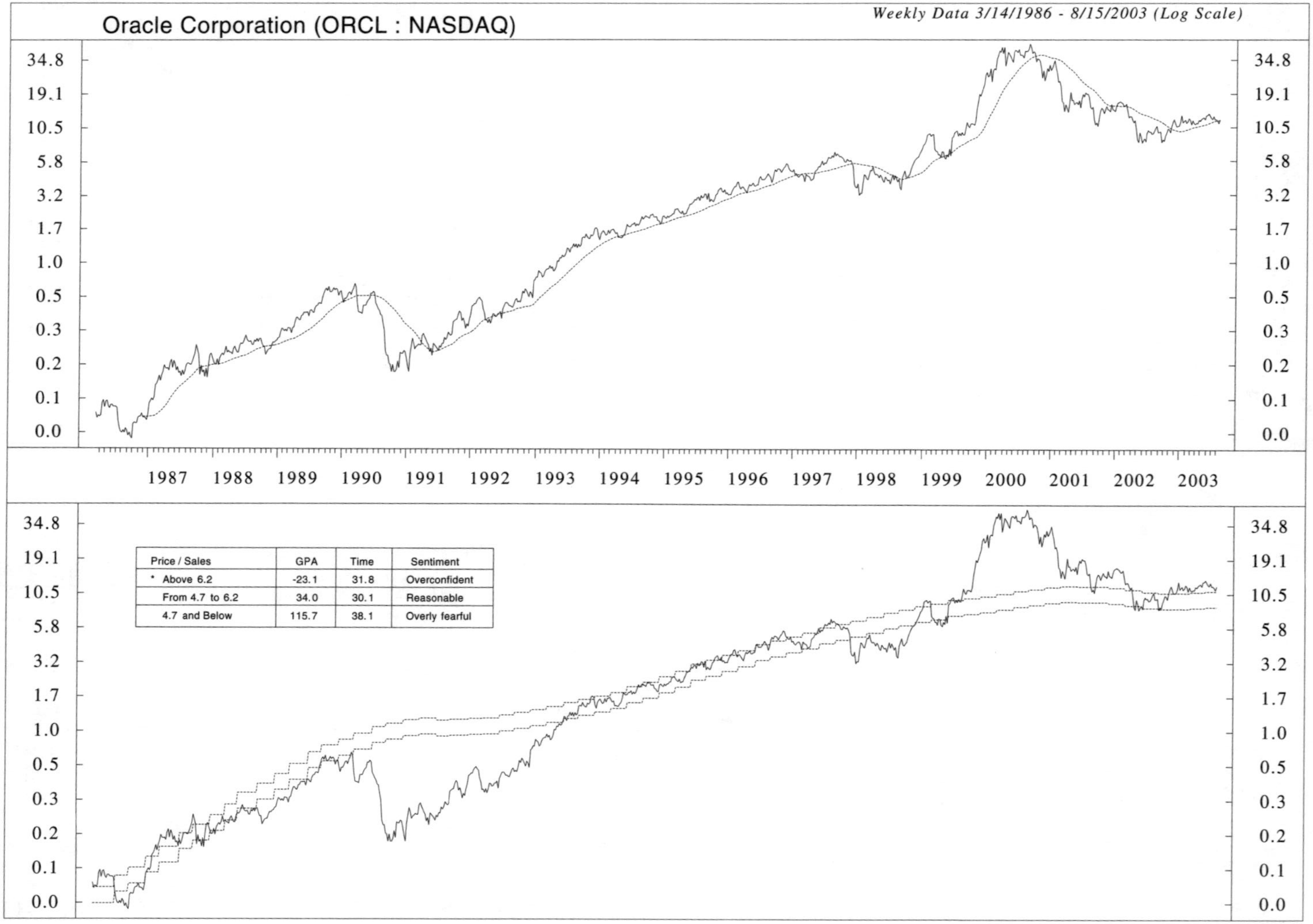

Price / Sales	GPA	Time	Sentiment
* Above 6.2	-23.1	31.8	Overconfident
From 4.7 to 6.2	34.0	30.1	Reasonable
4.7 and Below	115.7	38.1	Overly fearful

150

FIGURE A-81 PPG Industries, Inc. (PPG).

© 2003 Ned Davis Research, Inc. All rights reserved.

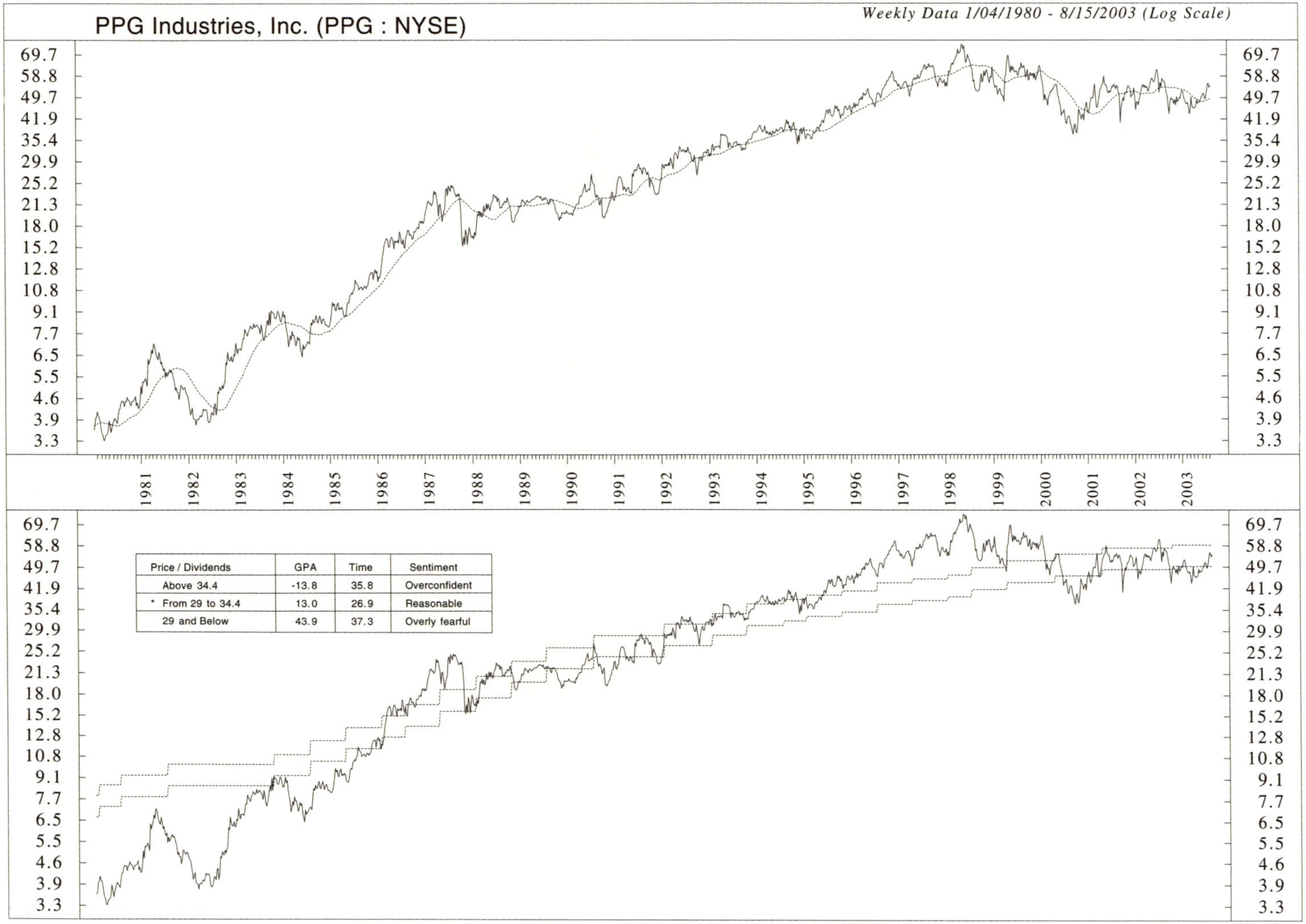

Price / Dividends	GPA	Time	Sentiment
Above 34.4	-13.8	35.8	Overconfident
From 29 to 34.4	13.0	26.9	Reasonable
29 and Below	43.9	37.3	Overly fearful

151

FIGURE A-82 PepsiCo, Inc. (PEP).
© *2003 Ned Davis Research, Inc. All rights reserved.*

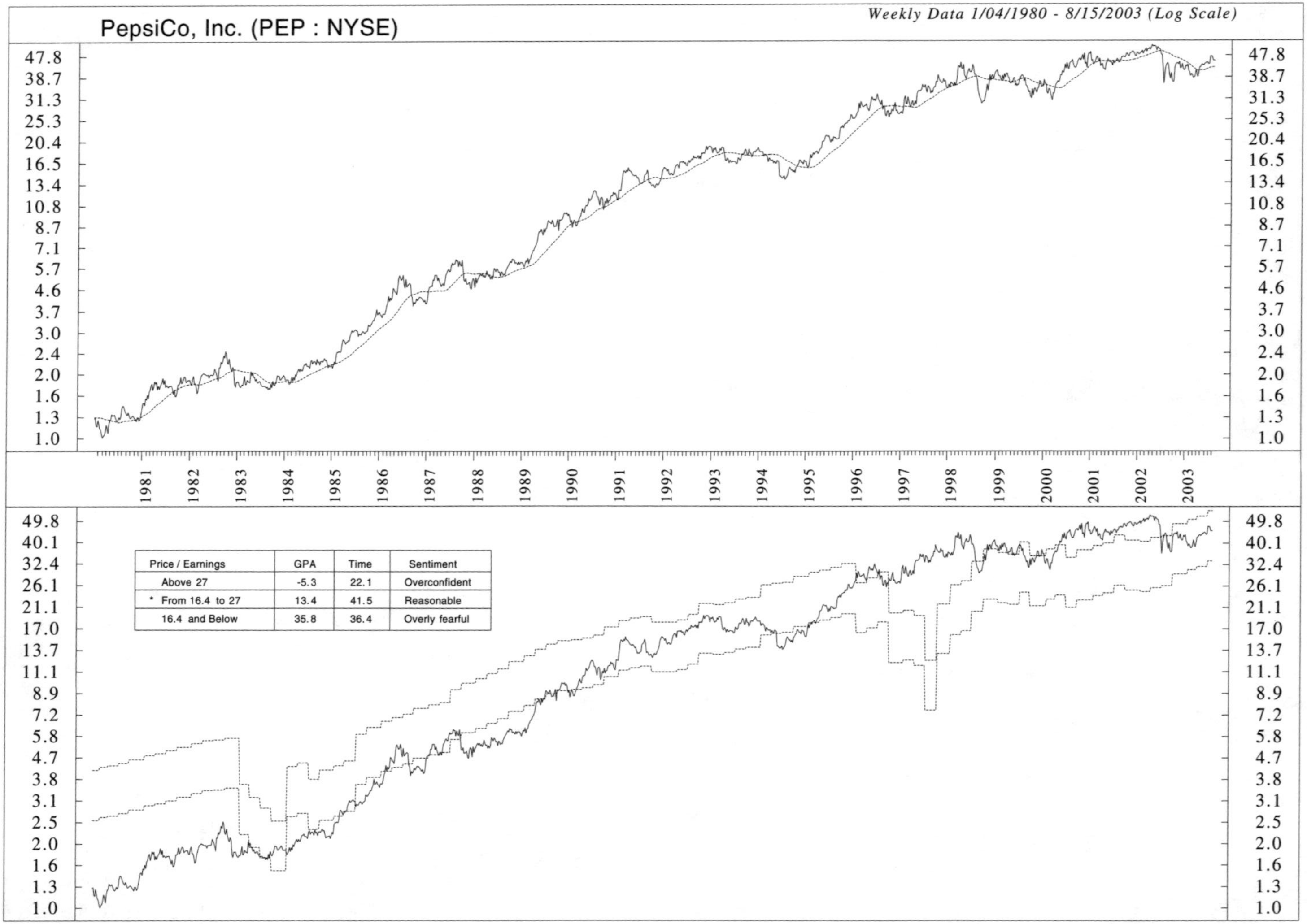

PepsiCo, Inc. (PEP : NYSE) — Weekly Data 1/04/1980 - 8/15/2003 (Log Scale)

Price / Earnings	GPA	Time	Sentiment
Above 27	-5.3	22.1	Overconfident
* From 16.4 to 27	13.4	41.5	Reasonable
16.4 and Below	35.8	36.4	Overly fearful

152

FIGURE A-83 Progressive Corporation, The (PGR).
© 2003 Ned Davis Research, Inc. All rights reserved.

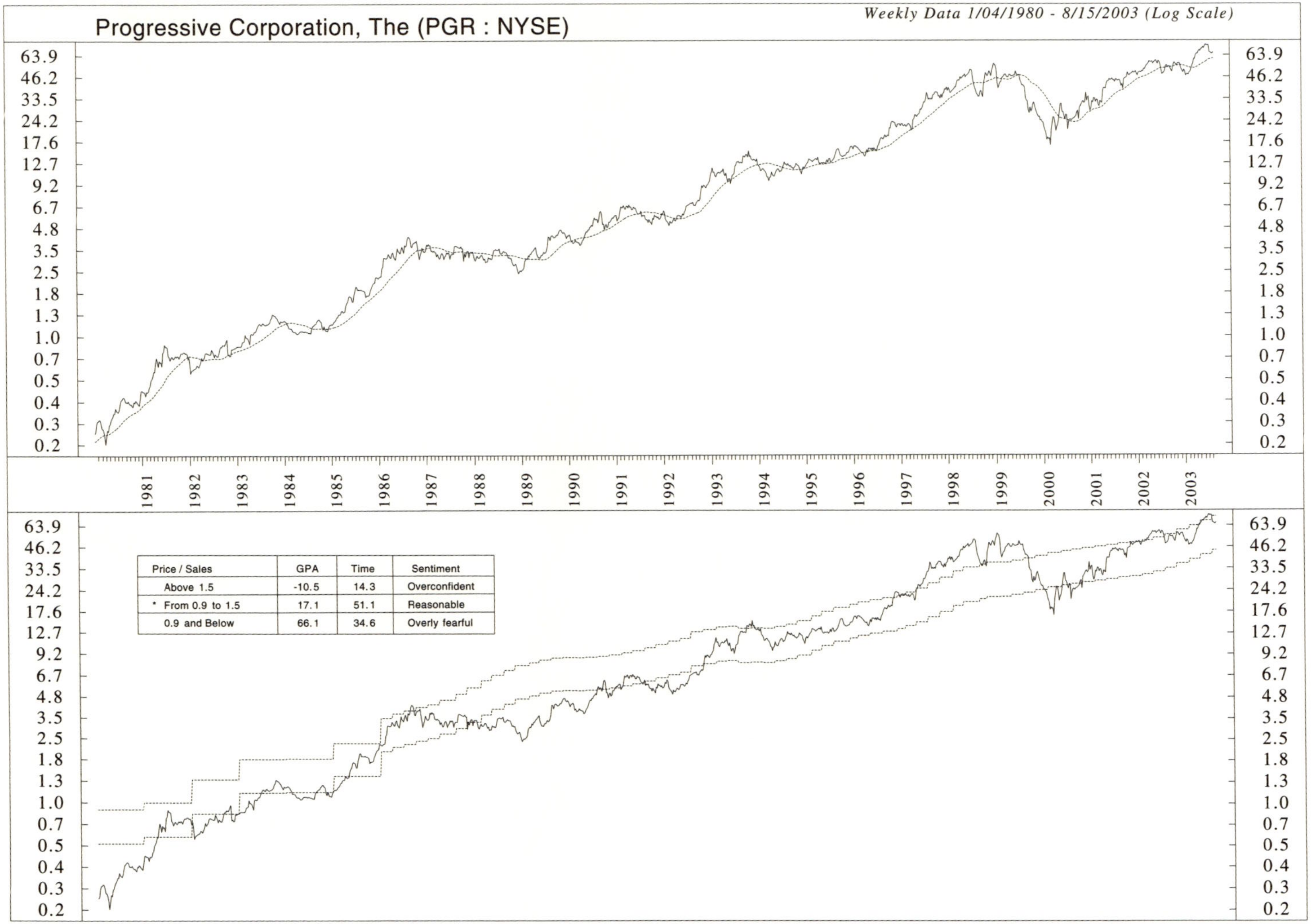

Progressive Corporation, The (PGR : NYSE)   Weekly Data 1/04/1980 - 8/15/2003 (Log Scale)

Price / Sales	GPA	Time	Sentiment
Above 1.5	-10.5	14.3	Overconfident
* From 0.9 to 1.5	17.1	51.1	Reasonable
0.9 and Below	66.1	34.6	Overly fearful

FIGURE A-84 RadioShack Corporation (RSH).
© 2003 Ned Davis Research, Inc. All rights reserved.

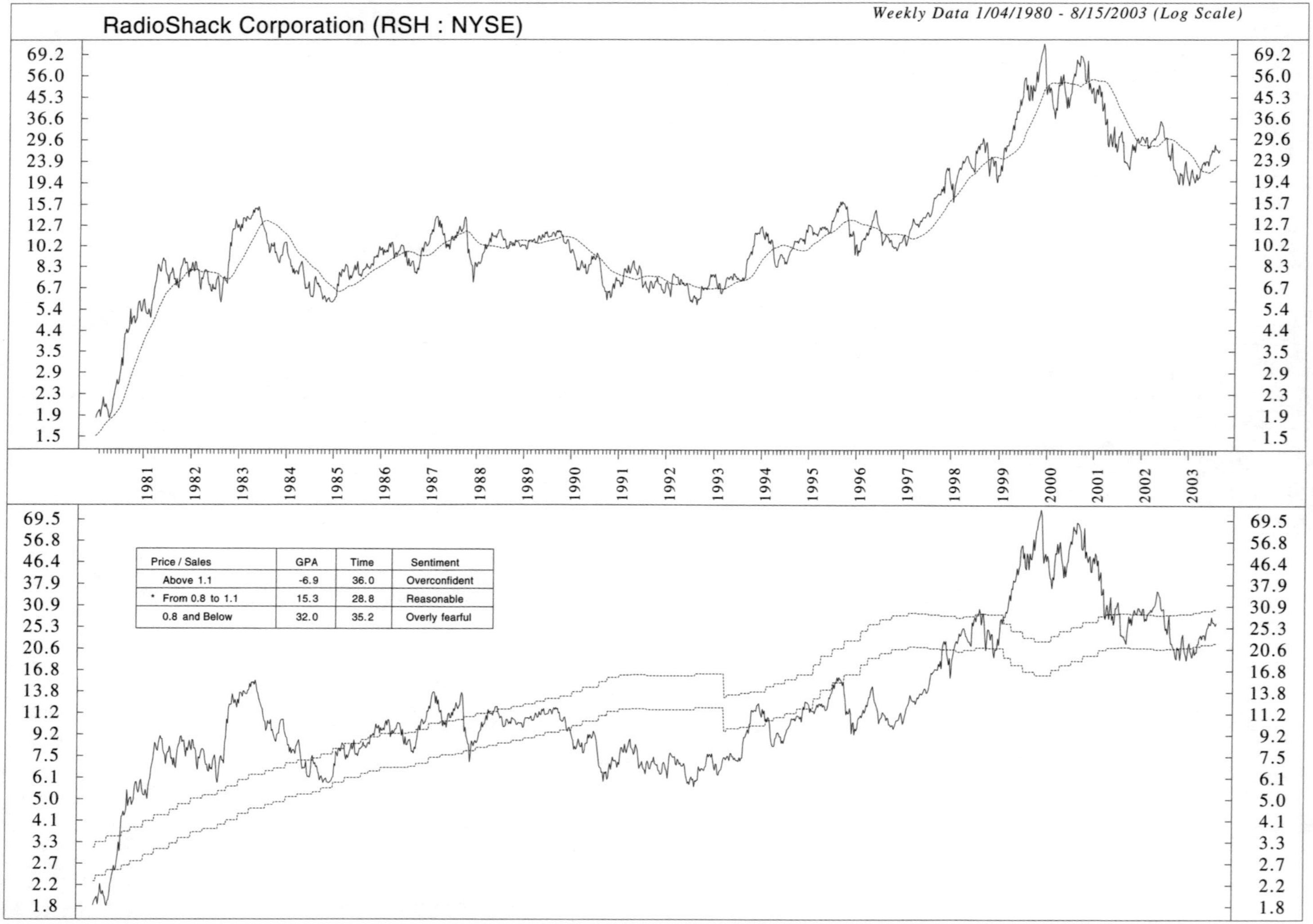

Price / Sales	GPA	Time	Sentiment
Above 1.1	-6.9	36.0	Overconfident
* From 0.8 to 1.1	15.3	28.8	Reasonable
0.8 and Below	32.0	35.2	Overly fearful

FIGURE A-85 Rohm and Haas Company (ROH).
© 2003 Ned Davis Research, Inc. All rights reserved.

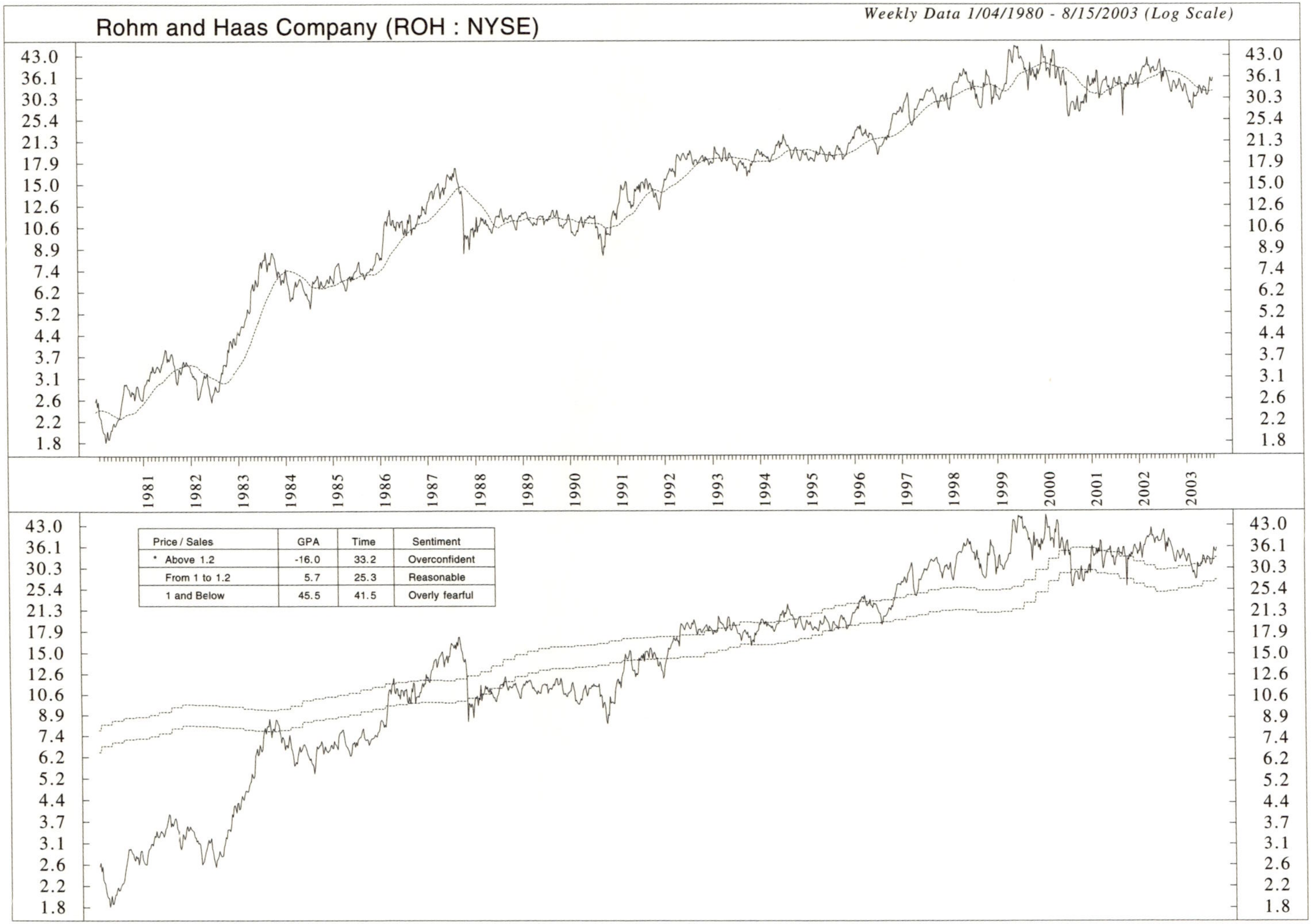

FIGURE A-86 Sara Lee Corporation (SLE).
© 2003 Ned Davis Research, Inc. All rights reserved.

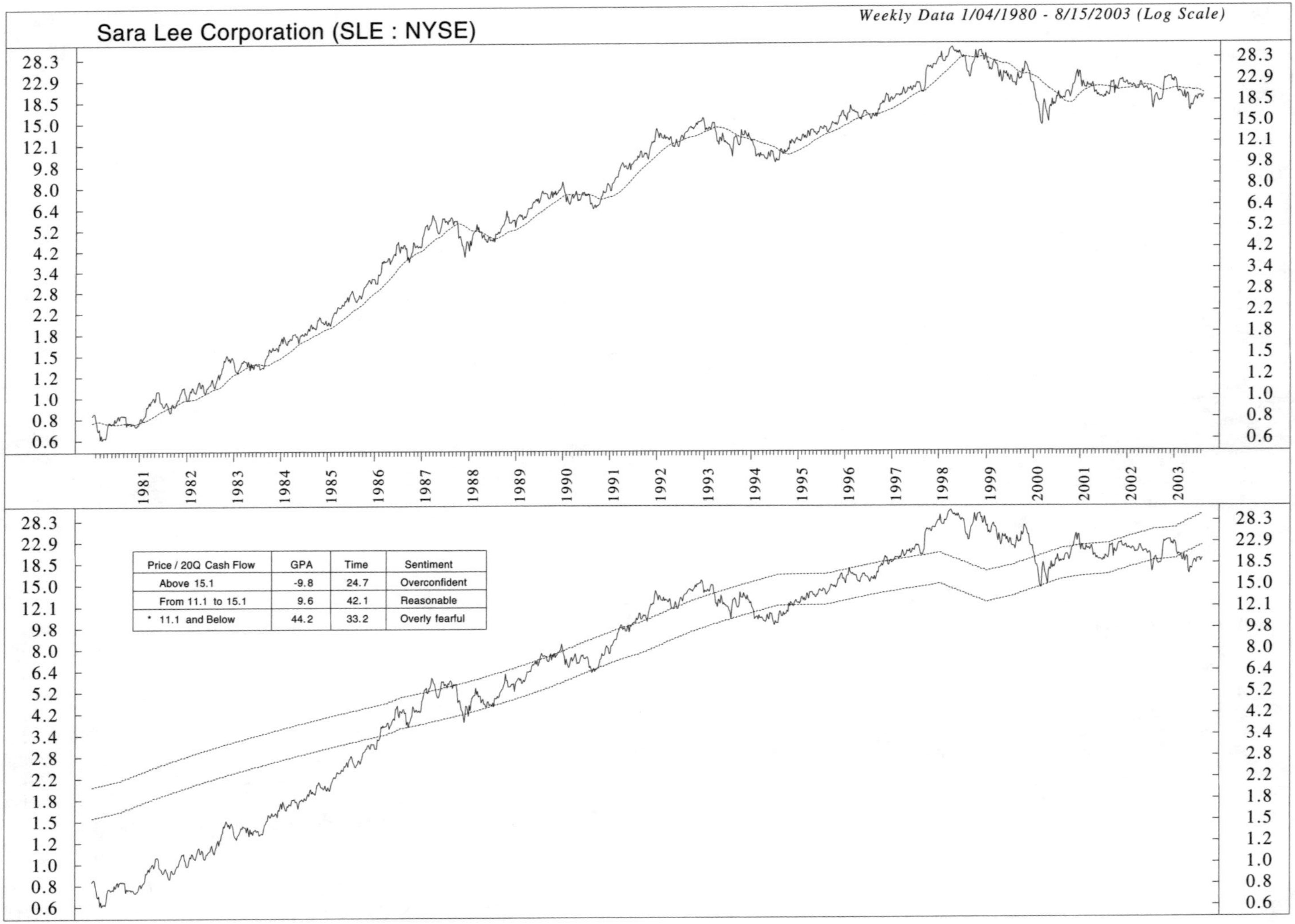

Sara Lee Corporation (SLE : NYSE)

Weekly Data 1/04/1980 - 8/15/2003 (Log Scale)

Price / 20Q Cash Flow	GPA	Time	Sentiment
Above 15.1	-9.8	24.7	Overconfident
From 11.1 to 15.1	9.6	42.1	Reasonable
* 11.1 and Below	44.2	33.2	Overly fearful

FIGURE A-87 Schering-Plough Corporation (SGP).
© 2003 Ned Davis Research, Inc. All rights reserved.

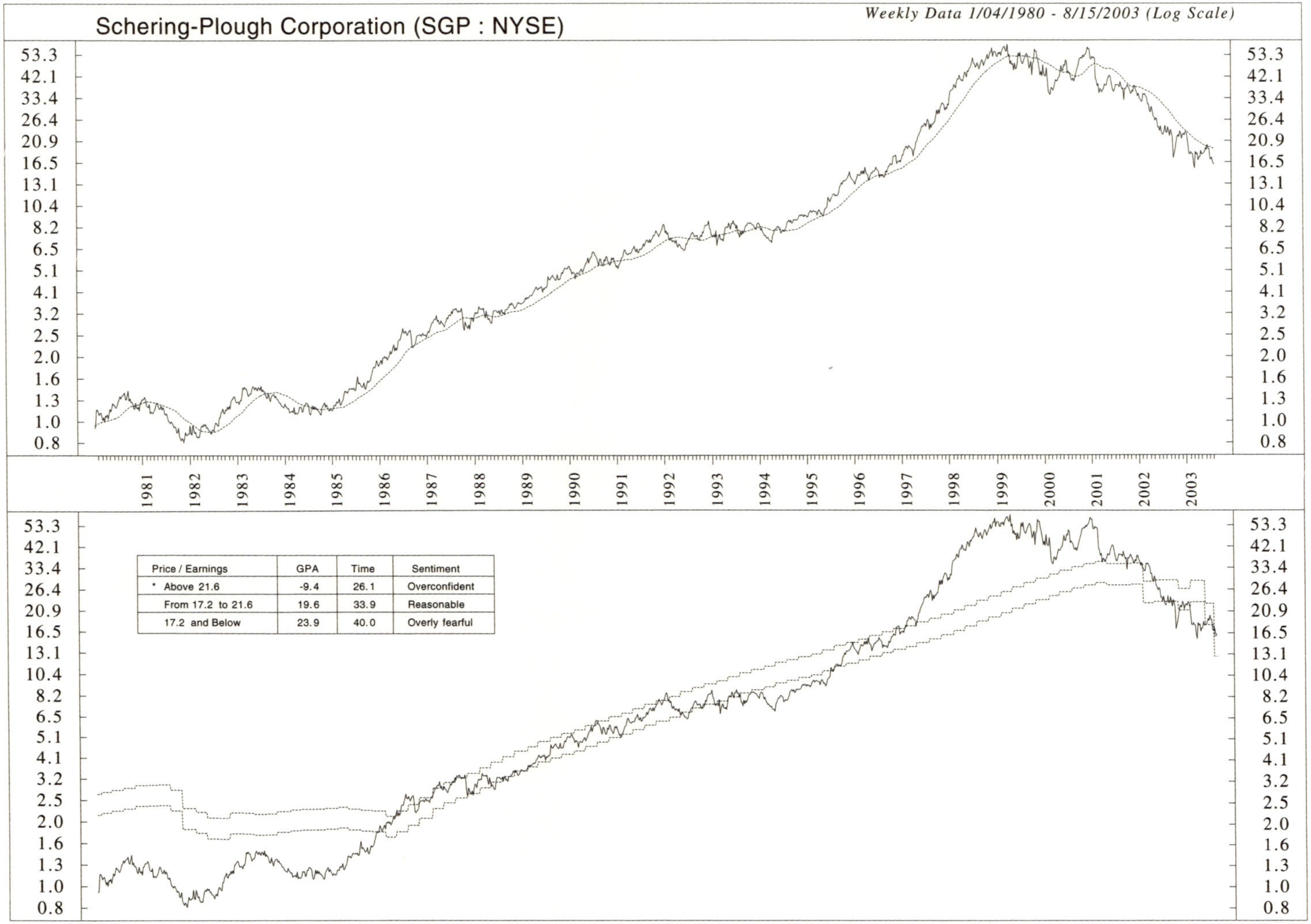

157

FIGURE A-88 Schlumberger Limited (SLB).
© 2003 Ned Davis Research, Inc. All rights reserved.

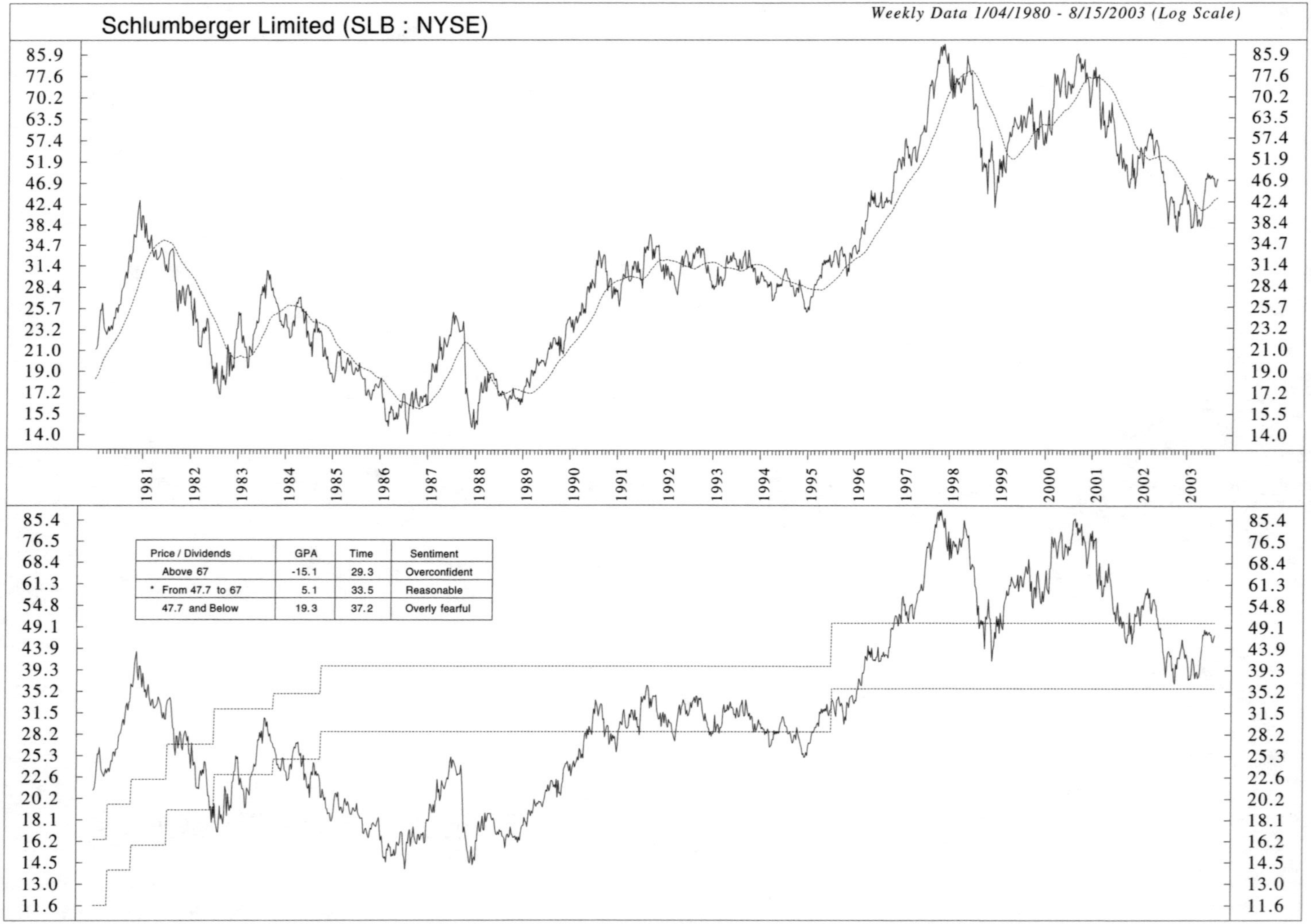

Price / Dividends	GPA	Time	Sentiment
Above 67	-15.1	29.3	Overconfident
From 47.7 to 67	5.1	33.5	Reasonable
47.7 and Below	19.3	37.2	Overly fearful

158

FIGURE A-89 St. Paul Companies, Inc., The (SPC).
© 2003 Ned Davis Research, Inc. All rights reserved.

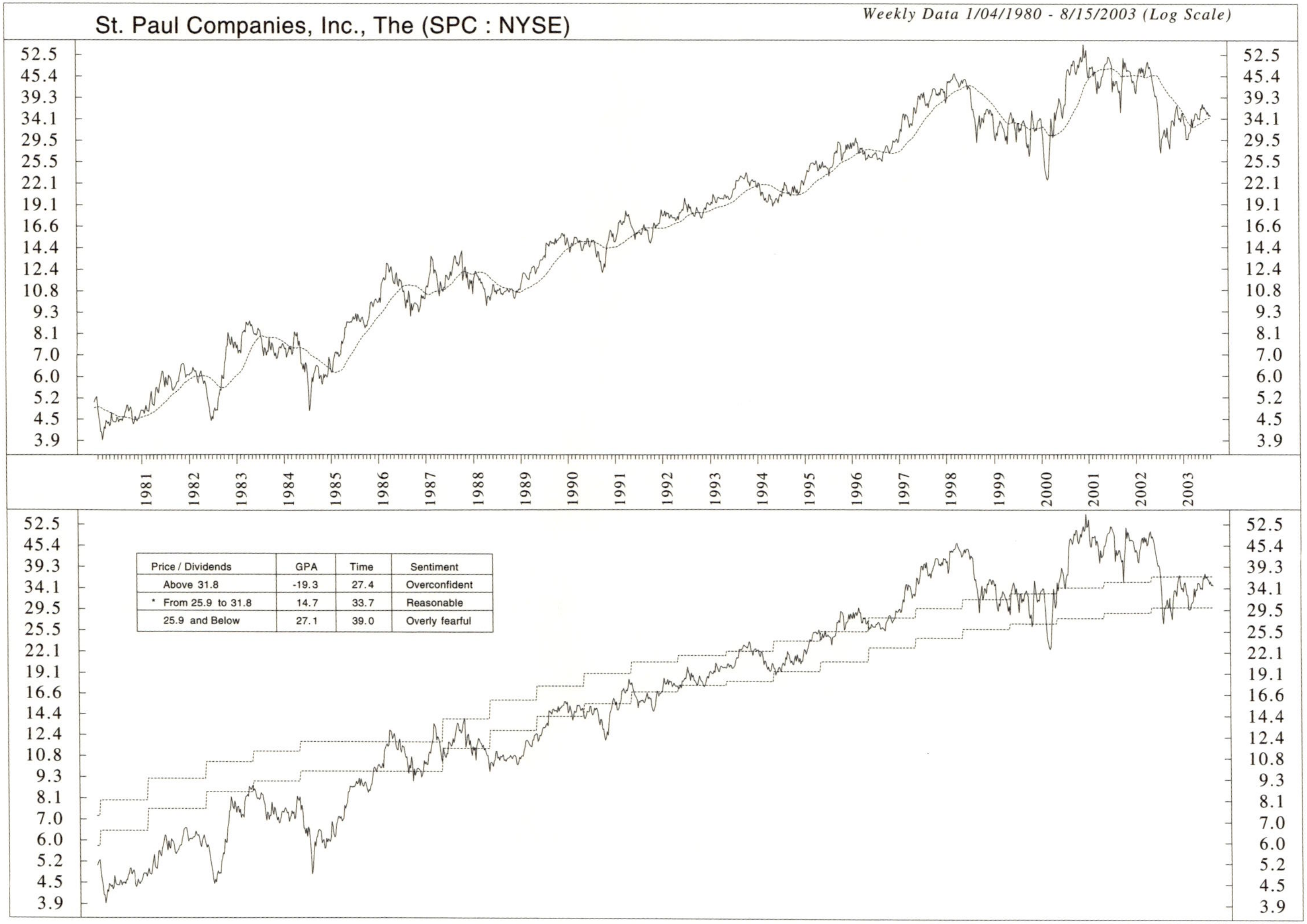

St. Paul Companies, Inc., The (SPC : NYSE) — Weekly Data 1/04/1980 - 8/15/2003 (Log Scale)

Price / Dividends	GPA	Time	Sentiment
Above 31.8	-19.3	27.4	Overconfident
* From 25.9 to 31.8	14.7	33.7	Reasonable
25.9 and Below	27.1	39.0	Overly fearful

FIGURE A-90 Sysco Corporation (SYY).
© 2003 Ned Davis Research, Inc. All rights reserved.

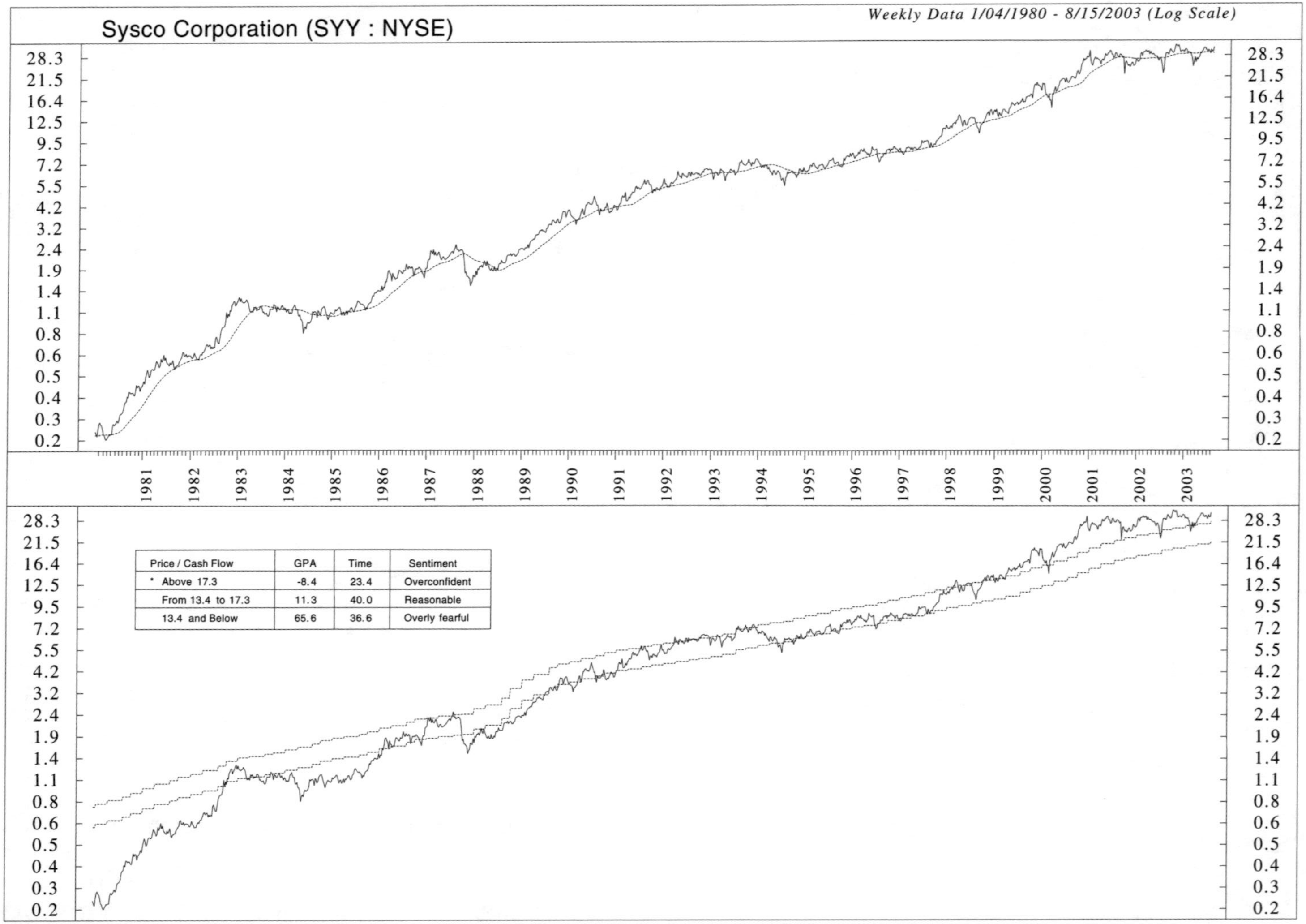

Price / Cash Flow	GPA	Time	Sentiment
* Above 17.3	-8.4	23.4	Overconfident
From 13.4 to 17.3	11.3	40.0	Reasonable
13.4 and Below	65.6	36.6	Overly fearful

FIGURE A-91 Target Corporation (TGT).
© 2003 Ned Davis Research, Inc. All rights reserved.

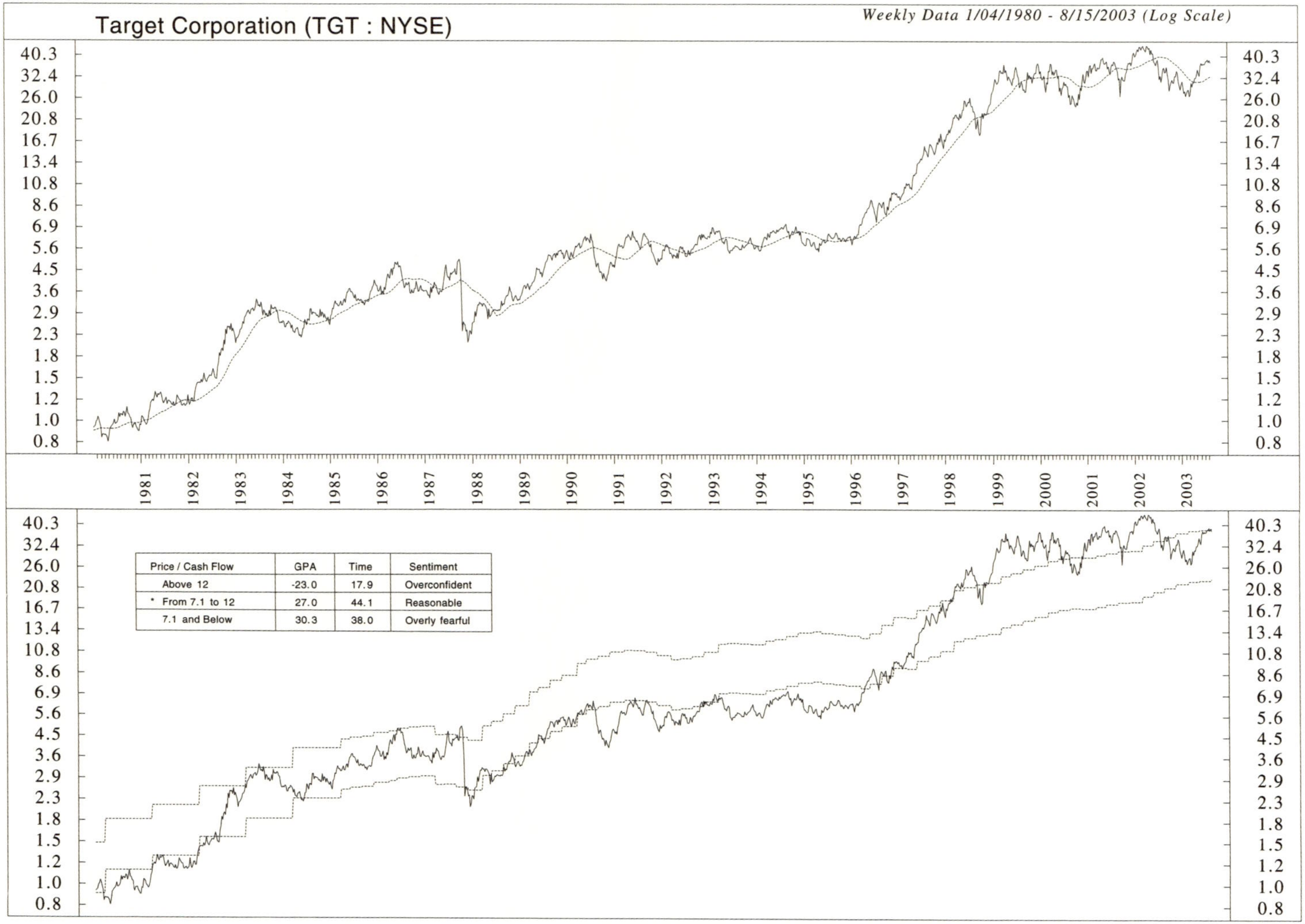

Price / Cash Flow	GPA	Time	Sentiment
Above 12	-23.0	17.9	Overconfident
* From 7.1 to 12	27.0	44.1	Reasonable
7.1 and Below	30.3	38.0	Overly fearful

FIGURE A-92 Union Pacific Corporation (UNP).
© 2003 Ned Davis Research, Inc. All rights reserved.

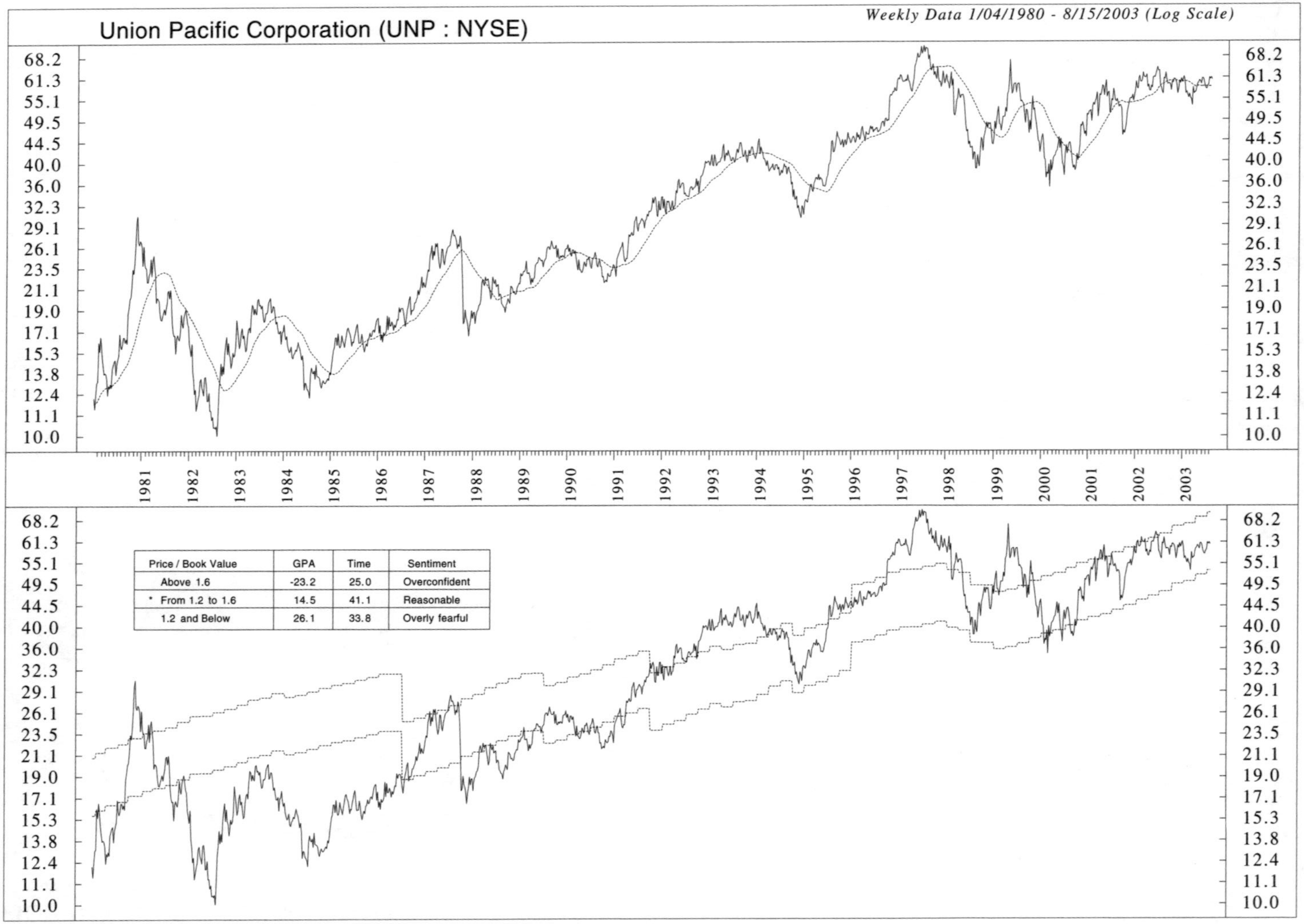

Union Pacific Corporation (UNP : NYSE)

Weekly Data 1/04/1980 - 8/15/2003 (Log Scale)

Price / Book Value	GPA	Time	Sentiment
Above 1.6	-23.2	25.0	Overconfident
* From 1.2 to 1.6	14.5	41.1	Reasonable
1.2 and Below	26.1	33.8	Overly fearful

FIGURE A-93 Verizon Communications, Inc. (VZ).

© 2003 Ned Davis Research, Inc. All rights reserved.

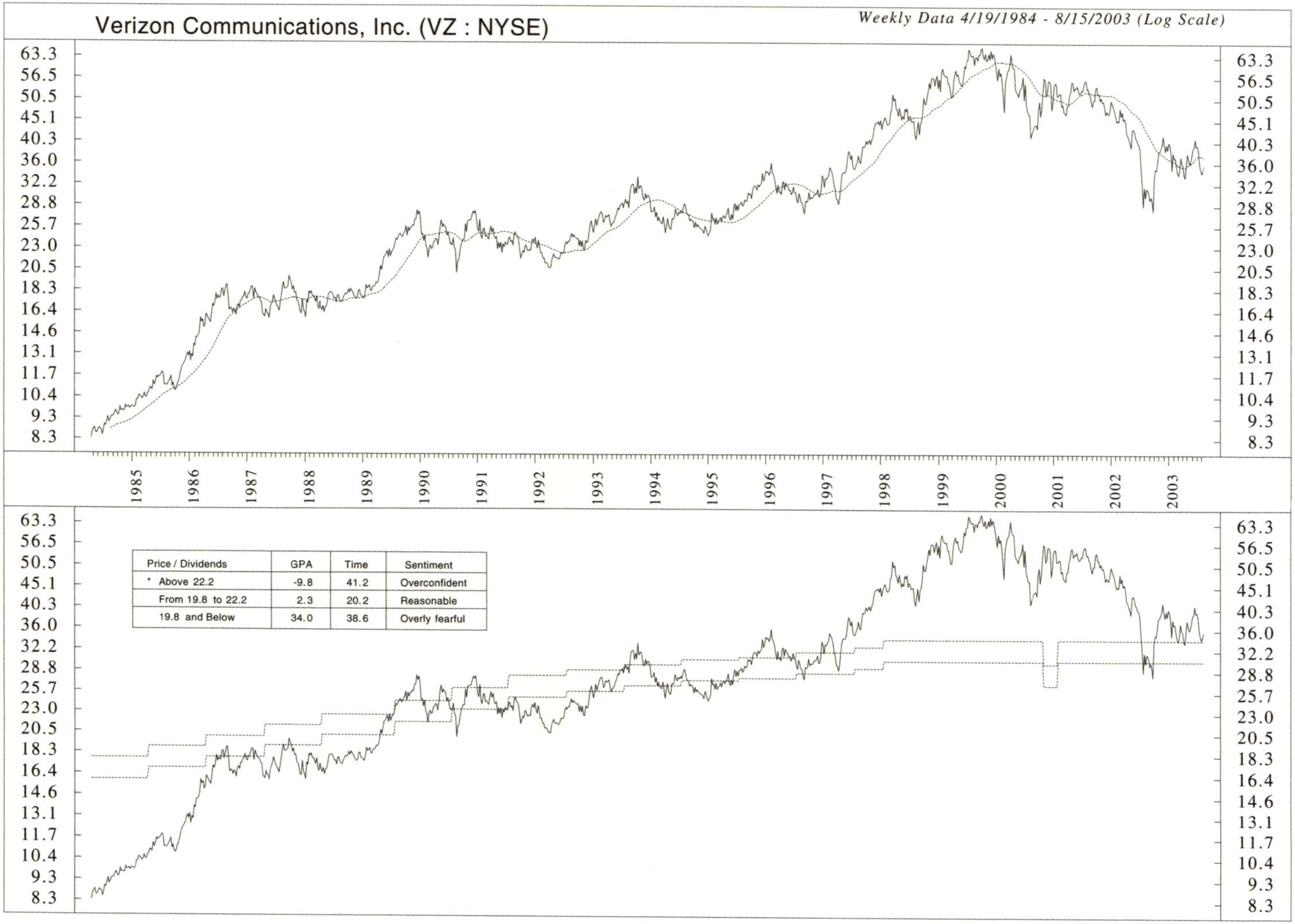

Weekly Data 4/19/1984 - 8/15/2003 (Log Scale)

Verizon Communications, Inc. (VZ : NYSE)

Price / Dividends	GPA	Time	Sentiment
* Above 22.2	-9.8	41.2	Overconfident
From 19.8 to 22.2	2.3	20.2	Reasonable
19.8 and Below	34.0	38.6	Overly fearful

FIGURE A-94 Viacom, Inc.—Class B (VIA.B).
© 2003 Ned Davis Research, Inc. All rights reserved.

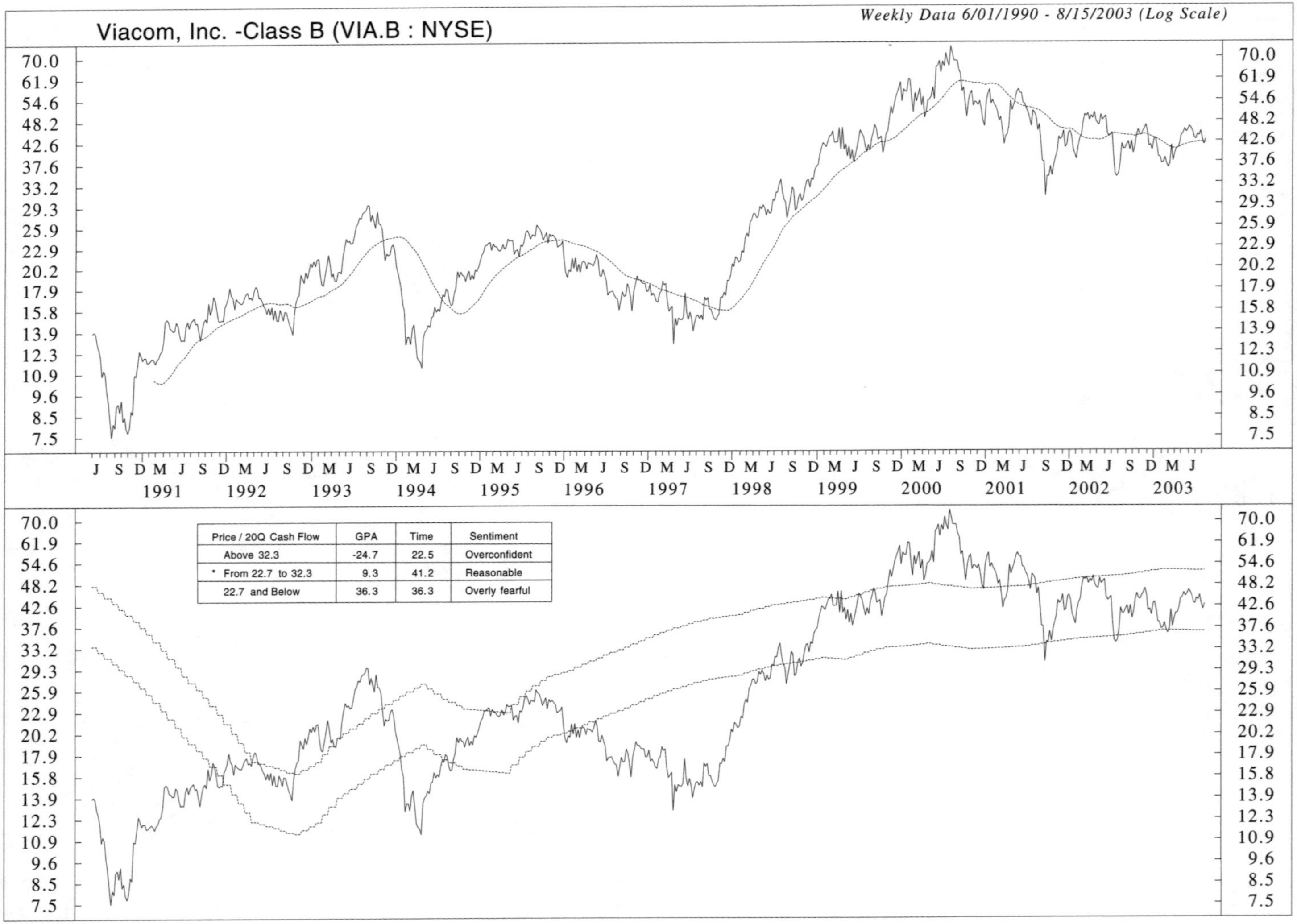

Viacom, Inc. -Class B (VIA.B : NYSE)

Weekly Data 6/01/1990 - 8/15/2003 (Log Scale)

Price / 20Q Cash Flow	GPA	Time	Sentiment
Above 32.3	-24.7	22.5	Overconfident
* From 22.7 to 32.3	9.3	41.2	Reasonable
22.7 and Below	36.3	36.3	Overly fearful

FIGURE A-95 W.W. Grainger, Inc. (GWW).
© 2003 Ned Davis Research, Inc. All rights reserved.

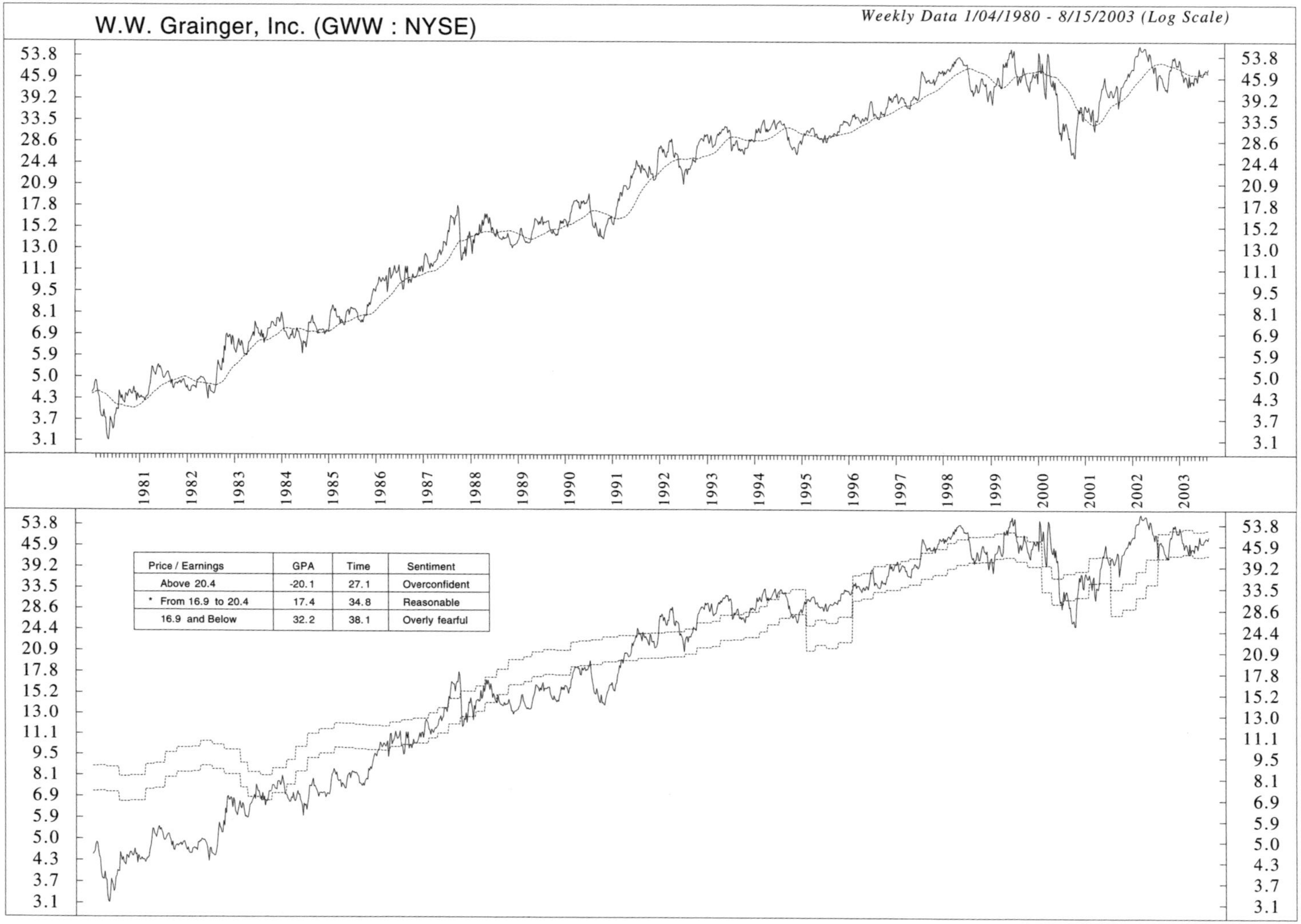

FIGURE A-96 Wachovia Corporation (WB).
© 2003 Ned Davis Research, Inc. All rights reserved.

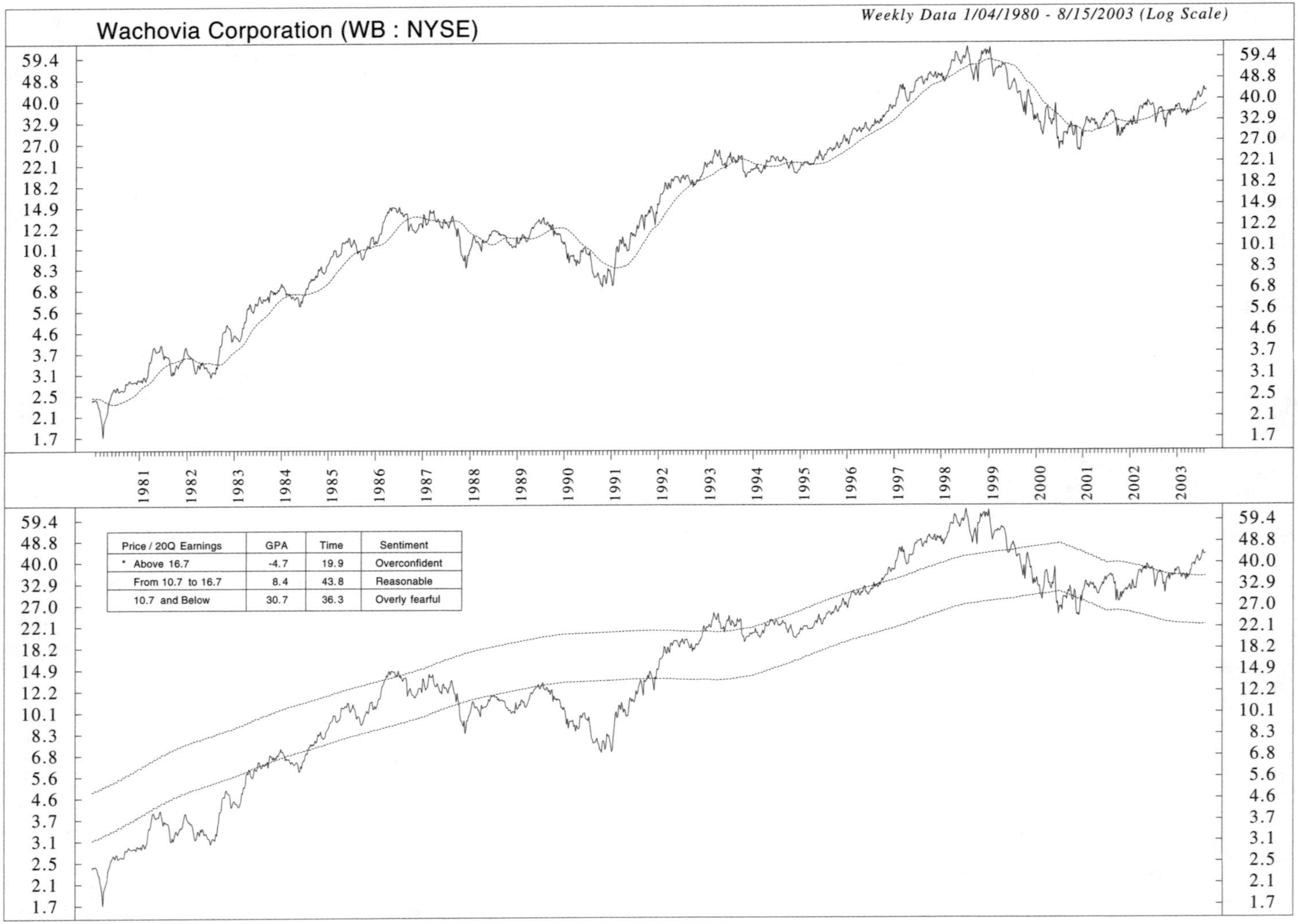

FIGURE A-97 Wal-Mart Stores, Inc. (WMT).
© 2003 Ned Davis Research, Inc. All rights reserved.

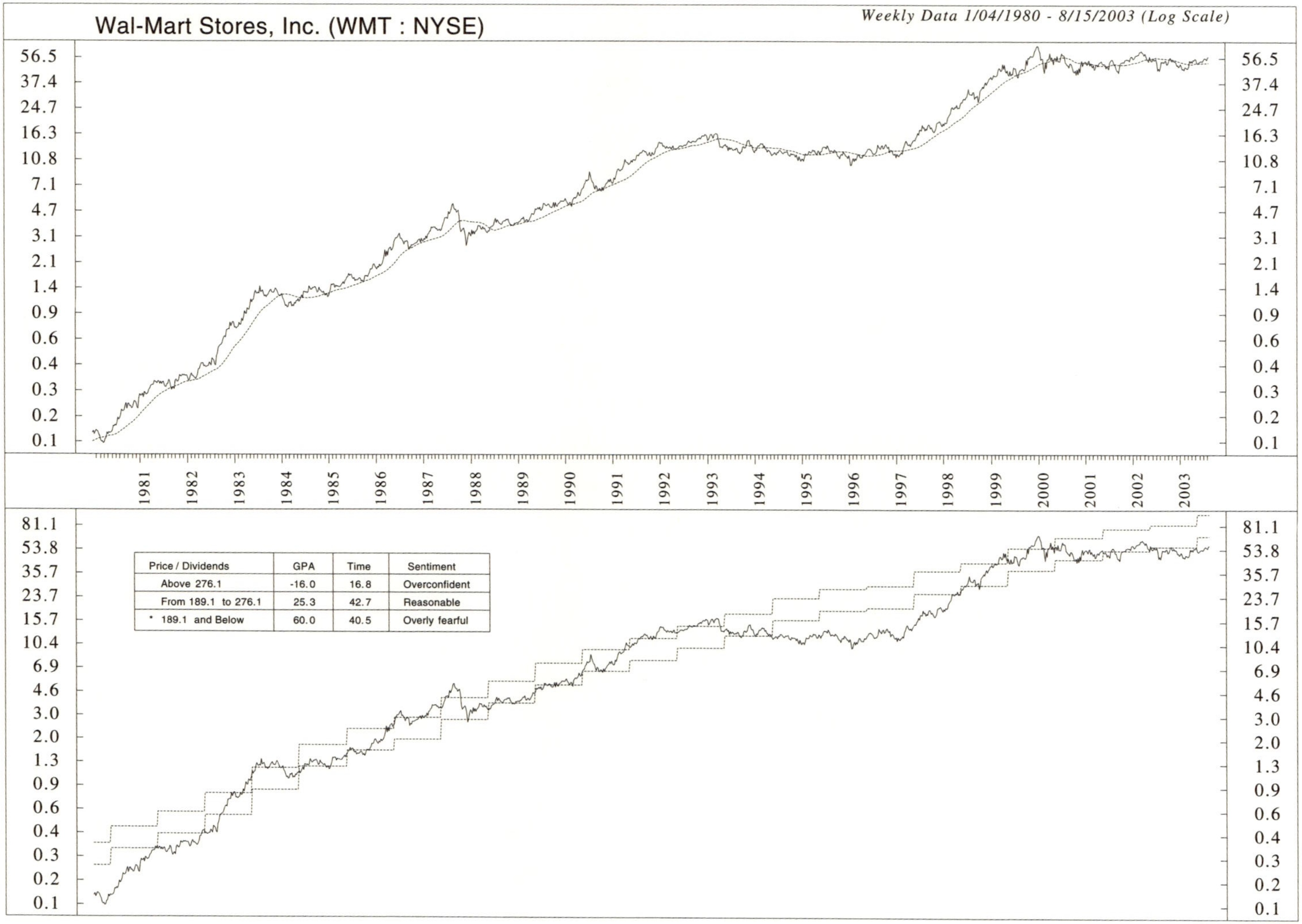

FIGURE A-98 Walt Disney Company, The (DIS).
© 2003 Ned Davis Research, Inc. All rights reserved.

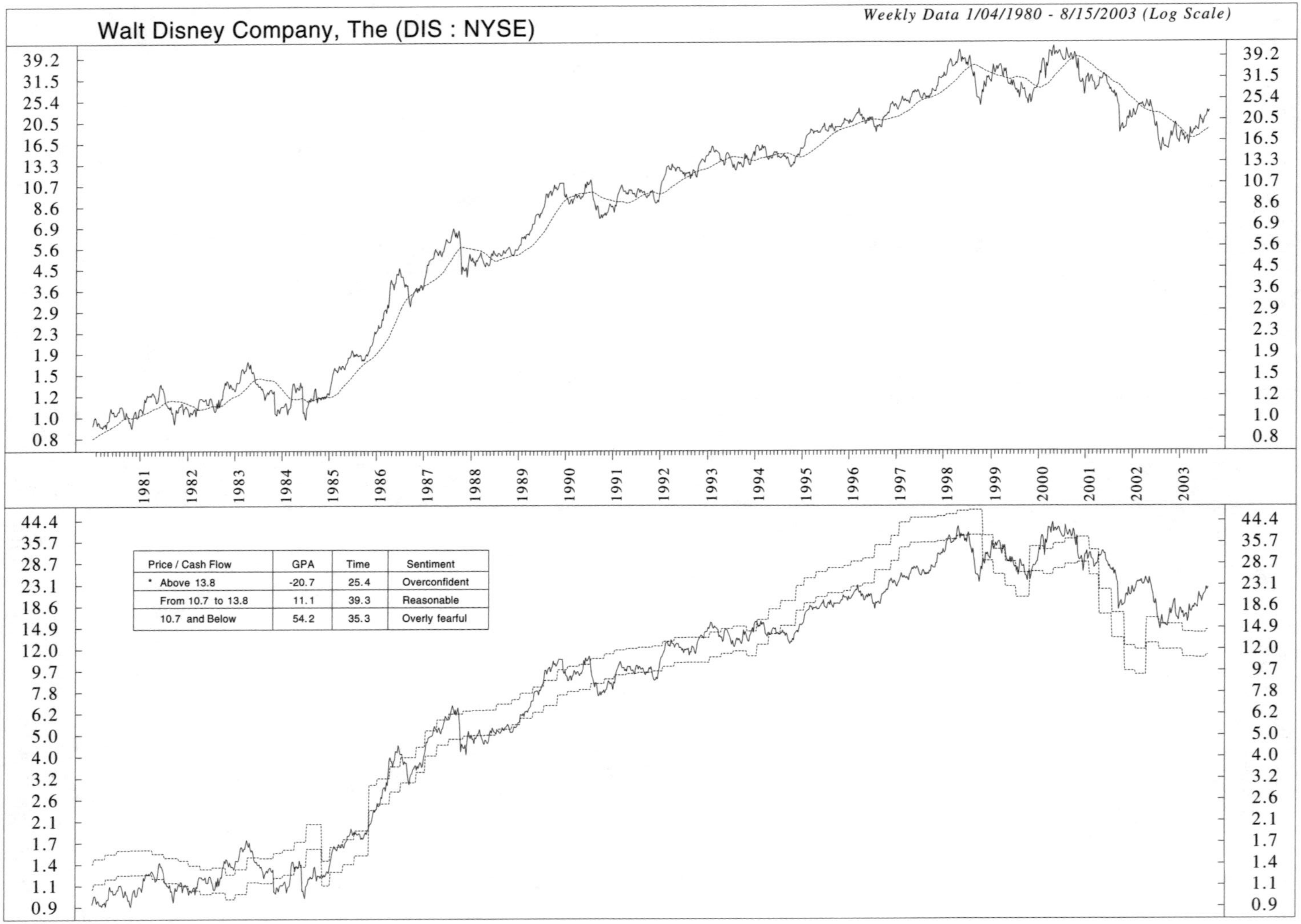

Weekly Data 1/04/1980 - 8/15/2003 (Log Scale)

Walt Disney Company, The (DIS : NYSE)

Price / Cash Flow	GPA	Time	Sentiment
* Above 13.8	-20.7	25.4	Overconfident
From 10.7 to 13.8	11.1	39.3	Reasonable
10.7 and Below	54.2	35.3	Overly fearful

FIGURE A-99 Weyerhaeuser Company (WY).
© 2003 Ned Davis Research, Inc. All rights reserved.

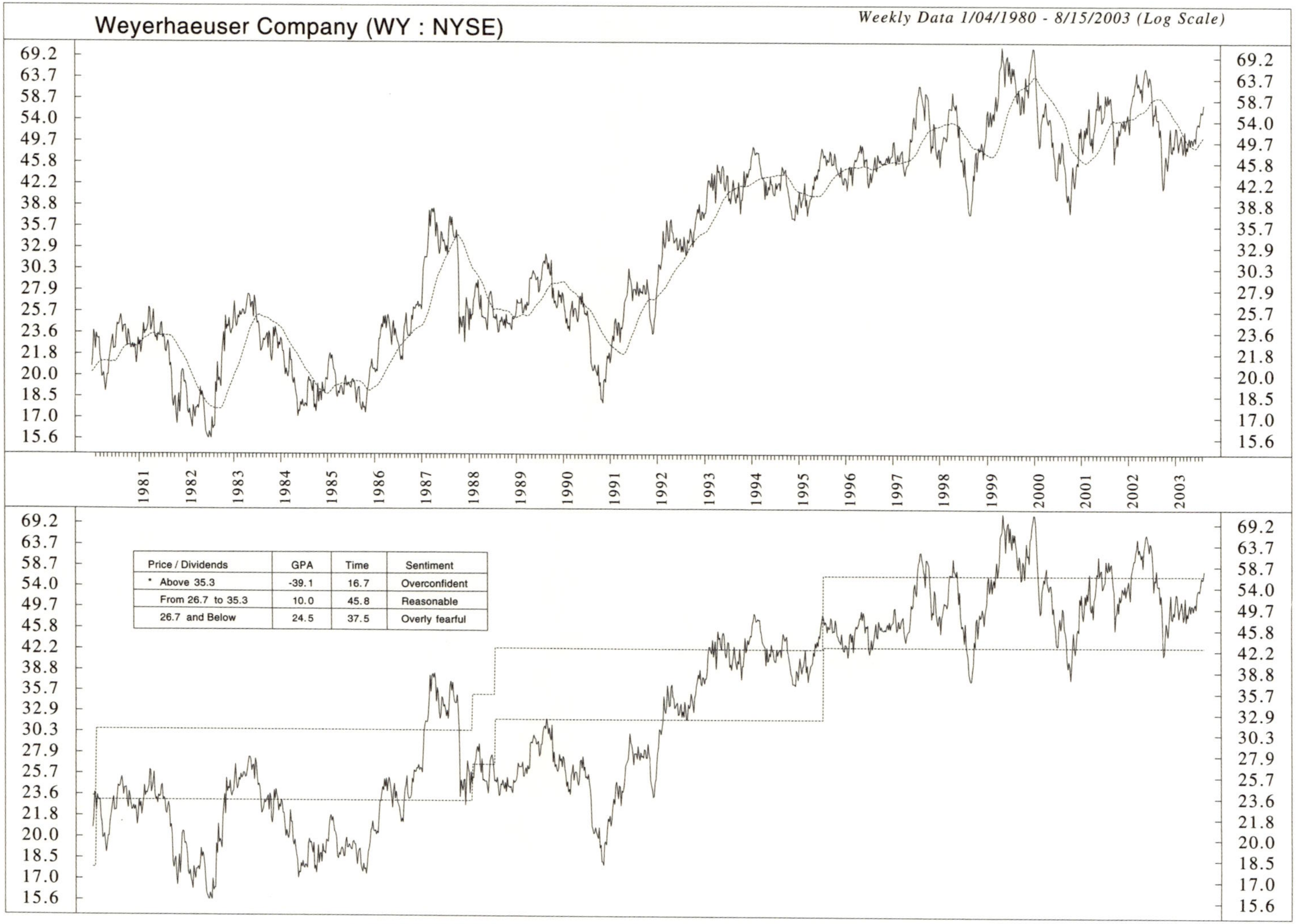

FIGURE A-100 William Wrigley Jr. Company (WWY).

© 2003 Ned Davis Research, Inc. All rights reserved.

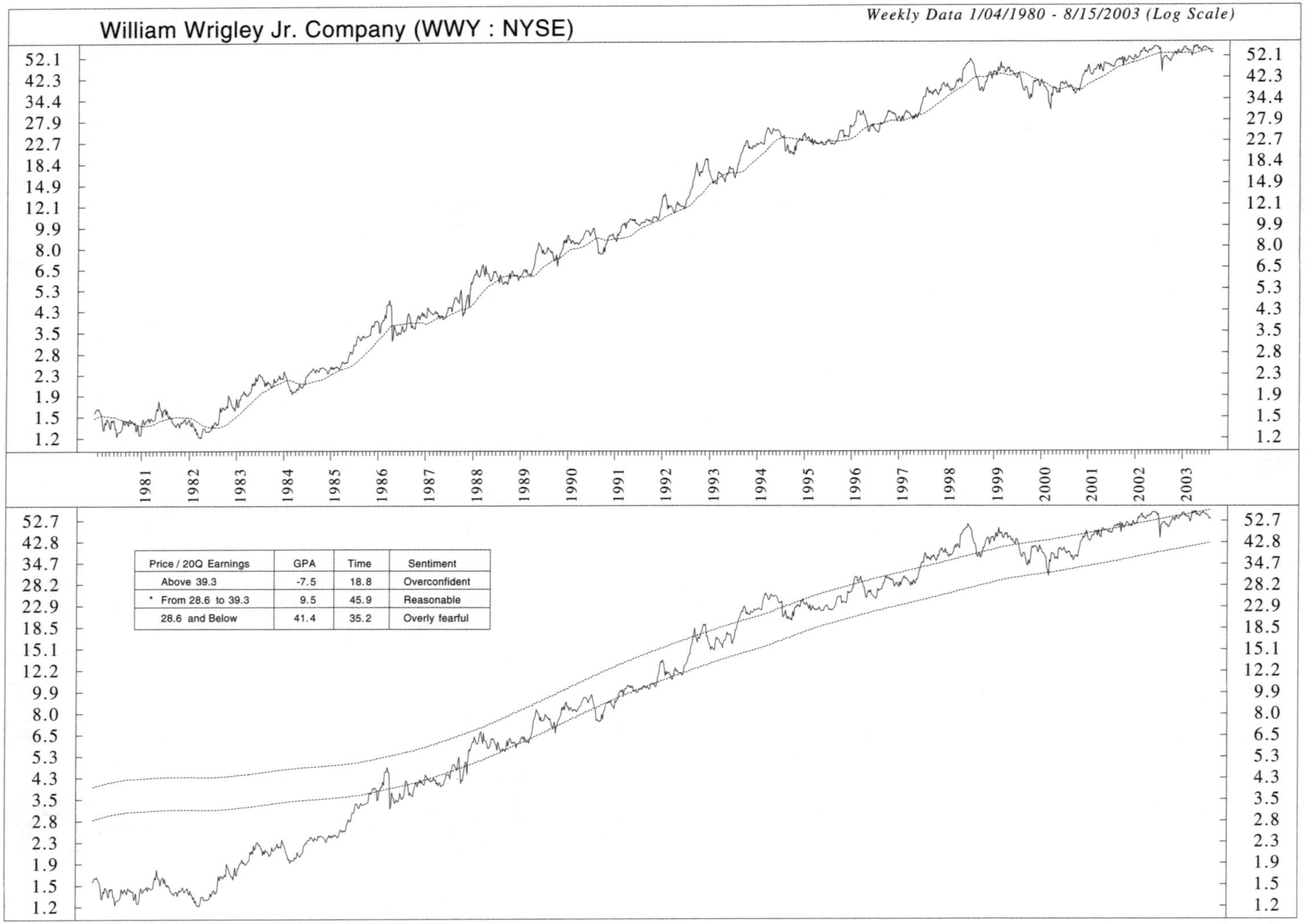

Price / 2OQ Earnings	GPA	Time	Sentiment
Above 39.3	-7.5	18.8	Overconfident
From 28.6 to 39.3	9.5	45.9	Reasonable
28.6 and Below	41.4	35.2	Overly fearful

REFERENCES

Bartlett, John. 1992. *Bartlett's Familiar Quotations.* Boston: Little, Brown and Company.

Casey, Douglas. 1995. *Media, Mania & the Markets.* Baltimore, Md.: Agora Financial Place of Publishing.

Cooper, Sherry. 2001. *Ride the Wave: Taking Control in a Turbulent Financial Age.* Upper Saddle River, NJ: Prentice Hall.

Dreman, David. 1998. *Contrarian Investment Strategies: The Next Generation.* New York: Simon & Schuster.

Getty, J. Paul. 1983. *How to Be Rich.* New York: The Berkley Publishing Group.

Hagstrom, Robert G., Jr. 1994. *The Warren Buffett Way: Investment Strategies of the World's Greatest Investor.* New York: John Wiley & Sons.

Hayes, Timothy. 2000. *The Research Driven Investor: How to Use Information, Data and Analysis for Investment Success.* New York: McGraw-Hill.

Le Bon, Gustave. 1982. *The Crowd: A Study of the Popular Mind.* Atlanta, Ga.: Cherokee Publishing Company.

Levy, Leon. 2002. *The Minds of Wall Street.* New York: Public Affairs.

Lynch, Peter, and John Rothchild. 1993. *Beating The Street.* New York: Simon & Schuster.

Mackay, Charles. 1989. *Extraordinary Popular Delusions and the Madness of Crowds.* New York: Barnes & Noble Books.

McConnell, James. 1980. *Understanding Human Behavior.* New York: Holt, Rinehart and Winston.

Menschel, Robert. 2002. *Markets, Mobs & Mayhem: A Modern Look at the Madness of Crowds.* New York: John Wiley & Sons.

Meyssan, Thierry. 2002. *9/11, the Big Lie.* New York: USA Books.

Neill, Humphrey B. 1992. *The Art of Contrary Thinking: It Pays to Be Contrary!* Caldwell, Idaho: Caxton Printers.

Raspberry, William. 1994. *Distinguished Commentary.*
Schwager, Jack D. 1989. *Market Wizards.* New York: New York Institute of Finance/Simon & Schuster.
Schwager, Jack D. 2001. *Stock Market Wizards.* New York: HarperCollins.
Shefrin, Hersh. 2000. *Beyond Greed and Fear.* Boston: President and Fellows of Harvard College.
Sobel, Robert. 1965. *The Big Board: A History of the New York Stock Market.* New York: Free Press.
Thaler, Richard. 1992. *The Winner's Curse.* New York: Free Press.
Zweig, Martin. 1986. *Winning on Wall Street.* New York: Warner Books.

INDEX

Abbott Laboratories, 72
Acton, Lord, 63
Adelphia Communications, 33
Advanced Micro Devices, Inc., 73
Affiliated Computer Services, Inc., 74
Air Products and Chemicals, Inc., 75
Airline industry, 29
Al-Qaeda network, 15
Alberto-Culver Company, 76
Alcan, Inc., 77
Alcoa, Inc., 78
Altria Group, Inc., 79
Amazon.com, 31, 43
American Association of Individual Investors (AAII), 48–49
American Express Company, 80
Amgen, Inc., 81
Analog Devices, Inc., 82
Anheuser-Busch Companies, Inc., 83
AOL Time Warner, 33
Archer-Daniels-Midland Company, 84
Art of Contrary Thinking, The (Neill), 8
Asch, Solomon, 20
Atlantic Monthly, cover stories, 41–42
Autokinetic effect, 19–20
Automobile industry, 29

Bank of America Corporation, 85
Bank One Corporation, 86
Barron's:
    cover stories, 38–39
    strategist forecasts, 2, 3
    Zweig and, xi
Bartlett, John, 61–62, 63
Baruch, Bernard, 8, 12
Baxter International, Inc., 87
Beating the Street (Lynch), 12–13
Behavioral finance, 21–23

Being Right or Making Money (Davis), 2, 6–8
Bell, Alexander Graham, 63
Beyond Greed and Fear (Shefrin), 21
Bezos, Jeff, 43
Bianco Research, 5, 7
Big Board, The (Sobel), 29
Bill of Rights, 62–63
Blake, Robert, 21
Blame avoidance, 22
Bloomberg News, 31
Boeing Company, The, 88
Boise Cascade Corporation, 89
Bubble Acts (England), 27
Budowski, Michael, 30–31
Buffett, Warren, 13, 62
Bush, George W., 15
Business Week:
    cover stories, 37, 40–41, 42
    forecasts, 4

Campbell Soup Company, 90
Carver, George Washington, 63
Casey, Douglas, 44
Chubb Corporation, 91
Cisco Systems, Inc., 31, 92
Citigroup, Inc., 93
Clinton, Bill, 44, 46
CNBC, 31
CNNfn, 31
Cohen, Steve, 13
Comcast Corporation Class A, 94
Commercial paper prices, 4950
Commercial traders, 5152
Commodity Futures Trading Commission (CFTC), 5152
Computer industry, 3034
Computer Sciences Corporation, 95
ConAgra Foods, Inc., 96

173

Conference Board, The, 6
Constitution, U.S., 62–63
Contrarian Investment Strategies (Dreman), 28
Contrary opinion (*see* Theory of contrary opinion)
Contrary Opinion Forum, 8
Coolidge, Calvin, 44
Cooper, Sherry, 30–31
Cootner, Paul, viii–x
Cover stories (*see* Headlines and cover stories)
Crash of 1929, 33–37
    headlines surrounding, 35–37
    nature of, 28–30
Creighton, Mandell, 63
Crowd, The (Le Bon), 8, 44
Crowd psychology, 19–23, 47–60
    anchoring the crowd, 19–20
    behavioral finance, 21–23
    cover stories and, 37–43
    group pressure, 20–21
    headlines and, 35–37
    indicators based on surveys and market data, 48–55
    Le Bon and, 8, 44
    market responses to crisis, 9–11
    politically motivated quotes and, 44–46
    successful users of, 11–13
    (*See also* Manias and panics)

Declaration of Independence, 62
Diagnostic Products Corporation, 97
Dow Chemical Company, The, 98
Dow Jones Industrial Average (DJIA):
    consumer confidence versus, 6
    crash of 1929 and, 29
    crisis events and, 9, 11
    headlines from 1960s and 1970s, 37, 38
    headlines from 1980s and 1990s, 39–41
    headlines from 1990s to late 2002, 41–43
    mania of 1924–1932, 29, 33–34, 36–37
    presidential performance versus, 15, 17, 44–46
Dreman, David, 28

Eastman Kodak Company, 100
eBay, 31
Economist, cover stories, 37
Edison, Thomas, 63
Einstein, Albert, 63
Elliott Wave Financial Forecast, 4
EMC Corporation, 99
Emerson, Ralph Waldo, 62
Emerson Electric Company, 101
Endowment effect, 33
England:
    Bubble Acts, 27
    gold mania (1979–1980), 33–34
    South Sea Bubble, 26–27
Enron, 33
Extraordinary Popular Delusions and the Madness of Crowds (Mackay), 12, 25–26

FactSet Research Systems, Inc., 102
Federal Reserve Board, The, 29–30, 41
Financial assets, stocks as percentage of total personal, 57, 59
First Data Corporation, 103
Fisher, Irving, 36
Ford, Gerald, 45–46
Ford, Henry, 63
Ford Motor Company, 104
Forecasting:
    by *Barron's* strategists, 2, 3
    by *BusinessWeek* survey, 4
    by *Fortune*, 5–6
    problems of, 2–8
    by *Wall Street Journal* survey, 5, 7
    by *Wall Street Week* panelists, 2–3
Forest Laboratories, Inc., 105
Fortune:
    cover stories, 39
    forecasts, 5–6
Fountainhead, The (Rand), 61
France, Mississippi Scheme, 25–26
Franklin, Ben, 63
Frost, Robert, 1
Fulton, Robert, 63
Futures contracts, 51–52

Gallup poll presidential approval ratings, 17
Gates, Bill, 62, 63
General Dynamics Corporation, 106
General Electric Company, 107
General Motors Corporation, 29, 108
Genuine Parts Company, 109
Georgia-Pacific Corporation, 110
Getty, J. Paul, 11–12, 62
Gillette Company, The, 111
GlaxoSmithKline plc, 112
Global Crossing, 33
Gold mania (1979–1980), 33–34
Gould, Edson, 8, 9
Grainger (W. W.), Inc., 165
Great Depression, 28–30
Great War, 28–29
Greenspan, Alan, 29–30, 33, 39
Group conformity research, 19–21
Group pressure, 20–21

H. J. Heinz Company, 113
Halliburton Company, 115
Harrah's Entertainment, Inc., 116
Harsco Corporation, 117
Hayes, Tim, 59–60
Headlines and cover stories:
    1960s-1970s, 37–39
    1980s-early 1990s, 39–41
    late 1990s-early 2000s, 41–43
    surrounding the Crash of 1929, 35–37
Hedgers, 51–52
Heinz (H. J.) Company, 113
Helson, Henry, 21

INDEX

Hewlett-Packard Company, 118
Hilton Hotels Corporation, 119
Home Depot, Inc., The, 120
HON Industries, Inc., 114
Honda Motor Co., Ltd., 121
Hoover, Herbert, 37
How to Be Rich (Getty), 11–12
Huis Clos (No Exit) (Sartre), 61
Hulbert ratings, vii

Illinois Tool Works, Inc., 122
Ingersoll-Rand Company Limited, 123
Integrated Device Technology, Inc., 124
Intel Corporation, 125
International Business Machines Corporation, 126
International Paper Company, 127
Internet companies, 30–34, 43
Intrinsic values, viii–ix
Intuit, Inc., 128
Investech Research Market Analyst, 2, 5, 29–30
Investment clubs, 58, 60
Investor expectations theory:
 nature of, viii
 predictive theory of, viii–ix
 reasons for effectiveness of, x–xi
 reflecting barriers theory and, viii–x
 (*See also* Theory of contrary opinion)
Investor Expectations (Zweig), vii
Investor sentiment, vii
 crowd psychology and, 20–23
 group conformity research and, 19–21
 on individual stocks, 67–70
 nontraditional, 55–60
 (*See also* Theory of contrary opinion)
Investors Intelligence, Inc., 49

Jabil Circuit, Inc., 129
Japan, Nikkei 225 (1983–1992), 33–34
Jarvik, Robert, 63
Jefferson, Thomas, 63
Jefferson-Pilot Corporation, 130
Johnson, Lyndon, 44
Johnson and Johnson, 132
Johnson Controls, Inc., 131
Jones, Paul Tudor, 13
Jones Apparel Group, Inc., 133

Kahneman, Daniel, 21
Kellogg Company, 135
Keynes, John Maynard, 13
Kipling, Rudyard, 63
KLA-Tencor Corporation, 134
Knight-Ridder, Inc., 136

Law, John, 25–26
Le Bon, Gustave, 8, 44
Lehman Brothers Holding, Inc., 137
Levy, Leon, 13
Limited Brands, Inc., 138

Lindbergh, Charles, 29
Liquidity:
 versus market indicators, 9, 10
 theory of contrary opinion and, 9–11
Loss aversion, 21–22
Louis XIV, King of France, 25–26
Lowe's Companies, Inc., 139
Lucent Technologies, 33
Lynch, Peter, 12–13

McConnell, James, 19–20
McDonald's Corporation, 141
McGraw-Hill Companies, Inc., 142
Mackay, Charles, 12, 25–26
Manias and panics, 25–34
 Crash of 1929, 28–30, 35–37
 Dow Jones Industrial Average (1924–1932), 33–34
 gold (1979–1980), 33–34
 Mississippi Scheme, 25–26
 NASDAQ Bubble, 20–23, 30–34, 42
 Nikkei 225 (1983–1991), 33–34
 Russian MMM mania, 27–28
 South Sea Bubble, 26–27
 tulip bulb mania, 33
Market crash of 1987, xi
Market indicators (*see* Dow Jones Industrial Average [DJIA]; NASDAQ Composite Index; S&P 500)
Market Wizards (Schwager), 13
Markets, Mobs, & Mayhem (Menschel), 26, 27
Mavrodi, Sergei, 28
May Department Stores Company, 140
Media, Mania & the Markets (Bezos), 44
MedImmune, Inc., 143
Menschel, Robert, 26, 27
Merck and Company, Inc., 144
Merrill Lynch and Company, 145
Meyssan, Thierry, 15
Microsoft Corporation, 146
Minds of Wall Street, The (Levy), 13
Mississippi Company, 26
Mississippi Scheme, 25–26
Mitchell, Charles A., 29
MMM company (Russia), 28
MMM Mania, 27–28
Monetary conditions, 49
Montgomery, Paul, 35, 37, 39
Morse, Samuel, 63
Motley Fool, 31–32
Motorola, Inc., 147

NASDAQ Composite Index:
 Advance/Decline Line, 32
 NASDAQ Bubble, 20–23, 30–34, 42
National Association of Investors Corporation, 58
National Bureau of Economic Research (NBER), 40–41, 42–43
National City Bank, 29
National Semiconductor Corporation, 148
Ned Davis Research, 14, 16–17, 47, 52–56, 59–60
Neill, Humphrey B., 8–9

Net aggregate position, 52
Netherlands, tulip bulb mania, 33
New Economy stocks, 20–23, 30–34, 42
New York Federal Reserve Bank, 29
New York Times, headlines and the Crash of 1929, 36, 37
Newell Rubbermaid, Inc., 149
Newsweek, cover stories, 37, 39, 41
Nikkei 225 bubble (1983–1992), 33–34
9/11, The Big Lie (Meyssan), 15
Nixon, Richard, 44–45
Noncommercial traders, 51–52
Nonprofessional investors, reflecting barriers theory and, viii–x
NYSE Advance/Decline line, 22

Old Economy stocks, 31
Oracle Corporation, 150
Osama bin Laden, 15
OurBeginnings, 30–31

PepsiCo, Inc., 152
Pets.com, 33
PPG Industries, Inc., 151
Price-earnings ratio (P/E), 55–57
Professional investors, reflecting barriers theory and, viii–x
Progressive Corporation, The, 153
Puts-calls ratio, vii

Quotations, politically motivated, 44–46

RadioShack Corporation, 154
Railroad industry, 33
Rand, Ayn, 61
Random walk within reflecting barriers, viii–x
Raskob, John J., 29
Raspberry, William, 15
Reagan, Ronald, 45–46
Reflecting barriers theory, viii–x
Regret theory, 21–22
Research Driven Investor, The (Hayes), 59–60
Ride the Wave (Cooper), 30–31
Roaring Twenties, 28–29
Rohm and Haas Company, 155
Rukeyser, Louis, 2
Russia, MMM Mania, 27–28
Rydex mutual funds, 50–51

St. Paul Companies, Inc., The, 159
Salk, Jonas, 63
Samuelson, William, 33
Sara Lee Corporation, 156
Sartre, Jean Paul, 61
Schering-Plough Corporation, 157
Schindler's List (movie), 14–15
Schlumberger Limited, 158
Schwager, Jack, 13
Sentiment indicators (*see* Investor sentiment)
September 11, 2001 terrorist attacks, 9–10, 15
Shefrin, Hersch, 21–22
Sherif, Muzafer, 19–20
Short-term bond prices, 49–50
Simpson, O. J., 15
Singer, Isaac, 63
Sobel, Robert, 29
South Sea Bubble, 26–27
South Sea Company, 27
S&P 500:
    versus 10-year Treasury notes, 55–58
    versus American Association of Individual Investors, 48–49
    versus bullish-bearish indicators, 49–50
    earnings yield, 55–57
    versus Ned Davis Research crowd sentiment poll, 53–54
    versus Rydex mutual funds, 50–51
    versus S&P price-earnings ratio, 55–57
    versus Speculator COT Index, 51–52
    versus stock mutual fund cash-assets ratio, 9, 10
    versus Wall Street strategist sentiment, 53
Speculator COT Index, 51–52
State of the Union addresses, 44–46
Statman, Meir, 22
Status quo bias, 33
Stock market indicators (*see* Dow Jones Industrial Average [DJIA]; NASDAQ Composite Index; S&P 500)
Stock Market Wizards (Schwager), 13
Sysco Corporation, 160

Target Corporation, 161
Technical analysis, 14
Terrorism:
    Al-Qaeda network, 15
    attacks of September 11, 2001, 9–10, 15
Thaler, Richard, 33
Theglobe.com, 31
Theory of contrary opinion:
    applications outside of markets, 13–14, 61–63
    creating own reality and, 14–15
    crowd psychology and, 8–9 (*See also* Crowd psychology)
    explanation of, 9–11
    Robert Frost and, 1
    liquidity and, 9–11
    Ned Davis Research and, 14, 16–17
    successful users of, 11–13
TheStreet.com, 31–32
Thomas, Clarence, 14
3M Company, 71
Time magazine, cover stories, 35–36, 39, 40, 42–43
Tulip bulb mania, 33
Tversky, Amos, 21

Understanding Human Behavior (Sherif and McConnell), 19–20
Union Pacific Corporation, 162
United Kingdom, gold mania (1979–1980), 33–34
United States:
    Constitution, 62–63
    Federal Reserve Board, The, 29–30, 41
    gold mania (1979–1980), 33–34
    Great Depression, 28–30

United States *(Cont.)*:
    NASDAQ Bubble, 20–23, 30–34, 42
    stock market crash of 1929, 28–30, 33–37
    stock market crash of 1987, vii
    stock market indicators (*see* Dow Jones Industrial Average [DJIA]; NASDAQ Composite Index; S&P 500)
    terrorist attacks of September 11, 2001, 9–10, 15

VA Software, 31
Valuation indicators, 55–57
Value Line Composite, 22
Verizon Communications, Inc., 163
Viacom, Inc. Class B, 164
Vietnam War, 40, 44

W. W. Grainger, Inc., 165
Wachovia Corporation, 166
Wal-Mart Stores, Inc., 167
Wall Street Journal:
    headlines and the Crash of 1929, 36

Wall Street Journal (Cont.):
    surveys, 5, 7
Wall Street Week, 2
Walt Disney Company, The, 168
Warren Buffett Way, The (Buffett), 13
Weyerhaeuser Company, 169
Whitney, Eli, 63
William Wrigley Jr. Company, 170
Winer, Larry, 33–34
Winner's Curse, The (Thaler), 33
Winning on Wall Street (Zweig), 13
World War II, 37
WorldCom, 33
Wright, Orville, 63
Wright, Wilbur, 63
Wright Aeronautical, 29

Zeckhauser, Richard, 33
Zweig, Martin, vii–xv, 13
Zweig Forecast, The (newsletter), vii

ABOUT THE AUTHOR

Louis Rukeyser has called Ned Davis, his guest on both *Wall $treet Week* and *Louis Rukeyser's Wall Street,* "one of the greatest market historians of the past century." A 58-year-old Phi Beta Kappa graduate of the University of North Carolina at Chapel Hill, Ned has been professionally involved in the stock market since 1966.

The institutionally oriented Ned Davis Research, based in Venice, Florida, produces nine different timing services and has built one of the largest independent research firms on Wall Street. Ned began Ned Davis Research in 1980 after 12 years as partner and Director of Technical Research at J. C. Bradford & Company. The research is marketed by Davis, Mendel and Regenstein, Inc. (NASD), of Atlanta, Georgia, of which Ned is Chairman of the Board of Directors. The focus of Ned's work is timing models and indicators. These computer-derived timing tools identify buying and selling junctures in such diverse markets as the Dow Industrials, the S&P stock index futures, the bond market, currencies, and gold, as well as 100 industry groups, individual stocks, inflation, the economy, and foreign stock markets.

All Ned Davis Research publications are fully illustrated by the rich graphics that have become their hallmark. Ned's approach, in general, differs from those of other technical analysts in that his models employ a broad spectrum of timing tools: price action, volume, investor psychology, valuation fundamentals, economic strain or ease, the bond-stock relationship, flow of funds studies, Federal Reserve policy, and monetary tools. In total, his research is best characterized as an objective, disciplined approach to investing that focuses on managing risk, staying in harmony with the primary trend, and avoiding major disasters.